AF361400

AQUINAS

ON EMOTION'S PARTICIPATION IN REASON

NICHOLAS KAHM

AQUINAS

ON EMOTION'S PARTICIPATION IN REASON

THE CATHOLIC UNIVERSITY OF AMERICA PRESS

Washington, D.C.

The paper used in this publication meets the minimum
requirements of American National Standards for Information
Science—Permanence of Paper for Printed Library Materials,
ANSI Z39.48-1984.

∞

Cataloging-in-Publication Data is available
from the Library of Congress
ISBN 978-0-8132-3157-0

For Denise, Grace, Martin, and Nina

CONTENTS

ACKNOWLEDGMENTS

First and foremost, I wish to thank my wife and best friend, Denise, for her love, humor, and unfailing support. I also wish to thank our three wonderful children for playing with me and making me forget about everything but them for long moments of time. Aquinas points out that metaphysics and child's play are the two highest natural activities possible, since they are most perfectly done for their own sakes—he should have added parents playing with their children. I wish to thank Msgr. John F. Wippel for his incredible kindness, generosity, and attention to detail in helping me with this book in its early stage. I also wish to thank Greg Doolan, Tobias Hoffmann, Brian Carl, and Kevin White, who have helped me work through various parts of the book. Many thanks to John Martino, Paul Higgins, and the anonymous readers at the Catholic University of America Press for their helpful comments and suggestions. In particular, I would like to thank Joe Butera, whose paper caused me to radically rethink this entire problem long ago, and for his comments on the book as a whole. I would also like to thank Daniel De Haan for his friendship and disagreement. Many thanks to the Department of Philosophy at St. Michael's College and, in particular, to Michael Olsen for his support and friendship. I would also like to thank Brian Lacey for creating and funding the endowed Henry G. Fairbanks Visiting position at St. Michael's College, which supported me for three years as I worked on this book. I would also like to thank my research assistant, Branden Young, for his attention to detail. And many thanks to those who have offered comments on matters in this book at various conferences over the last few years. And last but not least, I have to thank my parents for supporting me in countless ways.

Two portions of this manuscript have appeared in previous publications, and I thank these journals for granting the necessary permissions. Portions of chapter 1, especially section 2, use material from "Aquinas and Aristotelians on Whether the Soul Is a Group of Powers," *History of Philosophy Quarterly* 34, no. 2 (April 2017): 115–32. Some of the material of the third section of chapter 4 was published as part of "Aquinas on Quality," *British Journal for the History of Philosophy* 24, no. 1 (2016): 23–44.

Works by Thomas Aquinas

CT — *Compendium theologiae*

QDA — *Quaestiones disputatae de anima*

QDC — *Quaestio disputata de caritate*

QDM — *Quaestiones disputatae de malo*

QDP — *Quaestiones disputatae de potentia*

QDV — *Quaestiones disputatae de veritate*

QDVC — *Quaestio disputata de virtutibus cardinalibus*

QSC — *Quaestio disputata de spiritualibus creaturis*

De ebd. — *Super Boetii De ebdomadibus*

De ente — *De ente et essentia*

De princ. — *De principiis naturae*

De Trin. — *Super Boetii De Trinitate*

In Ethic. — *Sententia libri Ethicorum*

In Met. — *In duodecim libros Metaphysicorum Aristotelis expositio*

In Phys. — *In VIII libros Physicorum*

In Post. an. — *Expositio libri Posteriorum*

In Sent. — *Scriptum super libros sententiarum magistri Petri Lombardi*

Quodl. — *Quodlibeta*

SCG — *Summa contra gentiles*

ST — *Summa theologiae*

Editions of Thomas Aquinas Cited

Leonine	*Opera omnia* (Leonine Edition)
Mand / Moos	*Sentences commentary* (ed. Mandonnet and Moos)
Marietti	*Opera omnia* (ed. Marietti)
St. Paul	*Summa theologiae* (Editiones Paulinae)

Other

PL	*Patrologia Latina* (ed. Migne)

AQUINAS

ON EMOTION'S PARTICIPATION IN REASON

Emotions are so pervasively bound up with everyday life that we hardly ever stop to consider them. Their motivating power is undeniable. But what are they? Are they rational, irrational, somehow both, or neither? Sometimes they seem to be quite rational, but sometimes they seem utterly irrational and beyond our control. At times they seem to hew very closely to our thoughts, while at others they seem to arise contrary to our thoughts, or even out of nowhere. But even in some cases, such as anger, in which they do seem to follow our thoughts—as anger often follows from our perception that we have been unfairly treated—they nevertheless seem to quickly become irrational and troublesome. At other times, however, irrational emotions, such as some cases of love, do not seem to cause trouble but rather to be part of what makes life worth living. Yet the passion or emotion of love can also, of course, be very painful and burdensome. We may rationally wish to be rid of particular loves but feel powerless to do anything about them.

Can emotions somehow become more rational and subject to our control? Or are we, *à la* Hume, ultimately slaves to our passions, one way or another? Is it possible to tame and habituate our emotions? To what extent? Should we wish to tame them at all? In what sense can reason permeate emotion? If we can increase the rationality of our emotions and our control over them, can we habitually alter our emotional responses to the world around us? Can we habitually and always feel the right emotions toward the right things in the right ways? Aristotle thought this was possible. But if this is going too far, which is what Aquinas thought, to what extent is it possible to shape our emotional responses to the world around us? To what extent can they become more rational and more under our control? This book will explain Aquinas's answers to these perennial human questions, answers that I think are original, persuasive, and level-headed.

Turning to Aquinas, these questions can be fully answered only when we understand exactly what he means when he says that the sense appetites participate in reason. For Aquinas (and Aristotle), the sense appetites are the seat of the emotions or passions—that is, they are the faculties or principles of the emotions, just as mind is the principle or faculty by which we think. Practically all scholarship that touches on the relation between reason and emotion in Aquinas mentions the importance of the sense appetites participating in reason, but these publications fail to offer any real detail about what this participation entails.[1] I hope to clarify this important aspect of Aquinas's thought and ultimately to explain Aquinas's answer to these basic human questions.

There is one common thread that runs through the literature. Although the lack of detail often makes it impossible to say what most Aquinas scholars think the sense appetites' participation in reason entails, they at least usually agree about what this participation is not: it is not Kantian, nor is it Cartesian. But this rejection of Kant and Descartes follows a particular, classical line of interpretation of the history of philosophy. Let me explain.

Descartes's rejection of Aristotelian hylomorphism and formal causality is crucial. According to Descartes, the soul is not related to the body as form, but as an efficient cause—that is, the human soul is a "pilot soul" of sorts.[2] Aquinas scholars then loosely link this to a common

---

1. There have recently been three monographs on Aquinas's views on the passions: Diana Fritz Cates, *Aquinas on the Emotions* (Washington, D.C.: Georgetown University Press, 2009); Robert Miner, *Thomas Aquinas on the Passions: A Study of Summa Theologiae, 1a2ae 22–48* (Cambridge: Cambridge University Press, 2009); Nicholas E. Lombardo, *The Logic of Desire: Aquinas on Emotion* (Washington, D.C.: The Catholic University of America Press, 2011). Of these three Cates has the most to say about sense appetites' participation in reason (see 214–15, 220, 221), but she is just scratching the surface.

2. Even if Gilbert Ryle's famous quip about the ghost in the machine is an exaggeration, in what sense the soul is actually joined to the body is notoriously obscure in Descartes. On the one hand Descartes claims that man is nothing but a thinking thing (*res cogitans*), on the other hand he tries to explain the soul's union to the body (*res extensa*) in some more substantial way than efficient causality. Even though Descartes says that the soul is not joined to the body as a pilot is to a ship (*Discourses* VI, AT 59), it is very difficult to see how this is not the case. Whatever Descartes's ultimate position may have been, I am more interested here in how he has been interpreted in the history of philosophy, and in that respect Ryle's quip is right on the mark.

understanding of Kant. In the history of moral philosophy, Aristotle and Kant are usually placed at opposite ends of a spectrum. For Aristotle, the emotions can participate in reason, while for Kant, they cannot.[3] According to Kant's *Grounding for the Metaphysics of Morals*, the only intrinsically good thing is the good will.[4] The inclinations or passions are directed toward happiness (the fulfillment of inclination or passion), which ultimately has nothing to do with goodness. For example, Kant writes: "making a human being happy is something entirely different from making him good."[5] For Kant, what is moral is restricted to what is voluntary, and thus to the will. Universal volitions of duty (i.e., following the categorical imperative) impose themselves over and against our natural and contingent sensitive natures. In other words, we have a kind of Cartesian "ghost in the machine" or "pilot soul" where the will is (or at least ought to be) the domineering pilot.

Whatever Aquinas may mean when he says that the sense appetites participate in reason, it is apparently not as a pilot soul dominating sensitive nature by way of efficient causality. Any ethical theory that grants the soul too great a role as the efficient cause of the sensitive parts seems to imply this nonhylomorphic Cartesian-Kantian pilot soul—and thus, according to this interpretation of the history of moral philosophy, Scotus and the other medieval voluntarists were riding an express train headed straight for modernity. Aquinas, however, was not on this train, nor was he quasi-modern. Aquinas, apparently, was the last great Aristotelian.[6]

3. This reading of Kant, however, is no longer tenable. In the past couple decades, Kantians have drastically changed our understanding of Kantian virtue ethics. See Henry E. Allison, *Kant's Theory of Freedom* (Cambridge: Cambridge University Press, 1990), chap. 9; Nancy Sherwin, *Making a Necessity of Virtue: Aristotle and Kant on Virtue* (Cambridge: Cambridge University Press, 1997); Anne Margaret Baxley, *Kant's Theory of Virtue: The Value of Autocracy* (Cambridge: Cambridge University Press, 2010); and Michael Rohlf, "Emotion and Evil in Kant," *Review of Metaphysics* 66 (June 2013): 749–73. See chapter 12 below.

4. Kant, *Groundwork of the Metaphysics of Morals*, ed. and trans. Mary Gregor and Jens Timmermann (Cambridge: Cambridge University Press, 2012), 4:393 (9).

5. Ibid., 4:442 (53).

6. Alasdair MacIntyre, *After Virtue* (Notre Dame, Ind.: University of Notre Dame Press, 1981), calls Aquinas a "strict Aristotelian" (178), although he later softened his views. For some Thomists who subscribe to versions of this general metanarrative, see Servais Pinkaers, *The Sources of Christian Ethics*, trans. Sr. Mary Thomas Noble (Washington, D.C.: The Catholic University of America Press, 1995), and *The Pinkaers Reader: Renewing Thomistic Moral Theology*, ed. John Berkman and Craig Steven Titus (Washington, D.C.: The Catholic

Many scholars who believe some form of this metanarrative speak of "Aquinas's remarkably positive assessment of passion," and they are full of language about the harmony, intelligence, and basic goodness of the emotions, a direct result of Aquinas's Aristotelian hylomorphism.[7] In other words, because of the natural hylomorphic unity, there is a kind of mirrored natural unity between reason and the passions (which are partly bodily), as these mutually and synergistically reinforce each other in a kind of hylomorphic manner. These scholars are correct, in a certain sense, for Aquinas's account of the passions of the soul involves an extraordinarily complex, full-bodied, and interesting mixture of the rational, the irrational, the spiritual, and the material all acting together; his account does, in a way, mirror and reflect the human hylomorphic body-soul or matter-form union.[8]

However, I object to the transposition of this "hylomorphic understanding" (if one may say such a thing) of the passions onto particular accounts of morality and, in particular, the avoidance of anything remotely resembling dualism. By "dualism," which is a notoriously slippery term, they simply mean any account of moral virtue that grants too much control to reason over emotion—which would, in turn, seem to draw an excessive wedge between the soul and the body, that is, it would seem to call into question Aquinas's broadly Aristotelian hylomorphism. However, for Aquinas, it is simply not the case that because the soul is the form of the body it cannot also be an efficient cause of its motion, and there is strong textual evidence in Aquinas to show that the soul does efficiently move the body and the sense appetites: as we shall see, this is in fact part of what Aquinas has in mind when he says that the sense appetites participate in reason.

Moreover, Aquinas says repeatedly that the sense appetites only par-

---

University of America Press, 2005); Paul Gondreau, "The Passions and the Moral Life: Appreciating the Originality of Aquinas," *The Thomist* 71 (2007): 419–50; Craig Steven Titus, "Passions in Christ: Spontaneity, Development, and Virtue," *The Thomist* 73 (2009): 53–87; and Simon G. Harak, *Virtuous Passions: The Formation of Christian Character* (New York: Paulist Press, 1993).

7. Lombardo, *Logic of Desire*, 112; see also 100, 116, 272, etc.

8. The best and clearest depiction of this, in my opinion, is found in an article by Elisabeth Uffenheimer-Lippens: "Rationalized Passion and Passionate Rationality: Thomas Aquinas on the Relation between Reason and the Passions," *Review of Metaphysics* 56 (2003): 525–58.

ticipate in reason to the extent that they obey reason's *command*. I will investigate this in great detail in part 2, but this implies—and here I have been influenced by Bonnie Kent—that there is a kind of conscious self, so to speak, that can command or not command the lower parts of the soul and the body.[9] In other words, *I* experience a passion, but *I* then either freely accept or freely reject it, and then *I* command the lower powers and their virtues or vices. There is a kind of "pilot" for Aquinas (and for Aristotle), but it is not exactly the soul itself. Furthermore, as Plato and the Stoics illustrate, there is nothing particularly modern about the "pilot" problem. Moreover, given the medieval debates about the unity or plurality of substantial forms, it would seem that practically everyone medieval but Aquinas would be modern. I would rather think of this as a perennial philosophical problem. On the one hand, we seem to be mostly that which is conscious, rational, and free; on the other hand, we are substantial matter-form composites. Aquinas has a very interesting philosophical account of how these two positions come together. In this, he seems to me to have figured out how to have and eat his cake.

If I am right, this takes the pressure off of certain more "dualistic" passages in Aquinas. For example, he often explains how the soul rules the passions politically rather than despotically.[10] Most Thomists take this to mean that reason ought to respect the passions' own inherent goodness and autonomy, which are naturally ordered to virtue.[11] But in every single one of those passages, Aquinas is very explicit that their autonomy is problematic: they are rebellious (*rebellans*)[12] and at times fight

9. Bonnie Kent, "Losable Virtue: Aquinas on Character and Will," in *Aquinas and the Nicomachean Ethics*, ed. Tobias Hoffmann, Jörn Müller, and Matthias Perkams (Cambridge: Cambridge University Press, 2013), 108–9.

10. The passage is originally from Aristotle's *Politics* I.5, 1254b1–5. For Aquinas, see *Summa theologiae* (hereafter, *ST*) I, q. 81, a. 3, ad 2, in *Summa theologiae* (Rome: Editiones Paulinae, 1955) (hereafter, St. Paul), 391; *ST* I-II, q. 56, a. 4, ad 3 [St. Paul 781]; *Quaestiones disputatae de malo* (hereafter , *QDM*), q. 3, a. 9, ad 14, in *Opera omnia, iussu impensaque Leonis XIII P.M. edita* (Rome: S. C. de Propaganda Fide, 1882–) (hereafter, Leonine), etc. All translations of Aquinas's texts are my own.

11. Lombardo is a strong proponent of this position; see *Logic of Desire*, 112. Uffenheimer-Lippens is more tempered than Lombardo in "Rationalized Passion," but she nevertheless argues that the political understanding is paradigmatic. See also Gondreau, "Passions and the Moral Life," 422–24.

12. *Quaestio disputata de virtutibus cardinalibus* (hereafter, *QDVC*), q. 1, a. 4, ad 8, in *Opera omnia* (Rome: Marietti, 1926–65) (hereafter, Marietti), 719.

back (*repugnat*)[13] with some contradiction (*cum aliqua contradictione*),[14] and they can resist reason (*habet facultatem resistendi in aliquo imperio domini*).[15] The purpose of moral virtue is to diminish this resistance and rebellion as much as possible.[16] The goal is for reason and will to become *despotic* and for the passions to become slavish, so that reason and will can rule. Aquinas's texts are full of language of this sort. But scholars downplay these texts because they seem too dualistic. What they offer instead is a distortion of Aquinas's position, as if he espouses a kind of mutual respect for differing spheres of autonomy and thinks that a person is perfected by becoming more democratic and less autocratic. But this is to overlook Aquinas's basic point that there are higher and lower parts of the soul and that the higher parts (reason and will) should rule the lower ones (the sense appetites and their passions), which are problematic after the Fall.[17]

It is certainly true that Aquinas also says that the sense appetites *naturally* can obey reason,[18] but this must be reconciled with passages in which Aquinas says that they *naturally* often do not.[19] Both claims, properly understood, are true. Moreover, to argue that reason and will should rule the passions despotically does not in any way exclude the hylomorphic nature of the passions, nor does it exclude granting passions a positive role in the moral life. Passions may still be characterized as complex bodily-rational accidents and thus somehow quasi-hylomorphic, whether or not a person has political or despotic control over them. There is simply no connection between the degree or kind of control that reason has or should have over them, on the one hand, and Aquinas's metaphysics of hylomorphism, on the other.

---

13. *QDVC*, q. 1, a. 4 [Marietti 717].

14. *ST* I-II, q. 58, a. 2 [St. Paul 790].

15. *QDVC*, q. 4 [Marietti 717].

16. *QDVC*, q. 4, ad 7 [Marietti 718].

17. One could turn the hylomorphic argument on its head. In Aquinas's original account of human hylomorphism, the soul is not a material form but informs matter while transcending it. One could argue that because the immaterial soul clearly transcends the material body, it follows that the higher should rule and transcend the lower. In any case, although Aquinas nowhere makes such an argument, he could have. My point is simply that the connection between hylomorphism and virtue ethics is far from obvious.

18. For example, *QDVC*, q. 1, a. 8 [Marietti 728].

19. See, for example, *QDM*, q. 16, a. 2 [Leonine 23:288.230–37]; *Quaestiones disputate de anima* (hereafter, *QDA*), q. 8, ad 7 [Leonine 24.1:71.401–2].

Also, there has been no discussion of participation itself from the perspective of ethics, even though Aquinas is quite clear that there are three kinds of participation and there has been excellent scholarly literature on this from the perspective of metaphysics.[20] I propose that Aquinas has a precise meaning of participation in mind and develops his thinking on this matter throughout his writings, and that efficient causality becomes increasingly important in his mature texts. But this does not in any way contradict the demands of his hylomorphic metaphysics, nor does it preclude a positive role for the emotions in the moral life. Furthermore, understanding what exactly Aquinas means by participation in this context helps us to see his answers to perennial and practical ethical questions about the relation between reason and emotion.

For instance, Aristotle famously argued that the virtuous person always has the right emotions toward the right things, in the right ways, at the right times. Any contrary emotion would imply a lack of real virtue. To put it simply, someone who always feels like doing the right thing is virtuous, but someone who does not always feel like doing it, but still does it, is continent or something else—but certainly not virtuous. Many scholars think that this is also Aquinas's position, but I will argue that it is not. Aristotle's optimistic views about virtue seem to be unrealistic; it is fair to doubt whether there has ever been anyone who always feels like doing the right thing. But if this is not Aquinas's position, and if this is not what it means for the sense appetites to participate in reason, then what exactly does Aquinas think the moral virtues do to the emotions? I will argue that he substantially qualifies Aristotle's optimism and offers a far more realistic and plausible account. For Aquinas, unlike Aristotle, the virtuous person will not always have the right emotions—in fact, given Aquinas's understanding of participation and

---

20. There is, however, some literature on the manner in which reason participates in eternal law. While that is undoubtedly very important, this book focuses on how the sense appetites and their passions participate in reason, which is not the same topic. See John Rziha, *Perfecting Human Actions: St. Thomas on Human Participation in Eternal Law* (Washington, D.C.: The Catholic University of America Press, 2009); Martin Rhonheimer, *Natural Law and Practical Reason: A Thomistic View of Moral Autonomy*, trans. Gerald Malsbary (New York: Fordham University Press, 2000); Craig Boyd, "Participation Metaphysics in Aquinas's Theory of Natural Law," *American Catholic Philosophical Quarterly* 79 (2005): 431–45, and "Participation Metaphysics, The Imago Dei, and the Natural Law in Aquinas' Ethics," *New Blackfriars* 88 (2007): 274–87. For a full list of the literature on metaphysical participation see 21n2.

the emotions, that is simply impossible. But this does not mean that the virtues do not participate in reason in another sense and play a very important role in our emotional response to the world around us; it is just a role that is quite different than Aristotle proposed. I have now made many broad claims; but the devil (or the truth) is in the details, which I hope to bring out over the course of this book.

Overview

This book begins at the *locus classicus* of this whole discussion, Aristotle's famous description of the tripartite division of the soul in *Nicomachean Ethics* I.13. Aristotle says that all we need to know about the soul is that it has three parts: vegetative, sensitive, and rational. The sensitive part in the virtuous agent participates in reason, but in the continent agent, it does not. Aristotle immediately says that there is no need to go into greater precision about these parts. Aquinas, however, does exactly that: his ethics are chock full of complex metaphysical precisions about the three parts, which he thinks are important for understanding ethics. Although such detailed metaphysical discussions may be tangential to Aristotle's ethics, they are certainly not for Aquinas's. If the only point of ethics is to become virtuous, then perhaps, only just perhaps, such considerations are extraneous. But if the point of ethics is also speculative, that is, to know and understand what virtue ultimately is—which requires grasping its causes—then we simply must delve into these kinds of details.

After discussing why Aquinas's ethics are so much more metaphysically laden than Aristotle's and why an ethicist should bother with the details of the parts of the soul at all, I delve into the question of what exactly these parts that participate in reason are (chapter 1) and what kind of a whole they are parts of (chapter 2). Merely to ask how the soul has parts is to sail into uncharted scholarly waters and raise all kinds of philosophical problems about what the soul is. Aquinas scholars have been almost exclusively focused on what I (following Dom Lottin) would call the "static" view of the soul: it is the form of the body, the principle of substance, personhood, subsistence, and unity. For Aquinas, however, the soul as composed of parts or powers is a potential whole (*totum potentiale*), which is dynamic. The soul understood as the principle of motion and life must be composed of a complex, sophisticated, and dynamic cluster of powers that function together in a holistic fashion. As comprised of powers (*potentiae* or *dynameis*), the soul is dynamic in the sense of being self-moving, powerful, and alive. I am convinced that this dynamic view of the soul is utterly crucial for understanding Aquinas's moral ethics. For instance, in his famous prologue to his massive treatment on ethics, the second part of the *Summa*, Aquinas announces that he will now turn to consider man as he is the principle of his own operations (*suorum operum principium*), and the soul is, for Aquinas, the principle of its own operations (*operationis principium*) precisely insofar as it is a potential whole (*totum potentiale*).[21]

After dividing the soul into its parts (chapter 1) and examining how these parts are unified as a potential whole (chapter 2), the book considers the relevant sense in which the parts are naturally disordered (chapter 3) and then examines how these disordered parts become unified or ordered by good habits (chapter 4). From a metaphysical perspective, the potential whole can seem to be an incredibly complex and elegant unified whole, but from an ethical perspective, it can seem to be terribly inept and disorderly, not at all a unified, seamless whole. Thinking about the natural disorder of the potential whole illuminates why the sense appetites need habits in the first place. To put it very simply, if all the parts of the soul worked in perfect harmony, there would be no need for virtue. I also offer a brief theological detour to present Aquinas's views on how the Fall wreaked havoc on the order of the powers of the soul. Although this book is first and foremost concerned with Aquinas's philosophical thinking on reason, emotion, and virtue (hence I will sidestep the interesting and complex problem of the infused virtues altogether), the Fall places limits on how far virtue can go in ordering the soul's parts. The sense appetites will always be troublesome, and to think that virtues could perfectly solve the problem, as Aristotle does, is simply unrealistic; from Aquinas's theological perspective it is tantamount to claiming that we could habituate ourselves back to Eden. For Aquinas, habits can help us go quite far, but not that far.

Habits, of course, are a crucial part of the story of how the sense appetites can participate in reason. In Aristotle's paradigmatic example it

---

21. *QDA*, q. 9 [Leonine 24.1:81–82.247, 250, 288].

is habit, or more precisely virtue, that makes the difference. Sense appetites with temperance participate in reason, while those without do not. Although the full story of what habits actually do to the sense appetites unfolds throughout the second half of the book, I begin laying the groundwork in chapter 4 by explaining what a habit is in the first place. My view on Aquinas's philosophy of virtue qua habit is quite different than other scholarly treatments. On the one hand, Aquinas says that virtues are according to nature and perfections of nature, but on the other hand, he also says that virtues are perfections of powers. Aquinas scholars tend either to emphasize that virtues perfect nature or that they perfect powers. But as I see it, virtues are the perfection of powers insofar as these powers are part of nature precisely because nature is composed of powers, that is, virtues are perfections of nature or soul insofar as it is a potential whole.

As we seek to understand how emotion can participate in reason, part 2 begins with an introduction (chapter 5) to Aquinas's doctrine of participation to the extent necessary for our purposes. There are different kinds of participation, and given this, there are different possibilities concerning what can participate in what. Although I will conclude that Aquinas only means one kind of participation when he speaks of the sense appetites as participating in reason, chapter 5 is inconclusive. This is because the question of whether Aquinas actually means one kind of participation rather than another can only be fully resolved after we have gone through his explicit texts on the matter in chapters 6–10. Yet the possible interpretive options must be placed on the table and kept in mind while reading those chapters, before they are resolved most fully in the conclusion.

In order to trace the development in Aquinas's thought on exactly how the sense appetites participate in reason, chapters 6–10 follow the chronological sequence of Aquinas's ethical writings. Chapters 6–8 outline Aquinas's thought in Paris in the 1250s, first as he was teaching and composing his commentary on Peter Lombard's *Sentences* in 1251–56, and then later when he was Regent Master in theology and disputed a series of questions known as the *De veritate* in 1256–59. He did not write too much on ethics until his return to Paris in 1268. Chapters 9–10 trace his thought through the later period, 1268 until his death in 1274, which is marked by a large quantity of ethical writings. The second part of the *Summa* (1268–72) towers above all the rest of these and will necessarily consume the great bulk of my attention, but the *De malo* (1266–72) and *De virtutibus in communi* (1271–72) also have quite a few important texts, as does his commentary on the *Nicomachean Ethics* (1271–72).[22] These mature texts, written so close together (notably, the precise chronology of these texts is often not known), do not reveal much development of thought, or at least none that I have found significant. Thus I shall treat Aquinas's mature thought as a block and attempt to present it as clearly as possible.

Because Aquinas's ethical writings are neatly grouped into early and late texts, it is quite easy to trace their historical development, and thus it is odd that so little of the scholarship on Aquinas's ethics does this. I think it is dangerous not to, for if we want to know what Aquinas thought about anything, we ought at least to distinguish between his early positions on some matter and his late ones. A careful reading of his texts on almost any topic shows that Aquinas, like all serious thinkers, was constantly tinkering and developing his positions. There is, of course, great continuity between the early and the late texts, but there is also undoubtedly change, and on some topics more so than others. However, one cannot know whether he developed his thought until one rolls up one's sleeves and delves into the texts—I am far from believing that Aquinas sprung from the *nous* of Zeus all-knowing. Of course, if one restricts one's inquiry to the late texts, one can claim to have presented his mature position. But I strongly believe that thinking about how Aquinas clarified and developed his thought on any topic sheds light on why he ultimately settled on some particular position, which helps us to better understand that position. Nevertheless, I am also, out of straight historical curiosity, simply interested in seeing what his early and late opinions were and whether and how they developed. As there is so little scholarship on Aquinas's ethics that traces his historical and

---

22. I will only use this text sparingly, as I do not want to get too sidetracked on the question of whether or not Thomas is writing with a view to expositing Aristotle's views or putting forth his own personal positions. I will note the parallel passages in my footnotes, and I will only turn to this work when it adds something that is not present in the other texts. In such cases I will try to address the difficult question of whether or not Aquinas is speaking in his own voice.

philosophical development, I hope that these chapters contribute in this respect as well.

Part of the challenge of comparing Aquinas's early and late texts is that he often uses the exact same words in the early and late texts—for example, Aristotle's phrase "the sense appetites participate in reason"—but identical words can mask a difference in thought. Indeed, practically all of the medieval thinkers accepted Aristotle's claim that the sense appetites participate in reason, but of course, they often offered very different and original interpretations of what this meant. Aquinas develops his own thinking, to some extent, about each of the three terms, namely, sense appetites, participation, and reason. Thus we need to track how he uses these terms in his early texts and in his late texts. Although I offer a brief overview of the various powers of the soul in chapter 3, I offer a much fuller account of each of the relevant powers in chapter 6 before discussing the explicit texts in the *Sentences* commentary on how the sense appetites participate in reason in chapter 7. Additionally, before I discuss how the sense appetites participate in reason in the late texts in chapter 10, I return to the powers and show where I think Aquinas developed his understanding of some of the relevant participating parts in chapter 9. Thus, in chapters 6–10, I first discuss the relevant participating parts and then Aquinas's explicit texts on how the sense appetites participate in reason in the early and the late texts.

What I have discovered is that in his earlier treatments of how the sense appetites participate in reason, Aquinas explains the participation by way of exemplar causality, with the form of reason communicated to the sense appetites by way of some formal likeness. However, in these texts, it is unclear what exactly this formal communication is meant to explain in moral life. In the late texts, though, he shifts away from exemplar causality to discuss the entire matter in terms of efficient causality. In doing so, he also grants the will a far larger role to play in commanding the sense appetites to participate in or "obey" reason. What is crucial in the later texts is that the participation necessarily involves the joint and simultaneous efficient causality of reason and will commanding the sense appetites to do something specific. The sense appetites in turn participate in reason when they receive this command from reason and will. In other words, the sense appetites participate only insofar as they are actualized or moved by the very command of reason and will. This clears up many questions about the communication of reason to the sense appetites, as now there is no need to explain how the sense appetites are rational in the sense of having some mysterious diminished form of reason present in them by way of exemplar causality. Rather, the sense appetites receive their rationality from the actual causality of reason and will.

Chapter 11 discusses Aquinas's views on metaphysical participation and explicitly connects the dots to his ethics in light of the ground covered in chapters 6–10. Here, with Aquinas's doctrinal development in mind, I pinpoint the exact kind of participation Aquinas means when he says that the sense appetites participate in reason. I also explain that Aquinas's development in ethics mirrors his development in his metaphysics. Just as he shifts his metaphysical thinking on participation in *esse* from exemplar/formal causality to efficient causality, his thinking on the sense appetites' participation in reason follows suit.

Chapter 12 engages a large school of Aquinas scholars who think that when Aquinas says that the sense appetites participate in reason he means that the sense appetites of the virtuous agent always (by virtue of this participation) have the right emotions *vis-à-vis* the right objects, in the right way, at the right time, and so on. I think this is a fair account of Aristotle's position, but not of Aquinas's. If these scholars were right about Aquinas, such virtuous agents would always have rational emotions—in their words, the passions would be "spontaneously" good or rational apart from the immediate causality of reason itself. The current discussion has been centered on the problem of the so-called virtuous antecedent passions, where "antecedent" refers to the passions that arise very quickly prior to the judgment of reason. These scholars argue that a virtuous sense appetite, which participates in reason, would automatically have the right antecedent emotion about a particular thing prior to reason's deliberation about that particular thing.

I argue that, for a number of reasons, this cannot be Aquinas's position. First and foremost, there is no participation in reason apart from reason's actualizing the sense appetite by way of command; it is impossible for the sense appetites to participate in reason prior to the command. Aquinas, unlike Aristotle, is very adamant that we only use our habits when we will to do so and this means that virtues only participate in reason when they are commanded or actualized by prudential choices. Furthermore, a habit of moral virtue does not make the passions right, that is, desirous of the right thing in the right way at the right time (only reason can determine that mean in such circumstances); rather, what this habit does is simply lower the vehemence of the passions, that is, their strength or power, so that it becomes possible to deliberate clearly and command rightly. Because virtues are firmly bound to good choices, and good choices require clear deliberations, which are impossible with vehement antecedent passions, it is crucial that virtuous persons are not so moved by strong antecedent passions that they cannot think clearly about the relative merits of various possible courses of action. However, lowering antecedent passions is not participating in reason itself, nor does lowering the passions' vehemence order them to the right objects in the particular and messy circumstances in which choices must be made.

Chapter 13 argues for the plausibility of Aquinas's position by defending him against some important objections. Given that I draw a sharp contrast between Aquinas and Aristotle, and that some believe that departing from Aristotle implies an inevitable slide toward emotion-repressing Kant, I also briefly take up Kant and compare Aquinas with Kant. I argue that recent literature in Kantian ethics depicts a Kant who is, in some ways, surprisingly similar to my depiction of Aquinas. Indeed, Aquinas is closer to Kant in some ways, although in others he is closer to Aristotle. Here I challenge the popular metanarrative of the history of moral philosophy that maintains that Aquinas is the polar opposite of Kant and a faithful disciple of Aristotle on all questions of moral virtue. In my view, Aristotle is a little too optimistic about the possibility of habituating our emotions, while Kant is a little too pessimistic; Aquinas, however, strikes a plausible balance between the two. My discussion here is relatively brief and far more suggestive than comprehensive.

I end by addressing the important contemporary objections to virtue ethics from philosophers using studies in social psychology. Some have recently argued that studies in social psychology show that classical virtue ethics, and Aristotle's in particular, is an ephemeral and wishful fairy tale. If such virtue existed, they say, we should be able to find empirical evidence for it in such studies, but there apparently is none. Insofar as no one else has, I take up these important objections and level them at Aquinas. I argue that Aquinas's theory is better able to address these serious criticisms than Aristotle's theory. In fact, I think the data from the studies offers further evidence why Aquinas's theory of virtue is quite plausible. The last chapter, for those who are interested, can be read on its own, as it offers a kind of summary of Aquinas's position. All in all, in this chapter I try to show that Aquinas's position on this topic is realistic and makes good sense.

One of the problems in writing about how metaphysics, anthropology, and ethics are connected in Aquinas is the sheer quantity and complexity of tightly intertwined scholastic concepts that must be woven together—and weave we must, simply because these are so intertwined in Aquinas's thought. To oversimplify would be misleading and unscholarly, while to explain everything in detail would be tedious. For instance, I must briefly and summarily discuss Aquinas's distinction between essence and *esse* in order to ground a person's ontological unity, eliminate certain possible misunderstandings, and explain why substantial unity cannot be based on the soul's powers—*esse* rears its head again and again in many different relevant contexts. Such matters are not peripheral enough to excise, as without them the story cannot be told, but if I explained them fully no one would read the story. I have striven to keep my presentations of these terms brief, and accordingly, I fully admit to their ultimate inadequacy. There is, of course, an abundance of resources for those who wish to understand something particular in greater detail, and I have referred to many of these in my footnotes. Nevertheless, the balancing act—trying to help readers who are unfamiliar with scholastic and Aristotelian thought while not burdening those who are already familiar with these—has been difficult. I confess to catering more to the latter, but I also hope that I have offered enough to help the rest along. My apologies to those for whom I may have erred in one direction or the other.

I fully admit that parts of this book are expository, and that at times I hew very close to the original Latin, but I believe that staying close to a thinker like Aquinas needs no apology. Although our contemporary questions and discussions are not exactly the same as the questions asked in the thirteenth century, Aquinas wrote so much that it is possible to stitch together from various places a rather full account of what Aquinas would have said on many of our most pressing questions. Although it is always risky to cherry-pick passages and weave them together in a narrative, I have done my best to try to faithfully reconstruct Aquinas's voice in hope of making his position a plausible and interesting alternative to the many other voices in the conversation about reason, emotion, and habits in the moral life.

THE SOUL AS
A POTENTIAL
WHOLE

I

FRAGMENTATION OF THE SOUL INTO PARTS

Precision and Aristotle's Tripartite Division of the Soul

Why should someone interested in ethics bother with the parts of the soul at all? At the end of the first book of the *Nicomachean Ethics*, the *locus classicus* of this topic, Aristotle claims that if you want to know about human virtue there is one thing you need to know about the soul, namely, that it has three parts. We only need to know *that* this is so, and no more, for more precision about the three parts is unnecessary for the subject matter. However, Aquinas completely ignores Aristotle's warning and goes into an extraordinary amount of precision about these parts. Why does he ignore Aristotle's advice? Before we begin to answer this question, I must note that Aquinas's precisions about the parts of the soul are utterly crucial to the argument of this book. Not only do his details make sense; they also reveal the originality of Aquinas's ethical philosophy and precisely how Aquinas thinks that the emotions can participate in reason. Let us start, then, with Aristotle's claim about what it is that we do and do not need to know about the human soul and its parts and work our way to what Aquinas thinks we need to know.

The true student of politics, Aristotle argues, must study virtue above all else. This is because the student desires to make laws that will form virtuous citizens. Moreover, as the operation of virtue, or human happiness, is an operation of the human soul, the true student of politics must know a thing or two about the soul.[1] According to Aristotle, this student must know that one part of the soul is rational and that another part is irrational.[2] This student must also know that the irrational part is further subdivided into two parts: "For the vegetative element in no way shares in a rational principle, but the appetitive and in general the desiring element in a sense shares [or participates] in it, in so far as it listens to and obeys it."[3]

Moral virtue, as distinguished from intellectual virtue, concerns the appetitive or desiring part of the soul. Grasping moral virtue therefore requires recognizing something in the soul that can obey and listen to reason but at times "fights against and resists" it. It seems obvious enough that anyone can recognize this "part" of the soul:

There seems to be also another irrational element in the soul [the "appetitive" part mentioned above]—one which in a sense, however, shares in a rational principle. For we praise the reason of the continent man and of the incontinent, and the part of their soul that has reason, since it urges them aright and towards the best objects; but there is found in them also another natural element beside reason, which fights against and resists it. For exactly as paralyzed limbs when we intend to move them to the right turn on the contrary to the left, so it is with the soul; the impulses of incontinent people move in contrary directions. But while in the body we see that which moves astray, in the soul we do not. No doubt, however, we must none the less suppose that in the soul too there is something beside reason, resisting and opposing it. In what sense it is distinct from the other elements does not concern us. Now even this seems to have a share in reason, as we said; at any rate in the continent man it obeys reason—and presumably in the temperate and brave man it is still more obedient; for in him it speaks, on all matters, with the same voice as reason.[4]

Moral virtue, most generally, concerns the ordering of the appetitive to the rational part of the soul, specifically, how the appetitive part listens to, obeys, or shares in reason.[5] In Aquinas's Latin version of these texts,

---

1. Aristotle, *Nicomachean Ethics* (hereafter, *Nic.*) trans. David Ross, in *The Complete Works of Aristotle*, ed. J. Barnes (Princeton, N.J.: Princeton University Press, 1984), I.13, 1102a5–a25 [2:1741].

2. Ibid., 1102a25–27.

3. Ibid., 1102b29–1103a10 [2:1742].

4. Ibid., 1102b13–28 [2:1741–42].

5. Aristotle also entertains dividing the rational part somewhat differently in 1103a1–3

the phrase "shares in reason" is rendered as "participates in reason" (*participare ratione*).[6] Aquinas regularly used this phrase, *participare ratione*, to explain how the appetitive part is or ought to be related to the rational part, that is, how one part of the soul participates in another part. A natural starting point for this book, then, would be an examination of exactly what Aristotle or Aquinas meant by a "part" of the soul. However, as I mentioned, Aristotle warned his audience that the sense in which these parts (vegetative, appetitive, and rational) are distinct[7]—whether they are actually separable or only separable in thought[8]—"does not concern us."[9] That would be more precision than is necessary. In his commentary on the *Nicomachean Ethics*, Aquinas seems to agree with Aristotle about this. Aquinas notes that the end of practical science is not only knowledge but action.[10] More specifically, it is knowledge for the sake of action.[11] To bring up excessive details about the parts of the

---

[2:1741–42]: "And if this element [appetitive] also must be said to have reason, that which has reason also will be twofold, one subdivision having it in the strict sense and in itself, and other having a tendency to obey as one does one's father." This alternate division rests on Aristotle's claim that one could name the appetitive part in question rational, and thus the rational part itself would be divided in two. This passage in Greek is quite tricky, and Aristotle is playing on the different ways one can take *logon exein*, that is, to have reason. It can be taken in three ways: (1) to have reason, (2) to obey and follow reason, and (3) to originate a reason. The appetitive part obviously cannot fall under the third alternative, but it can certainly be conceived to fall under the first two. For if under "rational" is included that which is capable of being persuaded or influenced by reason (and in this way it could also be said to *have logos*), then one can call the appetitive power rational. In other words, it is possible to take the appetitive part as either rational or irrational depending on how strict one wants to be with the term "rational." Aristotle's tripartite division can be divided in two ways: either one can have two rational parts and one irrational part, or one can have two irrational parts and one rational part. In a certain sense it makes no difference if one wants to name this middle part irrational (as it is not reason, but granted that it is not vegetative) or rational (but by participation). That seems to be Aristotle's point. Cf. *Nic.* 1117b32–24.

6. Aquinas's Latin text of the first book of Aristotle's *Nicomachean Ethics* came from a version of Grosseteste's translation. For Grosseteste's translation see *Aristoteles Latinus* v. 26, f. 1, ed. R. A. Gauthier (Leiden: Brill, 1974). For this passage see 161–62. Grosseteste is simply translating the Greek *metecho* as the Latin *participo* (see the entry in the index of Greek-Latin terms on 716). The version of this text that Aquinas used was reconstituted and published in the Leonine (vol. 48) edition of Aquinas's commentary on the *Nicomachean Ethics*.

7. This is not the same tripartite division as the soul's tripartite division into vegetative, sensitive, and rational; more specifically, the appetitive part ought not to be equated with the sensitive part. See Aristotle's discussion in *De anima* III 432a17–432b9, esp. 432b5–7, and Aquinas's discussion of this in *In III De an.* 14 [Leonine 24.1:239.50–58].

8. Aristotle, *Nic.* I.13, 1102a29–32 [2:1741].

9. Ibid., 1102b24–25 [2:1742].

10. *Sententia libri Ethicorum* [hereafter "*In Ethic.*"] I.3 [Leonine 47.1:12.144–48].

11. Aquinas notes that it is necessary to know *that* concupiscence is curbed by abstinence,

soul would be a waste of time and energy, which ought rather to be focused on acts and virtue.[12]

Anyone who has casually glanced at Aquinas's ethical writings, however, will quickly notice that he ignores Aristotle's statement about the kind of precision that is necessary. Aquinas offers a helpful distinction in *ST* I (q. 14, a. 16) that accounts for his kind of precision:

Some knowledge is only speculative, some is only practical, but some knowledge is in a certain respect speculative and in a certain respect practical. It must be known on the following evidence that knowledge can be called speculative in three ways. First, on the part of the things known, which are not operable by the one knowing, as is man's knowledge of natural or divine things. Second, with respect to the mode of knowing, as for example if a builder would consider a house by defining, dividing, and considering its universal predicates. This indeed is to consider operable things in a speculative way and not insofar as they are operable: for something is operable through the application of form to matter, and not through the resolution of composed things into their universal formal principles. Third, with respect to the end: *for the practical intellect differs from the speculative by its end*, as Aristotle says in book three of the *De anima* [433a14].

For the practical intellect is ordered to the end of operation; the end, however, of the speculative intellect is the consideration of truth. Whence, if some builder were to consider how some house could come to be, not ordering it to the end of operation, but only in order to know, there will be, with respect to the end, speculative consideration, nevertheless of something operable. Knowledge therefore which is speculative by reason of the thing known is only speculative. But what is speculative either according to mode or according to end, is in a certain respect speculative and in a certain respect practical. But when it is ordered to the end of operation, it is simply practical.[13]

---

but it is not necessary to know why. For insofar as someone thinks *that* it possible to change his destructive inclinations, he may try to. Armed with this knowledge, a lawmaker may prohibit certain activities and promote others with the express intent of ridding citizens of certain habits which may be destructive to the common good and themselves. Thus it is necessary to know *that* this is the case (*quia*), but it is not necessary to know *why* (*propter quid*) this is the case. *Propter quid* knowledge of such things is reserved for the speculative sciences, see *In I Ethic.* 4 [Leonine 47.1:15.141–50].

12. *In I Ethic.* 11 [Leonine 47.1:39.86–95].

13. *ST* I, q. 14, a. 16 [St. Paul 85–86].

In the case of ethics, therefore, what is known need not be practical. Moral matters may be considered speculatively, as a house builder may consider universal truths about houses—that is, it is possible to consider universal truths about operable things, namely, things that can be made or done. Of course, for any object viewed speculatively, there is no limit to the amount of precision required, provided the details help one better understand the subject matter at hand. One may thus distinguish between ethical knowledge that is truly practical, insofar as it is for the sake of making persons virtuous, and knowledge of human ethics that is speculative, insofar as it aims to satisfy our natural desire to know what virtue is through an understanding of the principles and causes of virtue. Although speculative knowledge of human ethics must be presented quite differently than practical knowledge, it need not and does not positively exclude the latter.

This book looks closely at the detailed precisions in Aquinas's account of moral virtue's place and role within Aristotle's tripartite division of the soul in *Nic.* I.13 into the rational, the sensitive, and the vegetative. Specifically, this book examines how the part of the soul that is the principle of our emotions/passions (the sensitive part) participates in another part, reason. As this book is not strictly practical, it can ignore Aristotle's warning about the requisite precision.[14] Because I am investigating how the sense appetites, the seat of the emotions, can participate in reason, which involves one part of the soul (the sense appetites) participating in another part (reason), I first investigate these parts of the soul at Aquinas's level of precision in chapters 1–4. Then I examine participation in the context of the parts of the soul in chapters 5–11.

Soul qua *Simplex*: Soul as a Simple Unified Form

The most obvious candidate for the soul's parts are its powers. Aquinas is quite adamant that perfect knowledge about virtue requires knowledge about the powers of the soul.[15] And Aquinas often mentions

14. It is not as if Aquinas simply decided to proceed differently than Aristotle. Aquinas was, of course, part of a scholastic milieu that asked particular questions and expected highly detailed answers. He does, however, give a very good nonhistorical reason why he proceeds with the kind of detail that he does. Nor am I willing to say that the *Nicomachean Ethics* is simply a practical work.

15. *In I De an.* 11 [Leonine 45.1:55.122–24].

the powers of the soul as its parts—for example, reason, will, the internal and external sense powers, and so on,[16] but along with the powers he also mentions the supreme, active, contemplative,[17] rational, sensitive,[18] vegetative,[19] interior,[20] opiniative,[21] apprehensive, appetitive, etc., parts.[22] Clearly these are not parts of the soul in the exact same way. For example, the sense power of sight cannot be a part of the soul in the same way that the sensitive part is a part of the soul.

At times Aquinas seems to deny that the soul has parts, for he insists that the soul, as the form of the body, is simple (*simplex*) in its essence.[23] There is not more soul in the hand than in the power of sight—that is, the soul as immaterial is neither here nor there; it is the simple form of the whole body.

But if the soul is essentially simple, how can it also be the kind of thing that is composed of parts? Aristotle raised this question at the very beginning of his *De anima*:

We must consider also whether soul is divisible or is without parts, and whether it is everywhere homogenous or not; and if not homogenous, whether its various forms are different specifically or generically.... Further, if what exists is not a plurality of souls, but a plurality of parts of one soul, which ought we to investigate first, the whole soul or its parts? It is also a difficult problem to decide which of these parts are in nature distinct from one another.[24]

He returned to this question in the *De anima* again and again.[25] Whether Aristotle ultimately succeeded in distinguishing between the soul (or souls) and its parts is still disputed.[26] But it is quite clear, as shown by his

---

16. *In II De an.* 5 [Leonine 45.1:87.3–8].

17. *Scriptum super libros sententiarum magistri Petri Lombardi* [hereafter "*In Sent.*"] I, d. 3, q. 4, a. 1, ad 6, in *Scriptum super libros sententiarum magistri Petri Lombardi*, ed. R. P. Mandonnet and R. P. Maria Fabianus Moos (Paris: Lethielleux, 1929–47) (hereafter, Mand or Moos, for their respective edited volumes]; Mand 114.

18. *Summa contra gentiles* (hereafter, *SCG*) III.120 [Leonine manualis 371].

19. *De unitate intellectus* c. 1 [Leonine 43:292.116–18].

20. *ST* I-II, q. 80 [St. Paul 899].

21. *ST* I-II, q. 57, a. 4, ad 2 [St. Paul 786].

22. *ST* I-II, q. 22, a. 2, a. 1 [St. Paul 657].

23. *QDA*, q. 9, ad 14 [Leonine 24.1:85.483]; q. 8, ad 14 [Leonine 24.1:73.459–63]; q. 10, ad 17 [Leonine 24.1:94.401].

24. Aristotle, *De anima* I.1, 402b1–13 [1:641–42].

25. Ibid., 411b5–13 [1:655]; II, 413b14–29 [1:658]; III, 432a15–b9 [1:687]. Cf. *Nic.* I.13, 1102a26–32 and 1102b24–25 [2:1741–42].

26. Scholars are divided on this point. For example, some scholars argue that Aristotle's

repeated return to the question, that he considered it a very important question to ask. The remainder of this chapter and the next will concern itself with this question because Aquinas also thinks it is important for ethics, as we shall see.

Before Aquinas is willing to establish how the soul can have parts, he establishes how the soul does not have parts, namely, as it is the principle of substance and the form of the body. It is only after he has established this that he is willing to partition the soul. Thus Aquinas's major discussions of how the soul has parts always follow on the heels of his account of how the soul is a simple or partless form that is the principle of substance, namely, his discussion of why there can only be one substantial form (or soul) in any given substance.[27] In the coming sections we will see how the soul can have parts, but Aquinas insists that grasping in what sense the soul does have parts presupposes grasping in what sense it does not. Thus I will follow Aquinas's order and begin with an overview of his account of the role of soul in the problem of the unity of substantial form. In the remainder of this chapter I will discuss how the soul has parts and in the next chapter I will discuss how these parts are unified. My goal is to provide a general overview of his thinking on the unity of substantial form, which requires briefly discussing his most basic metaphysical principles. Because these principles will come up throughout the course of the book, this section also serves as a general introduction to them.

---

soul is a set of powers: William Charlton, "Aristotle's Definition of Soul," *Phronesis* 25 (1980): 170–86; J. L. Ackrill, "Aristotle's Definitions of *Psuche*," in his *Articles on Aristotle: 4. Psychology and Aesthetics*, ed. J. Barnes, M. Schofield, and R. Sorabji (London: Duckworth, 1979), 65–75; R. Sorabji, "Body and Soul in Aristotle," in *Aristotle's De Anima in Focus*, ed. Michael Durrant (London: Routledge, 1993), 162–69; Thomas Kjeller Johansen, *The Powers of Aristotle's Soul* (Oxford: Oxford University Press, 2012); Anna Marmodoro, "Aristotle's Hylomorphism without Reconditioning," *Philosophical Inquiry* 36 (2013): 18. See also Marmodoro's forthcoming *Aristotle on Perceiving Objects* (Cambridge: Cambridge University Press), chap. 1. For a more Thomistic approach (distinguishing between the soul and its powers) see Rebekah Johnston, "Aristotle's *De Anima*: On Why the Soul is Not a Set of Capacities," *British Journal for the History of Philosophy* 19 (2011): 185–200; Theodore Scaltsas, "Is a Whole Identical to its Parts?," *Mind* 99 (1990): 587–88. See Nicholas Kahm, "Aquinas and Aristotelians on Whether the Soul is a Group of Powers," *History of Philosophy Quarterly* 34 (2017): 115–32. See also Peter King, "The Inner Cathedral: Mental Architecture in High Scholasticism," *Vivarium* 46 (2008): 255–58, who argues that Aristotle's position is simply unclear.

27. Thus *Quaestio disputata de spiritualibus creaturis* (hereafter, *QSC*), a. 3, is presupposed for a. 4; *QDA*, q. 9, is presupposed for q. 10; and *ST* I, q. 76, aa. 1, 3, 4, 6, 7, are presupposed for a. 8. He opens *QDA*, q. 10, and *QSC*, a. 4, by noting that the truth of these questions depends on the previous ones.

Broadly speaking, for Aquinas, substances are (for the most part) what we intuitively think they are, namely, things like insects, trees, and people. They are not, however, artificial things like computers, books, or statues. In the broadest sense, substances are natural things that have their own intrinsic principle of motion and rest. These are the kinds of beings that are most fully and substantially beings—a person, say, ratherer than that person's T-shirt or paleness. For Aquinas, substantial form is the principle that makes such a being actually exist as this particular substance and as this kind of substance. The form of a human is the human soul, which makes the human exist as this human, that is, as this substance.

During the Middle Ages, there was a fierce debate about whether a substance could be composed of many substances. Unlike most of his contemporaries, Aquinas argued that there could only be one substantial form in any given substance.[28] This point is important for our purposes, because when Aquinas speaks of the soul's parts he is not speaking of other substances or substantial forms, nor, for that matter, does he think that substantial unity can be caused by the soul's parts. We will now see why.[29]

Substances come to be and pass away: this is called substantial change, that is, substantial generation and corruption. A substance cannot exist prior to generation (as it would have to exist before it exists) or after corruption (for then it would have to exist after it exists), and thus generation and corruption account for the coming to be and destruction of the whole substance. To say, however, that a substance comes to be where there was no substance before would seem to imply that a sub-

---

28. For Thomas's position see John F. Wippel, *The Metaphysical Thought of Thomas Aquinas: From Finite Being to Uncreated Being* (Washington, D.C.: The Catholic University of America Press, 2000), 327–51. For a helpful book-length review of all of the known scholastic positions on this topic from Gundissalinus (written ca. 1170–75) to the Condemnations of 1277, see Richard Dales, *The Problem of the Rational Soul in the Thirteenth Century* (Leiden: Brill, 1995). See also Anton Charles Pegis, *St. Thomas and the Problem of the Soul in the Thirteenth Century* (Toronto: Pontifical Institute of Mediaeval Studies, 1934).

29. The following paragraphs are a summary and paraphrase of Aquinas's main arguments. For Aquinas's best texts consult *QSC*, a. 3; *QDA*, q. 9; *ST* I, q. 76, aa. 3, 4, 6, 7; *SCG* II.71. See Bernardo Carlos Bazán, "The Human Soul: Form *and* Substance? Thomas Aquinas' Critique of Eclectic Aristotelianism," *Archives d'histoire doctrinale et littéraire du Moyen-âge* 64 (1997): 95–126; Dales, *The Problem of the Rational Soul*, 138–50; Pegis, *The Problem of the Soul*, 121–80; and Wippel, *Metaphysical Thought*, 327–51.

stance comes from nothing. Contra Parmenides's argument that something cannot come from nothing, Aristotle subdivides being into act and potency, enabling him to account for substantial generation. Being is divided into what actually is (act) and what can be (potency), and motion (the general umbrella under which generation falls) is the reduction of potency to act, or more simply, the actualization of the potential.

For instance, this page actually has these words printed on it, but it potentially has other words on it. To change these other words from potential words to actual words, all you have to do is to take out your pencil and scribble them on the margins, that is, you need an actual cause, your writing, and a potential cause, the capacity of the paper to receive ink. The written words do not come to be from nothing, but from the act of writing and capacity or potency of the paper to receive such forms. Or to use Aristotle's classic example, a bronze statue comes from the artist actually pouring the molten bronze into the mold thereby imposing the form on the matter, bronze, which has the capacity to be so formed.

These examples are highly oversimplified and somewhat misleading because scribbled pages and bronze statues are not substances, but artifacts. Artifacts are simply artificial arrangements of already existing substances, and Aquinas calls the coming-to-be of artifacts artificial generation in contrast to substantial generation. Both Aristotle and Aquinas, however, use artificial generation as helpful analogies to explain substantial generation. In other words, substantial generation is something like the making of a bronze statue, where the form of the statue is cast into the matter of bronze.

However, for Aquinas, in the case of real substantial generation, the potency principle or matter is radically different. Unlike the bronze of a statue this matter is not an already existing substance or group of substances. As Aquinas sees things, a substance simply cannot be composed of many substances without being many substances. The matter or potency principle in substantial generation therefore must be completely without any other substantial form. Such matter is called "prime matter" or "pure potency." Considered in itself prime matter has no form or existence (Aquinas sometimes calls it "relative nonbeing")—its existence is utterly dependent on whatever informs it, although it always exists under this or that substantial form. Aquinas's response to Parmenides, then, is that the potentiality from which substances come to be is not nonbeing or another substance; rather, it is relative nonbeing, pure potency, or prime matter.[30] Any material substance is thus composed of two intrinsic principles, form and prime matter. As prime matter is not a being, this hylomorphic composition is not a mereological composition of two separate actually existing entities, but is ontologically one and simple.

An accidental composition, however, is a composition of two actually existing entities: a substance and at least one accident. Accidents have a particular kind of being, namely, accidental being (*esse*), which is to be in some substance (*inesse*); it is a modification or qualification of an already existing substance (which has *esse*), for example, a person (a substance) is pale (an accident). Accidental form presupposes an actually existing subject or substance; it inheres in the substance in which it exists, and it depends on that substance for its existence. Thus, although I am pale, the form of paleness cannot exist apart from the substance (me) in which it exists. Once I spend some time in the sun, my paleness will vanish and be replaced by another skin hue. In the case of accidental change, unlike substantial change, the substance perdures though the change—I remain the same substance or person, regardless of whether I am pale, slightly tan, or tan.

From this perspective, as Aquinas likes to argue, to posit a multiplicity of substantial forms implies a confusion of the substantial and the accidental orders. For example, if one posited two substantial forms in a man, animal and rational, then either that man would be not one man but two men (insofar as substantial form is what makes a substance be one, as will be explained shortly) or one of these forms would have to be an accident and the other would have be a substance—but that is impossible, as man substantially *is* an animal: man is not accidentally animal. One medieval alternative for positing many substantial forms was to

---

30. For a helpful discussion of prime matter, see Aquinas's *De principiis naturae* (hereafter, *De princ.*), esp. 85–89 [Leonine 43:41.70–89]. For a full discussion of prime matter and an overview of Aquinas's texts see Wippel, *Metaphysical Thought*, 295–371. For a helpful general argument for the existence of prime matter, see Andrew J. Jaeger, "Back to the Primitive: From Substantial Capacities to Prime Matter," *American Catholic Philosophical Quarterly* 88 (2014): 381–95. See also Edward Feser, *Scholastic Metaphysics: A Contemporary Introduction* (Heusenstamm: Editiones Scholasticae, 2014), 160–208.

suppose that generation unfolds according to a process of adding substantial forms: first the animal is generated, and then an additional substantial form of rational is added to generate man. But Aquinas insists that in any such series the last added form must really be an accidental form that comes to and inheres in a preexisting substance, namely, an animal. In other words, any articulation of a process of a later addition of a substantial form to an already existing subject cannot be substantial generation but is in fact an accidental change of some preexisting substance.

I should also note that some contemporary metaphysicians consider body to be composed of powers, which are accidents.[31] But for Aquinas, this is to put the cart before the horse, because accidents can only exist in substances. He would ask: what are the substances that these accidents inhere in? Because powers are accidents, they must inhere in substances, and thus this position implies that body is really many substances. But if so, Aquinas would ask, what is it that unites them as one substance? Substances must be simple, and any composition of powers or substances must end up being a metaphysical hodgepodge.

One crucial facet of Aquinas's understanding of the unity (or nonplurality) of substantial forms is that it is the same substantial form that makes the substance exist and makes it one. This point presupposes Aquinas's thinking on the convertibility of one and being,[32] for which we can briefly turn to Aquinas's famous discussion of the transcendentals in *De veritate*, q. 1, a. 1. Aquinas notes that one way in which one can predicate something of being that is not included in the meaning (*ratio*) of being itself is according to what he calls the general modes of being, which follow upon each being in itself. One of these general modes is signified by the term "one." The term one is primarily negative. It signifies nothing other than undivided being (*ens indivisum*), that is, it signifies a being as not divided from itself.[33] In other words, if there were a

---

31. Marmodoro, "Aristotle's Hylomorphism," 12–18; Johansen, *The Powers of Aristotle's Soul*, chap. 1, holds a similar position, although he does not engage contemporary metaphysics. See Kahm, "Aquinas and Aristotelians," 121–24.

32. See *QSC*, a. 3 [Leonine 24:38.233–34]; *SCG* II.58 [Leonine manualis 154]; *QDA*, q. 9 [Leonine 24.1:89.310–14]. See Wippel, *Metaphysical Thought*, 338–39, and Jan A. Aertsen, *Medieval Philosophy and the Transcendentals* (Leiden: Brill, 1996), 233–34.

33. *Quaestiones disputatae de veritate* (hereafter, *QDV*), q. 1, a. 1 [Leonine 22.1:5.124–42].

plurality of substantial forms in any particular being, that being would not, according to Aquinas, be an undivided being; rather, it would be divided. This is important because a substance's unity cannot be grounded on a mereological complex of substances or powers; it must be simple and undivided. It is the simple substantial form that makes a being be one in the unqualified sense (*simpliciter*).

But how exactly does this work? It would seem that for Aquinas, it is God as creator (rather than substantial form) who makes beings be by efficiently causing their existence (*esse*), that is, it is ultimately God who makes all beings be *simpliciter* and makes them be one. In order to understand in what sense a human being is ultimately one, we must broaden our perspective to include not only Aquinas's account of matter-form composition, but also his thinking on essence-*esse* composition.

In general, *esse* for Aquinas is actuality in the particular sense of the actual existence of a being. Essence, however, is the "formal" determination of that existence, that is, what the being is or the way (or mode) in which the being has its existence. Finite beings are composed of two ultimate intrinsic metaphysical principles, *esse* (accounting for their actual existence) and essence (accounting for the way they have existence or what they are). Aquinas insists that a being or essence cannot cause its own existence, for then it would have to be prior to itself, and thus a being's existence must be caused by something else (ultimately by God). And, of course, essence cannot actually exist without existence. Aquinas's essence/existence distinction (inherited from Avicenna) points to the radically contingent nature of all finite beings, for granting that *esse* must be caused by something else, there is no necessity that any essence or being actually exists.[34] Aquinas offers a succinct account of his position in the first article of his disputed question *De spiritualibus creaturis*:

It is clear that the first being, namely, God, is an infinite act having in himself the whole fullness of existing which is not contracted to some generic or specific nature. Thus it is necessary that his *esse* is not an *esse* that is, as it were, instilled in some nature [or essence] which is not its own *esse*, since then it would be limited to that nature. Thus we say that God is his own *esse*, and this cannot

---

34. The literature on the *esse*/essence distinction is vast. For a good starting point see John F. Wippel's "Essence and Existence," in *The Cambridge History of Medieval Philosophy*, ed. R. Pasnau (Cambridge: Cambridge University Press, 2010), 2:622–34.

be said of anything else. For as it is impossible to understand that there are many separate whitenesses—for if there were a whiteness separate from any subject or recipient, it could only be one—so it is impossible that there be more than one *ipsum esse subsistens*. Everything that is after the first being, since it is not its own *esse*, has an *esse* received in something, by which the *esse* is limited. And thus in every created thing, the nature of the thing which participates in *esse* is other than the participated *esse* itself. And since each thing participates by assimilation in the first act insofar as it has *esse*, it is necessary that the participated *esse* in each thing is related to the nature that participates in it as act to potency.[35]

Thus in every being, with one possible exception, there is a real distinction and composition between essence and *esse*. Aquinas emphasizes that the correlation between essence and *esse* is one of potency to act. Essence as potency receives and limits *esse*, which is its act. With these distinctions in mind, let us return to the question concerning how both God and substantial form could make a being be one. We can reformulate the question like this: how can essence, which is related to *esse* as potency, in turn give *esse* to the body, that is, be correlated as act to the body qua potency? Aquinas immediately proceeds to discuss this in the same article:

Therefore, in the nature of corporeal things matter does not participate per se in *esse*, but through form: for form coming to matter makes it actually exist [*ipsam esse actu*] as soul to body. Thus in composite things we can consider a twofold act and a twofold potency: first, matter is as potency with respect to form, and form is its act. Second, nature as constituted by matter and form is as potency with respect to its *esse* insofar as it receives it.[36]

Thus the solution, according to Aquinas, is straightforward: essence receives *esse* and in turn grants it or communicates it to the body. It should be noted that essence is not the same as soul. Essence includes both matter and form, but the human soul does not include matter at all, for soul is understood in contrast to matter.[37] In the case of a human being, the *esse* that is of the whole composite, however, is also of the soul itself, and

35. *QSC*, a. 1 [Leonine 24.2:13–14.363–85].
36. Ibid., ll. 386–95.
37. *De ente et essentia* (hereafter, *De ente*) 2 [Leonine 43:370.38–57].

the soul communicates that *esse* in which it subsists to corporeal matter.[38] Thus anything is one insofar as it has *esse*.[39]

To conclude this section, from the perspective of any corporeal being's ontological unity we have four distinct principles: essence, *esse*, matter, and form. None of these can be called a part of the soul. In order for matter to be called a part of the soul, it would have to be included within the *ratio* of soul itself, which, of course, it is not. As far as we know, we have no reason at this point to think of the soul as having parts. The soul is simple (*simplex*) or partless as it grounds substantial unity and informs the body. What we do know from this quick overview of Aquinas's position on the unity of substantial form is that if the soul has parts, these parts cannot be other substantial forms, for the soul informs prime matter directly without any mediate forms. And from the perspective of grounding substantial unity these parts cannot be powers, as powers (and any accidents) presuppose a unified substance in which they inhere. In terms of a being's ontological unity, there are no parts to the soul. What is required are the being's intrinsic principles: essence and *esse*, and for corporeal beings, also matter and form. That the soul is the form of the body, that there is only one substantial form in any finite being, and that its being and its oneness are convertible offers no help in dividing the soul into parts. In this sense the soul itself is simple, as Aquinas puts it, and if we wish to posit parts, at the very least we know something about what those parts are not.

Soul qua *multiplex*: The Soul Must Have Parts

Now that we know something about what the parts of the soul are not, let us continue following Aquinas's thread to see what they are. The depiction of the soul up to this point is the standard Thomistic view, but this is where it starts to get interesting. This metaphysical depiction or perspective is in a certain sense static. With the previously mentioned principles, we can account for a substance's existence, unity, and its role in forming the body, but we cannot say anything about what that being does. Aquinas, however, claims that each thing is for the sake of its op-

---

38. *ST* I, q. 76, a. 1, ad 5 [St. Paul 351]. For more on how *forma dat esse*, see John F. Wippel, "Thomas Aquinas on Creatures as Causes of Esse" in his *Metaphysical Themes in Thomas Aquinas II* (Washington, D.C.: The Catholic University of America Press, 2007), 172–94.

39. *ST* I, q. 103, a. 3 [St. Paul 482]; *In VI Metaph.* [Marietti 1176].

eration.[40] Or, as he puts it, *esse* is proportioned to operation; it is granted according to the mode that suits the being's operation, for each being operates insofar as it is a being.[41] Perhaps a better way of putting it is this: if we ask why any particular being has this kind of existence rather than that kind of existence, one answer Aquinas gives, in the line of final causality, is that the being exists in this way so that it can operate in this way.[42] In a certain sense, operation is essential to the soul; in a certain sense, however, it is not.

Consider the very general philosophical question: what is soul? The most common way to begin to answer this question is by making a distinction: animate beings are distinct from inanimate beings. A one-year-old child, for example, makes this distinction naturally. He takes far more interest and delight in a living animate thing that visibly moves itself, for example, an insect, than in an inanimate thing that does not—say, the dirt on which the insect is crawling. This is the distinction between what has a nature and what does not, according to Aristotle's definition of nature as that which has its own internal principle of motion and rest.[43] A living being, according to Aquinas, is precisely that which moves itself.[44]

But if we want to grasp more firmly what exactly this internal principle of motion or operation that Aristotle has called "nature" or "soul" is, we immediately run into some aporias.[45] To say that the soul has an in-

---

40. *QDVC*, q. 9 [Marietti 731]: "omnis res est propter suam operationem"; *ST* I-II, q. 3, a. 2 [St. Paul 569].

41. See, for example, *QDA*, q. 9 [Leonine 24.1:82.278–80]; *QSC*, a. 2 [Leonine 24.2:29.300–303]; *QDA*, q. 10, ad 2 [Leonine 24.1:92.287–89]; *In II De an.* [Leonine 45.1:88.50–54]; *SCG* III.13 [Leonine manualis 365].

42. His first answer to this is because the being has this kind of essence rather than any other. And in the order of discovery, one can reason from its distinctive kind of operation to its distinctive kind of essence. Aquinas, as the texts in the previous notes show, will answer the question in both ways: it acts like this because it exists in this way (because its essence has determined or limited its *esse*), or he answers that it exists in this way so that it can operate in this way, this latter answer being in the line of final causality.

43. For Aristotle's definition of nature, see *Physics* II, 192b14. See Aquinas's agreement with this definition in *In VIII libros Physicorum* [hereafter "*In Phys.*"] II [Marietti 145] and *In II De an.* 2 [Leonine 45.1:75.78–80]. More generally, nature is simply the intrinsic principle of motion or operation: see *ST* I, q. 29, a. 1, ad 4 [St. Paul 150]; *ST* III, q. 2, a. 1 [St. Paul 1871–72]; etc.

44. *ST* I, q. 18 [St. Paul 99].

45. This discussion will be restricted to the metaphysical and more general understanding of motion as the act of potency insofar as it is potency, rather than the understanding of

ternal principle of motion amounts to saying that the soul moves itself.[46] But if it moves itself, it appears that there are two parts, one that moves and another that is moved. Notice that as soon as we speak of motion, we must posit parts. But which part is soul? If it is the moving part, then how can the soul be said to move *itself*? If it is the moved part, then what causes the motion? Can the living soul be both?

Let us look at Aquinas's commentary on Aristotle's discussion of this problem in *De anima*:

All philosophers who recognized soul from observing motion held this common principle, namely, that everything which moves, is moved. Thus, because it is natural for the soul to move, they believed that it was also connatural to it that it be moved; and that is that which the soul has from its own substance. That is why those philosophers placed motion in its definition, saying that the soul moves itself.[47]

For Aquinas this is not quite right, or perhaps it is better to say that it is not quite precise enough. Aquinas would never deny in a general way that, say, an animal moves itself and truly exercises its own agency, for that is what it means to be alive. But positing agency does not commit one to the position that motion or operation is of the essence of any substance. First, Aquinas says, Aristotle disproved the claim that everything that moves is moved by proving the existence of the unmoved mover in *Physics* VIII. Further, Aquinas notes, there is a very brief way to disprove it:[48]

If something moves and is moved, it is obvious that insofar as it moves it is in act, and insofar as it is moved it is in potency. But then the same thing in the same respect would be both in act and in potency, which is unacceptable [*inconveniens*].... In something which moves itself there are two things: one

---

motion from physics, e.g., everything in motion is divisible qua material. The problem with arguments from physics is that one always has to ask whether or not they apply to the human soul, which belongs partly to metaphysics, and partly to physics (see *In I De an.* 2 [Leonine 45.2:9.22–45, 161–243, 262–64] and *Sentencia De sensu* intro. [Leonine 45.2:73–79]), as it is the form of the body as well as the cause of immaterial and material powers and operations. For a fuller discussion of whether or not the study of the soul ultimately belongs to metaphysics or physics see John F. X. Knasas, "Aquinas on the Cognitive Soul: Metaphysics, Physics, or Both?," *American Catholic Philosophical Quarterly* 72 (1998): 501–27.

46. *In VII Phys.* [Marietti 535].

47. *In I De an.* 6 [Leonine 45.1:28.57–65]. He is commenting on I.3, 405b31.

48. Ibid., ll. 69–73.

moving and another moved. It is impossible that the one moving is itself moved per se.[49]

In other words, when it is said that a nature is that which has its own internal principle of motion, it cannot mean that the nature itself qua itself moves itself qua itself. In his commentary on Aristotle's *Physics* VIII, Aquinas explains that a hot thing cannot heat as a whole, for "if the whole were to move itself as whole, it follows that the same thing insofar as it is the same thing is at the same time hot and not hot; because insofar as it is moving it will be actually hot, and insofar as it is moved it will be potentially hot."[50] If a finite being moves itself *per se*, in the sense that it moves itself by itself as whole, then it must be the case that either the substance is prior to itself (in which case it would be simultaneously existing and not existing), or we would have to claim that it was in both act and potency at the same time in the same respect—which, of course, is impossible. In other words, it is impossible for the soul to be the *per se* cause of its own motion.

Thomas then says something quite interesting: we arrive at an understanding of *per se* motion by negating *per accidens* motion. It may be helpful, then, to consider what exactly we are negating. He gives an overview of this in his commentary on Aristotle's *Physics* VIII. Concerning moving and mobile things, he notes that some move or are moved *per accidens* and some are moved *per se*. Here, he says, Aristotle takes *per accidens* broadly, insofar as it also means *according to a part*. Then he subdivides moving and being moved *per accidens*:

First, things are said to move *per accidens* whenever they are said to move because they are in some movers, as when it is said that a musical man heals because there is music in one who heals, and likewise things are said to be moved *per accidens* because the things that are moved are in things that are moved, either as what is located and moved in a place, as we say this person is moved because he is in a moving ship, or as an accident is in a subject, as we say white is moved because a body is moved. There is, however, another way to say that something moves or is moved *per accidens*, since it moves or is moved according to a part [*secundum partem*], as a person is said to strike or be struck, since his hand is struck or strikes. Something is said to move or be moved *per se*, how-

49. Ibid., ll. 74–78 and 92–94.
50. *In VIII Phys.*, l. 7 [Marietti 553].

ever, through negation of the two aforementioned kinds of *per accidens* motion.[51]

All three kinds of *per accidens* motions are applicable to natures. But when it is said that a nature moves itself, this is obviously not to be understood in the sense in which a man moves because he is on a moving ship or in the sense that the accidental whiteness moves. What is meant is that natures must move by means of their parts.

Per se motion, grasped by negating the kinds of motion that we know, is in a certain sense unintelligible, for it seems to be in act and in potency at the same time and in the same respect.[52] In the familiar natural motion of a living being, the mover must be distinct from the moved, and thus there must be division and parts.[53] Wherever there is finite self-motion or operation, be it on a physical or metaphysical plane, there must be parts.[54]

But what about the soul itself: does this mean that it must have parts? In my discussion of the soul as the form of the body, I had no way to divide it into parts. For the soul as a whole completely informs prime matter, and prime matter is not a part of the soul. As the form of the body it is simple. But as a nature, that is, a principle of motion that moves itself in a *per accidens* manner, it must have parts.[55] This was garnered from strictly metaphysical arguments based on act and potency.[56]

---

51. Ibid. [535].

52. There is, however, another kind of *per se* motion in the sense that an act is proper to a specific nature, e.g., reasoning and willing are proper *per se* actions of man: *In VIII Phys.*, l. 7 [Marietti 535]. Also along this line of thinking is Thomas's claim that *per se* actions only come from beings which *per se* subsist, see *SCG* II.51 [Leonine manualis 144], and by this he has in mind an immaterial mode of existing (and its consequent actions), and the contrary, *per accidens* implies a material mode of existing (and its consequent actions). Thus Thomas at times affirms that man acts in a *per se* manner and at times denies it. When he affirms this it is usually to signify man's immortal soul and its immaterial operations. When he denies it, it is according to the strong sense of *per se* self-motion, as a whole cannot move itself as whole. These uses of *per se* are not to be confused with *per se* causality.

53. *In VIII Phys.*, l. 7 [Marietti 537]: "Quia movens ad motum se habet, sicut agens ad patiens: cum autem agens sit contrarium patienti, necesse est quod dividatur id quod est aptum natum agere, ab eo quod est aptum natum pati."

54. *In VIII Phys.*, l. 10 [Marietti 553]; *QDV*, q. 22, a. 3 [Leonine 22.3:618.63–65].

55. *In II De an.*, c. 1 [Leonine 45.1:73.380–92].

56. *In VIII Phys.*, l. 10 [Marietti 553]: "Si igitur totum moveat se secundum totum, sequitur quod idem sit simul actu et potentia; quod est impossibile. Ex hoc ergo concludit principale intentum, quod moventis seipsum una pars movet et alia movetur." See also *SCG* I.13 [Leonine manualis 13].

Aquinas was very careful to make this distinction between these two ways of viewing the soul: the soul qua form (*forma*) is simple (*simplex*), but the soul qua mover (*motor*) is manifold (*multiplex*). Scholarship has been exclusively focused on the soul as the form of matter and also as a principle of subsisting while practically ignoring the soul as mover.[57] I hope to bring out this important aspect of Aquinas's thought. In sum, at this point we may conclude that (1) operation, namely, self-motion, is crucial to living natures, and (2) natures cannot move themselves as wholes, but must move themselves *per accidens* by means of parts, which means, of course, that they must have parts.

The Distinction between the Soul and Its Powers

For Aquinas, the parts of the soul are powers, which are principles of acts. Rather than asking if the soul has parts, the scholastics asked a slightly different question, namely, whether the powers of the soul are the same thing as its essence. I shall focus on my favorite of Aquinas's full and mature answers to this question: article 11 of his disputed questions *De spiritualibus creaturis* (1267–68).[58] Aquinas begins this article by noting a common but incorrect opinion:

57. Most Thomistic scholarship on the soul revolves around two questions: (1) in what way the soul is a principle of subsisting and existing and, closely connected, whether or not the separated soul is a person, and (2), in what way is Aquinas to be contrasted with Descartes and whether or not he can be placed in some kind of modern category, e.g., nonreductive materialism. Much of this large body of literature is very good, but none of it focuses on or even brings out this distinction, which Aquinas took great pains to clarify. Adam Wood in "The Faculties of the Soul and Some Medieval Mind-Body Problems," *The Thomist* 75 (2011): 585–636, briefly discusses it, but he does not go into much detail.

58. For the dating see Jean-Pierre Torrell, *Saint Thomas Aquinas, vol. 1: Person and Work*, rev. ed., trans. Robert Royal (Washington, D.C.: The Catholic University of America Press, 2005), 428. For a more comprehensive overview of the different kinds of arguments Aquinas gives see Pius Künzle, *Das Verhältnis der Seele zu ihren Potenzen* (Freiburg: Universitätsverlag, 1956), 97–170, and Wippel, *Metaphysical Thought*, 266–94. E.-H. Wéber asserted that Thomas changed his mind on this and ultimately denied the real distinction between the soul and its powers: see *La controverse de 1270 à l'Université de Paris et son retentissement sur la pensée de S. Thomas d'Aquin* (Paris: Vrin, 1970), and "Les discussions de 1270 à l'Université de Paris et leur influence sur la pensée philosophique de S. Thomas d'Aquin," in *Die Auseinandersetzungen an der Pariser Universität im XIII. Jahrhundert*, Miscellanea Mediaevalia 10 (Berlin: De Gruyter, 1975), 285–316. This thesis was effectively refuted by B. Carlos Bazán in "Le dialogue philosophique entre Siger de Brabant et Thomas d'Aquin: à propos d'un ouvrage récent de E. H. Wéber," *Revue philosophique de Louvain* 72 (1974): 55–155. See also Wippel, *Metaphysical Thought*, 288–94. But Jaekying Lee in "The Intellect-Body Problem in

Some people think that the powers of the soul are nothing else than the soul's essence, and thus the same essence of the soul, insofar as it is the principle of sensitive operations is called sense, but insofar as it is the principle of intellectual operation it is called intellect, etc. Avicenna noted that these people seem especially to have been moved by the simplicity of the soul, as though this simplicity would not permit so much diversity as appears in the powers of the soul.[59]

Aquinas's approval of Avicenna's opinion that the problem seems to be a misguided emphasis on the simplicity of the soul is worth noting. Another way of putting this view is that there really is no difference between the soul qua form and the soul qua mover. For if the soul acts directly without parts, there is no need to speak of parts of the soul or to emphasize its manifold (*multiplex*) nature. Thus, on this view, we may speak of things like sense and intellect, but those are really just naming the soul in terms of how it is immediately operating. To use the given example, a person does not really think with his or her intellect, but rather with his or her soul. There are no parts of the soul (like intellect or sense) in any real way; these are simply helpful ways of articulating the simple soul in its capacity for its manifold operations. But Aquinas rejects this position:

First, indeed, since it is impossible that the very essence of any created substance is the same as its own operative power. For it is manifest that diverse acts

---

Aquinas," *Archiv Fur Geshichte der Philosophie* 88 (2006): 239–60, has recently tried to revive the controversy. He argues that when Aquinas claims that the intellect is the form of the body, he does not mean the intellective soul, but the intellective power. Although I will not engage his argument directly, it should be clear from the later section on "souls" why I agree with Bazán that Aquinas means the intellective soul. I am intentionally staying away from the argument in *QDA*, q. 12, because I am uncomfortable with the claim that when an accident is produced, the proximate principle for that accident must be another accident [Leonine 24.1:109.152–63]. See King, *Cathedral*, 265; Wippel, *Metaphysical Thought*, 285–88; and Dominik Perler, "Faculties in Medieval Philosophy," in *The Faculties*, ed. D. Perler (Oxford: Oxford University Press, 2015), 106 and 115. Künzle argues that the ultimate ground for the real distinction between the soul and its powers is Aquinas's real distinction between essence and esse; see *Verhältnis*, 158, 195, 205, 216. While Aquinas undoubtedly thinks that wherever there is a real distinction between essence and *esse* there will also be a real distinction between the soul and its powers (or between essence and its operative principles) and that wherever there is no distinction between essence and *esse* there is no distinction between the soul and its power, I have not seen a compelling argument that one can move directly from the essence/*esse* distinction to the distinction between the soul and its powers. For a position similar to Künzle's see Richard R. Baker, "The Thomistic Theory of the Passions and their Influence Upon the Will" (PhD diss., University of Notre Dame, 1941), 8–9n12.

59. *QSC*, a. 11 [Leonine 24.2:118.190–99]. See Avicenna, *Liber de Anima seu Sextus Naturalibus*, ed. S. Van Riet, Avicenna Latinus 1.1 (Leuven: Peeters, 1972), pars 5, cap. 7 (155.44–46).

come from diverse principles. This is because act is always proportioned to that whose act it is. As *esse* itself is the certain actuality of an essence, so *operari* is the actuality of an operative potency or power. Each of them is in act in this way: essence according to *esse*, power according to *operari*. But since in no creature is its own *operari* its own *esse*, for that is only true of God; it follows that the operative power of no creature is its essence. Only in God is essence the same as operative power.[60]

Aquinas here assumes that *esse* is the same as *operari* only in God, and thus there is a real distinction between *esse* and *operari* in all created beings. If one grants such a distinction in creatures, the potency that is ordered to *operari* cannot be identical with the potency that is ordered to *esse*. If we ask why this is so, a number of arguments can be given.

First, let us consider the distinction between *esse* and *operari*. It is obvious from introspection that there is a real distinction between *esse* and *operari* in ourselves. Take thinking, for example. It is an action, and it is obviously not the same as existing. A person can stop thinking without ceasing to exist.[61] What about God? We have no such recourse to introspection there. However, in the argument that no nature can move itself qua itself, as everything that moves must be moved by another, we have already been reasoning along the same lines as the first half of the first proof of God's existence in *ST* I, q. 2, a. 3.[62] If we grant the second half of the argument, that is, if we deny the possibility of an infinite regress in *per se* ordered efficient causes, we can accept that God, as the uncaused cause, is pure act.[63] From this Aquinas argues to divine simplicity by negating any possible composition in God, as any composition

---

60. *QSC*, a. 11 [Leonine 24.2:118.200–214]. This argument is apparently from Alexander of Hales, *Summa theologica* Ia–IIae, inq. 4, tract. 1, sect. 2, q. 1 [Quaracchi 2:424]. For a discussion of this argument and medieval reactions to it see Wood, *Faculties of the Soul*, 597.

61. *ST* I, q. 77, a. 1 [St. Paul 363].

62. The first half of the argument is a defense of the axiom that everything (other than God) which is moved is moved by another because nothing can reduce itself from potency to act. For a presentation of this argument and a discussion of their critics, see Wippel, *Metaphysical Themes*, 413–25 and 444–62. Of course, because everything which moves is moved by another, nothing created can be immediately *per se* operative, so there must be a real distinction between the soul and its powers as the potency for *esse* and the potency for *operari* have to be really different.

63. On the infinite regress, see Wippel, *Metaphysical Thought*, 422–23, esp. n63. See also Caleb Cohoe, "There Must Be a First: Why Thomas Aquinas Rejects Infinite, Essentially Ordered, Causal Series," *British Journal for the History of Philosophy* 21, no. 5 (2013): 838–56.

implies imperfection and consequently potency of some sort.[64] But as God is pure act, there can be no composition in God. If *esse* and *operari* were really distinct in God, they would have to enter into some kind of composition; but that would force us to attribute some potency to God. Thus, they cannot be distinct in God.[65]

What about the principles of *esse* and *operari*? As *esse* and *operari* are not distinct in God, one can hardly argue that they require distinct principles. But what about creatures? What Aquinas said in the above passage is that diverse acts come from diverse principles as an act is always proportioned to its principle. Aquinas simply says that this is "manifest." If we grant this, because it has already been proven that *esse* and *operari* are really distinct, they must have distinct principles. This is not so complex. A human obviously has the capacity to actually think, even when not actually thinking. In other words, humans have a potency that may or may not be actualized. Furthermore, because humans cannot be immediately operative but must act by means of powers, it follows that there must be some causal proportion between the part or power as a principle and its effect, namely, action.

But let us return to the beginning of Aquinas's article and consider what it means to say that essence is identical to operative power. Those who claim that the soul is immediately operative are saying that the soul operates without parts and thus operates in a *per se* manner. As Avicenna noted, these thinkers are overly impressed by the simplicity of the soul, and Aquinas adds that they ultimately wind up applying to the soul a characteristic that is only applicable to God himself.

Here we must remember Aquinas's claim that one only has knowledge of *per se* motion in the strong sense by negating *per accidens* motion. To say that God acts in a *per se* manner is simply to deny that he acts by means of his parts. In other words, the kind of operation that is found in a being that is not composed of act and potency is going to be radically different from the kind of operation that is found in a creature that is so composed. What it means to operate in a *per se* fashion is a purely negative concept for us. Something being immediately operative in this

___

64. For example, as we saw in *QSC*, a. 1, the highest level of composition, essence and *esse*, is a composition of potency and act.

65. A real distinction corresponds to extra-mental reality apart from the mind's consideration.

per se way, as is God, is in a real sense unimaginable in any of the ways in which we are familiar with motion and act, for we are immediately confronted with the question of how something can reduce itself from potency to act.

In all of Aquinas's arguments for the distinction between the soul and its powers, he contrasts the way in which God is immediately operative with the way in which all finite beings operate by means of parts. Negating God's mode of simple and immediate operation in the case of creatures makes it evident that humans, in contrast, operate in a complex, mediate way (by means of powers). The powers of the soul, then, are the means by which humans are able to operate according to their own finite natures. These are the parts of the soul through which the soul, qua mover, is operative.[66]

Aquinas continues his argument in *QSC*, a. 11, but here he restricts it to apply to the human soul in particular. Let us look at the third argument:

Third, the same is apparent from the order of the powers of the soul and their relation to one other. For it is found that one power moves another, as reason moves the irascible and concupiscible powers, and intellect moves the will. This would not be possible if all the powers were the very essence of the soul, since the same thing in the same respect does not move itself, as Aristotle proved. It follows therefore that the powers of the soul are not its very essence.[67]

This argument assumes that the powers move one another. In anger, as Aquinas sees it, a perceived injustice (in the intellect) will often cause (or move) a kind of bodily desire in the irascible power for revenge. At the very least one can distinguish between thinking about the injustice and recognizing the concomitant boiling of the blood, as Aquinas (following Aristotle) describes the passion of anger. Without the perceived injus-

---

66. Before moving on to Thomas's second argument I would like to note a recent objection to Thomas's psychology. Peter King has argued that Thomas's faculty psychology (i.e., psychology of powers) is not sufficiently rooted in his metaphysics to be able to withstand the philosophical objections that have been leveled against it in the wake of Descartes (King, *Cathedral*, 273). I shall simply note that King has not discussed any of the above-mentioned arguments from the broad concept of motion, i.e., Aquinas's strongest arguments for the necessity of positing powers of the soul that are rooted in his metaphysics of act and potency. For another effective criticism of King's paper see Wood, *The Faculties*, 585–636; see also Perler, *Faculties in Medieval Philosophy*, 98–100 and 134–39.

67. *QSC*, a. 11 [Leonine 24.2:118–19.229–38].

tice, the somatic passion would not occur. If there were no powers, but the soul was immediately operative, then the soul would be both moving (intellect) and moved (irascible powers) in the same respect. There would be no difference between cause (perceived injustice) and effect (somatic passion). In other words, that would force us to posit the kind of *per se* self-motion that we recently excluded from all finite beings based on the reason that something cannot be in act and in potency at the same time and in the same respect.

In the second half of *QSC*, a. 11, Aquinas gives a more positive account of what these powers are. For Aquinas, being is divided between substance and the nine accidents, between what does not exist in another and what does exist in another. Granting this division, because a power of the soul is not the essence of the soul or another substance, it can only be an accident.[68] More specifically, he notes that it is in the second species of quality. Thus, from a metaphysical perspective in which being is divided between substance and accidents, a power of the soul is an accident: the kind of being it has is *inesse*.[69]

---

68. *QSC*, a. 11 [Leonine 24.2:119.243–58].

69. However, this position was by no means common in Aquinas's time. Albert was the first person to forcefully argue that the powers of the soul were predicamental accidents (Künzle, *Verhältnis*, 157–58). But many masters denied this claim. Bonaventure (see ibid., 127), e.g., agrees that the powers are not identical with essence. He agrees that the soul cannot be immediately operative in his *I Sent.*, d. 3, p. 2, a. 1, q. 3, ad 3 [Quaracchi 1.86–87] (note the similarity to Thomas's *ST* I, q. 77, a. 1), but the parts which one is then forced to posit are not accidents (see Bonaventure, *I Sent.*, d. 3, p. 2, a. 1, q. 3, ad 6 [Quaracchi 1.87]), but are in the category of substance by reduction (ibid., ad 3 [Quaracchi 1.86]). This line of thinking would ultimately lead to the development of Henry of Ghent's intentional distinction and Scotus's famous formal distinction; see Stephen Dumont, "John Duns Scotus," in *A Companion to the Philosophy in the Middle Ages*, ed. J. Gracia and T. Noone (Oxford: Blackwell, 2005), 358. These thinkers saw a need for a distinction that was weaker than a real distinction but stronger than a distinction that was merely rational. Aquinas was willing to admit that the powers were predicable substantial properties, but he insisted that they were nevertheless really distinct predicamental accidents (for this see *QSC*, a. 11 [Leonine 24.2:119–20.239–90]) that is, they were really distinct. Because the soul is the substantial form of prime matter, the potency principle in the genus of substance is limited to matter. Powers had to be excluded from substance, and thus they also had another mode of existing, namely, *inesse*. Bonaventure's metaphysics of substance, however, is far more accommodating to the inclusion of other forms. For the soul itself directly informs spiritual matter, and there are a multiplicity of forms included in substance before it is united to the *form* of the body. All of these forms are included in the genus of substance. The powers, according to Bonaventure, are essential because the subject cannot be thought to have *perfect esse* without them; *I Sent.*, d. 3, p. 2, a. 1, q. 3, ad 1–2 [Quaracchi 1.86]. Although it seems that Aquinas never directly challenged Bonaventure's position (see Bazán's note in Aquinas's *QDA* [Leonine 24.1:108n119]) it is not

But he also notes that the powers of the soul can be considered as "properties" of the soul and that in this sense they signify an accidental relation of the predicate to its subject. The accidental predicate signifies the subject because it is caused by the subject, as the powers naturally and inseparably follow from (or "flow from," as Aquinas often says) the essential principles of the species, in this case, form. And form, of course, is a principle of the subject of substance. Properties are neither the essence nor part of the essence, nor are they common accidents in the sense that they might happen (*accidit*) to an individual substance or a person in the way that someone might become cold or happen to be in London.[70] Rather, they signify the subject in the manner in which we might say that a property of humans is that they are rational or risible, which signifies the power of reason without signifying the essence of the person or subject.[71]

This chapter began with the claim that to understand how the emotions participate in reason, we need to understand how the "emotional part" of the soul (the sense appetites) participates in the "rational part." Bracketing participation until later chapters, I emphasized that Aquinas thinks that details about the soul's parts matter for ethics. In order to examine these parts, I followed Aquinas's argument that the soul as the principle of substance and the form of the body must be simple and partless, and I then further considered his arguments for the existence of parts of the soul, which we now see are really distinct from the soul. This is a real distinction, namely, a distinction corresponding to extra-mental being—it is not simply a distinction drawn in thought. But if the soul is really distinct from its parts, how can they be parts of the soul at all? Let us turn to this problem next.

---

hard to see how it would conflict with his philosophy of prime matter and the unicity of substantial form.

70. See *QSC*, a. 11 [Leonine 24.2:119–20.258–90], and ad 5 [121.350–56]; see also *ST* I, q. 77, a. 1, ad 5 [St. Paul 363].

71. I will discuss these inseparable accidents or properties in greater detail in the fourth section of chapter 2.

2

THE UNIFICATION OF THE SOUL'S PARTS

The Potential Whole

Having divided the soul from its parts, let us now consider how Aquinas unifies these parts into a whole. Can the powers, which are really distinct from the soul, be parts of that very same soul? Aquinas does, after all, call them the parts of the soul. As Aquinas divides finite being between substance and accidents, how can something in a genus of accident, namely, a power, be part of something in the category of substance, namely, the soul?

For Aquinas, the powers of the soul are called its parts, not as parts of the essence of the soul, but as parts of its total power (*totalis virtutis eius*)—as it might be said that the power of the bailiff is part of the total power of the royal court.[1] When Aquinas calls the powers parts of the soul, he does not mean that these are parts of the soul itself. The word "soul" is used in a different sense here than it is used when distinguishing the essence of the soul from its powers, that is, when substance is divided from accidents. When Aquinas uses the term "essence of the soul" (*essentia animae*) he is almost always distinguishing between the soul and its powers. However, when the powers are the soul's parts, the word "soul" includes the powers, its inseparable accidents. Here the whole soul signifies the soul's total power. The image is that of an entire court in

---

1. *QSC*, q. 11, ad 19 [Leonine 24.2:123.462–65].

which the power of all of its various members add up to some kind of total force. But what kind of a whole is this?

There are three kinds of wholes: the universal whole which is present to each part according to its whole essence and power. This kind of whole is properly predicated of its parts, as when it is said that "man is animal." Another whole is an integral whole, which is not present to any part of it, neither according to the whole essence, nor according to its whole power. This whole can in no way be predicated of its part: one would be forced to say something like "the wall is the house." The third whole is the potential whole, *totum potentiale*, which is a medium between these two. For it is present to its own part according to its whole essence, but not according to its whole power. Thus it is predicated in a middle way, sometimes of its parts, but not properly. In this way it is sometimes said that the soul is its own powers, or conversely.[2]

Here is a preliminary answer to the question of what kind of a whole the soul and its powers is: it is a potential whole (*totum potentiale*). We shall soon return to this important passage in great detail at the end of this chapter. The soul as a potential whole, which has been completely ignored in the scholarship, is the subject of this chapter, and I will further develop it in the following two chapters. But let us first backpedal a bit to see how Aquinas arrived at the potential whole in the first place.

The Distinction between Soul as Form and Soul as Mover

In order to grasp the sense in which the soul as a potential whole has parts, we must examine the distinction between the soul as form (*forma*) and the soul as mover (*motor*), for the soul qua mover corresponds to the potential whole. This distinction between form and mover almost always occurs in a context where Aquinas is discussing whether the soul is immediately or mediately united to the body—which, in turn, is con-

---

2. *QSC*, q. 11, ad 2 [Leonine 24.2:120.317–32]. See also *In I Sent.*, d. 1, q. 3, a. 4, ad 1 [Mand 1:116–17], and *ST* I, q. 77, a. 1, ad 1 [St. Paul 363]. But there are many other passages that discuss the *totum potentiale*. There is an article by Carl A. Lofy, "The Meaning of 'Potential Whole' in St. Thomas Aquinas," *The Modern Schoolman* 37 (1959): 39–47, but it is almost exclusively interested in how the virtues are classified as potential parts. Robert Pasnau briefly mentions it in *Thomas Aquinas on Human Nature* (Cambridge: Cambridge University Press, 2002), 144–45. The most notable statements are those of P. Künzle and D. Lottin; I shall discuss those below. For a recent treatment see David Svoboda, "Thomas Aquinas on Whole and Part," *The Thomist* 76 (2012): 273–304, esp. 277–80.

nected to the problem of the unity of substantial form.[3] According to Aquinas, one must first understand that there is only one substantial form in a substance and that the soul is immediately united to prime matter; then one may consider in what sense the soul is a mover and has potential parts:

If it is the case that the rational soul is united to the body only as mover [*motor*] by virtual contact,[4] as some have said, then there is no problem in holding that there are many intermediaries between the soul and body, and even more so between the soul and prime matter. But if it is held that the soul is united to the body as a form, then it is necessary to say that the soul is united to it immediately. For every form, whether substantial or accidental, is united to matter or to the subject. For every thing is one according to this, namely, according to which it is being. Each thing, however, is a being in act through its form, whether according to substantial *esse* or according to accidental *esse*. Thus every form is an act, and consequently the reason for the unity by which something is one. As one should not say that there is some other medium by which matter has existence through its own form, so it cannot be said that there is some other medium uniting form to matter or its subject. Insofar as the soul is the form of the body there cannot be some other intermediary between soul and body. But insofar as it is mover [*motor*] one may posit there many intermediaries: for it is obvious that the soul through the heart moves the other members of the body, and it also moves the body through its spirit.[5]

Depending on how soul is understood, either as form or as mover, a different answer will be given to the question of whether there are intermediate forms between it and the body. In the soul's capacity as a mover, Aquinas notes, it is obvious that there are such intermediate forms, for the soul moves the heart, which in turn moves the other organs, and so forth. In the soul's capacity as a form, however, there are no such medi-

---

3. As noted above, thus *QSC*, q. 3, is presupposed for q. 4; *QDA*, q. 9, is presupposed for q. 10; and *ST* I, q. 76, aa. 1, 3, 4, 6, 7, are presupposed for a. 8. He opens *QDA*, q. 10, and *QSC*, q. 4, by noting that the truth of these questions depend on the previous ones. I intend to follow that order. On the question of the soul's mediate or immediate union to the body in these texts see Kevin White, "Aquinas on the Immediacy of the Union of Soul and Body," in *Studies in Thomistic Theology*, ed. Paul Lockey (Houston: Center for Thomistic Studies, 1996), 209–80.

4. On virtual contact see *ST* I, q. 75, a. 1, arg. 3 and ad 3 [St. Paul 343–44]; *QSC*, q. 2 [Leonine 24.2:26–27.244–56]; *SCG* II.56 [Leonine manualis 150–51].

5. *QSC*, q. 3 [Leonine 24.2:38–39.224–48].

ating forms. Any attempt to introduce intermediating forms robs the substance of its unity. This is because there is no real reason to posit unity between movers and moved.[6] It is only because the soul is the form of the body that its substantial unity is safeguarded and may be defended philosophically.

But it is the very same soul that is both form and mover: although "the soul is a form insofar as it is act and likewise insofar as it is a mover, and thus it is according to the same thing that it is form and that it is mover, but nevertheless its effect insofar as it is form and insofar as it is mover differs."[7] The effect of the soul as form is substance with its inseparable accidents, and the effect of the soul as mover is operation.

From the broadest metaphysical perspective Aquinas notes:

Since it is the same form which grants *esse* to matter which is also the principle of action, and because each thing acts insofar as it actually is, the soul, as is true of any other form, must also be a principle of operation. It must be noted that, because operation comes from something that actually exists, in accord with the level [*gradus*] of forms in their perfection of existing is their grade in power of operation. And so insofar as some form enjoys greater perfection in granting *esse*, to that degree does the form have a greater power in acting.[8]

Here I wish to draw attention to Aquinas's point that the *actus essendi*, the kind of existence that the soul communicates to the body, corresponds to or is proportionate to the composite's power of action or operation.[9] This is rooted in the principle that each thing acts according to the way that it actually is. In other words, in order for a soul to perform the operation of galloping, for example, the soul must communicate to matter the *esse* of horse; that is, the soul must make the horse exist as a horse, which includes the power to operate befitting to a horse. It is the same soul that makes a horse exist as a horse (*forma*) that also makes the horse gallop (*motor*). Following his account of this proportion between *esse* and operation, Aquinas notes that there is a corresponding degree of complexity:[10]

---

6. *SCG* II.56 [Leonine manualis 151].

7. *QDA*, q. 9, ad 2 [Leonine 24.1:83.324–30]; see also *QSC*, a. 3, ad 7 [Leonine 24.2:45.500–502].

8. *QDA*, q. 9 [Leonine 24.1:81.246–56].

9. *QDA*, q. 10, ad 2 [Leonine 24.1:92.287–89]; *QDA*, q. 9 [Leonine 24.1:82.278–80].

10. This only holds for the genus of material beings. Prime matter is the simplest. Elements are less simple, then mixed bodies, etc. The more simple a being, the more imperfect as

Whence more perfect forms have more operations that are more diverse than less perfect forms. Consequently, a diversity of accidents suffices for the diversity of operations in less perfect things, but in more perfect things there is further required a diversity of parts and so much the more so as the form will be more perfect. For we see that diverse operations belong to fire according to diverse accidents, such as to be borne upwards according to lightness, to heat according to heat, etc.[11] But each of these operations belongs to fire according to some part of it. But in animate bodies, which have more noble forms, diverse parts are assigned for diverse operations, as in plants the operations of the roots, the stem, and its branches are diverse. And so, to the extent to which ensouled bodies are more perfect, to that extent will be found, because of that greater perfection, a greater diversity of parts. Thus, since the rational soul is the most perfect of all material forms, in a human there will be found the greatest distinction of parts on account of its diverse operations. The soul grants substantial *esse* to each of them according to that mode that is fitting for the operation of these parts.[12] … it is necessary that the order of instruments be according to the order of operations.… But insofar as it grants *esse* to the body, it immediately grants substantial and specific *esse* to all the parts of the body. And this is what many say, namely, that the soul is united to the body as form without medium, but as a mover though a medium.[13]

The powers of the soul, then, are the soul's parts insofar as the soul is a mover through its parts; the soul, however, has no parts insofar as it is a form.[14] Building on the proportion between the perfection of existing and the power of operation, this passage adds that there is a corresponding complexity and multiplicity in parts. Humans, as the highest materi-

---

it is closer to prime matter. Thus perfection and multiplicity go hand in hand. This is not the case in immaterial beings. There God is most simple and perfect, and all others are characterized by multiplicity and to that extent imperfection. See *QDA*, q. 7 [Leonine 24.1:59.277–311].

11. Even the forms of elements are not immediately operative; see *ST* I, q. 67, a. 3 [St. Paul 320].

12. *QDA*, q. 9 [Leonine 24.1:81.256–82], and ad 14 [Leonine 24.1:85.482–94].

13. *QDA*, q. 9 [Leonine 24.1:82.283–98].

14. There is a helpful summarizing passage in *QDA*, q. 9, ad 14 [Leonine 24.1:85.482–94]: "licet anima sit forma simplex secundum essentiam, est tamen multiplex uirtute secundum quod est principium diversarum operationum. Et quia forma perficit materiam non solum quantum ad esse, set etiam ad operandum, ideo oportet quod, licet anima sit una forma, partes corporis diuersimode perficiantur ab ipsa, et unaquaeque secundum quod competit eius operationi. Et secundum hoc etiam oportet esse ordinem in partibus secundum ordinem operationum, ut dictum est. Set iste ordo est secundum operationem corporis ad animam ut est motor."

al beings, are the most complex beings—their complex bodily and spiritual operations require an extraordinary diversity of parts or powers. But a plant, in contrast to a human being, has far fewer parts corresponding to its far simpler operations.

It is important to note that when Aquinas speaks of the soul as the mover, this is not to be restricted to bodily motion, nor is it to be restricted to the motive power, a particular power of the soul by means of which, for example, a person wills the hand to move.[15] The rational soul as the principle of operations includes completely immaterial motions (volition and intellection) as well as bodily motions (digestion, imagination, etc.).[16] As mover, the soul is the principle of any reduction of potency to act—the exception, of course, being its granting of *esse* to matter and to its powers. It should also be noted that when I say that the soul qua *motor* has parts, I do not mean to say, for example, that the soul sees or that the eye sees. Neither of these is true, strictly speaking. It is the person or agent who sees.[17] This is because of the metaphysical point that actions are of the supposit or person;[18] however, if one asks how someone sees, it is by means of parts.

Thus, there are two ways of considering the soul that correspond to its twofold role. On the one hand, the soul is the form of the body and the principle of substance, and as such, it has no parts. On the other hand, the soul is the principle of actions, and as such, it must have parts. The higher the grade of material existence, the more complex will be its acts, which will require a corresponding sophistication in the parts.

Souls

At times, Aquinas seems to speak as if humans are composed of multiple souls, for example, the rational soul, the sensitive soul, and the nutritive soul. At other times, he calls the human soul "the rational soul." There is, however, only one soul, and these "souls" are always potential

15. On the motive power see *ST* I, q. 78, a. 1 [St. Paul 370]; *QDA*, q. 13 [Leonine 24.1:119–20.346–53].

16. See, for example, *QSC*, q. 3, ad 4 [Leonine 24.2:45.464–76]; *QDA*, q. 9, ad 6 [Leonine 24.1:83–84.363–97]; *In II De an.* 1 [Leonine 45.1:70.177–81].

17. Jason T. Eberl emphazises this point in "Aquinas on the Nature of Human Beings," *Review of Metaphysics* 58 (2004): 338.

18. See, e.g., *QSC*, q. 4 [Leonine 24.2:52.187]; *ST* I, q. 76, a. 8 [St. Paul 361], etc.

parts of that soul.[19] Let me briefly explain Aquinas's peculiar use of these "souls."

Because human beings do not have direct access to the essences of material beings, they must grasp essential differences from the properties or powers of the soul.[20] Aquinas assumes that one can know something about an essence by reasoning to its powers from its operations.[21] And he occasionally names the soul from one of its powers, namely, from the one that tells us the most about the soul. Thomas explains why it is possible to predicate a power of the soul and which one to choose:

In powers this is commonly found, that what can do more can do less, but not conversely, as "he who can carry a thousand pounds can carry one hundred," as Aristotle said in the first book of his *De caelo*. And so, if some thing ought to be designated through its own power, it is necessary that it be designated by the ultimate of its own power. But the soul of plants has only the lowest level among powers of the soul; thus from this power it is named the nutritive or vegetative soul. But the soul of an animal reaches a higher level, namely, sense. That is why it is called the sensitive soul or sometimes even sense. But the human soul attains to the highest level among the powers of the soul and is named from this. Thus it is called the intellective soul and sometimes also intellect, and in like fashion mind, insofar as from that soul such a power naturally flows, which is proper to it before other souls.[22]

It is because the powers or properties flow from or are caused by the essence of the soul that it is possible to reason from effect to cause to signify the essential differences of souls. For Aquinas, awareness of this causal relationship is crucial for any human knowledge of soul.[23] Be-

---

19. *ST* II-II, q. 48, a. 1 [St. Paul 1301]. See also *In I De an.* 1 [Leonine 45.1:7.231–46].

20. *QDV*, q. 10, a. 1 [Leonine 22.1:296–97.107–11]. See *ST* I, q. 77, a. 1, ad 7 [St. Paul 363–64]. Note the qualification *interdum* in the text: this order seems to admit of exception. See *ST* I, q. 85, a. 1 [St. Paul 416].

21. This line of thinking is Aristotelian; see *De anima* I, 402b22–25. See also Richard W. Field, "St. Thomas Aquinas on Properties and the Powers of the Soul," *Laval théologique et philosophique* 40 (1984): 203–15.

22. *QDV*, q. 10, a. 1 [Leonine 22.1:296–97.107–11]. Cf. Aristotle's *On the Heavens* I, 281a7–15.

23. The one "natural" exception being the separated soul's infused knowledge which may be called natural according to the separated state. See *QDM*, q. 5, a. 3 [Leonine 23:136.84–85]. See also John F. Wippel, "Thomas Aquinas on the Separated Soul's Natural Knowledge," in *Approaches to Truth*, ed. J. McEvoy and M. Dunne (Dublin: Four Courts Press, 2002), 114–40, esp. 132–34.

cause the higher power can do, in a sense, what the lower power can do, and more, the soul can be named by its highest power. For example, if one wanted to describe a very fast car, one would describe how fast it was by the fact that it has the power to accelerate from zero to sixty miles per hour in three seconds. It would not be incorrect to say that it has the power to accelerate from zero to sixty in seven seconds, but that would not properly describe the car.

When Aquinas names the soul the "intellective" soul, he names it from the perspective that it is the kind of soul from which flow intellect and will. When he names it the "sensitive" soul, he names it insofar as it is the kind of soul from which sensitive powers naturally flow.[24] Because these "souls" always signify the one soul insofar as it causes certain kinds of powers, and because the existence of the higher power implies the existence of all the lower powers, the part can be substituted for the whole—and in this way the whole may be denominated or named by the part. Thus one can say, as Aquinas occasionally does, that the intellect is the form of the body, meaning thereby the intellective soul.

It is the causal relation between the soul and its powers that permits some flexibility in predication. At times Aquinas emphasizes the soul itself, albeit understood as the principle of certain kinds of powers. At other times he emphasizes the powers themselves and speaks of souls as if they were a kind of cluster of powers.[25] Either way, Aquinas's "souls" can never fully prescind from the powers of the soul, that is, from the soul qua *motor* as a potential whole.

The Soul as a Potential Whole

Let us now return, as promised, to the important text on the potential whole, *QSC*, a. 11, ad 2.[26] In general, a whole can be predicated of its parts according to the way that the whole is *present* to its parts. In a universal whole, the whole can be predicated of its parts according to its whole essence and whole power because the whole is present to its parts according to its whole essence and power. In a potential whole, however, the whole is predicated of its parts according to its whole essence, but

24. *Quaestiones disputatae de potentia* (hereafter, *QDP*), q. 3, a. 11, ad 2 [Marietti 75].

25. *ST* I, q. 79, a. 1, ad 1 [St. Paul 375]; q. 77, a. 1, ad 7 [St. Paul 363–64]; II-II, q. 48, a. 1 [St. Paul 1301].

26. See 37–42.

not according to its whole power because the whole is present to its parts according to its essence, but not according to its whole power.

Immediately, one wonders what Aquinas means by distinguishing between how one predicates a whole's *essence* of its part from how one predicates a whole's *power* of its part, and what kind of corresponding presence this entails.[27] Because he offers the same examples in most of his texts, they are worth considering. Concerning the universal whole and its parts, which are called subjective parts, he notes that the whole is predicated of the part as animal is predicated of man. As we have seen, it is the same soul that is both man and animal.[28] Thus, the whole is predicated of the part according to its essential content because the whole is the part.

It is more difficult, however, to understand what Aquinas means by saying that this whole is also predicated of the part according to its full power (*virtus*). What does he mean by "power" here? In *ST* III, q. 90, a. 3, Aquinas notes that "the whole power of the whole is present, simultaneously and equally, to each particular subjective part, in the way in which the whole power of animal, insofar as it is animal, is preserved in each of the species of animal, which simultaneously and equally divide animal."[29] As I understand this, the entire force (*virtus*) of the whole intelligible content is present to each of its parts in an undiminished fashion. The distinction between predicating the universal whole of its parts according to essence and predicating it according to power seems to me to be mostly one of emphasis.[30]

The distinction concerning the potential whole, however, is quite different.[31] Aquinas's favorite examples of potential parts are the powers of the soul[32] or the "souls."[33] According to Aquinas, the potential

---

27. This distinction seems to come from Aristotle's *De anima* III.9, 432b1–4 [1:678].

28. This mode of predication accords with the first mode of *per se* predication, that is, when the predicate is included in the definition of the subject; see *In II De an.* 14 [Leonine 45.1:124.42–56]; *Expositio I libri Posteriorum* (hereafter, *In post. an.*) 10 [Leonine 1.2:39.25–67].

29. *ST* III, q. 90, a. 3 [St. Paul 2372].

30. In the above-mentioned case the distinction between its wholes and parts is clearly not a real distinction, but a logical distinction, although it need not be so; see *QSC*, q. 4 [Leonine 24.2:52.227–34].

31. In the classification of the virtues into their parts (e.g., subjective, potential, and integral parts) one cannot, in the same sense, claim that the parts are ontologically distinct.

32. *QDA*, q. 12, ad 15 [Leonine 24.1:112.321–25]; *QDA*, q. 19, ad 4 [Leonine 24.1:166.254–58]; *SCG* IV.36 [Leonine manualis 490].

33. *ST* II-II, q. 48 [St. Paul 1301].

whole is present to its parts according to its complete essence, but not according to its complete power. Let us begin by asking how the whole is present to its parts according to essence. Aquinas usually puts it this way: the whole is present to its potential parts according to its whole essence as the whole soul is present to its powers.[34] He further adds that the essence of the soul is present to its powers as their origin, as the powers flow from the essence.[35] Thus it is the manner in which the soul is present to its powers that shows us the relationship between the potential whole and its potential parts. Because the powers of the soul are potential parts, in this case, the relation between the soul and its powers not only is *as*, but in fact *is* that of a potential whole and its parts.

If we choose to predicate the potential whole of its potential part, we would be predicating according to what became known as the second mode of *per se* predication (following Aristotle's *Posterior Analytics* 73a34–b5), in which the subject is included in the definition of the predicate.[36] If we say that a person is intellect,[37] it is clear that that person is necessarily included in the definition of intellect, for the accident must include the subject in its definition as its cause.[38] This follows because the subject serves as the receiving principle that grants being to the accident, but in the case of inseparable accidents that follow upon the species (i.e., the powers of the soul), the subject is also included in the definition of the accident as its active and efficient cause.[39] This second mode of *per se* predication is rooted in the necessary causal connection between the soul and its powers or properties,[40] for the powers of the soul have a permanent cause in their subject,[41] that is, they are caused by its substantial form. This guarantees that as long as the subject exists,

---

34. *ST* III, q. 90, a. 3 [St. Paul 2372]; *In IV Sent.*, d. 16, q. 1, a. 1, qc. 3 [Moos 4:774].

35. *In I Sent.*, d. 3, q. 4, a. 2, ad 1 [Mand 1:116–17].

36. *In II De an.* [Leonine 45.1:124.55–56].

37. For example see *QDA*, q. 12, ad 13 [Leonine 24.1:111.310–14]: "homo dicitur intellectus esse quia intellectus est id quod est potius in homine, ... Non autem hoc dictum est eo quod essentia anime sit ipsa potentia intellectus."

38. *In II De an.* [Leonine 45.1:124.56].

39. *Super Boetii De Trinitate* (hereafter, *De Trin.*), q. 5, a. 4, ad 4 [Leonine 50:156.277–86]. For a helpful discussion of all of Thomas's texts on how the soul causes its powers see Wippel, *Metaphysical Thought*, 266–75. Perler denies that the soul efficiently causes its powers (*Faculties in Medieval Philosophy*, 128).

40. *In I post. an.* 14 [Leonine 1.2:53–54.14–46].

41. *QDA*, q. 12, ad 7 [Leonine 24.1:111.265–87].

the powers do so as well. That is why they are said to be inseparable from the subject—for they are ultimately caused by the same cause that causes the soul itself.[42]

As we saw above in *De veritate*, q. 10, a. 1,[43] according to our mode of cognition, it is through the powers of the soul that we name the soul and know something about it.[44] According to the order of nature, however, the soul causes the powers. Because every agent produces something like itself,[45] and because the soul produces the powers, there is some kind of likeness between the soul and its powers. Thus it is possible to reason from effect to cause, namely, from some power to the soul. Reason, of course, is not present in the power of the soul that is named "reason" in the same way as it is in the soul itself, but it is present in the soul itself as an effect is virtually present in its cause, that is, insofar as the soul has the power to produce these powers. Thus we learn of humans' essential differences from their accidental powers—for example, humans are rational. This is the manner in which the soul is present to its powers, as their receiving cause but more importantly as their active cause.[46] As Aquinas says in *QDA* 10, ad 10, "a power of the soul is rooted in the essence, thus wherever there is some power of the soul, there is the essence of the soul."[47]

Thus, in this way, as he said in *QSC*, q. 11, ad 2, the whole is predicated of the potential whole according to its whole essence. Let us now turn to consider the further claim in that text that the potential whole is *not*

42. See Wippel, *Metaphysical Thought*, 275.

43. See 50n22.

44. For a more complete discussion of human knowledge of the soul see Therese Cory, *Aquinas on Human Self-Knowledge* (Cambridge: Cambridge University Press, 2013).

45. For a discussion of this axiom, see 124n14.

46. This cannot be limited to the subject's receiving causality, for a subject equally receives, say, the power of the intellect as it does the accident of being in a place. From the first kind of accident it is possible to deduce far more about man's essence than the latter. When we say man is rational from that fact that he has reason, it is the necessary causal connection between the soul and its powers which adds over and above whatever knowledge can be garnered from receiving causality. The second mode of *per se* predication is only applicable to properties; it cannot be predicated only in terms of receiving causality. In fact, what distinguishes properties from all other accidents and allows for this mode of predication is precisely their unique causal status as "flowing from" or as being actively and absolutely necessarily caused by the soul. That is, it is because a human soul is the kind of thing which always necessarily produces the power of reason that we can call it the rational soul.

47. *QDA*, q. 10, ad 10 [Leonine 24.4:93.335–37].

present to its potential part according to its complete power, and thus the whole cannot be properly predicated of its part.[48] This contrasts with an early text, *In II Sent.* d. 9, q. 1, a. 3, ad 1, where Aquinas notes that the potential whole is present according to essence to each part, but according to complete power it *is* in the supreme part, as the superior power always has in itself more completely what the inferior power has.[49] Aquinas's early texts affirm that the whole power is present in the highest potential part, but his later texts deny this. Why?

Here I ought to mention something about Aquinas's context. For Bonaventure, for example, who denied that the powers are ontologically distinct from the soul, the question about what kind of a whole the powers comprise is simply not that pressing.[50] Furthermore, Odon Lottin has pointed out that there was very little use of the potential whole prior to Aquinas's teacher Albert: it was Albert who first argued that the powers of the soul were predicamental accidents[51] and who really brought the potential whole to the fore.[52] I would like to suggest that as soon as powers of the soul were understood to be predicamental accidents that had an accidental being that was really distinct from their subject's substantial being, the problem of the soul's parts, as Aristotle raised it in the *De anima*, took on a new dimension. Albert's solution, passed on to Aquinas, was the potential whole. Broadly speaking, I think Lottin was right to say that to a large extent Aquinas adopted Albert's solution to

48. See 45n2.

49. *In II Sent.*, d. 9, q. 1, a. 3, ad 1 [Mand 2.237]: "sed totum potentiale adest quidem secundum essentiam cuilibet parti, sed secundum completam virtutem est in parte suprema, quia semper superior potentia habet in se completius ea quae sunt inferioris." *In IV Sent.*, d. 38, q. 1, a. 2, qc. 2 [Busa 611]; *Expositio super Isaiam ad litteram* 1.1 [Leonine 28:8.52–59].

50. Bonaventure, *In I Sent.*, d. 3, p. 2, a. 1, q. 3, ad 1–2 [Quaracchi 1.86] and ad 6 [Quaracchi 1.87]. Bonaventure is interesting because he does not think the soul is immediately operative; see *In I Sent.* d. 8, p. 2, q. 2 [Quarrachi 1.168], but he is nevertheless not willing to make the powers ontologically distinct. See Fidèle d'Eysden, "La distinction de la substance et de ses puissances d'opération d'après saint Bonaventure," *Etudes Franciscaines* 2 (1951): 5–23, 147–71. See d'Eysden's point (169) that habits, for Bonaventure, also have the same ontological status as powers and the soul; *In I Sent.*, d. 3, p. 2, q. 2, ad 2 [Quaracchi 1.92].

51. Künzle, *Das Verhältnis*, 154–58. For most of the schoolmen, the categories were understood to be not only logical but also ontological. For Thomas, see *QDV*, q. 1, a. 1, in which he says that they are *modi essendi*.

52. Odon Lottin, "Identité de l'âme et de ses Facultés," in his *Psychologie et morale aux XIIe et XIIIe siècles* (Leuven / Gembloux: Abbaye du Mont César / J. Duculot, 1948), 1:497–502. It is Boethius who seems to have coined the term; see 56n54. For a discussion of some earlier medieval treatments of the potential whole see Wood, *Faculties*, 595–98.

this problem, which was to distinguish between the soul as static and the soul as dynamic[53]—the former excludes the powers, while the latter includes them.

A quick look at Albert's position will manifest his obvious influence on Aquinas:

It must be said that according to Boethius there is a certain potential whole, and that is in a certain way a medium between a universal whole and an integral whole. For the universal whole is in each of its parts, and is predicated of it, as Aristotle proves in Book VII of the *Metaphysics*, that what is *per essentiam* is the same for the universal and for the particular. The integral whole, however, is not in any of its parts, nor is it predicated of them. But the potential whole is in each part, although not equally powerfully [*aequipotenter*], but in the first part according to less [power], in the second more powerfully, and in the ultimate according to the whole power [*secundum totum posse*].[54]

Although Albert does not explicitly distinguish between presence and predication according to essence and according to power, he does distinguish between there being some intelligible content that is completely present to each part of the whole and the fact that the whole power is not present to all parts: there is a hierarchy of more or less power in individual parts, with the whole power only being present to the ultimate part. Aquinas's use of the distinction between predicating *per essentiam* and *per virtutem* adds a little precision to Albert, but it does not change much—they are more or less, at least according to Aquinas's early texts, saying the same thing.

While there can be no doubt of the Albertian provenance of the potential whole, I think it is worth asking how Albertian Aquinas's use of the potential whole ultimately was. I will mention two reasons for thinking that Aquinas did not simply adopt Albert's position. First, for

53. Lottin, *Psychologie*, 1:500.

54. Albert, *De coaequaevis*, tract. IV, q. 36, a. 2, p. 1, part 1, sol. [Borgnet 34:540]. This text is slightly incorrect in Stanley B. Cunningham, *Reclaiming Moral Agency: The Moral Philosophy of Albert the Great* (Washington, D.C.: The Catholic University of America Press, 2008), 107. For the reference to Boethius, see *Anicii Manlii Severini Boethii De Divisione Liber*, ed. John Magee (Leiden: Brill, 1998), 38–41, in Patrologia Latina, ed. J.-P. Migne (Paris: 1844–79) (hereafter, PL), 64:888, and Magee's comments on 144–46. For a discussion of this text see Andrew Arlig, "Medieval Mereology," *The Stanford Encyclopedia of Philosophy* (Fall 2015 edition), ed. Edward N. Zalta, available at plato.stanford.edu/archives/fall2015/entries/mereology-medieval/.

Aquinas, the potential whole concerns the soul as *motor* in contradistinction to the soul as *forma*. This distinction is collapsed or at least is very different in Albert's thought. Unlike Aquinas, Albert was unwilling to make the soul the form of matter, for he thought, like many of his contemporaries, that such a position would force the soul to be a material form. Albert's solution was to lean on Avicenna's twofold way of viewing the soul: on the one hand, in itself, and on the other hand, insofar as it is the *motor* and act of the body.[55] The reason he bound the soul as *motor* of the body to the soul as act of the body is that he understood the soul to be united to the body by means of its powers.[56] But for Aquinas, as we have seen, the soul is immediately united to prime matter. For Albert, unlike Aquinas, the potential whole has to account not only for the soul's motion but also, in a certain sense, for its union with the body.[57] Second, Aquinas wrestled with this issue of the potential whole. A comparison of his early and late texts shows that Aquinas's position did not stabilize until later in his career.[58] This suggests that he was not quite satisfied with whatever he may have inherited from Albert.

55. Albert, *De homine* 4.1, sol. [Borg 35:34]. See Steven Baldner in "St. Albert the Great on the Union of the Human Soul and Body," *American Catholic Philosophical Quarterly* 70 (1996): 106n10, for more texts.

56. Albert, *De anima* III, tr. 2, c. 12 [Borg 7.1:193.41–49]. See Bazán's comments in the notes of *QDA*, q. 9 [Leonine 24.1:74].

57. For Albert what accounts for the soul's substantial being is that the soul itself is composed of *quod est* and *quo est* (neither of which is matter, but the former acts like spiritual matter), in other words, the soul is a substance. This makes it difficult for Albert to explain how the body has anything to do with the soul's subsisting. The soul, however, does have a natural affinity for the body. But this is mostly in the manner in which a sailor needs a ship. Albert wants to say something like this: a sailor can, of course, exist without his ship, but he is nevertheless a sailor, so he must have a ship (a body). The soul's role of granting being to the body is subsumed under its role as *motor*. By far the best treatment of this is by Steven Baldner in "St. Albert the Great on the Union," 103–20. Baldner argues that Albert held to this position throughout the course of his career. See also Pegis's treatment of Albert for a helpful collection of the important texts in *The Problem of the Soul*, 77–121. See also Dales, *The Problem*, 89–98; and Künzle, *Das Verhältnis*, 149. For Thomas the soul as *forma* and the soul as *motor* are two different ways of viewing the same principle; if anything, the emphasis is the opposite in Thomas, for him the soul as form seems predominant. For Albert the soul is only united to the body because the soul is the mover of the body.

58. For examples of his mature position see *ST* I, q. 77, a. 1, ad 1 (1267–68) [St. Paul 363]; *QSC*, q. 11, ad 2 (1267–68) [Leonine 24.2:120–21.312–32]; and if you are persuaded of its authenticity, the *Lectura Romana* 3.3.4 ad 1 (1265–66) [Boyle 120.37–40]. Aquinas's earliest text *In I Sent.*, d. 3, q. 4, a. 2, ad 1 (1252–56) [Mand 116–17] is interesting because rather than predicating a whole of its part according to essence and/or power, the division is between predicating by the presence of the whole to its part according to *esse* and according to power.

Albert and Aquinas were both trying to provide an account of how the powers of the soul are like their cause and related to their cause, the soul itself, which is partly a question about how to interpret Aristotle's obscure passage about the virtual possession of souls as geometrical forms: the sensitive soul is in the rational soul as the tetragon is in the pentagon (*De anima* II.3, 414b28–31). For Aquinas, the virtual possession of these souls can be understood in terms of the soul itself, as these clusters of powers are caused by one soul. Wherever the cluster of higher powers exist, the clusters of lower powers must also exist, the lower "souls" exist virtually in—that is, in the power [*virtute*] of—the higher "souls." That is, any soul that produces the higher powers has the power (*virtus*) to produce the lower powers as well, and thus the rational "soul" virtually contains the sensitive and vegetative "souls." This is why the potential whole is present to the whole according to essence, that is, according to soul itself.[59]

Shifting their perspective from the essence of the soul to the powers themselves, Aquinas and Albert both asked whether the higher powers virtually contain the lower powers. Aquinas's mature position was that they do not. That is, the whole power of the potential whole is not contained or present in its highest power or part. For example, the highest

---

The language of essence and power normalizes by *In II Sent.*, d. 9, q. 1, a. 3, ad 1 (1252–56) [Mand 237], but there he notes that the whole is present to the highest part according to complete power and essence; he later drops the claim that the potential whole is present to its highest part, as we have discussed. At the very least it is clear that Aquinas wrestled with this issue, and it cannot be said that he simply took whatever Albert gave him. But the later texts, some of which we have been examining, show that Aquinas firmly settled on an answer. See n63 and n67 for more evidence that it took Thomas some time to settle his position.

59. For Albert, all of the powers flow from the soul itself, and thus all of the powers are somehow contained in the highest power because the soul is united to the body via powers. Specifically, the soul is united to the body in the heart. See *De prin. mot.* 2.11 [Colon 12:72.69–77]; this text with helpful discussion is in Baldner "St. Albert the Great on the Union of the Human Soul and Body," *American Catholic Philosophical Quarterly* 70 (1996): 112. Virtual possession, as Albert interprets the geometrical forms of the *De anima* II, ought to be understood primarily in terms of powers, not in terms of "souls." For a discussion of this see Ingrid Craemer-Ruegenberg, "The Priority of Soul as Form and Its Proximity to the First Mover: Some Aspects of Albert's Psychology in the First Two Books of His Commentary on Aristotle's De Anima," in *Albert The Great: Commemorative Essays*, ed. Francis J. Kovach and Robert W. Shahan (Norman: University of Oklahoma Press, 1980), 60. See also S. Baldner, "Is St. Albert the Great a Dualist on Human Nature?," *Proceedings of the American Catholic Philosophical Association* 67 (1993): 219–29. For Aquinas, e.g., *ST* I, q. 77, a. 4 [St. Paul 366], not all the powers inhere in the essence of the soul; some inhere in the composite, and thus they cannot be united in the highest power in the same way as they can in Albert.

power, reason, does not have the power to cause someone to do something. If someone is to act, that person must also use a host of other internal and external sense powers and bodily organs, and so forth, to choose and perform this action here and now.[60] Each power has a limited sphere of operation. Although a lower power may derive its power of causing from a higher power, it is certainly not the case that the highest power formally has the power to do whatever the lower powers can do. This hierarchical complex of diverse powers is not united in the highest power, but in the soul itself as the mover, the principle of operation of the whole person. That is why the whole power of the potential whole is not present in its highest part, that is, its highest cluster of powers, the rational powers (reason and will).

In considering the soul as a potential whole, Aquinas wants us to see that the soul has various powers that operate in unison through the soul itself to perform highly complex operations in an integrated manner. The potential whole is a kind of sum total of what the soul can do,[61] and there is no need to force the highest power to have or do whatever the lower powers have or can do[62]—it is only the soul itself, as the principle of all of these powers, that virtually (but not formally) has the full power of all of these powers. Nevertheless, the soul moves one part by means of another, and it often moves the lower by means of the higher. Each power plays its proper role in the whole power of the creature. In a late passage in his commentary on Aristotle's *De sensu* (1268–70), Aquinas gives a clear account of this. Notice the hierarchy, order, and mutually exclusive but complementary operative roles of the soul's parts:[63]

60. See, e.g., *QDA*, q. 9, ad 6 [Leonine 24.1:83–84.363–97]. At the very least the will is required, say, if I simply will to think about something. But for any other action a great number of powers are required.

61. *Sentencia libri De anima* 1.14 [Leonine 45.1:67–69.65] "anima enim est quoddam totum potenciale et pars accipitur ibi potencialis respectu tocius potestatiui."

62. The highest power in some way controls the lower powers but not in such a way that it does not need the lower powers for its own operation; see *QDA*, q. 13, ad 9 [Leonine 24.1:121.426–31].

63. There are some texts in which Thomas describes the relation between the potential whole and its parts in terms of participation. His accounts of this participation generally fit his earlier view of one part of the potential whole as completely possessing its full power. It is the other powers which then participate in this complete and perfect power. *In IV Sent.*, d. 24, q. 2, a. 1, qc. 1, ad 2 [Busa 1:573]: "sed totius potestativi; cujus haec est natura quod totum secundum completam rationem est in uno, in aliis autem est aliqua participatio ipsius." There are a fair number of early texts in which he notes that the relation between the potential

Wherever there are diverse ordered powers, the inferior power is related to the superior power in the manner of an instrument because the superior moves the inferior. For action is attributed to the principal agent through the instrument, as we say that the builder cuts with the saw. It is in this way that Aristotle says here that the common sense senses through sight and hearing, and the other proper senses, which are diverse potential parts of the soul, but they are not parts of some continuum.[64]

It is in this way that the powers of the soul mirror the soul itself. The "potential whole" refers to the soul's complete power, which is composed of a group of powers, but a group that is ordered. Aquinas sometimes refers to this as the order of the powers of the soul (*ordo potentiarum*). Nature or life, understood as ordered and acting for the sake of an end but not immediately operative, must be composed of a soul plus a complicated ordered group of really distinct powers. It is this ordered hierarchy of material and immaterial powers, ordered in the sense of operating in unison, with each power playing its part for the sake of the person's end, that Aquinas calls the "potential whole." As he notes in *QDA* 13, ad 7: "every soul has some particular end, as the human soul has the intelligible good. But it has other ends ordered to this ultimate end as the sensible is ordered to the intelligible. And since the soul is ordered to its objects through its powers, it follows that also the sensitive pow-

---

whole and its parts is one of participation. *In III Sent.*, d. 33, q. 3, a. 1, qc. 1–2 [Moos 1081]; *In III Sent.*, d. 33, q. 3, a. 3, qc. 1 [Moos 1087]; *In IV Sent.*, d. 4, q. 2, a. 1, qc. 1, ad 2 [Moos 168], and d. 38, q. 1, a. 2, qc. 2 [Busa 1:611]; *Expositio super Isaiam ad litteram* 1.1 [Leonine 28:8.52–59]; etc. But I have only found one later passage, *QDVC*, q. 1, a. 12, ad 27 [Marietti 747] (from 1271–72) where Thomas espouses this relation of participation. But in this later passage he is making the point that the cardinal virtues are virtues in a complete and perfect way, while the potential parts of virtue participate in that perfection deficiently. Despite the different context (the classification of the virtues), this passage does not commit him to holding that the highest part completely contains the power of the whole, but nor does it positively exclude it. All that it requires is that what principally and more perfectly belongs to one, is deficiently had by another, in a participative manner. That is in accord with Thomas's later thinking on the potential whole, and his general thinking on participation as outlined in the *De hebdomadibus*, c. 2, in which Aquinas gives the general description of participation: "When something receives in a particular fashion what pertains universally to another, it is said to participate in that" [Leonine 50:271.71–73]. For one can have a hierarchy of parts in which the higher parts principally and more perfectly have the power of the whole without having to commit to the point that one power must have the full and complete power of the whole. However one wants to interpret this passage from the *De virtutibus*, the language of participation, with that one exception, is not present in his later discussions of the potential whole.

64. *Sentencia libri I De sensu et sensato* 18 [Leonine 45.1:89.130–40].

er in man is for the sake of the intellective, and so on for the others."[65]

The natural order of the powers of the soul[66] is the soul's ordination to its end via its parts. Perhaps one should put this as follows. On the one hand, one can rank all being according to materiality and immateriality and, more generally, in terms of various degrees of act and potency. Because *esse* is act, this order is also understood in terms of various degrees of *esse*, which is usually imagined in a rather vertical fashion, with humans *above* irrational animals but *below* angels. On the other hand, the teleological order is imagined in a rather horizontal sense: this is always done for the sake of that—for example, I am driving for the sake of getting over *there*. While this is a helpful way of thinking, I wish to emphasize its unhelpfulness as well. Being is not vertical, nor is teleology horizontal. The imagination should be repressed here. It is because a human is a particular kind of being that he or she can and must act for the sake of a particular kind of end. Aquinas's distinction between the soul as *form* and the soul as *motor* allows one to keep the two perspectives related and distinct, but ultimately both are united in one being that is ranked in an ascending order of being according to varying degrees of *esse*.

Conclusion

I would like to conclude this chapter by mentioning an important series of mature texts that discuss the soul as a potential whole or mover: *ST* I, q. 76, a. 8; *QSC*, q. 4; and *QDA*, q. 10. These texts presuppose, summarize, and discuss most of what we have already covered in this chapter. They ask how the soul is divisible—for on the one hand, the soul is fully and in the same way present to all of its parts, while on the other hand, the soul seems unequally and hierarchically distributed to its various parts.[67] This is the tension between the soul's role in the Aristotelian hylomorphic union and the soul's parts, as Aristotle divides and outlines them in his *De anima*. Aquinas's answer, as we have seen, is

---

65. *QDA*, q. 13, ad 7 [Leonine 24.1:121.407–14].

66. *ST* I, q. 77, a. 4 [St. Paul 365].

67. One wonders if his lack of mentioning the potential whole as a whole in his first treatment of this problem in *SCG* II.72 (I have not found any earlier treatments) manifests a desire to distance himself from his teacher. On the other other hand, one could read into the text in *SCG* that he has simply subsumed the role as mover under the role as form. In any case, this is another example of Aquinas developing his thought on this topic.

the potential whole. It is interesting, and perhaps surprising, that Aquinas says that this is also Aristotle's solution to the problem.[68] At the very least it is a plausible and defensible interpretation of Aristotle.[69]

In this set of texts, Aquinas outlines three kinds of wholes and parts: of quantity, of essence, and of power.[70] The human soul, of course, is not a quantitative whole divisible by quantitative parts as quantity, for Aquinas, is material. As a whole of essence, however, it is completely in each part. Because the soul, according to its own essence, is the form of the body, it is in each part of the body and in the whole body. But as the potential whole, the human soul is not entirely in each part of the body nor is it in the whole body. This is because the human soul exceeds the capacity of the body and has the power for certain nonbodily operations, namely, of intellect and will.[71]

This general point is crucial for Aquinas's understanding of the soul. Considering the soul as form, we can account for a person's existence, the person's being one person, and the person's bodily nature. But such a perspective falls short of accounting for the most important and distinctive aspects of human nature, in particular, that humans are rational and capable of immaterial operations. It is only from the perspective of the soul as mover or as a potential whole that we can judge that a rational soul is not a material form, or as Aquinas says, that it is not completely immerged or immersed in matter. Both perspectives are crucial, and they complement one another. There is no contradiction in one principle (*anima*) having two different effects (by serving as *forma et motor*).[72] Without the soul as form, a person will have no hylomorphic or substantial unity,[73] but without the soul as mover, we cannot ultimately grasp

---

68. *In I De an.* 14 [Leonine 45.1:65.63–75].

69. See Kahm, "Aquinas and Aristotelians," 115–32, for a further discussion of this.

70. In these texts the threefold division of wholes is somewhat different than the previous texts I have been considering. Be that as it may, I am interested in the potential whole, and I have no doubt that he is speaking of that in all of these texts. Also, it should be noted that both groups of texts are quite similar in that both exclude *per accidens* wholes, whether it be an integral whole, a whole of quantity or even a whole of place, but both texts affirm that the only *per se* wholes are the universal whole/totality of essence and the potential whole. For *per se* and *per accidens* totality, see *ST* I, q. 76, a. 8 [St. Paul 361].

71. *QDA*, q. 10 [Leonine 24.1:92.252–58].

72. See 47n8.

73. *QDA*, q. 9, ad 3 [Leonine 24.1:83.331–32]: "ex motore ex mobili non fit unum per se in quantum huismodi."

the distinct and dignified characteristics of humans and, ultimately, Aquinas's unique account of the relation between the human body and soul—namely, that the soul is immediately and intimately united with the body, but nevertheless is not completely immerged and immersed in it. It is from the perspective of the soul as mover that we can see Aquinas's unique account of human hylomorphism.

I would also like to point out that the potential whole is crucial for grasping Aquinas's account of substance. One of the broad ways that Aquinas distinguishes substances from nonsubstances is simply by the fact that a substance has its own intrinsic principle of motion. Living animals move themselves most fully, but other substances do so as well, although to a lesser extent. Consider the elements, the most basic substances, which have at least one power: the substance of fire, for instance, has the power to heat. In contrast, artifacts are not potential wholes because they do not have the power of real self-motion—they are not substances.[74] It is only beings that are natures, that is, self-moving beings with powers, that are substances at all. There is, of course, a world of difference between a human's living self-motion and the determinate self-motion of fire's heating, but for Aquinas, substances are nevertheless always and only the kinds of things that have an intrinsic power of self-motion of some sort or other and thus must have powers and be potential wholes. While a knife has the power to cut, it clearly does not have a soul that moves the knife by itself to cut. While teeth have the power to cut, my teeth are part of a whole that can move itself to chew. Real substantial beings are themselves ordered to and move themselves to operation: once again, *esse* is ordered to *operari*. If a being cannot move itself, it is not fully a being—or more precisely, it is not substan-

---

74. Artifacts are accidental wholes, that is, arrangements of already existing substances. As Eleonore Stump points out, something having substantial form must have irreducible causal powers. Thus water has different causal powers than the causal powers of hydrogen and oxygen. It is true that we can make water from hydrogen and oxygen, but the substantial generation of something like water or styrofoam is caused by the causal properties of prior substances working on each other and prime matter. For instance we can make wood burn, but burning wood is, of course, natural; see *In II Sent.*, d. 7, q. 3, a. 1. See Eleonore Stump, "Substances and Artifacts in Aquinas's Metaphysics," in *Knowledge and Reality: Essays in Honor of Alvin Plantinga*, ed. Tom Crisp, Matthew Davidson, and David Vander Laan (Dordrecht: Springer, 2006), 63–80, and "Emergence, Causal Powers, and Aristotelianism in Metaphysics," in *Powers and Capacities in Philosophy: The New Aristotelianism*, ed. Ruth Groff and John Greco (London: Routledge, 2013).

tially a being. While the potential whole cannot account for substantial unity, we can at least say that wherever there are real powers, these powers must be rooted in a real substance and must be its potential parts.[75]

I would like to point out here that God constitutes the soul as form and the soul as mover or potential whole through his divine idea. A divine idea exemplates and causes a particular essence (including matter and form) and its inseparable accidents, that is, the whole substance including its powers.[76] Considered in another way, God's divine idea of a person is one particular way that God knows himself capable of being participated in.[77] For a person, it is as a living, free, and operating being, that is, as the principle of his own actions (*suorum operum principium*), that a human imitates and participates in God, who is the human's exemplar,[78] and it is as a mover that a human is the principle of his or her own actions (*principium operationis*).[79] In other words, an important part of humans' likeness to God is the human considered as mover.

The primary focus of ethics, which, for Aquinas, considers humans as they are ordered to their end, is not going to be on the soul as form, but on the soul as mover, or as the potential whole. Of course, the soul as form is presupposed for the soul as mover, but it is nevertheless somewhat peripheral to ethics. As I mentioned in the introduction, Aquinas stated in the prologue to his massive treatment of ethics in the *Summa* that he would turn to consider humans insofar as they are the principle of their own operations (*suorum operum principium*), and it is precisely insofar as the soul is a potential whole (*totum potentiale*) that the soul is the principle of its own operations (*operationis principium*).[80] This is the context in which Aristotle's tripartite division of the soul is set and in which Aquinas will argue that the middle part of the soul *can* participate in reason. Humans are *naturally* ordered to their end or actualization through potency—specifically, through the powers of the soul. Virtue is precisely such an actualization, a becoming of what a human ought to be, and one can only say what something ought to be if it can

---

75. I am not going to take up the question of transubstantiation.
76. *QDV*, q. 3, a. 7 [Leonine 22.1:114.66–87].
77. *ST* I, q. 15, a. 2 [St. Paul 87–88].
78. *ST* I-II, prol. [St. Paul 556].
79. *QDA*, q. 9 [Leonine 24.1:82.289]. See also ibid., ad 14 [ll. 483–94].
80. *QDA*, q. 9 [Leonine 24.1:81–82.247, 250, 288].

be that—in this case, the predication of possibility is very literally based on metaphysical potency.[81] This is why Aquinas says that moral virtues are according to nature, that is, as nature is ordered to its end through its powers.[82]

It is worth emphasizing that Aquinas's account of human hylomorphism is not threatened by this or that account of how these powers operate together. Most particularly, it is not threatened (as many scholars think) by an account that would seem to grant reason great power for efficiently moving the body, as if too much efficient causality would force Aquinas into rejecting hylomorphism and only viewing the soul as some sort of Cartesian ghost in the machine. The soul is simultaneously both form and mover, and it is precisely as mover that the soul efficiently moves the body via its powers.

In sum, in order to grasp how the sense appetites participate in reason, I have sought to understand how the soul has parts (sense appetites and reason). From a metaphysical perspective, God causes natural substances that are composed of form and matter, that is, soul and body. The soul plays a crucial role as an intrinsic formal principle that makes the substance subsist as the particular kind of substance it is. But Aquinas also insists that teleology is crucial, for the existence of material substances is ordered to action. Because the soul is the principle of life and action it must, for Aquinas, include operative powers. Thus, Aquinas uses the word "soul" in different senses: the powers are excluded from soul as the form of the body and the principle of substance; however, the powers are included in the soul as mover or a potential whole. The latter is the sense in which Aquinas considers the soul to be the dynamic principle of life's self-motion, which must include a complex group of holistic operative powers. Somehow this has been neglected in the scholarship, and I hope to have made some progress toward a fuller understanding of Aquinas's thinking on soul.

---

81. Excluding absolute contradictions (that something cannot be and not be at the same time and in the same respect), possibility is predicated according to the passive and active *potentiae*: *In I Sent.*, d. 42, q. 2, a. 3 [Mand 994]; *QDP*, q. 1, a. 3 [Marietti 14]; etc.

82. This will be further developed in chapter 4.

3

DISORDER IN
THE POTENTIAL
WHOLE

The soul as a potential whole is a remarkable complex of operating powers ordered to the person's end. However, its order does not amount to total harmony, especially in the ethical realm. It is obvious that we often do not feel particularly ordered; in fact, we often feel naturally disordered. If we are ordered in this way, why do we often want the wrong things? Why does the potential whole so often seem to stumble along or go terribly wrong? This chapter will focus on some of the ways in which the potential whole often derails and acts in a disorderly rather than orderly fashion. In particular, I will focus on the relevant powers for our inquiry, those that require habits to somehow become more rational—namely, the sense appetites. The point of this chapter, following the previous chapter's discussion of the natural order of these powers, is to bring out their natural disorder. For it is this natural disorder that requires moral virtues as a remedy, through the sense appetites' participation in reason.

I will start with a general overview of the powers of the soul, then discuss the natural disorder of the relevant powers, first from a philosophical perspective, and then briefly from a theological perspective. Although this book is first and foremost philosophical, the story would somehow be incomplete without a slight detour through Eden and Aquinas's views on the Fall's effect on the powers of the soul.

Introduction to the Parts of the Potential Whole

From the most general perspective, the powers of the soul are *poten-tiae*. In the Latin it is much more obvious that these potencies are understood in contrast to actualities. That is, the powers of the soul map nicely onto Aquinas's metaphysical distinction between act and potency, between what exists (act) and what can exist but does not (potency).[1] The reason that powers are not called, say, "actualities" but are rather relegated to the realm of potentiality is because they are not always actual. This is quite obvious. I am not always thinking, although I clearly have the potential or the power to do so. The act of thinking is the act of the *potentia*, that is, it is the actualization of my potential to think.

But the primary metaphysical distinction between act and potency is not the sole reason why a power of the soul is called a *potentia*. There is another meaning of *potentia* that is not necessarily a correlative of "act." For example, *potentia* is one of the names of God, and God, of course, is pure act. Aquinas suggests that this other understanding of *potentia* came first. In the first book of his commentary on the *Sentences*, Aquinas notes that the name *potentia* was first taken to signify the power (*potestatem*) of man, as we say that some men are powerful.[2] *Potentia* was thus first used to signify humans' power to act,[3] their agency or principle of acting.[4] Thus, in its most general sense, *potentia* signifies a principle of some sort, and principle qua principle is not the kind of thing that is necessarily understood to be ordered to potency.[5]

For the most part, these are two different ways of thinking about the same thing: on the one hand, as potency as ordered to act, and on the other hand, as a principle or agent of action. But *potentia* (understood as agent) is limited in how potential (understood as distinct from act) it may be. Pure *potentia* understood as distinct from act is in a way not

---

1. *De princ.* I [Leonine 43:39.1–4]; *In III Phys.* 2 [Marietti 145]; *In XI libros Metaphysicorum Aristotelis expositio* [hereafter "*In Met.*"], XI.9 [Marietti 544].

2. *In I Sent.*, d. 42, q. 1, a. 1 [Mand 983]. For a discussion of this text see Pasnau, *Human Nature*, 147.

3. It is worth noting that just as Thomas had said that the word *potentia* was first taken from human power, so Aquinas notes that the word *actus* was first taken from operation. See *QDP*, q. 1, a. 1 [Marietti 9]; *In IX Met.* 1 [Marietti 424].

4. *QDP*, q. 1, ad 2 [Marietti 9].

5. See *ST* I, q. 33, a. 1, and esp. ad 1 [St. Paul 167].

compatible with pure *potentia* understood as principle or agent, for if it is purely passive, it appears that it is not really an agent.

Aquinas resolved this tension by distinguishing between different kinds of principles or *potentiae*: active and passive ones. Thus, prime matter, which in Latin is often rendered *potentia pura*, is a purely passive principle of a substance, and God is a purely active principle of creation. It makes sense that pure actuality is completely active and pure potentiality is completely passive, but it would be misleading to simply identify passivity with potentiality and activity with actuality.[6] For the most part, these two different intelligibilities align, but sometimes they do not. This is because very few things are purely active, as the agent intellect and God are, or purely passive, like prime matter; rather, practically everything is partly active and partly passive.

The basic definitions of the two general kinds of principles can be stated simply: an active power is a principle of motion in another insofar as it is other; a passive power is a principle by which something is moved by another insofar as it is other.[7] In his clarification of Aristotle's apparently redundant formulation of other qua other, one can see that Aquinas is very much concerned with the case of natural agents that cause self-motion, that is, souls and their parts. There is no reason to rehearse the arguments for why an agent cannot be immediately operative, but it is evident enough that in living agents there must be something that moves and something that is moved, and hence some kind of division between active and passive principles. This division between active and passive principles or powers is the first and most general division of the powers of the soul.

The powers are then further specified according to their acts, which in turn are specified according to their objects. This is quite simple: diverse acts require diverse principles or powers.[8] As potency is only

---

6. For example, the nutritive powers are active and the possible intellect is passive; it is not the case that the nutritive powers are higher than the possible intellect on the hierarchy (according to act and potency) of being as they are more material and thus less subsistent.

7. I am here taking motion broadly to include any kind of reduction of potency to act. For Aquinas on the distinction between active and passive power see *In IX Met.* [Marietti 425]; *ST* I, q. 25, a. 1 [St. Paul 134]; *SCG* II.7 [Leonine manualis 97]; *QDP*, q. 1, a. 1 [Marietti 9]. See James E. Royce, "St. Thomas and the Definition of Active Potency," *The New Scholasticism* 34 (1960): 431–37. See also McLaughlin, *Act*, 217.

8. *QDA*, q. 13 [Leonine 24.1:118.281–83].

intelligible by reference to act, one can only know what a power is by what it does. And we only know what the power does by the object of its action. Thus the specification of a power is tightly bound to the specification of its action, which in turn is specified according to the *ratio* of its objects.[9]

An object is related to the act of a passive power as its principle and moving cause, but the object is related to the active power as its term and end.[10] It is from these two kinds of objects (moving cause or end) that actions are first specified.[11] This is intuitive. We have some powers that actively do things or tend toward an end, and some powers that undergo or "suffer" passively, and their objects will correspondingly be the cause that actualized them.[12]

Let us consider Aquinas's division of the powers in *ST* I, q. 78, a. 1. Aquinas specifies the powers by beginning with the three "souls" and their corresponding acts. The rational soul, acting by means of immaterial powers, causes immaterial actions. The vegetative soul, acting by means of corporeal qualities, causes material actions. The sensitive soul must use these material qualities, but its actions are not completely reducible to material causes.[13]

Aquinas then divides the powers into genera by focusing on the universality (or lack thereof) of their objects. The object of the vegetative powers is not universal; it is the very body of the composite in which they inhere. Examples of vegetative powers are nutrition, generation, and growth. The sense powers, in contrast, are ordered to a more universal object, namely, sensible body in general and not simply the body of the composite. Here we have the five external senses and the four internal senses, which include the sense appetites. If, however, the object is not only sensible being but universally all being, then one has the rational

---

9. *In III De an.* 8 [Leonine 45.1:240.124–25].

10. *ST* I, q. 77, a. 3 [St. Paul 364–65].

11. *QDA*, q. 13 [Leonine 24.1:115.166–76]. In this text he roots this classificatory schema in the fact that an agent acts to induce its likeness in another. In other words, there will be a likeness between cause and effect, as the active principle always causes its likeness in the passive principle. That is why it is possible to reason from objects and ends to their respective active or passive principles.

12. For a somewhat different presentation of the division of the powers of the soul along the lines of act and potency, see Pasnau, *Human Nature*, 145–49.

13. *ST* I, q. 78, a. 1 [St. Paul 369]. Cf. Aristotle *De anima* II, 416b25.

powers, that is, intellect and will. Thus the second and third genera of powers transcend the composite and are concerned with external objects.[14]

Aquinas then subdivides the rational and sensitive powers (the second and third genera) according to the manner in which they relate to their external objects. The agent can be joined or related to the external object in two ways. In one way, the object is present to the soul by way of likeness. These are the apprehensive powers and there are two kinds, namely, sensitive powers, with respect to sensible body, and intellect, with respect to the most common object, universal being. The other way that the soul can be joined to an external object is as the soul inclines and tends toward the exterior thing. This can happen in two ways. One way is by means of the appetitive powers through which the soul desires and seeks an external thing as an end. The other, however, is through the motive power by which the soul is moved according to the category of place, or to put it more simply, it moves from here to there.[15]

It is possible, in a rough way, to neatly divide the powers. The appetitive powers are actively related to their ends, and the apprehensive powers are passively related to their objects. Broadly speaking this is correct, but there is a way in which the apprehensive powers actively move the appetitive powers and a way in which the appetitive powers are passively moved by the apprehensive powers.[16] In other words, what appears to be a passive power (e.g., intellect) is partly active and what appears to be an active power (e.g., will) is also partly passive.[17] On the one hand, the rational appetite (will) and sensitive appetites (concupiscible and irascible) are passively moved by rational and sense cognition, respectively; on the other hand, these appetitive powers actively move toward the cognized objects. We will discuss these powers in far greater detail in chapters 6 and 9, but it is important to note that not all powers are simply active or passive; some are partly active and partly passive. In any case, this, in broad brushstrokes, is the soul as a potential whole.

As the sense appetites are utterly crucial to our inquiry, for these are the powers that participate in reason and they are the principles of

14. *ST* I, q. 78, a. 1 [St. Paul 369–70].
15. Ibid.
16. See, for example, *QDV*, q. 25, a. 1 [Leonine 22.3:728.114–29].
17. *QDM*, q. 6 [Leonine 23:148.307–31]. I shall investigate this in more detail shortly.

emotion or passion, it is worth briefly distinguishing between the two sense appetites and outlining their passions. The concupiscible appetite explains our basic attraction to or repulsion from sensible things. The irascible appetite concerns these same things but as difficult, that is, as requiring some kind of thrust or effort to attain or avoid. The motions of these powers, their actualizations, are the passions, and there are eleven of them.

When you apprehend an attractive apple, the first passion that you experience is (1) love, *amor*, that is, you immediately like it; the second passion that follows from this is (2) desire, *desiderium*, that is, you want the apple, and if your desire causes you to actually pick up and eat the apple, then the last passion experienced is (3) delight, *delectatio*. But let us say that the apple is moldy, that is, you apprehend it as bad or evil. Your first passion in the sense appetite following this apprehension will be (4) hatred, disgust, or dislike, *odium*; the second passion will be an (5) aversion from it, *fuga/abominatio*; and if for some reason you were to actually eat the apple, you would finally feel (6) pain, *dolor/tristitia*. The passions of the irascible appetites take their origin in the concupiscible appetite, but concern these insofar as they are apprehended as difficult in some way. So when something is apprehended and loved in the concupiscible appetite, but also apprehended as something difficult or arduous, there are two possible irascible passions. If the difficult good seems obtainable, there is (7) hope, *spes*, but if this same good seems unattainable, there will be (8) despair, *desperatio*. Going back to the concupiscible appetite once again, if there is hatred or dislike of some apprehended evil, but with difficulty, two possible passions can arise in the irascible appetite, if the difficulty seems avoidable, there is (9) daring, *audacia*, but if that difficulty seems unavoidable, there is (10) fear, *timor*. And just as these irascible passions arise in the concupiscible appetite, they also terminate in them: when the difficult good is attained, there is pleasure, but if the difficult evil is attained, there is pain. Of course, once the difficult good or evil has been attained, they are no longer difficult, and thus we are back in the concupiscible appetite. But notice that all of the passions start with the first motion of the concupiscible appetite, namely, love or hatred, or, we could say, liking or being disgusted. Because evil, for Aquinas, is the privation of good, evil is only evil because some good is being deprived, for example, the "evil" mold has destroyed the goodness of the apple. Thus, Aquinas insists that all of the passions are rooted in love: fear is born of love because we only fear to lose what we love, and so forth.[18]

There is, however, one irascible emotion, anger, that falls outside of this neat schema. Anger (*ira*) is caused, says Aquinas following Aristotle, by the apprehension of a perceived slight or injustice—that is, the evil is already present; it has already been done. The emotion of anger seeks to cause vengeance, which also terminates in pleasure, namely, the pleasure in getting even or in righting a wrong through justice. It is an irascible emotion whose thrust is a desire to overcome some damage that has been done.[19]

As the whole purpose of the potential whole is action, let us now consider how it acts. The soul, qua mover or as potential whole, moves by means of cognition and appetite; in humans, the soul moves by means of intellect and will.[20] When the intellective part, comprising reason and will, moves the body, it can only do so by means of the sensitive part, the internal and external sense powers, for reason apprehends what is universal, but motion concerns what is particular.[21] In the particular case of locomotion, the soul moves the body by means of the motive power, which in turn is moved by reason's command.[22]

However, it is not the case that the sensible soul in humans is identical to the sensible soul in animals, as if a human were just an advanced animal but with two additional complex powers, reason and will, sprinkled on top. The sensitive soul in a human is more excellent than the sensitive soul in an irrational animal because, as we have discussed, a human's sensitive soul is the rational soul.[23] Aquinas notes that the sensitive souls in animals and humans are not even in the same genus, as genus and species are taken from the composite, that is, matter and form.

---

18. *ST* I-II, q. 23, a. 4 [St. Paul, 661–62].

19. Ibid.

20. *QSC*, q. 3, ad 4 [Leonine 24.2:45.464–76].

21. *QDA*, q. 9, ad 6 [Leonine 24.1:83–84.368–91].

22. In humans the motive power moves by way reason and will's command; see *QDV*, q. 25, a. 4 [Leonine 22.3:737.74–76]; *SCG* III.10 [Leonine manualis 236]; *ST* I, q. 76, a. 4, ad 2 [St. Paul 357]; etc.

23. *QDA*, q. 11, ad 12 [Leonine 24.1:103.348–51]; *QDP*, q. 3, a. 11, ad 1 [Marietti 74]; *ST* I, q. 76, a. 5 [St. Paul 358].

If they were in the same genus, this would be so only logically speaking.[24] If we ask how this is, he gives us an answer:

The sensible soul in man is not an irrational soul, but it is simultaneously a sensible and a rational soul. But it is true that certain powers of the sensitive soul are indeed irrational according to themselves, but they participate in reason insofar as they obey reason. The powers of the vegetative soul, however, are completely irrational because they do not obey reason, as is apparent from the Philosopher in book I of the *Ethics*.[25]

The sensitive powers are, then, irrational taken alone, but because the sensitive soul from which they flow is the rational soul, they are not completely so, because they can participate in reason and are meant to do so. Aquinas, following Aristotle, apparently wants to characterize some of the sense powers as partially rational and partially irrational. As rooted in the soul's essence, the rational soul, the sense powers ought to participate in reason; however, as sensitive powers they are nevertheless somehow irrational.

Arguing along the same lines in *QDVC*, q. 8, Aquinas notes that the sense appetites are naturally obedient to reason and thus naturally receptive to virtue, by which they are perfected to follow a good of reason.[26] In the following article Aquinas explains, rather mechanically and somewhat simplistically, how the sense appetites participate in reason. One sees the natural aptitude to virtue, he says, from the order of the powers of the soul. In the intellect, there is the quasi-passive possible intellect that is actualized by the agent intellect. The actualized intellect in turn moves the will, for the understood good is the end that moves the will. The will, which has been moved by reason, in turn naturally moves the sensitive appetite, which in turn naturally obeys reason.[27] He says a little later that virtue in the appetitive part, if rightly considered, is nothing else than a disposition or a form, sealed or signed and impressed (*sigillata et impressa*) on the appetitive power by reason.[28]

Although this is highly simplified, I wish to emphasize that humans'

---

24. *QDA*, q. 1, ad 14 [Leonine 24.1:103.358–65].
25. *QDA*, q. 11, ad 15 [Leonine 24.1:103.366–74].
26. *QDVC*, a. 8 [Marietti 728]; *QDVC*, a. 10, ad 11 [Marietti 737].
27. *QDVC*, a. 9 [Marietti 731].
28. Ibid.

aptitude for virtue is intelligible from the perspective of the rational soul qua *motor*, that is, the potential whole that includes all of the powers operating together in unison as rooted in the soul. It is from this perspective that virtue and the sense appetites' participation in reason is natural to humans and is according to their nature. Moral virtue is only natural when it is grasped that the sensitive soul is identical with the rational soul. When the sensitive powers are grasped by themselves, however, Aquinas seems to want to say that they are rather irrational. But there should be nothing too surprising about their natural irrationality, of course, for they are not, strictly speaking, rational powers.

The Human Divided Nature

Let us take a step back and consider how the sense appetites may be both irrational and rational, as this is a large part of the reason why virtues are needed to perfect them and enable them to participate in reason. Aquinas opens his disputed questions *De virtutibus in communi* with some prefatory remarks explaining that virtue is a perfection of a power. He then turns to explaining which kinds of powers can be perfected by habits and which cannot; the crucial point is the manner in which a power is a principle of an act. Powers are constituted in three ways: active, passive, and partly active and partly passive.[29] If a power is completely active (e.g., the agent intellect), or completely passive (e.g., an external sense), then it cannot be perfected by a habit. In the case of a completely active power, the power itself is already complete and does not need an additional habit to be perfected or fully actualized. In fact, the virtue of such a power is the power itself.[30] Nor can a completely passive power have such a perfection, because such a power completely receives its perfection from its corresponding active power.[31] Its perfection is utterly dependent on the active cause, and as soon as that cause ceases to cause, its perfection vanishes. In other words, it does not make sense to speak of a perfection of a completely passive or a completely active power as they both always do exactly what they are supposed to do. Only powers that are partly active and partly passive need perfecting habits.

---

29. *QDVC*, a. 1 [Marietti 708–9].
30. Ibid.
31. Ibid.

Aquinas says that those powers that are partly active and partly passive (*agentes et actae*) are moved by their active causes but (in the case of humans) not deterministically, or as he puts it, they are not determined by those causes to one thing (*ad unum*). They are moved movers, but not deterministically. These powers are perfected by a superimposed habit, but by this habit (I will discuss habits in great detail in chapter 4) the power is not compelled to one thing (*ad unum*), as then the power would not be in control of its own acts (*domina sui actus*).[32] Aquinas does not mean to say that the power itself completely controls its own act (although it does so to a certain extent), for he notes that the virtues of these powers are habits to the extent that someone can act when he or she wills to do so, and humans only have control (*dominum*) of their actions to the extent that they have free decision.[33]

Thus it is not only because of the fact that some powers have an active and a passive element that perfecting habits are possible; it is also because these powers are in rational agents that one can speak of such perfections at all.[34] Consider the case of nonrational animals: their sense appetites are partly active and partly passive, but they have no need for habits. In some sense an animal's sense appetite is more perfect than a human's, as it always does what it is supposed to do, that is, it impels the animal toward a particular perceived object as suitable (*conveniens*) to its animal nature. More complex animals (excluding humans) have an estimative power that instinctually judges what is good or bad for them—a kind of instinctual cognition that their sense appetites always immediately and naturally follow.[35] Aquinas notes that animals can have this kind of instinctual judgment about what is truly good and bad for them because of the weakness of their active principle, that is, their soul.[36] Because material forms (i.e., souls) have material goods, they can have instinctual judgments about particular goods, for example, wolves are always evil for sheep. The goods that their sense appetites are nat-

---

32. Ibid.

33. Ibid.

34. See *ST* I-II, q. 51, a. 3 [St. Paul 764].

35. The estimative power in higher animals accounts for their relatively complex judgments, which are too complex to be explained by the external senses. For more on the estimative power see chapter 6.

36. *QDVC*, a. 6 [Marietti 722].

urally attracted to or repelled by are really what is good or bad for the animal qua animal. It is not the same in the case of a human, whose soul is the form of the body but is nevertheless not a material form; that is, a human soul is not completely immersed in matter. Although the sense appetite orders humans to what is good for their animal nature, it is impossible for there to be a determinate inclination to particular good things that are in fact good for humans qua humans. A human's good would consist in particular material things if the human were a material form, but this is not the case.[37]

Because a human's bodily goods are ordered to the good of the human's soul, the human's bodily determination of their goodness or badness, that is, the sense appetite's natural determination, is necessarily always insufficient and incomplete. Any material good must always be placed in the extraordinarily complex and often messy circumstances of human actions, and in that context only reason informed by prudence is able to order material goods to the good of the soul.

Humans' sense appetites are, however, in some way rational, *aliquo modo rationales*, as we discussed, because they can participate in or obey reason.[38] Thus there are two ways of construing what the sense appetites naturally do. On the one hand, they are naturally drawn toward particular objects as sensible goods.[39] On the other hand, a human's sense appetite may *naturally* obey the human's reason and will, in spite of its normal *natural* inclination toward some particular good.[40] Humans are naturally divided in a way that animals are not. Consider how *QDVC*, q. 4, brings out the divided nature of humans to argue for the need for perfecting habits in the sense appetites:

Any act of which man is master [*dominus*] is properly a human act; not, however, those of which man is not master [*dominus*], although they happen in man,

---

37. *ST* I-II, q. 2, a. 5 [St. Paul 565].

38. *ST* I-II, q. 50, a. 3, ad 1 [St. Paul 758]; q. 56, a. 4 [St. Paul 780]. There are many passages that say the same; we shall see them in part 2.

39. See *ST* I-II, q. 31, a. 1 [St. Paul 686]; q. 34, a. 1 [St. Paul 700–701].

40. *QDM*, q. 4, a. 2, ad 1 [Leonine 23:111.316–23]: "aliquid potest esse naturale homini dupliciter: uno modo in quantum est animal, et sic naturale est ei quod concupiscibilis feratur in delectabile secundum sensum communiter loquendo; alio modo in quantum est homo, id est animal rationale, et sic naturale est ei quod concupiscibilis feratur in delectabile sensus secundum ordinem rationis." *In II Sent.*, d. 30, q. 1, a. 1, ad 4 [Mand 768]; *ST* I-II, q. 50, a. 3, ad 1 [St. Paul 758].

as to digest, and to grow, and other things of this sort. Therefore, in that which is the principle of such action of which man is master [*dominus*], it is possible to place human virtue.

Nevertheless it must be known that there is a threefold principle of this sort of act. *One* [is] as first mover and commanding: it is by this that man is master [*dominus*] of his own act, and this is reason and will. *Another* is a moved mover, such as the sense appetite, which is also moved by the superior appetite insofar as it also obeys it, and then in turn it moves the exterior members through its own command. *Third*, however, is what is only moved, namely, the exterior member.

When, however, both, namely the exterior member and the inferior appetite, are moved by the superior part of the soul, they are moved in different ways. For according to the order of nature, the exterior member on command obeys the commanding superior without any resistance, unless there is some impediment, as is apparent with a hand or a foot. But the inferior appetite has its own inclination from its own nature, whence it does not follow the superior appetite on command, but sometimes it resists [*repugnat*, literally "fights back"]. Whence Aristotle says in his *Politics* [I.3] that the soul dominates the body by a despotical rule, as a master [*dominus*] dominates [*dominatur*] his slave, who does not have the capacity to resist a command of his lord. But reason dominates the inferior parts of the soul by a regal and political rule, that is, as kings and princes of states lord over [*dominatur*] free men, who have the right and power to resist [*facultatem repugnandi*] with respect to some precepts of a king or a prince.

Therefore in the exterior member there is no need of something perfective of the human act, except its natural disposition, by which it is naturally moved by reason. But in the inferior appetite, which can resist reason, it is necessary that there is something by which it follows an operation which reason commands without resistance [*repugnantia*]....

Thus when it is necessary that the act of a man is concerned with things that are objects of the sense appetite, it is required for the goodness of the act that there be some disposition or perfection in the sense appetite by which it easily obeys reason. And this we call virtue.[41]

Aquinas here speaks of the sense appetite as passive or as a moved mover in two ways: (1) insofar as it is moved by the sensible good apprehended by the external senses (or imagination, we might add),[42] and

---

41. *QDVC*, a. 4 [Marietti 717–18].

42. *ST* I, q. 80, a. 2 [St. Paul 388]. In both cases, the sense appetite is moved via the internal sense powers.

(2) insofar as it is moved by the command of reason. As it is moved by the command of reason it can be ordered to diverse things, and in this respect it can have habits by which it is disposed in a good or a bad way.[43] Except for the *per accidens* concordance of (1) and (2),[44] either it is drawn toward what reason commands or it is drawn toward the sensible object. Moral virtue, in this passage, is a kind of obedience or docility on the part of the sense appetites, the ability to always be moved by reason without resistance and pain. It seems that the purpose of virtue is to make the person more able to do as he or she freely chooses and to make the sense appetites more slavish and less able to fight back (*repugnare*) against the person's free decision about what is best. The perfection of the sense appetites is precisely to become obedient to reason without pain, resistance, or repugnance.

Moral virtue strives to overcome a kind of natural evil:

Thus it follows that there is in each thing a natural inclination to evil in the unqualified sense, because it is composed of two natures of which the inferior has an inclination to some particular good suitable to that inferior nature and repugnant to the superior nature insofar as it seeks the unqualified good, as in man there is a natural inclination to that which is suitable to the carnal sense against the good of reason.[45]

It is important to point out that there is a sense in which these two appetites are somehow essentially contrary to each other. The lower appetite, insofar as it pulls a person toward some particular good, always threatens to draw that person away from the universal good. On its

---

43. *ST* I-II, q. 50, a. 3 [St. Paul 758]: "Respondeo dicendum quod vires sensitivae dupliciter possunt considerari: uno modo, secundum quod operantur ex instinctu naturae; alio modo, secundum quod operantur ex imperio rationis. Secundum igitur quod operantur ex instinctu naturae, sic ordinantur ad unum, sicut et natura. Et ideo sicut in potentiis naturalibus non sunt aliqui habitus, ita etiam nec in potentiis sensitivis, secundum quod ex instinctu naturae operantur. – Secundum vero quod operantur ex imperio rationis, sic ad diversa ordinari possunt. Et sic possunt in eis esse aliqui habitus, quibus bene aut male ad aliquid disponuntur." Cf. *QDV*, q. 20, a. 2 [Leonine 22.3:576.122–23], and *QDVC*, a. 4, ad 6 [Marietti 718]. In these passages the phrase to operate by instinct of nature *ex instinctu naturae* is used to signify determinate natural operation in contrast to indeterminate free operation (see *QDV*, q. 20, a. 2, cited above); the instinct describes the manner in which a human sensitive appetite can be directly moved by external sensitive powers, which are "secundum dispositionem suae naturae ordinantur ad suos actus determinatos" (*ST* I-II, q. 50, a. 3, ad 3 [St. Paul 758]). Cf. *In I Sent.*, d. 39, q. 2, a. 2 [Mand 932].

44. *QDM*, q. 2, a. 4 [Leonine 23:40.196–220].

45. *QDM*, q. 16, a. 2 [Leonine 23:288.230–37]; *ST* I-II, q. 71, a. 2, ad 3 [St. Paul 850].

own, because of its partly material nature, the sense appetite has a kind of resistance or repugnance to the immaterial reason and will[46]—for it is always naturally pushing toward what it wants irrespective of reason's consideration. The harmonizing of these two appetites is not a question of giving each equal reign, as in a democracy; it is rather the control of the one over the other.[47] It is simultaneously a repression of a kind of natural evil and the perfection of a kind of natural good, that is, it is the classical idea of letting the higher part of the soul govern the lower.

Vicious agents who habitually follow their passions have forfeited their humanity by reversing this order. Such agents have chosen to act according to material necessity—for sensible objects determine their passions, which in turn, in a habitual manner, determine their volitions.[48] When that happens, God governs them exactly like brutes (animals), that is, through heavenly bodies, which are material causes.[49] The vicious have anchored their immaterial wills to material necessity. Sin allows the sense appetites to operate naturally according to material necessity, but from the perspective of their ability to obey reason they are depressed, that is, drawn or dragged down to the flesh. In contrast, when the sense appetites are perfected by virtues they are elevated, in a way, from this material necessity.[50] The wise rule the stars, Aquinas says, but fools are ruled by them.[51]

---

46. *QDA*, q. 8, ad 7 [Leonine 24.1:71.401–2].

47. *In II Sent.*, d. 24, q. 3, a. 2 [Mand 620]; note how sensuality diminishes man's *dominium*.

48. *In II Sent.*, d. 39, q. 2, a. 2 [Mand 993]; *QDVC*, a. 4, ad 1 [Marietti 718].

49. Aquinas thinks that for the most part astrologers can predict vicious and incontinent action because such agents are ruled by material necessity in accordance with the material heavenly bodies. He generally places this in the context of predicting wars, i.e., predictions of large numbers of people who for the most part act, he thinks, according to their passions and not reason. Because humans are free, however, such predictions are very inaccurate in particular cases. On Aquinas's view, a materialistic science of behavior that was sufficiently sophisticated, say neuroscience in a few hundred years (or perhaps a few thousand years), could have substantial predictive success among large populations. However, such science must always be blind to virtuous (and continent) acts because they are free and thus not determined by prior internal and external material causes. See *ST* I, q. 115, a. 4, ad 3 [St. Paul 536]; *ST* I-II, q. 9, a. 5, ad 3 [St. Paul 603]; *QDV*, q. 5, a. 10, ad 7 [Leonine 22.2:171.241–53], *De sortibus*, c. 4 [Leonine 43:233–34.124–54].

50. *QDVC*, a. 4, ad 4 [Marietti 718]. See also *QDM*, q. 4, a. 3 [Leonine 23:111.265–74]: *In II Sent.*, d. 24, q. 3, a. 2 [Mand 621].

51. *In II Sent.*, d. 25, q. 1, a. 2, ad 5 [Mand 650–51]. He means the heavenly bodies; see two notes above.

The vicious agent has chosen to act as a material form. Such people really think that they are their sensitive natures—this is precisely what perverted self-love is.[52] Virtuous agents, however, do their best to live according to the demands of their rational human nature. For virtue, according to Aquinas, is the good that is according to their human form.[53] But before we consider how virtue is according to form, in the first section of chapter 4, let us examine the human divided nature from another perspective.

A Theological Excursus:
Human Natural Powers in
Light of the Fall

In Eden, human natural powers were insufficient in the sense that humans could only attain their ultimate end from God's liberality.[54] Created in grace, however, they were freely given that which they naturally lacked, that is, grace completes or adds what nature naturally lacks.[55] In a rather peculiar fashion, Aquinas considers nature within this graced state—this is what Aquinas means by integral nature, that is, nature in its full or whole integrity but in abstraction from grace.[56] It is worth pointing out that Aquinas first denies that this state is natural (for otherwise it would have remained after the Fall), but then affirms that it is not only according to nature, *but also* according to the supernatural gift of God (*non solum secundum naturam, sed secundum supernaturale donum gratiae*).[57] Here he denies that this state is natural in the sense that humans are its active cause, but he nevertheless affirms that it is according to human nature. It is apparently only in the context of grace that we can see how nature (even as mover) is supposed to fully thrive:

Man's nature can be considered in two ways. In one way, in its integrity as it was in the first parent before sin. In another way, insofar as it is corrupted in us af-

---

52. *ST* II-II, q. 25, a. 7 [St. Paul 1203]; *ST* I-II, q. 71, a. 2, ad 3 [St. Paul 850].

53. *ST* I-II, q. 18, a. 5 [St. Paul 635–36]; see also *In II Ethic* 2 [Leonine 47:80.41–49]; *ST* I-II, q. 50, a. 2, ad 1 [St. Paul 757], and q. 71, a. 2 [St. Paul 850]; *In II Ethic* 5 [Leonine 47:91.128–33].

54. *QDV*, q. 14, a. 10, ad 2 [Leonine 22.2:467.221–28].

55. *SCG* IV.52 [Leonine manualis 508].

56. Torrell, *Nature and Grace*, 171–72. Note also *QDM*, q. 4, a. 2 [Leonine 23:113.502–3]: "Rectitudo enim gratiae non est sine rectitudine naturae."

57. *ST* I-II, q. 95, a. 1 [St. Paul 959].

ter the sin of the first parent. According to both states, however, human nature needs divine help, as the first mover, to do and to will any good, as was said. But in the state of integral nature, with respect to the sufficiency of his operative power, man could by means of his own powers will and do the good proportionate to his nature, which is the good of acquired virtue, not, however, the exceeding good, which is the good of infused virtue. But in the state of corrupt nature man even falls short of what he can do according to his own nature, so that he cannot fulfill the whole good of this sort through his own natural powers.[58]

Most generally, Aquinas says that what is characteristic of this state is the body's total subjection to and lack of interference with the soul.[59] Metaphysically viewed, original justice is an accident that inheres directly in the essence of the soul.[60] Thus it manifests itself in the soul's two roles, as form and as mover. Qua form, integral justice enabled the soul to overcome the body's natural march toward death.[61] Qua mover, reason was perfectly subject to God, and the inferior powers were perfectly subject to reason.[62] Consider this description of nature in Eden:

Man was constituted in his own condition by God in such a way that his body would be entirely subject to the soul; and again, among the parts of the soul the lower powers would be subject to reason without any repugnance, and man's reason would be subject to God. Yet because the body was totally subject to the soul, it came to pass that no passion could happen in the body which would resist the dominion of the soul over the body; whence there was neither death nor sickness in man. But from the subjection of the inferior powers to reason there was in man a complete tranquility of mind, because human reason was not perturbed by any inordinate passion. From the fact that the will of man was subject to God, man referred all things to God as to the ultimate end, in which his justice and innocence consisted. The last of these three was the cause of the others; for the cause of this was not from the nature of the body, if its components are considered, because there was no place for dissolution or passion repugnant to life, since it would be composed of contrary elements. Likewise, it was not from the nature of the soul that the sensible powers were subject to reason without repugnance, since the sensible powers are naturally

---

58. *ST* I-II, q. 109, a. 2 [St. Paul 1052].

59. *ST* I, q. 94, a. 2 [St. Paul 458].

60. *ST* I, q. 100, a. 1 [St. Paul 474]; I-II, q. 110, a. 2, ad 2 [St. Paul 1061], and q. 50, a. 2 [St. Paul 757–58].

61. *ST* I, q. 97, a. 1 [St. Paul 467], *QDM*, q. 4, a. 8 [Leonine 23:127.189–96].

62. *ST* I, q. 95, a. 1 [St. Paul 461].

moved to those things that are delightful according to the senses, which are often repugnant to right reason. Therefore, it came from a superior power, namely, that of God, who, just as he joined the rational soul to the body, transcending all proportion of body and of bodily powers (sense powers are powers of this sort), so he granted power to the rational soul so that beyond the condition of the body it could restrain the body and the sensible powers, insofar as it was fitting for a rational soul.[63]

Notice that the purpose of the sense appetites' subjection to reason is negative: they are *not to impede* reason from its journey to and contemplation of God.[64] In Eden, the sense appetites did not behave as free men who had the power to resist; rather, they were always well behaved, docile, and utterly obedient. Adam and Eve thus in some way had all the virtues, whose purpose, Aquinas states, is to subject reason to God and the lower powers to reason.[65] Aquinas grants that Adam and Eve had passions that do not imply any imperfection (e.g., delight, but not fear),[66] but what was truly extraordinary about Eden was the supernatural peace (*omnimoda mentis tranquillitas*) experienced by Adam and Eve in their wills. For Aquinas, we all naturally desire peace,[67] a peace that can only consist in having the highest good in which nothing further is desired.[68] This peace, in which all our appetites (including the sense appetites) are satisfied and rest, can only be granted as a gift of grace.[69] Adam and Eve did not experience the beatific vision, of course, but they knew and loved God with a desirable peace that is not possible for postlapsarian humans; the powers of Adam's and Eve's souls operated together in harmony and delight without conflict.

The Fall destroyed this harmony and left its parts in a mess; the natural order of the powers of the soul was undone (*per deordinationem potentiarum*).[70] Original sin is precisely the destruction of an internal harmony,[71] a motion away from an internal unity and equilibrium,

---

63. *Compendium theologiae* (hereafter, *CT*) I.186 [Leonine 42:153–54.1–35].
64. See also *In II Sent.*, d. 30, q. 1, a. 1 [Mand 767]. Cf. *QDVC*, a. 5, ad 8 [Marietti 721].
65. *ST* I, q. 95, a. 3 [St. Paul 462].
66. Ibid., a. 2.
67. *ST* II-II, q. 29, a. 2 [St. Paul 1225].
68. Ibid., a. 3.
69. *ST* II-II, q. 29, a. 3 [St. Paul 1226], and ad 1.
70. *ST* I-II, q. 85, a. 5 [St. Paul 919].
71. *ST* I-II, q. 82, a. 1 [St. Paul 906].

where virtues are connected, to a disordered multitude.[72] Humans were at peace, but now they are torn asunder in different directions. Nature left to itself is disordered.[73]

Because Adam turned from the unchangeable good, he lost the gift of original justice, indeed from this he was inordinately turned to the changeable good and the inferior powers, which should have been drawn towards and elevated by [*erigi*] reason, were turned downward to inferior things ... the superior part of the soul lacks its fitting order to God, which was through original justice, and the inferior powers are no longer subject to reason, but are turned to inferior things according to their own motions.[74]

The cause of this disorder is something like the removal of the cornerstone of a bridge.[75] Original justice was a chain or a fetter (*vinculum*) holding the sense appetites in check.[76] Concupiscence, or the *fomes* of sin, is the name of the disorder caused by its removal.[77] In *QDM*, q. 4, a. 2, ad 4, Aquinas explains that concupiscence was held in place by original justice just as a bit restrains a horse from galloping. Once the rein was broken, the horse was no longer restrained by the bit and the rider no longer had control of the horse, which then galloped forth at full speed.[78] This analogy may make it seem that grace does not perfect nature, but rather violently restrains it, but as Aquinas sees things, humans were created to be in a state of original justice, that is, with grace.[79]

It was not, however, God's intention that humans be so disordered. Aquinas explains this as follows. Someone who makes a saw chooses steel because it has the right material qualities for cutting. Humans, in the same way, have a body for the sake of their intellect, which requires phantasms to operate. Although steel rusts, the fact that it rusts

---

72. *ST* I-II, q. 73, a. 1 [St. Paul 862].

73. *ST* I, q. 82, a. 1, ad 2 [St. Paul 906]. "Sibi relinquitur" is found in *QDM*, q. 5, a. 1, and *ST* I-II, q. 87, a. 7.

74. *QDM*, q. 4, a. 3 [Leonine 23:111.265–74]; *In II Sent.*, d. 30, q. 1, a. 3, ad 2 [Mand 775].

75. *ST* I-II, q. 82, a. 1, ad 3 [St. Paul 906]: "per remotionem prohibentis, idest originalis iustitiae, quae prohibat inordinatos motus." *In II Sent.*, d. 32, q. 1, a. 3 [Mand 831]: "subtrahatur rectitudo illa quae omnes vires animae in unum continebat."

76. *ST* I-II, q. 82, a. 4, ad 1 [St. Paul 908]. See also ad 3, and *In II Sent.*, d. 32, q. 2, a. 1 [Mand 833–34].

77. *ST* III, q. 15, a. 2 [St. Paul 1943].

78. *QDM*, q. 4, a. 2, ad 4 [Leonine 23:112.343–55].

79. *QDV*, q. 14, a. 10, ad 2 [Leonine 22.2:467.221–28].

was not intended by the maker. By the same token, although material bodies, which are composed of contraries, naturally tend to dissolution and death, that was not the intent of our maker who made our souls immortal. However, creating humans in grace, God gratuitously gave us the supernatural power to overcome these natural bodily imperfections. Provided that we not sin, he would forever grant that power.[80]

In Eden, the rectitude of the will[81] was the cause of the rectitude of the passions; these were related as form and matter, for by will we are immediately ordered to our end, and our sense appetites receive this order from the will insofar as the sense appetites obey or listen to reason (*aliqualiter rationi obaudibiles*; Aristotle's phrase from *Nic.* I.13).[82] Because the sense appetites naturally ought to receive their order from the will, when they are unfettered from the will (by the will's own disordered turn from God), their disorder (their inordinate turn toward created goods) necessarily also follows.[83] A turn away from God must always be a turn toward something else. This necessarily follows, as whatever we will we will for the sake of something we deem good (*sub ratione boni*). Thus the aversion from the immutable and conversion to the commutable are related as matter and form, and they cannot in any meaningful way be separated.[84]

What was lost in original sin—bodily immortality, obedient sense appetites, knowledge, and the rectitude of the will—was only partially restored by grace. Only the rectitude of the will was reinstituted. Death, ignorance, and disordered powers are now permanent aspects of earthly life.[85] The flesh will always rebel against the spirit (*rebellio carnis ad spiritum*), and perfect liberty (*perfecta libertas*) will not be restored until the next life.[86] There is now material necessity in the internal fight (*pugna*) between contrary desires[87]—we cannot help but experience them. Through grace we are given rectitude of will, but our sense appetites lag

---

80. *ST* I-II, q. 85, a. 6 [St. Paul 920].

81. Aquinas defines the rectitude of the will as the will's fitting order to its ultimate end; *ST* I-II, q. 4, a. 4, and q. 5, a. 7.

82. *In II Sent.*, d. 30, q. 1, a. 3, ad 4 [Mand 775].

83. Ibid. [Mand 774].

84. *ST* I-II, q. 82, a. 3 [St. Paul 907].

85. *In II Sent.*, d. 32, q. 1, a. 1, ad 1 [Mand 825].

86. See ibid., a. 2 [Mand 828].

87. *QDA*, q. 8, ad 7 [Leonine 24.1:71.401–10]; *QDA*, q. 8 [Leonine 24.1:69.304–13].

behind, often being stubbornly recalcitrant. Rectitude of the will and rectitude of the sense appetites are no longer related as matter and form; however, rectitude of the sense appetites is not possible without rectitude of the will. Moral virtue, whatever it may be, cannot eliminate the rebellion of disordered passions, for if it did, it could eliminate original sin. Nonetheless, it is a partial and incomplete restoration of what was lost.

Original sin threw a wrench into the well-made cogs of the potential whole.[88] "Original sin infects diverse parts of the soul insofar as they are parts of one whole, just as original justice kept together all the parts in one."[89] The soul, which was once a peaceful autocracy, has, as a result of original sin, become a noisy and often tumultuous democracy with each constituent asking to have his or her wish become law. Moral virtue, however, is an attempt, as much as is possible, to reinstitute peace and quiet and to enable the soul's natural leaders to rule.[90] The stronger the moral virtues in any person, the weaker the *fomes* becomes.[91] Moral virtue can never completely eliminate contrariness and disorder from the sense appetites, as it cannot eliminate original sin, but it can make them a little more obedient than they would otherwise be. In other words, it can help them to participate in reason.

As a result of original sin, the sense appetites are now inherently problematic, as they are naturally attracted to sensible-particular-bodily goods, which are inherently in tension with the soul's natural appetite for the intelligible-universal-immaterial good. This is a permanent characteristic of earthly life that cannot and will not be overcome. Aristotle suggests, however, that a person with the moral virtues will simply never experience such tension; he or she will be habitually, effortlessly, and pleasantly attracted to the right objects, in the right ways, at the right

88. *ST* I-II, q. 85, a. 1 [St. Paul 916]: "Sed quantum ad inordinationem agentis, oportet dicere quod talis inordinatio causatur per hoc quod in actibus animae aliquid est activum et aliquid passivum, sicut sensibile movet appetitum sensitivum, et appetitus sensitivus inclinat rationem et voluntatem, ut supra dictum est. Et ex hoc causatur inordinatio, non quidem ita quod accidens agat in proprium subiectum; sed secundum quod obiectum agit in potentiam, et una potentia agit in aliam, et deordinat ipsam."

89. *ST* I-II, q. 82, a. 2, ad 3 [St. Paul 907].

90. *ST* I-II, q. 55, a. 2 [St. Paul 776]: "virtus est quaedam dispositio ordinata in anima: secundum scilicet quod potentiae animae ordinantur aliqualiter ad invicem"; *ST* I-II, q. 77, a. 3 [St. Paul 887].

91. *ST* III, q. 15, a. 2 [St. Paul 1943].

times, and so forth. For Aquinas this would be paradise regained—that is, it is simply going too far; it is unrealistic. We would like this; we naturally desire it; but it is not going to happen in this life. Yes, the moral virtues can make our sense appetites better as they participate in reason more and more, and I will investigate exactly what this entails in the following chapters, but they cannot restore us to Eden and grant us complete emotional harmony and equilibrium. Aquinas also offers good reasons, which we will also investigate later, why such an account of moral virtue is impossible on strictly philosophical grounds. But these passages also show us how the powers of the potential whole have become disordered and unhinged from one another, which is a permanent effect of the Fall and thus why there is a disconnect between our natural desire for complete emotional harmony/paradise and the ability of acquired moral virtue to satisfy this desire.

4

———

ORDER IN

THE POTENTIAL

WHOLE

In chapter 1, I considered how the soul must somehow be divided into parts. In chapter 2, we saw how these parts are part of a naturally ordered whole, namely, the potential whole. But in chapter 3, I considered how this whole is also naturally disordered. In the present chapter, I will consider how habits can, to some extent, help to remedy this disorder by ordering the parts according to nature. In full disclosure, I will only begin to say how this works, and the entire story of how Aquinas thinks habits work must wait until the very last chapters. The kinds of habits I am most interested in are virtues, of course, and as we have seen, Aquinas says that virtues are according to nature. Because nature is ambiguous, in the particular sense of being both ordered and disordered, I will begin by considering what Aquinas means by nature when he says that virtues are "according to nature." After that, I will move on to an investigation of the nature of habits in great detail, and I will offer a new interpretation of them in the context of the potential whole. On my reading, when Aquinas says that virtues are according to nature, what he means is that they can only be understood in the context of the potential whole. In fact, the potential whole is crucial for understanding Aquinas's views on habits.

How Is Virtue according to Nature?

As we have seen, virtue is according to nature, but as we have also seen, we are by nature disordered. Nature thus cuts both ways: on the one hand, it is problematic, but on the other hand, it somehow orders us to the good. What exactly, then, does Aquinas mean when he says that virtue is according to nature? Sin (*peccatum*), for example, is nothing other than a failure to achieve what is according to one's nature.[1] In the broadest sense (when nature is divided from art), it is the very "inclination of nature itself" that provides the mark that is missed in a *peccatum*.[2] Is it this same inclination of nature that drives the manner in which virtue is according to nature, and more particularly, the manner in which the moral virtues qua habitual participations in reason are according to nature?

Does Aquinas mean natural inclination or appetite in a broad sense or in some more restricted sense? It would seem that the phrases "according to nature" and "the inclination of nature itself" mean the same thing. For instance, in *ST* I-II, q. 49, a. 2, Aquinas says that a habit is according to nature, and here he seems to be using "according to nature" in a broad sense as essence.[3] But in other places he seems to mean something more restricted. For example, he says that human acts that are according to nature are those that are according to reason, man's highest part; indeed the phrase *secundum naturam* and *secundum rationem* are often interchangeable for Aquinas.[4] Moreover, Aquinas often says that virtue is according to the natural inclination of the rational appetite itself, that is, the will.[5] Which of these alternatives does Aquinas mean when he says that virtue is according to nature?

One way of approaching this is to consider that Aquinas speaks of the principles (*semina*) of virtue, which are in reason and will.[6] These principles are the natural inclination of the will and the habitual knowl-

1. *ST* I-II, q. 109, a. 8 [St. Paul 1057], and a. 2, ad 2 [St. Paul 1052].

2. *QDM*, q. 2, a. 1 [Leonine 23:29.175–87]; *QDM*, q. 2, a. 4 [Leonine 23:39.117–62].

3. *ST* I-II, q. 49, a. 2 [St. Paul 753].

4. *QDM*, q. 14, a. 2, ad 8 [Leonine 23:262.217–19]; *ST* I-II, q. 54, a. 3 [St. Paul 773].

5. *CT* I, c. 122 [Leonine 42:126.1–2, 9–18]; *QDM*, q. 1, a. 4 [Leonine 23:20.163–67]; *ST* I-II, q. 94, a. 3 [St. Paul 956]; etc.

6. *QDA*, q. 19, ad 17 [Leonine 24.1:167.357–58]: "omnium enim virtutum semina sunt in voluntate et ratione."

edge of the first principles of practical reason,[7] synderesis, which are rendered actually intelligible to the possible intellect by the agent intellect.[8] One good way to account for Aquinas's claims that virtue is both according to will and according to reason is simply to trace the will's natural volitions to reason's naturally known first principles as illuminated by the agent intellect. Thus, as we just saw, in *QDVC*, q. 9, the agent intellect is the first principle of motion in the case of virtue: the agent intellect moves the possible intellect by impressing intelligible content on it and, as actualized, the possible intellect then moves the will, which in turn moves the sense appetites. Do this enough times and a habit of virtue will be formed. Because we may predicate the whole of its highest part, reason, the phrases *according to nature* and *according to reason* may be substituted for one another. And because will follows intellect, as the rational appetite, we could further substitute the phrase *according to will* for *according to reason*.[9] Of course, this is not speaking properly or strictly, but it is well within Aquinas's usage.[10] Here, then, is one provisional answer to how virtue might be according to nature, reason, and will.

Such an account would undoubtedly please Thomists of a more intellectualist bent, but is the natural inclination of the will ultimately reducible to synderesis? I wish to momentarily focus on the "naturalness," if one may say such a thing, of the natural inclination of the will—the other *semen* of virtue. This will be very important in later chapters. Let us consider two texts that discuss the will as nature, that is, the will's natural inclination toward its end. The first text traces the cause of the natural inclination of the will to God, while the second traces the same natural inclination to man's nature, that is, to his essence. First, however, I should point out that the will's natural willing of the end is distinct

7. *ST* I-II, q. 63, a. 1 [St. Paul 810]; *QDVC*, q. 1, a. 8 [Marietti 728].

8. *QDVC*, q. 1, a. 8 [Marietti 727–28]. For more on reason and synderesis see *QDV*, q. 16, a. 1 [Leonine 22.2:503–5], and *ST* I, q. 79, a. 12 [St. Paul 386]. For a helpful introduction to synderesis see Tobias Hoffmann, "Conscience and Synderesis," in *The Oxford Handbook of Aquinas*, ed. Brian Davies and Eleonore Stump (Oxford: Oxford University Press, 2012), 255–64.

9. This possible way of taking the phrase "according to reason," which is admittedly somewhat intellectualist, fits better with his earlier texts. I will examine this in greater detail in part 3.

10. See *QSC*, q. 11, ad 2 [Leonine 24.2:120.317–32].

from the will's willing of the means (choice, *electio*) to this end—we are not discussing free decision here, but the will's natural volition of the end prior to free decision. It is through this natural volition that the will sets in motion the process of deliberation that ultimately results in a free decision.

The will of a rational creature is determined to one in those things toward which it is naturally moved, as every man naturally wills to exist, to live, and happiness. These are the things to which the creature is naturally first moved either to be understood or to be willed since natural action is always presupposed for other actions. And so if the angel would have sinned in the first instant of his creation, this would seem to be attributed to his nature and thus it would also somehow be referred to the Author of nature.[11]

Will is divided against nature as one cause against another. For some things come about naturally and some come about voluntarily. However, there is another mode of causing that is proper to the will which is mistress of its own act [*domina sui actus*] beyond the mode which is in accord with nature, which is determined to one. But since the will is grounded in some nature [*voluntas in aliqua natura fundatur*], it is necessary that the motion proper to nature, with respect to something, is participated in by the will. Just as what belongs to a prior cause is participated in by a posterior cause. For in each and every thing, the act of existing itself [*esse*], which is from nature, is prior to volition [*velle*], which is from the will, and thus it is that the will naturally wills something.[12]

In the latter passage we see that the will naturally wills something because it is rooted in human nature, or our essence, which is determined to one, *ad unum*; in the former passage we see that this determination of nature in turn is caused by God. Aquinas thus traces the natural and necessary aspects of human volitions straight back to the cause of the inseparable power of the will itself—the essence of the human soul—and to its *esse*, which is immediately and always created by God. Thus the natural appetite of the will is rooted in human nature and caused by God.[13] I wish to point out, however, that the "naturalness" of the natural appetite of the will can be accounted for in two ways: (1) as

---

11. *QDM*, q. 16, a. 4, ad 5 [Leonine 23:300.401–10].

12. *ST* I-II, q. 10, a. 1, ad 1 [St. Paul 605].

13. If one objects that the two texts above are not explicit enough one can find confirmation here: *ST* I, q. 60, a. 1, and ad 3 [St. Paul 283]: cf. *QDV*, q. 22, a. 5 [Leonine 22.3:624.190–94].

following upon what is naturally cognized as good, and (2) as following from nature as essence and ultimately also from God's causality. In other words, the natural appetite of the will comes from two directions, or two kinds of causes, as it were: from the intellect on the one hand and from nature and God on the other.

I would like to add two points to this. First, for Aquinas, it is axiomatic that wherever there is form, there is inclination following upon that form,[14] and thus, second, the powers of the soul, which are accidental forms, have their own "natures" and therefore have their own natural inclinations or appetites.[15] This is how the will has its own natural appetite, and one way to account for its naturalness is by tracing it back to the agent's nature, as we just saw. But then we must also ask whether (granting the first point) there is also an inclination that follows upon human nature itself, that is, upon humans' substantial form. For Jorge Laporta the answer is "yes," while for Lawrence Feingold it is "no"— Aquinas's texts are quite difficult on this point.[16]

In the case of humans' natural appetite, Feingold argues that whenever Aquinas divides appetite into rational, sensitive, and natural, either he is positively excluding a natural appetite following human nature itself and limiting natural appetite to beings that lack cognition, or he is restricting natural appetite to the nature of the powers of the soul.[17] It must be granted to Feingold that some of the texts that Laporta cites appear, upon closer inspection, to support Feingold's interpretation.[18] In these texts, Aquinas is emphasizing that the natural appetite that follows upon material forms is strictly proportionate and determined to material goods, that is, "natural" is here used in the sense of "mate-

---

14. *ST* I, q. 80, a. 1 [St. Paul 387]: "quamlibet formam sequitur aliqua inclination." See also *Sentencia libri De anima* II.5 [Leonine 24.1:88.107–9].

15. *ST* I, q. 80, a. 1, ad 3 [St. Paul 388], and q. 78, a. 1, ad 3 [St. Paul 370]; I-II, q. 30, a. 1, ad 3 [St. Paul 683]; *QDV*, q. 25, a. 2, ad 8 [Leonine 22.3:734.239–42].

16. Jorge Laporta, *La Destinée de la nature humaine selon Thomas d'Aquin* (Paris: Universitätsverlag, 1965), 23–46, and "Pour trouver le sens exact Des Terms Appetitus Naturalis, Desiderium Naturale, Amor Naturalis, etc. chez Thomas D'Aquin," *Archives d'histoire doctrinale et littéraire du Moyen-âge* 48 (1973): 66–71; Lawrence Feingold, *The Natural Desire to See God According to St. Thomas and His Interpreters* (Ave Maria, Fla.: Ave Maria Press, 2010).

17. Feingold, *Natural Desire*, 12–13.

18. *In II Sent.*, d. 24, q. 3, a. 1 [Mand 617]; *QDV*, q. 22, a. 3, ad 2–3 [Leonine 22.3:619.104–32]; *QDV*, q. 23, a. 1 [Leonine 22.3:653.135–61]; *QDV*, q. 25, a. 1 [Leonine 22.3:729.131–58]; *SCG* II.55 [Leonine manualis 149]; *SCG* III.23 [Leonine manualis 249]; *ST* I, q. 19, a. 1 [St. Paul 103]; q. 59, a. 1 [St. Paul 280]; q. 81, a. 2 [St. Paul 390]; *In I Ethic.* 1 [Leonine 47.1:5.165–83].

rial."[19] As a human soul is not a material form, this sense of natural appetite must be positively excluded.[20] Furthermore, there are texts in which Aquinas seems to say that humans' natural appetite is the natural appetite of the will itself.[21]

There are quite a few ambiguous passages, and I do not have the space here to adequately argue about the details of this massive set of texts. But there are texts, most of which concern divine providence, in which Aquinas states that natural appetite follows upon *all* things, that is, all natures or substances.[22] Thus we may conclude, contra Feingold, that natural appetite that follows upon nature need not be restricted to material beings, nor need it be restricted to material actions.[23]

But the more difficult question is whether or how this natural appetite in humans should be distinguished from the natural inclination of the will itself. Aquinas's texts generally proceed like this: there is natural inclination following on form; different kinds of forms have different kinds of inclinations; the inclination that follows human form is will.[24]

19. The reason these texts are so hard to pin down is because of the way that Thomas often distinguishes between the three kinds of appetite; natural, sensitive, and rational. When he draws the line between natural and rational appetite, for example, he contrasts the natural and material appetite of a rock with the immaterial rational appetite of man. The example of the rock makes the distinction quite clear, but what is less clear is the exact scope of natural appetite. For the difference between material and immaterial is not the same as the difference between being moved by one's own cognition and being moved by God's cognition (by natural appetite). Animals have material forms, but they are nevertheless, in a real way, moved by the object of their own cognition and simultaneously by their natural appetite. It is true that material beings are never *freely* moved by their own cognition, as that requires reason, but it is less clear, what exactly the role of natural appetite is in rational and irrational animals.

20. E.g., *ST* I-II, q. 17, a. 6 [St. Paul 629].

21. *In II Sent.*, d. 39, q. 2, a. 2, ad 2 [Mand 994]; *QDV*, q. 22, a. 5 [Leonine 22.3:174–93]; *SCG* I.72 [Leonine manualis 69]; *SCG* III.26 [Leonine manualis 254]; *QDP*, q. 7, a. 10, ad 6 [Marietti 211]; *ST* I, q. 41, a. 2, ad 3 [St. Paul 201], and q. 60, a. 1, ad 2–3, and a. 2 [St. Paul 283–84]; *ST* I-II, q. 1, a. 5 [St. Paul 560]; q. 10, a. 1, ad 3 [St. Paul 605]; q. 16, a. 4 [St. Paul 628]; *De caritate*, a. 1 [Marietti 755]; *QDVC*, q. 1, a. 5, and ad 2 [Marietti 720–21]; *QDM*, q. 3, a. 1 [Leonine 23:67.150–54]; *QDM*, q. 3, a. 3 [Leonine 23:73.221–33]; *QDM*, q. 6 [Leonine 23:148.269–96]; *In V Metaph.* l. 6 [Marietti 226]; *In I Ethic.* l. 2 [Leonine 47.1:7–8.20–52].

22. One could hardly interpret the following passages to be refering to the will: *In III Sent.*, d. 27, q. 1, a. 2 [Moos 861]: "amor naturalis est in omnibus potentiis et omnibus rebus." *ST* I-II, q. 27, a. 2, ad 3 [St. Paul 673]: "amor naturalis, qui est in omnibus rebus, causatur ex aliqua cognitione, non quidem in ipsis rebus naturalibus existente, sed in eo qui naturam instituit." *In IV Sent.*, d. 49, q. 1, a. 3, qc. 1 [Busa 1:681]. Cf. *Super primam epistolam ad II Corinthios lectura*, c. 5, l. 2 [Marietti 477]; *QDV*, q. 22, a. 1 [Leonine 22.3:613–14.191–207].

23. The following is also a strong text which distinguishes between the inclination of man's nature and the the will: *ST* I-II, q. 85, a. 1, ad 2 [St. Paul 916]; cf. a. 2 [St. Paul 917].

24. *ST* I, q. 80, a. 1 [St. Paul 387–88]; *QDM*, q. 16, a. 5 [Leonine 23:304.233–38]. See also

Does this mean that there is no natural appetite following upon human nature that is distinct from the natural appetite of the will? Wherever there is a rational soul, there will always be a will inseparably flowing from it. One could, of course, say the same about all the powers of the soul insofar as they are all inseparable accidents, but only the will could be man's natural appetite because it alone is naturally ordered to the good of the whole person and the good of all of the other powers.[25]

However, appetite is a principle of operation, and the soul, it should not be forgotten, is a form that is a principle of operation.[26] Furthermore, because the soul is a real *per se* first (although not proximate) principle of operation that is prior to the powers, it must have its own end and action that is not caused by the natural inclination of the powers or by their cognition, as these are "posterior" to the soul in the causal chain.[27]

Here we must recall from chapter 1 that no living soul can be immediately operative. In other words, there is no operation of the soul without a distinct power, and there is no operation of a power without the soul. This means that man's nature only operates by means of the powers, and the natural appetites of the powers only operate by means of man's nature or soul—these are distinguishable in thought and really distinct, but inseparable in reality.[28]

As Aquinas puts it in *ST* I-II, q. 10, a. 1, ad 1, the natural motion of the will participates in the motion of nature, as the will is founded (*fundatur*) in nature and is posterior to it. The soul causes the powers

---

ST I, q. 60, a. 1, and ad 2 [St. Paul 283]; *SCG* I.72 [Leonine manualis 69]; *SCG* III.26 [Leonine manualis 254]; *ST* I-II, q. 1, a. 5 [St. Paul 560]; *QDM*, q. 6 [Leonine 23:148.269–84]; *De caritate*, a. 1 [Marietti 755]; *In V Metaph*. l. 6 [Marietti 226]. See also *In III Sent.*, d. 27, q. 1, a. 2 [Mand 861–62, esp. n43], and ad 1.

25. *ST* I-II, q. 10, a. 1 [St. Paul 605].

26. *ST* I, q. 77, a. 1, ad 4 [St. Paul 363]: "hoc ipsum quod forma accidentalis est actionis principium, habet a forma substantiali. Et ideo forma substantialis est primum actionis principium, sed not proximum."

27. *QDM*, q. 4, a. 4, ad 3 [Leonine 23:117.140–43]: "forma substantialis est primum principium actionis. Et sic etiam essentia anime est per prius principium actionis quam potentia."

28. Note that the following passage is not restricted to the sense appetites. *ST* I-II, q. 41, a. 3 [St. Paul 728]: "aliquis motus dicitur naturalis, quia ad ipsum inclinat natura. Sed hoc contingit dupliciter. Uno modo, quod totum perficitur a natura, absque aliqua operatione apprehensivae virtutis; sicut moveri sursum est motus naturalis ignis, ... Alio modo dicitur motus naturalis, ad quem natura inclinat, licet non perficiatur nisi per apprehensionem: quia, ... motus cognitivae et appetitivae virtutis reducuntur in naturam, sicut in principium primum. Et per hunc modum, etiam ipsi actus apprehensivae virtutis, ut intelligere, sentire et memorari, et etiam motus appetitus animalis, quandoque dicuntur naturales."

and their natures or natural inclinations. But also, when Aquinas says that the soul, and not the powers of the soul, is the first principle of operation, he means that the soul itself causes the operations of the powers of the soul through the natural inclinations of each power.[29] Although the soul itself is the primary cause of the will's volitions, one would never be able to experience or notice, at least in properly human acts, the difference between the natural inclination of the will and the soul itself. This is because the soul cannot tend toward its end without the will's volition and the will cannot and does not will its natural end without the soul as first cause—that is, they require each other in their simultaneous inclination to the same end.[30] Any human action is an action of the person that includes the simultaneous synergistic causality of both soul and power, or, we should more accurately say, soul and powers.

Although Aquinas often speaks in the later texts of God as moving the will directly,[31] it must be supposed that he does this through the soul itself—for otherwise Aquinas could not also say that the soul itself is the first principle of operation prior to the powers of the soul and that every operation of the soul is through its powers.[32] Because God causes the soul, which in turn causes its powers, so God moves the soul through its powers. Although Aquinas does not explicitly say this, it is certainly implied; there is no problem, of course, for Aquinas to hold that God moves the will through the soul.

But nevertheless, is there such a thing as a simple natural unconscious metaphysical appetite following upon the human soul? This is important, because if human nature has one simple inclination to its end, then we would have an easy standard by which to measure human virtue and goodness, which Aquinas repeatedly says is according to our nature. It seems to me that if there were such a thing, Aquinas would have treated

---

29. *In I Phys.*, l. 5 [Marietti 68]: "Nihil est igitur aliud appetitus naturalis quam ordinatio aliquorum secundum propriam naturam in suum finem. Non solum autem aliquid ens in actu per virtutem activam ordinatur in suum finem, sed etiam materia secundum quod est in potentia; nam forma est finis materiae." See also *QDV*, q. 25, a. 2 [Leonine 22.3:732.97–110].

30. These are an ordered series of causes, which means that the first is present in the second; see *QDV*, q. 22, a. 5 [Leonine 22:625.151–59, 174–83, 190–203].

31. *QDM*, q. 6 [Leonine 23:149.381–91, 407–17], and q. 16, a. 8 [Leonine 23:321.235–38]; *ST* I-II, q. 9, a. 4 [St. Paul 602]; etc.

32. *ST* I-II, q. 55, a. 4 [St. Paul 778]: "omnis operatio est ab anima per aliquam potentiam."

it in his extraordinarily full treatments of the human soul in his disputed questions *De anima* (1265–66) and *De spiritualibus creaturis* (1267–68) and in his treatment of the human soul in the *prima pars* of the *Summa* (1266–68). But one can only seek in vain for unequivocal statements affirming such an appetite. I think there are good reasons why this is so.

An appetite is a stretching out toward or a desire for something; moreover, it must be a desire for something not already had. In the broadest terms Aquinas says, "act is in a certain way in potency … since for each thing existing in potency, insofar as it is this kind of a thing, there is in it appetite for its own act."[33] He goes as far as saying that matter (which is utterly passive potency) inclines to and even seeks (*appetit*) form.[34] But he also speaks of the appetite of highly active potency, for example, the will. The general point is that potency somehow seeks and tends toward actualization, an actualization not presently had, whether this seeking or tending is in an active or a passive way. All potency is ordered to a particular kind of actualization, and we may call this natural order of potency to some kind of actualization "appetite."

Therefore, in order to find the natural appetite of the soul, we must find how it is naturally in potency. As we recall from earlier, form grants *esse* to the body. In this respect, the soul is in act and the body as prime matter is in potency to the soul as its substantial form. But form grants *esse* to the body for the sake of action (*operari*),[35] and in this respect the soul is in potency, with respect to its operations. I mean that the soul grants the kind of being that is able (is in potency) to act. Because a soul can only act by means of powers, the soul is in potency to act through its powers. Simply put, it is in potency by its potencies to other acts (operations).[36] And, as we have seen, more complex souls (at least souls that inform bodies) have more complex and diverse powers. In the case of the human soul, it is united to the body for the sake of its highest oper-

---

33. *ST* I-II, q. 27, a. 1 [St. Paul 673]; *In III De an.* [Leonine 45.1:203.131–34].

34. *ST* I-II, q. 59, a. 2 [St. Paul 280–81]; *QDV*, q. 22, a. 1 [Leonine 22.3:614.247–69].

35. See, e.g., *QDA*, q. 9 [Leonine 24.1:82.278–80]; *QSC*, q. 2 [Leonine 24.2:29.300–303]; *QDA*, q. 10, ad 2 [Leonine 24.1:92.287–89]; *SCG* IV.13 [Leonine manualis 365].

36. See *ST* I, q. 77 [St. Paul 363]: "Non enim, inquantum est forma, est actus ordinatus ad ulteriorem actum, sed est ultimus terminus generationis. Unde quod sit in potentia adhuc ad alium actum, hoc non competit ei secundum suam essentiam, inquantum est forma; sed secundum suam potentiam."

ation, *intellegere*.[37] The complex of diverse powers (soul qua *motor*) are ordered to one another for the sake of an end, namely, *intellegere*.[38] This end, then, can be said to be the end of its nature qua principle of operation. In this regard, the soul is a bit like a carpenter. Carpenters need a particular set of tools to operate. Without the tools, they cannot be carpenters. A carpenter cannot act without the tools, nor can the tools act without a carpenter. It is the same with the soul; in order to reach its end, it needs particular powers, and these cannot act without the soul, just as the soul cannot act without its powers.

As potency and appetite are coextensive, one can simply consider that there are two kinds of potencies involving the soul: (1) prime matter, which it actualizes, and (2) the powers of the soul corresponding to (a) first act (*esse substantiale*) and (b) second act (*operari*). It is true that matter seeks form, but in such a case matter seeks to exist under substantial form—this could hardly be characterized as the natural appetite of nature itself for something not possessed.[39] Qua form, the soul is in act. But insofar as it is ordered to its end, *intellegere*, it is ordered as motor, as a whole composed of parts. The soul is so ordered by inseparable accidents that are added to the soul. In other words, the soul's natural appetite for its end is *multiplex*, not *simplex*. The soul is in potency to its end; it naturally seeks its end through the manner in which it is naturally in potency, that is, through its powers.[40]

This complex of material and immaterial parts works together in unity (or, at times, disorder) toward one end. Hence, I do not think there is such a thing as a natural simple metaphysical appetite following from man's essence. What is simple (*simplex*) is the manner in which the soul informs the body and the end toward which the soul, via its parts, is ordered. What naturally flows from the soul as it is ordered to its end is complex (*multiplex*). The soul is immediately ordered to its simple end in an extraordinarily complex fashion. Rather than seeking for a simple natural appetite, natural appetites are best understood in grasping that one person, considered as an agent, is a complex of material and imma-

---

37. *QDA*, q. 8, ad 15 [Leonine 24.1:73.468–74].

38. *QDA*, q. 13, ad 7 [Leonine 24.1:121.408–18]; *QDA*, q. 10, ad 17 [Leonine 24.1:94.400–413].

39. See *ST* I, q. 59 [St. Paul 280–81].

40. *QDA*, q. 12, ad 10–12 [Leonine 24.1:111.295–309].

terial parts ordered toward a simple end. When Aquinas says that virtue is according to nature, that is, according to humans' natural appetite, he means that it is according to this complex human inclination to its simple end. In other words, the best way to grasp how virtue is according to humans' natural appetite is to consider the human being as a potential whole that is composed of multiple powers ordered to a single end in a complex fashion. I will develop this further in the remainder of the book.

The Categories

Habits play a crucial role in ordering this complex of powers to its end. For our purposes, I am interested in a particular subset of these powers, namely, the sense appetites. As we saw in chapter 3, the sense appetites considered by themselves are problematic because they naturally seek sensible bodily goods that may or may not be compatible with the human good, which is not simply bodily. The moral virtues apparently solve this problem, at least to some extent. With the moral virtues, the sense appetites participate in reason, and this habitual participation somehow resolves the natural tension between the sensible and the rational. It is the habit that makes the difference. But how, exactly, does this habit help the sense appetites participate in reason? The full answer to this question will carry us through to the very end of the book. However, we should now seek to understand what habit is in order to begin to answer this question.

For Aquinas, habits are essentially bound up with nature. Aquinas does not mean that we are naturally born with them, but rather that we are naturally the kinds of beings that can and should have them. As we have seen, Aquinas repeatedly insists that they are according to nature, *secundum naturae*, and what exactly this means has puzzled interpreters. However, it seems clear to me that what Aquinas means by nature here is nature as a principle of motion, that is, the soul as the potential whole in exactly the way we have been discussing it. I will offer a new interpretation of Aquinas's views on habits by contextualizing them in his thinking on the potential whole, for I think this resolves many of the ambiguities that have been dogging interpreters; it offers a better account of Aquinas's position and also puts us in a good place to ultimately evaluate how habits can help the sense appetites participate in reason.[41]

41. For some scholarship on Aquinas views on habits see Vernon J. Bourke, "Habitus as

Let us begin, then, with the most basic question: What is a habit? For Aquinas, there are two ways to answer the question. From an ethical/teleological perspective, habits are principles of good or bad actions ordering us toward or away from our end; from a metaphysical perspective, however, they are modes of existing (*modi essendi*) that exist in substances as accidents in the genus of quality.[42] When we speak of a habit as a virtue, we speak of it with reference to that entire substantial being's end or perfection, but in speaking of a habit as a predicamental accident in the genus of quality, we are speaking according to a division of being whereby we predicate being of an accident by reason of its reference

a Perfectant of Potency in the Philosophy of St. Thomas Aquinas" (PhD diss., University of Toronto, 1938), and "The Role of Habitus in the Thomistic Metaphysics of Potency and Act," in *Essays in Thomism*, ed. Robert E. Brennan (New York: Sheed and Ward, 1942), 103–9; Bernard Ryosuke Inagaki, "*Habitus* and *Natura* in Aquinas," in *Studies in Medieval Philosophy*, ed. John F. Wippel (Washington, D.C.: The Catholic University of America Press, 1987), 166–67; Servais Pinkaers, "Virtue Is Not a Habit," trans. Bernard Gilligan, in *Cross Currents* 12 (1961): 65–81; see also *The Pinkaers Reader*, 304–20. Bourke's dissertation is the best work on this list. However, much of this literature focuses on the *dynamic* nature of habits (see Bourke's article for the origin of this) and it is very hard to understand what is meant by this. Many (Pinkaers is a good example) wish to replace the English word habit with *habitus*, but I find this to be obscure. Inagake claims that the key to understanding habit is through nature, but his views on nature are unclear. I hope that my account of habit is far more straightforward and helpful. See also David Decosimo, *Ethics as a Work of Charity* (Stanford, Calif.: Stanford University Press, 2014), chap. 3, who emphasizes powers.

42. For Aquinas the predicamental categories are not primarily logical; they are determinate modes of existence founded upon the existence of things; *QDV*, q. 21, a. 1 [Leonine 22.3:593.135–36]. But what does Thomas mean by a mode of existing? John Tomarchio argues that *modus* is always tied to Thomas's metaphysics of *esse*. Tomarchio emphasizes this point by translating *QDV*, q. 21, a. 6, ad 5, as follows: "Whenever there is something received, it is necessary that there be a mode, because the received is limited according to the receiver; and thus because both the accidental and the essential existence of a creature is received, mode is found not only in accidents but also in substances" (Tomarchio, *Modes*, 592). Tomarchio comments on this text as follows: "Note that in considering a perfection as received, one is *ipso facto* considering it according to a distinct individual existence and not abstractly, as one does when considering the *ratio* of the perfection in itself. The notion of the mode of perfection, nature, essence, or form enters in with the consideration of its relation to existence" (593). Tomarchio's formulation clarifies the existential nature of the term *modus*. Thus the word *modus*, at least in this context, simultaneously connotes both formal determining aspects and strong existential aspects. These two aspects cannot be separated from each other *in re*: this mode of existence is formally different from that mode of existence. Any predicament, as it exists in a being, is a way in which that being either has a certain kind of being (accidental being or *inesse*) or the way in which a being is a certain kind of being (substantial being, *esse*). For an account of these modes cast in more contemporary terms see Jeffery Brower, *Aquinas's Ontology of the Material Word: Change, Hylomorphism and Material Objects* (Oxford: Oxford University Press, 2014), 42–54.

to substance.[43] These are simply two different ways of considering the same habit, and both are important for grasping how the sense appetites participate in reason. Let us begin with the metaphysical perspective and work our way toward the ethical perspective.

According to the classical Parmenidean line of thinking, being is not a genus that can be divided by some differentia outside of itself, for such a difference would have to be nonbeing. But according to Aquinas, something can be added to being insofar as it expresses a mode of being that the name "being" itself does not express, that is, some particular mode of existence (*modus essendi*). The name "substance," for example, does not add a difference that is external to being; rather, it expresses a particular mode of existing, in this case, existing *per se*.[44]

Aquinas says: "Some things are found to add something to being since being is contracted to the ten categories, each of which adds something beyond being, not indeed some accident or some difference that is beyond the essence of being, but a determinate mode of existence [*modum essendi*] that is founded in the very existence of the thing [*fundatur in ipsa existentia rei*]."[45] In other words, the categories are divided by the existential modifications already intrinsic to being itself—not by something external to being. Thus, substance is distinct from the other categories because it exists in itself, whereas an accident exists in another.[46] The mode or way in which a substance has existence is different than the way in which an accident has existence. Any predicament, as it

43. For Aquinas's derivation of the categories see John F. Wippel, "Thomas Aquinas's Derivation of the Aristotelian Categories (Predicaments)," *Journal of the History of Philosophy* 25 (1987): 13–34, and *Metaphysical Thought*, 208–28; Gregory Doolan, "Aquinas and the Categories as Parts of Being," in *The Metaphysics of Aquinas: Philosophical and Theological Perspectives* (New York: Fordham University Press, forthcoming); E. P. Bos and A. C. van der Helm, "The Division of Being over the Categories according to Albert the Great, Thomas Aquinas and John Duns Scotus," in *John Duns Scotus (1265/6–1308): Renewal of Philosophy: Acts of the Third Symposium Organized by the Dutch Society for Medieval Philosophy Medium Aevum (May 23 and 24, 1996)*, ed. Bos, Elementa Schriften zur Philosophie und ihrer Problemgeschichte 72 (Amsterdam: Rodopi, 1998), 187–89. Paul Symington, "Thomas Aquinas on Establishing the Identity of Aristotle's *Categories*," in *Medieval Commentaries on Aristotle's Categories*, ed. Lloyd Newton (Boston: Brill, 2008), and *On Determining What There Is: The Identity of Ontological Categories in Aquinas, Scotus and Lowe* (Piscataway, N.J.: Ontos Verlag, 2010).

44. *QDV*, q. 1, a. 1 [Leonine 22.1:5.15–23]. See also *In V Metaph.*, l. 9 [Marietti 238].

45. *QDV*, q. 21, a. 1 [Leonine 22.3:593.129–36].

46. For a full account of Aquinas's distinction between substance and accidents, see Wippel, *Metaphysical Thought*, chaps. 7–8, esp. 228–38.

exists in a being, is a way in which that being either has a certain kind of being (accidental being, *inesse*) or the way in which a being is a certain kind of being (substantial being, *esse*). For Aquinas, the general rule is quite simple: "Once it is known whether something is [*an est*], it remains to inquire how it is [*quomodo est*], in order to know what it is [*quid est*]."[47] In other words, in order to know what something is, one must know how it has existence: this is different than that because this way of existing is different than that way of existing. Thus a claim about which category something belongs to is also a claim about how something actually has existence, that is, about its particular *modus essendi*.

Granting Aquinas's theory of knowledge, the modes of existing are proportionate to our ways of predicating, that is, the modes of predication follow the modes of existing.[48] However, Aquinas does not simply think that all speech signifies extra-mental being. Following Aristotle, he argues that the modes of signification signify the modes of existence of things through a mediate mode of understanding, for words are likenesses of what is understood, and what is understood is a likeness of things.[49] Therefore, through a careful investigation of human speech and thought (while being mindful of our mistakes), it is possible to uncover the most elemental modes of existing. Aquinas would thus have us employ, as John Wippel puts it, a "logical technique" within his metaphysics to discover the ultimate categories of being.[50] In however many ways being is predicated, in so many ways is *esse* said to be, which is why the modes of existing are called "predicaments." Of these modes of predication, some signify what something is, that is, substance; others signify how much it is, that is, quantity; yet others signify how it is, that is, quality; and so on.[51]

---

47. *ST* I, q. 3, prol.

48. *In V Metaph.*, l. 9 [Marietti 238].

49. *In VII Metaph.*, l. 1 [Marietti 317]. See Aristotle's *De Interpretatione* I, 14a3–9, and Aquinas's commentary on this text in *Expositio libri peryermenias*, lib. I, l. 2 [Leonine 1.1:10–11.95–112].

50. Wippel, *Metaphysical Thought*, 211. For more on Aquinas's use of logic within his metaphysics, see Gregory Doolan, "Aquinas on the Metaphysician's vs. the Logician's Categories," *Quaestiones Disputatae* 4, no. 2 (2014): 133–55; Rudi te Velde, "Metaphysics, Dialectics and the *Modus Logicus* According to Thomas Aquinas," *Recherches de Theologie et Philosophie Medievales* 63 (1996): 15–35; Giorgio Pini, *Categories and Logic in Duns Scotus: An Interpretation of Aristotle's Categories in the Late Thirteenth Century* (Leiden: Brill, 2002), chaps. 1–2; and James C. Doig, "Aquinas on Metaphysical Method," *Philosophical Studies* 13 (1964): 20–36.

51. *In V Metaph.*, l. 9 [Marietti 238].

Aquinas uses this "logical technique" to derive the ten supreme predicaments or categories. He argues that a predicate can be related to a subject in three fundamental ways: (a) the predicate is the subject, (b) the predicate is taken from something in the subject, or (c) the predicate is taken from something extrinsic to the subject. In the case of the first way, we can say "Socrates is an animal," and here the predicate signifies (1) first substance, which is a particular substance of which everything else is predicated. In the case of the second way, the predicate can be in the subject *per se* and absolutely considered either as following matter, that is, (2) quantity, or as following form, that is, (3) quality. The predicate can also be in the subject not absolutely, but with respect to something else, that is, (4) relation. The third way can be further subdivided. If the predicate is taken from something that is altogether outside of the subject but does not measure the subject, we have (5) habit (think of the Franciscans' habit)—for example, Socrates is clothed. If the external thing measures the subject in some way, there is (6) time and (7) place, and if the order of the subject's parts in that place are taken into consideration, there will be (8) position. If the predicate is taken from something in the subject that is a principle of action in another, there is (9) action, but if the predicate is taken as the subject receives the terminus of an action from another, there is (10) passion, for passion terminates in the subject.[52]

For our purposes here, then, quality comes from the mode of predicating in which the predicate is taken from something in the subject, namely, form: quality follows (*consequens*) form. We will return to this important point later.

The Genus of Quality

In his *De ente* 6, Aquinas explains how one takes genus, difference, and species *vis-à-vis* accidents. Genus is first taken from the mode of ex-

---

52. Ibid. [239] and *In III Physic.*, l. 5 [Marietti 159]. For Aquinas's derivation of the predicaments see Wippel, *Metaphysical Thought*, 208–28; Doolan, "Aquinas and the Categories"; Bos and van der Helm, "The Division of Being," 187–89; Symington, *The Identity of Aristotle's Categories*, 119–44; and Giorgio Pini, "Scotus on Deducing Aristotle's Categories," in *La tradition médiévale des Catégories (XIIe–XIVe siécles). XIIIe Symposium européen de logique et de sémantique médiévales. Avignon 6–10 juin 2000*, ed. J. Biard and I. Rosier-Catach, Philosophes médiévaux 45 (Louvain-la-Neuve / Leuven: Éditions de l'Institut supérieur de Philosophie / Éditions Peeters, 2003), 23–35.

isting insofar as being is said in different ways of the ten predicaments.[53] "But their differences are taken from the diversity of principles by which they are caused.... But since the proper principles of accidents are not always manifest, so sometimes we take the difference of accidents from their effects."[54] In other words, the genus of accidents is taken from their particular accidental mode of existence. In the case of quality, this is the kind of accidental being (*inesse*) that follows form, as we saw in Aquinas's general derivation of the ten categories. The differences that divide this genus, however, are taken from the different principles that cause the specific accidents. Yet there are times when the causes of these accidents are obscure, and in such cases the differences are taken from their effects. It is through these differences (through causes or effects) that we divide the genus of quality into its four species.

In *ST* I-II, q. 49, a. 2, Aquinas articulates what it means for a habit to be in the first species of the predicament of quality. The question, even for Aquinas's metaphysics-laden ethics, is extraordinarily metaphysical. Aquinas begins his division of the genus of quality in a. 2 by noting that measure precedes mode and that mode implies a determination according to some measure. Although the terms "mode" and "determination" are somewhat synonymous, "mode" has a stronger existential aspect, while the emphasis of "determination" is more formal. Aquinas notes that "just as that according to which the potency of matter is determined according to *esse substantiale* is called quality, which is a *differentia* of substance, so that according to which the potency of a subject is determined according to accidental *esse* is called accidental quality, which is also a certain *differentia*." Thus, the key lies with the measure, as it is the determining principle or cause of the particular mode of existing. To put this in the terms of *De ente* 6 that have just been discussed, the measure is the principle, cause, or difference by which the genus of quality is divided into its species.

In the case of quality, the mode or determination of the subject according to accidental *esse* can be taken according to four measures or differences corresponding to the four species of quality. When nature is the measure, we have the first species of quality (habits and dispositions).

53. *De ente* [Leonine 43:381.132–35].
54. Ibid., ll. 139–40 and 156–59.

When action and passion (which follow upon the principles of nature, matter, and form) are the measures, we have the second (capacity and incapacity) and third (passion[55] and sensible qualities) species, respectively. When quantity is the measure, we have the fourth species of quality (form and figure).[56] Aquinas thus follows Aristotle's schematic division of quality in *Categories* 8 into four species, each of which is subdivided further.[57]

The first two species of quality are the relevant ones for our purposes. To avoid confusion, however, I should note that the passions in the third species are not the passions of the soul, that is, our emotions—which I will examine in chapter 9. The word "passion" here means property, in particular, a sensible property, for instance, the property of this is that it is hot. Passions qua emotions are in the category passion, not in the category quality.[58] I should also point out that the fourth species of quality simply refers to the shape or dimensive quantity of natural bodies or artificial things. Let us briefly consider the second species of quality before turning to the first in more detail.

The second species of quality is divided into *potentia* and *impotentia naturalis*, which can be translated as capacity and incapacity or as power and defective power. These qualify a subject in the sense that something is said to be able or not able to do something by means of them—so, of course, it is by means of these qualities that a substance can in fact do or not do something.[59] These powers are all the powers of the soul, including vegetative, sensitive, and rational powers.[60]

---

55. For Aquinas, a passion, as a movement of a sense appetite, is not a quality, although Aristotle seems to suggest as much in *Categories* 8 (9a34–b7). For Aquinas the redness caused by the passion of shame is a sensible quality of the third species, but the passion itself is not a quality. Because a passion is a movement, it is in the category of action, in particular, alteration, which is the motion from one sensible quality to another, say from pale to red; see *QDV*, q. 26, a. 1 [Leonine 22.3:747.173–77]; *In III Sent.*, d. 15, q. 2, a. 1, sol. 1 [Moos 483].

56. *ST* I-II, q. 49, a. 2 [St. Paul 753–54].

57. See also Nicholas Kahm, "Aquinas on Quality," *British Journal for the History of Philosophy* 24, no. 1 (2015): 23–44.

58. Because such a passion is a motion, in particular, of the species of alteration; see *QDV*, q. 26, a. 1 [Leonine 22.3:747.173–77]; *In III Sent.*, d. 15, q. 2, a. 1, sol. 1 [Moos 483], it is in the category of passion, *In V Metaph.*, l. 20 [Marietti 278]. Cf. *In III Phys.*, l. 5 [Marietti 158–60].

59. *SCG* IV.77 [Leonine manualis 542, *adhuc*]

60. Notably, Aquinas sometimes uses *potentia naturalis* in the sense in which natural is contrary to rational, i.e., to denote the vegetative or sensitive powers; cf., e.g., *ST* I-II, q. 50, a. 3, and q. 55, a. 1, and ad 1; II-II, q. 104, a. 1. This is not the sense in which the powers of the

A defective power is a power that is defective or deprived,[61] for example, blindness or a weak power of reason.[62] The word "natural" is important here, implying as it does not just any lack of power, but a lack of or deficiency in the powers that such and such a nature ought to have.[63] Thus, although one might call, say, our inability to look at the sun or our inability to see in darkness an *impotentia*, one cannot call it an *impotentia naturalis*, as humans are not naturally capable of either.[64]

Let us turn to the first species of quality, which generically is a disposition.[65] Paraphrasing Aristotle's *Metaphysics* V, Aquinas notes that disposition signifies order; more specifically, he says that a disposition is "nothing else than an order of parts in that which has parts."[66] Aquinas specifies this further and says that every such disposition is said to be toward something (*ad aliquid*) and thus involves a relation, although it is not a relation itself.[67] It is a certain way of being related (*modus se habendi*), either in oneself or to something else.[68]

Moreover, such dispositions are dispositions to "what is perfect in its own nature in relation to what is best, that is, the end, which is operation."[69] Likewise, in q. 49, a. 2, Aquinas says that a quality of the first species, in contrast to the other three, is according to nature (*secundum naturam*), and included in the understanding of nature is the end (the *rationem finis*).[70] The first species is thus inherently teleological and is ordered to the end of nature.[71] Because it is ordered to the end of nature,

---

soul are in the second species of quality. He also uses the phrase *potentia naturalis* to mean the rational powers; cf. *ST* II-II, q. 23, a. 2, and q. 24, a. 2.

61. *In V Metaph.*, l. 14 [Marietti 256]; *QDP*, q. 1, a. 1, ad 17 [Marietti 10].

62. *QDP*, q. 1, a. 3, ad 2 [Marietti 15]; *In II Metaph.*, l. 5 [Marietti 93].

63. *In V Metaph.*, l. 14 [Marietti 257–58].

64. *In II De an.*, l. 21 [Leonine 45.1:156–57.121–35].

65. *ST* I-II, q. 49, a. 2, ad 3 [St. Paul 754].

66. *In V Metaph.*, l. 20 [Marietti 277]; see also *ST* I-II, q. 49, a. 1, ad 3 [St. Paul 754].

67. *In VII Phys.*, l. 5 [Marietti 470–71]. On relations in Aquinas, see Mark G. Henninger, "Aquinas on the Ontological Status of Relations," *Journal of the History of Philosophy* 24 (1987): 491–515.

68. *ST* I-II, q. 49, a. 1 [St. Paul 752].

69. *In VII Phys.*, l. 5 [Marietti 471].

70. *ST* I-II, q. 49, a. 2 [St. Paul 753].

71. Ibid.: "Non autem consideratur in his [the second and third species of quality] aliquid pertinens ad rationem boni vel mali, quia motus et passiones non habent rationem finis, bonum autem et malum dicitur per respectum ad finem – Sed modus et determinatio subiecti in ordine ad naturam rei, pertinet ad primam speciem qualitatis, … ideo in prima specie consideratur et bonum et malum; … Metaphys. philosophus definit habitum, quod

whether it attains, or falls short of its end, goodness or badness can be predicated of it.[72] Because the other three species of quality have no such teleological ordering, they cannot be said to be good or bad in this way.

In his commentary on the *Metaphysics*, Aquinas notes that a quality of the first species is a disposition according to which one is disposed well or poorly either with respect to oneself or with respect to something else; for example, by the disposition health one is well disposed to oneself and by the disposition robustness one is well disposed to do something. Not only is this first species of quality concerned with the disposition of the whole (as the material dispositions of health or robustness are dispositions of the whole body), but it also includes the dispositions of the whole's parts; as the good dispositions of the parts of animals are parts for the sake of the whole animal, so are the virtues good dispositions of the parts of the soul, for example, temperance in the concupiscible appetite, courage in the irascible appetite, and prudence in reason.[73] A disposition is thus an order of that which has parts to the whole of which the parts are a part. Nature taken in different senses can be considered as a universal whole composed of subjective parts (form and matter), an integral whole composed of integral parts (the various different bodily parts of the animal), and a potential whole composed of potential parts (as the soul is a whole composed of powers).[74] Qualities of the first species are always dispositive perfections of these parts to the whole of which they are a part, that is, to nature.

This is not the perfection that necessarily follows upon creation, that is, a being's first perfection, but the perfection that a creature may or may not attain, that is, its second perfection. In other words, it is a dispositive perfection or actualization that a creature is naturally in potency toward but may not actually have. Furthermore, this perfection can only be in a potency that can be actualized in different ways, in other

---

est dispositio secundum quam aliquis disponitur bene vel male.... Quando enim est modus conveniens naturae rei, tunc habet rationem boni, quando autem non convenit, tunc habet rationem mali. Et quia natura est id quod primum consideratur in re, ideo habitus ponitur prima species qualitatis."

72. Ibid., and ad 1 [St. Paul 753].

73. *In V Metaph.*, l. 20 [Marietti 277]: "non solum habitus dicitur dispositio totius, sed etiam dispositio partis, quae est pars dispositionis totius; ... virtutes etiam partium animae."

74. See the discussion of habits in angels in *ST* I-II, q. 50, a. 6 [St. Paul 761], esp. ad 3: here he clearly means potential parts of the potential whole.

words, in a potency that can be disposed either according to nature or contrary to it.[75]

More specifically, this perfection concerns a dispositive actualization of two kinds of potency: (1) as the body is in potency to the soul, or (2) as the being is in potency toward operation through its powers. Thus Aquinas distinguishes two ways of taking "according to nature": as either (1) according to form (*ad formam*) or (2) according to operation (*ad operationem*).[76] The former may be subsumed under the latter, as the perfections of the body are ordered to the soul, which is itself ordered to operation.[77]

What is common to the first species, then, is that it is according to nature (*secundum naturam*). The primary way that Aquinas divides this species is into dispositions that are ordered to form and dispositions that are ordered to operation. Dispositions toward form (*ad formam*) are called "dispositions" and dispositions toward operation (*ad operationem*) are called "habits." Habits and dispositions can be distinguished both by their respective potencies, which they perfect, and by their respective causes.

Let us first consider dispositions toward form (*ad formam*). Qualities of the first species that are according to form are in the body as it is related to the soul, for example, health and beauty.[78] Because a habit or disposition can only be in a potency that can be disposed in different ways, it is impossible for there to be a disposition in the rational soul as it is ordered to the body. This is because the soul, as the form of the body, is already perfectly actualizing the body—there is no potency for a perfecting disposition.[79] The body, however, being inherently potential and composed of contrary elements, is always unstable; that is why there is room for perfecting dispositions in the body. Furthermore, such dispositions do not have stable causes.[80]

Health, for instance, is a certain proportion of humors, heat, and

75. *ST* I-II, q. 49, a. 4 [St. Paul 755].
76. *ST* I-II, q. 50, a. 1 [St. Paul 756]: "habitus est quaedam dispositio alicuius subiecti existentis in potentia vel ad formam, vel ad operationem." See also ibid., a. 2 [St. Paul 757]; *ST* I-II, q. 54, a. 2 [St. Paul 772]. This distinction is ubiquitous in *ST* I-II, qq. 49–66.
77. *ST* I-II, q. 49, a. 4, ad 1 [St. Paul 755]; ibid., a. 3 [St. Paul 754]; ibid., ad 3 [St. Paul 755].
78. *ST* I-II, q. 50, a. 1 [St. Paul 756].
79. Ibid., a. 2 [St. Paul 757].
80. *ST* I-II, q. 49, a. 2, ad 3 [St. Paul 754].

coldness that is according to nature.[81] There is no reason to insist on the details of medieval medicine, but the general point is still correct. Health involves a certain proportion of material parts to one another. When someone is sick, for example, it is fair to say that something material and internal is somehow out of proportion; it is disordered. Beauty (*pulchritudo*) is also included in this species, but as the proper figure of the body and the proportion and color of the members of the body.[82] Aquinas even considers strength and weakness to belong to this species of quality, as a kind of fitting commensuration of nerves, flesh, and bones.[83]

These are all material dispositions of the body and its parts as they are ordered to the soul, and they all have changeable and corruptible material causes.[84] Although they concern the relation of the body to the soul, Aquinas insists, as we noted, that they also concern the manner in which the soul is ordered to operation.[85] Closely related to these dispositions are the natural dispositions of the organs of the sensitive powers, for example, the manner in which some have a natural *inchoatio* to virtue, such as a natural mildness that may help someone be temperate.[86]

Because one of the distinguishing marks of habits is that they have immutable or permanent causes and these dispositions have changeable causes, they are not truly habits and they do not perfectly have the nature of habits,[87] although Aquinas often calls them "habits."[88] Aquinas

81. The humors are the four fluids of the body. On health see *QDV*, q. 27, a. 1, ad 4 [Leonine 22.3:791.190–93]; *QDVC*, q. 3 [Marietti 823]; *In II Physic.*, l. 4 [Marietti 87]; *In librum Beati Dionysii De divinis nominibus exposito*, lib. 4, l. 22 [Marietti 215]; *In I Sent.*, d. 19, q. 5, a. 1 [Mand 486]; *QDV*, q. 11, a. 2 [Leonine 22.2:353.78–82].

82. *ST* I-II, q. 49, a. 2, ad 1 [St. Paul 753–54]; *Super Psalmo* 44, n. 2 [Parma 14:520]; *SCG* III.139 [Leonine manualis 397, *sed si*].

83. *ST* I-II, q. 54, a. 1 [St. Paul 771]; See also *In X Ethic.* 3 [Leonine 47.2:559.46–55]; *In II Ethic.*, l. 7 [Leonine 47.1:98.12–21], *De regno*, l. 1, c. 3 [Leonine 42:452.47–50]. In *QDM*, q. 8, a. 4 [Leonine 23:206.55–58], he also discusses beauty's opposite, *turpitudo*. *Pulchritudo* always has some pleasing relation to an apprehensive power; see *ST* I-II, q. 27, a. 1, ad 3 [St. Paul 672], in this case sight. But Aquinas does distinguish between spiritual and sensible beauty in *ST* I-II, q. 27, a. 2 [St. Paul 673]: spiritual beauty is apprehended by the intellect whereas sensible beauty is apprehended by sight (and presumably the internal senses). For example, see *ST* II-II, q. 145, a. 2 [St. Paul 1647].

84. *ST* I-II, q. 49, a. 2, ad 3 [St. Paul 754], and q. 50, a. 1 [St. Paul 756].

85. *ST* I-II, q. 49, a. 3, ad 3 [St. Paul 755]; *In VII Phys.*, l. 5 [Marietti 471].

86. *ST* I-II, q. 51, a. 1 [St. Paul 762], and q. 63, a. 1 [St. Paul 810].

87. *ST* I-II, q. 50, a. 1 [St. Paul 756].

88. See, for example, *ST* I-II, q. 49, a. 1 [St. Paul 752]; *In VI Ethic.*, l. 10 [Leonine 47.2:371.131]; *In III Sent.*, d. 23, q. 1, a. 1 [Moos 699].

says that these dispositions are *as* habits (*ut habitus*),[89] and at times he refers to them as "habitual dispositions" (*habituales dispositiones*).[90]

Habits proper, as we have noted, concern the manner in which the soul is ordered to operation or action. Thus, Aquinas contrasts dispositions that are in the body with habits that are in the soul. However, as we have also noted, habits can only be in a potency that can be determined in different ways. As the soul itself as form is always actual, habits cannot be in the soul as it informs the body, and thus Aquinas denies that habits inhere in the essence of the soul.[91] But as we discussed in chapters 2 and 4, the soul is in potency to operation through its potencies.[92] Thus habits are in the soul, but only in the soul understood as a potential whole composed of powers and ordered to operation.[93]

One way to grasp this is to contrast habits with powers and consider why habits are in the first species and powers are in the second. Natural powers or potencies are also ordered to a kind of natural perfection, namely, their actualization; thus will is ordered to willing and the intellect to understanding, and so on. Furthermore, the powers of the soul are the parts of the potential whole. Then, it might be asked, is not the actualization of such a part ordered to the whole of which it is a part? The answer is "no"; powers are ordered to or inclined to their own actualization,[94] but they are not ordered to the end of nature, that is, the end of human life.[95] An example may be helpful: the intellect may be actualized by understanding the quiddity of a dog, but such an actualization is neither according to nor opposed to the end of human life. Even if someone understands the good, that actualization is not necessarily ordered to the end of human nature because the incontinent can understand the good.

89. *ST* I-II, q. 50, a. 1, ad 2 [St. Paul 757].

90. *ST* I-II, q. 49, a. 3, ad 3 [St. Paul 755], and q. 50, a. 1 [St. Paul 756].

91. Grace is the only exception. It is important to note that grace is not immediately ordered to operation, but to *esse spirituale*. See *QDV*, q. 27, a. 2, ad 7 [Leonine 22.3:795.192–202]; *ST* I-II, q. 110, a. 3, ad 3 [St. Paul 1062] and *In II Sent.*, d. 26, q. 1, a. 4, ad 1 [Mand 678].

92. *ST* I-II, q. 50, a. 1, ad 2 [St. Paul 757–58], and q. 49, a. 4, ad 1 [St. Paul 755].

93. *ST* I-II, q. 50, a. 2 [St. Paul 757]: "Si vero accipiatur habitus in ordine ad operationem, sic maxime habitus inveniuntur in anima: inquantum anima non determinatur ad unam operationem, sed se habet ad multas, quod requiritur ad habitum, ut supra dictum est. Et quia anima est principium operationum per suas potentias, ideo secundum hoc, habitus sunt in anima secundum suas potentias." See n00 in this chapter.

94. *ST* I-II, q. 51, a. 1 [St. Paul 762].

95. *ST* I-II, q. 50, a. 5, ad 1 [St. Paul 760]: "necessarium est ad finem humanae vitae, quod vis appetitiva inclinetur in aliquid determinatum, ad quod non inclinatur ex natura potentiae."

What is required for the existence of a habit is an indeterminate but determinable potency. But this potential indeterminacy is not a property of the nature of a power or potency itself. Let us consider the sense appetites. It is true that the sense appetites have something indeterminate with respect to their objects, as it is possible to be attracted to this or that, but this is not the kind of potential indeterminacy that is relevant to habits. This kind of indeterminacy, for this or that object, is simply part of the nature of the power itself. But even granting this particular indeterminacy, the sense appetites can nevertheless be considered to operate in a deterministic fashion *ad unum*.[96] For when a certain sensible object is perceived and presented to the sense appetite, the sense appetite is either naturally attracted to it or it is not. For instance, it is indeterminate whether we smell and see fruit; however, granting the presence of fruit, we are naturally attracted to fresh and ripe fruit and repulsed by rotting and moldy fruit.

But the kind of potential indeterminacy that is relevant to habits, which can be said to be according or opposed to nature, is only grasped when the sense appetites are considered in the context of the whole of which they are a part, that is, the rational soul as a potential whole, which includes reason and will.[97] This is why the very *ratio* of habit necessarily includes will and reason, which is the principle of the soul's rational acts.[98] Any act of a habit of the soul proceeds from synderesis and the natural inclination of the will. In fact, it must be commanded, and thus a habit of the soul necessarily includes reason and will in its definition as its cause. Habits cannot be severed from free decision, for without free choice a human's potency is determined by nature. That is, when goodness and badness are predicated of operative habits, this is only intelligible in reference to the whole soul, including all its powers, as they are ordered to nature's end. There is no such reference to the end of nature in the powers of the soul;[99] thus habits are in the first species of

---

96. *ST* I-II, q. 50, a. 3 (text, 78n43, in chapter 3). See also ibid., ad 2.

97. Ibid. Cf. chapter 3 above.

98. *ST* I-II, q. 50, a. 5 [St. Paul 760]: "Ex ipsa etiam ratione habitus apparet quod habet quendam principalem ordinem ad voluntatem, prout habitus est quo quis utitur cum voluerit, ut supra dictum est." See also ibid., a. 3, ad 2 [St. Paul 758], and a. 1, ad 1 [St. Paul 756–57].

99. Synderesis is not an exception because it is a habit. The only exception is the natural inclination of the will as the will naturally inclines to the good of virtue, the good of all of the other powers and the good of the whole person; see *ST* I-II, q. 10, a. 1 [St. Paul 615].

quality and powers are in the second. To return to the example of fruit, when the witch brought Snow White the apple, there were obviously other considerations that Snow White should have taken into consideration. If she were virtuous, her natural desire for the delectable apple would have been tempered by prudential considerations (i.e., there is something suspicious about this evil-looking witch), which would have to involve the sense appetites precisely as related to reason and will.

The habits of the soul, which are ordered to operations, perfect and determine the powers of the soul according to nature as nature is ordered to operation through its powers. The nature (*ratio*) of these virtues includes other powers, in particular, reason and will, and the immutable principles or seeds of these habits are the natural inclination of the will and synderesis.[100] Thus, the proper division between virtues and dispositions is as follows: dispositions are dispositions of the body as it is related to the soul that have mutable causes, while habits are dispositions of the soul that inhere in the powers of the soul as it is ordered to operation and that have immutable causes. When Aquinas says that a disposition cannot become a habit, he is distinguishing between them in this way.[101] One has mutable causes while the other has immutable causes, and thus they are different species of the genus of disposition.

However, Aquinas also grants that there is another proper way to draw the distinction between habits and dispositions. One may further divide each of these two species into what is perfect and what is imperfect, or what is perfectly in that species (*perfecte inest*) and thus cannot be easily lost and what is imperfectly in it (*imperfecte inest*) and thus can be easily lost.[102] This is a reference to the medieval discussion of the intension and remission of accidental forms. The point is that one way we may speak of the perfection or imperfection of accidents (the *esse* of

However, this natural inclination is determined *ad unum* and operates by way of an *instinctus naturae*. I will discuss this in detail in chapter 9.

100. *ST* I-II, q. 63, a. 1 [St. Paul 810], and q. 51, a. 1 [St. Paul 762].

101. *ST* I-II, q. 49, a. 2, ad 3 [St. Paul 754]; *QDM*, q. 7, a. 3, ad 4 [Leonine 23:168.243–51] and ad 11 [ll. 292–95]; ibid., a. 2, ad 4 [Leonine 23:164.265–69]; *Quaestio disputata de virtibus in communi*, q. 1, a. 1, ad 9 [Marietti 710].

102. *ST* I-II, q. 49, a. 2, ad 3 [St. Paul 754]; *In IV Sent.*, d. 4, q. 1, a. 1 [Moos 150]; *QDM*, q. 7, a. 6, ad 5 [Leonine 23:175.117–20]. However, it is important to note that the division between perfect and imperfect also applies to the distinction between habits of the soul and habits of the body, as habits of the soul are inherently more perfect than habits of the body; see *QDM*, q. 7, a. 3, ad 4 [Leonine 23:168.243–50].

which is *inesse*) is in terms of the degree to which the accidents inhere in a subject. That is, any given accidental form may be more or less firmly entrenched *in* the subject[103]—or one can say that the accident is more or less perfectly in the subject. Thus we may say that any given subject has more or less temperance as temperance inheres more or less firmly in the soul. According to this way of making the division, habits have firm *in-esse* and are thus immobile while dispositions have weak *inesse* and thus are easily removable. According to this division, the same disposition can become a habit.[104]

As is readily apparent, there is a tremendous amount of flexibility in Aquinas's usage of the terms "habit" and "disposition," and it can be difficult to know which way he is using them. Moreover, at times he seems to use the terms interchangeably and imprecisely.[105] But the two ways of making the division make sense: (1) between dispositions of the body as it is ordered to the soul with mutable causes and habits of the soul as it is ordered to operation with immutable causes, and furthermore, within this division, (2) we may speak of any given disposition or habit as a habit if it has firm *inesse* or as a disposition if it has weak *inesse*. Thus health is a disposition, as it is a bodily disposition ordered to the soul, but we may speak of it as a habit if it is firmly entrenched in a subject. Similarly, in the process of acquiring virtue, a novice may have the habit of temperance, but if that person barely has the habit, we may call the habit a disposition, as metaphysically, it has weak *inesse*.

Habits and the Potential Whole

In Aquinas's general derivation of the ten categories, quality is in the subject as following (*consequens*) form.[106] Form, of course, is a principle of substance. Inspired by Aristotle's *Metaphysics* 1020b14–25, Aquinas's hierarchical ordering of the genus of quality, from first to fourth, follows

---

103. *QDM*, q. 7, a. 2, ad 4 [Leonine 23:164.273–76]; *ST* II-II, q. 24, a. 4, ad 3 [St. Paul 1191]; *ST* I-II, q. 54, a. 4, ad 1 [St. Paul 774].

104. *QDM*, q. 7, a. 2, ad 4 [Leonine 23:164.265–71]. For an argument suggesting that the mature Aquinas thought that a disposition could not become a habit see McKay Knoble, "Pagan Virtues," 347. To that I would note that this *De malo* text is a late text: Torrell dates it to roughly 1270, which is contemporaneous to the parallel passage in *ST* I-II, q. 49, a. 2, ad 3 [St. Paul 754].

105. E.g., *QDM*, q. 7, a. 3, ad 11 [Leonine 23:168.292–94].

106. See 101n52.

from taking the subject or substance in two senses: (1) as abstracted from motion, and (2) as a difference of things in motion as they are in motion. This maps neatly onto Aquinas's distinction between form qua *motor* and form qua *forma*.

The fourth species of quality reduces to substance in abstraction from motion,[107] for the form or figure of something, say a cube, is obviously not a consideration of that thing in motion.[108] However, the first to third species of quality reduce to things in motion as they are in motion. The third species of quality always involves motion, namely, alteration; so does the second species, as powers or *impotentiae* are inherently ordered to operation;[109] and the first species, habits and dispositions, imply being moved well or badly, for, as Aristotle says (*Metaphysics* 120b24–25), "Good and bad indicate quality especially in living things, and among these especially in those that have choice." This broad division forms a kind of spectrum, where substantial form in complete abstraction from motion lies at one extreme (fourth species) and qualities concerned with beings that above all move themselves by choice lie at the opposite extreme (first species), with the various ways in which substances actively move (second species) and are passively moved (third species) in between.

Dispositions of the first species are according to nature (*secundum naturam*), and included in the understanding of nature is the end (the *rationem finis*),[110] which is operation.[111] The first species of quality, disposition, is thus inherently teleological; it considers the order of the whole to its end. Nature, in the relevant way that Aquinas takes the term here, is precisely an intrinsic principle of motion by which a substance moves toward its end.[112]

Even given his distinction within the first species between dispo-

---

107. *In V Metaph.*, l. 16 [Marietti 263].

108. *QDVC*, a. 1 [Marietti 709].

109. *Quodlibeta* (hereafter, *Quodl.*) X, q. 3, a. 1 [Leonine 25.1:131.43–50]. See Kahm, "Quality," 10–12.

110. *ST* I-II, q. 49, a. 2 [St. Paul 753].

111. *In VII Phys.*, l. 5 [Marietti 471].

112. *SCG* III.23: "natura enim est principium motus in eo in qua est" (Leonine manualis 249). *De Ente* 1 [Leonine 43:370.45–49]: "nomen autem nature hoc modo sumpte videtur significare essentiam rei secundum quod habet ordinem vel ordinationem ad propriam operationem rei, cum nulla res propria destituatur operatione." See also *ST* III, q. 2, a. 1, etc.

sitions to form (*ad formam*) and dispositions to operation (*ad operationem*), Aquinas still subsumes the former under the latter. Consider health, for instance: although it is a disposition of the body as ordered to the soul, health is nevertheless ultimately for the sake of living well, namely, for operation. Aquinas would have us think similarly of all bodily dispositions. It is thus final causality that causes the first species and divides it from the other three. Because dispositions are so related to the end of nature, whether or not they are ordered to that nature's end, operation, we may predicate goodness or badness of them.

Given that the first species is bound to the soul as mover, that is, as the potential whole, it makes sense that what divides the first species from the other three is that it is according to nature, *secundum naturae*, where by "nature," in this particular context, Aquinas means *human* nature as it is a principle of human self-motion. Moreover, self-motion for humans must ultimately be through free choice. In general, for Aquinas, if we do not freely move ourselves through choice, then we are ultimately moved by something else. The self-motion of free choice requires reason and will in considering various ends, the various means to those ends, and ultimately choosing the means and following through with action. Because such self-motion must be free motion, habits of the first species are necessarily bound to reason and will, and they must either support free human acts toward the good or hinder such acts in some way. This is how habits of the first species are according to nature, that is, rational human nature, or opposed to it.[113]

If we wish to properly divide the first species, dispositions, into its two subspecies, we have dispositions that are in the body and we have transmutable causes or habits of the soul that inhere in the powers of the soul and have permanent causes, namely, reason and will. Habits of the soul, of course, perfect the potential parts of the potential whole, the powers of the soul. But habits perfect the powers of the soul insofar as they are parts of a whole, and this whole is judged good or bad depending on how well it operates, as that is the whole point of the potential whole.

This is crucial: a habit is not simply the perfection of some power

---

113. This is why Aquinas denies that animals can have habits, as they do not have rational souls, but he affirms that they can have dispositions of the body ordered to their own natures.

by itself; it is the power's perfection as understood in the context of the complex of powers operating together. Notice how the cause that further divides the habits from dispositions includes other powers, namely, the natural inclination of will and synderesis. I will discuss this particular causality in great detail in chapters 7 and 10. But here I want to emphasize that the perfection of any particular power is necessarily bound up with other powers, as this perfection is precisely the perfection of the part qua part of an operative whole, not in abstraction from this whole. This is why the potential whole is so crucial for understanding Aquinas's views on habits.

The scholarship on Aquinas's philosophy of habit has missed this point. Scholars tend to either overemphasize habits' roles as perfections of powers[114] or to overemphasize habits' relation to nature qua soul.[115] What has not been understood is that Aquinas is using "nature" in this context to mean the rational soul as a mover, which includes other powers of the soul, in particular, the rational powers. Habits help the soul's parts operate together as a unified whole according to our human nature. Nature's end is *simplex*, as discussed at the beginning of this chapter. This is why we can use one end to measure all of the different dispositions. But as I also mentioned there, the soul is ordered to its simple end in a *multiplex* fashion through its various powers. Thus, multiple habits are needed in these different powers to help them act in unison toward the soul's simple end. Each part of the soul has to be perfected to play its role in the whole's complex march toward its simple end.

One trend in Thomistic scholarship is to emphasize the "dynamic"

114. Bourke, "Habitus as a Perfectant"; see also his "The Role of Habitus in the Thomistic Metaphysics of Potency and Act," in *Essays in Thomism*, ed. Robert E. Brennan (New York: Sheed and Ward, 1942), 103–9. Decosimo, *Ethics*, chap. 3, emphasizes virtue is as the *ultimum potentiae*, the perfection of a power.

115. Bernard Ryosuke Inagaki, however, in an oft-cited article on habits criticizes Thomists (and Bourke) for neglecting Thomas's most significant and original claim, namely, that virtue is according to nature; indeed, "the uniqueness of Aquinas's position can hardly be overemphasized." See his "*Habitus* and *Natura* in Aquinas," 166–67. Inagaki cites the following passage on 168, from *ST* I-II, q. 49, a. 3: "non est de ratione habitus quod respiciat potentiam, sed respiciat naturam." However, I must confess that I do not understand much of Inagaki's article, and much of what I understand I am unwilling to embrace. For example, I do not agree with his thesis that habit is the best way to arrive at an understanding of nature (that no quidditative knowledge comes from knowledge of the acts of the soul, but it does come through knowledge of habits, 161–62). It is unclear to me what exactly he ultimately thinks nature is.

nature of habits. This, however, is metaphysically mysterious. "Dynamic" is, of course, simply a transliteration of the Greek *dynamis*, which is perfectly well translated into Latin as *potentia*. But these scholars seem to mean that habits have some sort of special dynamic quality over and above *potentia*. One oft-cited source for this "dynamic" language is Vernon Bourke's claim that a habit is a "metaphysical perfectant," by which he means to emphasize the manner in which a habit perfects a power.[116] It is not completely in potency (as it is actually a quality), but it is also not completely in act (as it is in potency to operation); hence the term "perfectant"—not quite perfect but becoming so, not quite potency and not quite act. According to Bourke, this is a kind of "metaphysical scandal."[117]

Oddly enough, this "scandal" is similar to contemporary metaphysicians' distinction between categorical and dispositional properties. The term "categorical" does not refer back to Aristotle's *Categories*, but rather means categorical as opposed to hypothetical. Thus a categorical property is a property that the subject *actually* has, and a dispositional property is one that the subject has in *potentiality*. For instance, to say that sugar is soluble is not to say anything about an actual categorical quality or property of the sugar itself; what is meant is that sugar is potentially dissolved if (or on the condition or hypothesis that) you submerge it in water. The underlying assumption in the literature seems to be that something cannot be simultaneously categorical and dispositional, namely, in act and in potency.

For Aquinas, however, this analytic distinction is too strong. It is precisely because sugar is actually or categorically the kind of thing it is that it has the potentiality or power to dissolve in water: there is nothing metaphysically scandalous about the same property being in act and potency at the same time provided these are in different respects.

I think the way forward along lines that are more congruent with Aquinas's thought is what John Heil calls the "identity theory of pow-

116. Bourke, "Habitus as a Perfectant," 106.
117. Bourke, "The Role of Habitus," 104. Although I do not think this is so very scandalous, as habits are passive and active in different respects, he is absolutely right to point out that virtues are metaphysical perfections of the powers of the soul with active and passive elements.

ers," also advocated by C. B. Martin and William Jaworski.[118] This theory argues that one and the same property has both categorical and dispositional descriptions and theoretical roles; that is, the same power can be described both as an actuality and as a potentiality, but in different respects. For instance, a diamond's actual categorical hardness grants it the dispositional power to scratch glass: in simpler terms, it is precisely because the diamond is hard that it can scratch glass. Humans, for instance, actually have the power of sight, but this is not manifested or actual when our eyes are closed. We can describe the categorical actuality of that power in one way, as inhering in the soul or as the structural-material makeup of its organ, the eye, but the very same property or power is in potency to being actualized or not, that is, to seeing or not seeing. In the latter sense, we are speaking of the causal-dispositional role of the very same categorical property.

This is simply another way of getting at Aquinas's point that *esse* is proportioned to *operari*: beings exist in the ways that they do (as modes of existing, *modus essendi*) for the sake of operation. Certainly, we can distinguish between categorical and dispositional facets, between a property's actuality and potentiality, but it is the same actual power that is in potency to a further actualization simply because it is that kind of a thing. There is no need to force a massive wedge between the categorical and dispositional, as the contemporary analytic discussion tends to do. Nor is there anything particularly scandalous about a power or habit being both in act and potency at the same time, provided these are so in different respects. If this is what is meant by "dynamic," then practically all powers and dispositions are dynamic, and there is nothing especially dynamic about habits *per se*.

---

118. John Heil, *From an Ontological Point of View* (Oxford: Oxford University Press, 2003), 111–25; C. B. Martin and John Heil, "The Ontological Turn," *Midwest Studies in Philosophy* 23 (1999): 34–60; C. B. Martin, "On the Need for Properties: The Road to Pythagoreanism and Back," *Synthese* 112 (1997): 193–231, and *The Mind in Nature* (Oxford: Oxford University Press, 2007); William Jaworski, "Hylomorphism and the Metaphysics of Structure," *Res Philosophica* 91 (2014): 179–201, and *Structure and the Metaphysics of Mind* (Oxford: Oxford University Press, 2016), chap. 4.

PARTICIPATING IN REASON

5

PARTICIPATION

Now that I have considered in what way the soul has parts that might participate in one another, let us turn to participation and see how the sensitive part of the soul might participate in the rational part. I begin part 2 with a discussion of Aquinas's philosophy of participation and his distinction between the different kinds of participation in chapter 5. However, to determine which kind of participation Aquinas means when he says that the sense appetites participate in reason will require delving into the explicit passages discussing this, in chapters 6–10.

I began my research by generating a chronological list of Aquinas's *ex professo* treatments of the sense appetites' participation in reason; indeed, Aquinas uses some form of Aristotle's phrase from *Nic.* I.13 in Latin translation, *participare rationem*, hundreds of times in various contexts. It is impossible, however, simply to march through these texts in strict chronological order: there are too many of them and they are in too many diverse contexts, not to mention that such a listing would be tedious and unreadable. Rather, I will present the fruit of my research by using the most important and representative passages to depict three synoptic overviews of his teachings, namely, his early position in the *Sentences* (1251–56) in chapters 6–7, his views in the *De veritate* (1256–59) in chapter 8, and then his more mature teaching in the later texts (1268–74) in chapters 9–10. Because I have not found any evidence to suppose otherwise, I will assume that Aquinas is philosophically consistent within texts that were written very close to one another.

I present these three overviews in a straightforward manner: first, I discuss the tripartite division of the soul, then the relevant participating parts of this division and also passions and habits. After this I discuss how the sense appetites participate in reason from the rather abstract metaphysical/causal perspective, and then I shift to what this means from a more concrete ethical and personal perspective. I do this once for the *Sentences* commentary, once for the *De veritate*, and then once again for the late texts.

Because I will follow the texts quite closely, these chapters are somewhat expository. They are also somewhat asymmetrical as each section mirrors the strengths, idiosyncrasies, and particular emphases of each set of texts.[1] As my intention is to bring out the similarities and differences between texts in order to chart Aquinas's historical and philosophical development, there will be some overlap between sections. There is overlap to bring out difference, and where there is no difference, there is no overlap. For instance, I will not return to discuss the passions and internal sense powers in the late texts because I have not found a significant difference from the early texts. However, I will return to the will's role *vis-à-vis* reason because I think Aquinas shifts his position in ways that are significant for understanding how the sense appetites participate in reason.

Chapter 11 ties together the material from part 2. At this point we will have a clear idea of what exactly Aquinas means when he says that the sense appetites participate in reason. I will highlight the important developments in Aquinas's thought and tie it to parallel developments that happened in his metaphysics of participation.

In the third part of the book I will use the conclusions garnered from the first and second parts to distinguish Aquinas from his contemporaries, to engage the contemporary scholarship on Aquinas, to distinguish him from both Kant and Aristotle, and to situate Aquinas's thinking on virtue in the current debate about virtue ethics and social psychology. I also hope to convince readers that Aquinas's views on reason, emotion, and moral virtue are plausible.

---

1. As his thought matures and the quantity and detail of his treatment of our topic increases there are later texts for which there are no simply no earlier parallel discussions. This adds a bit to the asymmetrical treatment.

Participation

There can be no doubt that participation is first and foremost a metaphysical doctrine for Aquinas. Its importance can hardly be exaggerated. It is Aquinas's ultimate answer to the Parmenidean riddle of how being can be both one and many in the context of created and uncreated being; it is his reconciliation of Platonic participation with Aristotle's division of being into act and potency. Participation is the causal undergirding of Aquinas's analogical predication of being and of the divine names. There is much good scholarship on this topic, notably by Wippel, Montagnes, and Fabro, and many summaries of the topic—there is no need to replicate what has already been done.[2] However, I will take from the scholarship on participation (most notably from Montagnes and Wippel) their general conclusions and comments about the nature of participation as it is helpful for understanding how the sense appetites participate in reason. For the sake of clarity, I shall stay close to Aquinas's own terminology.[3]

2. The best treatment is Wippel's third chapter, "Participation and the Problem of the One and the Many," from *Metaphysical Thought*, 94–132. To get the sense of the grandeur of its scope within its Parmenedian context one ought to read the first part of Wippel's book (65–197). Wippel has been influenced by Cornelio Fabro and Bernard Montagnes's excellent book *The Doctrine of Analogy of Being according to Thomas Aquinas* (Milwaukee, Wis.: Marquette University Press, 2004). Montagnes was, in turn, influenced by Cornelio Fabro. For a summary of Fabro's thinking on participation see "The Intensive Hermeneutics of Thomistic Philosophy," *Review of Metaphysics* 27 (1974): 449–91. See also his *Participation et causalité selon s. Thomas d'Aquin* (Louvain: Publications Universitaíres de Louvain, 1961). For a recent dissertation on Fabro see Jason A. Mitchell, "Being and Participation: The Method and Structure of Metaphysical Reflection according to Cornelio Fabro" (PhD diss., Pontifical Athenaeum Regina Apostolorum, 2013). Fabro disagrees greatly (concerning the role of essence with respect to *esse*) with Louis B. Geiger, *La participatione dans la philosophie de s. Thomas d'Aquin* (Paris: Librairie Philosophique J. Vrin, 1953) who has influenced Rudi A. te Velde, *Participation and Substantiality in Thomas Aquinas* (New York: E. J. Brill, 1989). See Wippel's effective response to Geiger and te Velde in *Metaphysical Thought*, 128–30. For an excellent and very clear overview of participation and a summary of the scholarship see Doolan, *Divine Ideas*, 192–212. See also Rziha, *Perfecting Human Actions*, the first chapter of which is a summary on participation and its scholarship. There is a summary of the dispute between Fabro and Geiger in Helen John James, *The Thomist Spectrum* (New York: Fordham University Press, 1966). For some discussions of the Platonic and Neoplatonic provenance of participation see W. Norris Clarke, "The Meaning of Participation in St. Thomas," *Proceedings of The American Catholic Philosophical Association* 26 (1952): 147–57; Robert J. Henle, *Thomas and Platonism* (The Hague: Martinus Nijhoff, 1956); and Arthur Little, *Platonic Heritage* (Dublin: Golden Eagle Books, 1949).

3. I shall neither use Geiger's terminology of participation by similitude or composition, nor shall I use Fabro's language of predicamental or transcendental participation (although I will briefly discuss Fabro's views in chapter 11). As Wippel has noted, these divisions of par-

The best place to start is Aquinas's commentary on Boethius's *De hebdomadibus*, c. 2 (1271–72). It is the only place in his corpus where he lays out an account of participation (*rationem participationis*).[4] Although the passage is explicitly concerned with participation in *esse*, the passage is also useful for its general comments on participation and his classification of participation into three modes or kinds.

He introduces the *rationem participationis* with an etymological play on words. To participate is, in a sense, to take a part (*Est autem participare quasi partem capere*).[5] He then clarifies this: "And so when something receives in a particular way that which pertains to another universally, it is said to participate in that."[6] From this general definition one can readily grasp how vast the application of participation can be. He then proceeds to offer three such ways or modes of participation: (1) as man is said to participate in animal because he does not have the *ratio* of animal according to its complete universality. For the same reason Socrates participates in man. (2) Likewise a subject participates in an accident and matter participates in form, as substantial or accidental form, which is common when considered by itself, is determined to this or that subject. (3) An effect is said to participate in its own cause, especially when it is not adequate or equal to the power of its own cause, for example, as air participates in the light of the sun because it does not receive it according to the same brightness which is in the sun.[7]

---

ticipation are not Aquinas's own terms (*Metaphysical Thought*, 127), and I do not think they would be particularly helpful here.

4. *Super Boetii De ebdomadibus* (hereafter, *De ebd.*), l. 2 [Leonine 50:271.70].

5. See n7.

6. Wippel aptly puts this in other words: "In other words, when we find a quality of perfection possessed by a given subject in only partial rather than in total fashion, such a subject is said to participate in that perfection. If in fact other subjects also share in that same perfection, it is because each of them only participates in it. None is identical with it. Thus, appeal to a participation structure is also a way of accounting for the fact that a given kind of characteristic or perfection can be shared in by many different subject, or of addressing oneself to the problem of the One and the Many." Wippel, *Metaphysical Thought*, 96–97. For similar general descriptions see *In I Metaph.*, l. 10 [Marietti 46] and *In De caelo*, lib. 2, l. 18 [Marietti 233].

7. *De ebd.*, l. 2 [Leonine 50:271.69–85]: "Que quidem differencia sumitur secundum rationem participationis. Est autem participare quasi partem capere. Et ideo quando aliquid particulariter recipit id quod ad alterum pertinet universaliter, dicitur participare illud, sicut homo dicitur participare animal quia non habet rationem animalis secundum totam communitatem; et eadem ratione Sortes participat hominem. Similiter etiam subiectum participat accidens et materia formam, quia forma substantialis vel accidentalis, que de sui

In the first kind of participation an individual shares in the intelligible content of a species, and the species shares in the intelligible content of a genus. In Wippel's helpful rephrasing:

In each of these examples we are dealing with a less extended intelligibility which is said to share in a more universal or more extended intelligible content. Since in each of these instances we are dealing with the fact that one intelligible content shares in another without exhausting it, we may describe it as a case of participation; but since we are only dealing with intelligible contents, the participation is logical or intentional, not real or ontological.[8]

In this first case, the kind of form communicated is univocal; that is, when animal is predicated of horse and cow the word animal is the same in name and definition or intelligible content.[9] This is not the case in the third mode of participation, that of equivocal causality.[10] According to this third mode of participation, in which the effect virtually exists in its cause but in a more eminent way, there is a likeness between cause and effect, but not so much likeness as to be univocal; nor is there so much unlikeness as to be equivocal, that is, accidentally sharing the same name.[11] The kind of likeness at stake in the third kind of participation is analogical likeness, where the intelligible content is "partially diverse and partially not diverse"; or as Aquinas puts it, these contents are diverse insofar as they have diverse relations, but they are not diverse insofar as these diverse relations are referred to one and the same thing.[12] Thus secondary analogates are always related to one prime analogate.[13] And this prime

---

ratione communis est, determinatur ad hoc vel ad illud subiectum. Et similiter etiam effectus dicitur participare suam causam, et precipue quando non adequat virtutem sue cause, puta si dicamus quod aer participat lucem solis quia non recipit eam in ea claritate qua est in sole."

8. Wippel, *Metaphysical Thought*, 97. For some parallel passages, discussion, and scholarship on this first mode of participation see ibid., n9. For an interpretation that ties this first mode of participation to analogy of being see Fabro, *Intensive Hermeneutics*, 484–86.

9. See *In IV Metaph.*, l. 1 [Marietti 151].

10. On equivocal causality see *SCG* I.29 [Leonine manualis 30–31]; *QDV*, q. 10, a. 13, ad 3 [Leonine 22.2:343.158–70]; *DP*, q. 7, a. 5 [Marietti 198]; *ST* I, q. 4, a. 2 [St. Paul 22]. See Fabro, *Participation et Causalité*, 338; Wippel, *Metaphysical Thought*, 517–18; Doolan, *Divine Ideas*, 175.

11. The example Aquinas uses is the star *canis* major and Latin word for dog, *canis*. These two accidentally share the exact same name but there is no real likeness between in intelligible content or definition, hence they are only equivocally alike. *In IV Met.*, l. 1 [Marietti 151]; *De princ.*, c. 6 [Leonine 43:46.29].

12. *In IV Met.*, l. 1 [Marietti 151]. Cf. *ST* I, q. 13, a. 5 [St. Paul 64–65].

13. *In IV Met.*, l. 1 [Marietti 151].

analogate is not merely one in intelligible content, but it actually exists as a real equivocal efficient cause of the secondary analogates.

The analogical likeness between equivocal effects and their causes is rooted in Aquinas's axiom that every agent produces something like itself, *omne agens agit sibi simile*.[14] Thus there is a real likeness between effect and its cause, at least enough so that effect and cause may share the same name, provided one is mindful of negating univocal significance to both terms. This analogical predication according to the third mode of participation is usually expressed according to the language of *per prius* and *per posterius*: something is predicated of its cause *per prius* and predicated of its effect *per posterius*.[15] In most general terms, this is one of the ways that Aquinas says that something can share in particular what belongs to something else universally; something can share in an intelligible content without being forced to predicate univocal likeness while simultaneously avoiding having to say that the likeness is simply logical.

When it is said, however, that a subject participates in an accident (the second kind of participation), it is said univocally. Thus when a painting and a human participate in whiteness, it is the exact same color that is meant in both predications. The intelligible contents of both are identical. Univocity holds even in the case of intension and remission of accidents.[16] When it is said that something is whiter, the exact same intelligible content is signified as when it is less white;[17] the predication of more or less in accidental forms does not translate into analogical predication of *per prius* and *per posterius*.[18] The participation predicated in the intension and remission of accidental forms, say when someone participates more or less in temperance, obviously refers to the second kind of participation.

Another significant difference between the manner in which a sub-

---

14. See Wippel, *Metaphysical Themes II*, 152–72, and Daniel J. Pierson, "Thomas Aquinas on the Principle *Onme Agens Agit Aibi Simile*" (PhD diss., The Catholic University of America, 2015).

15. *ST* I, q. 13, a. 6 [St. Paul 65]. Sometimes, however, Aquinas expresses this as more or less: *In VII Met.*, l. 4 [Marietti 331] and *In II Sent.*, d. 3, q. 1, a. 5 [Mand 100]. For a discussion of the *per prius, per posterius* couplet see Montagnes, *Analogy*, 44–45. See also Fabro, *Intensive Hermeneutics*, 485.

16. Montagnes, *Analogy*, 30–31.

17. *QSC*, a. 8, ad 8 [Leonine 24.2:84.401–6]; *De ente*, c. 6 [Leonine 43:379.115–21].

18. Montagnes, *Analogy*, 31.

ject participates in an accident (second kind) and the participation of an equivocal cause in its effect (third kind) is that in the third kind the cause exists independently and separately from the effect that participates in it. This is not the case in the second kind of participation in which the participated perfection only exists in the subject. Accidental *esse* is *inesse*; it can never exist apart from its subject. There is no such thing as a whiteness separate from any white thing.[19] When it is said that a subject participates in whiteness, this means that a particular accidental form (which could never subsist on its own) inheres in a particular subject. If the subject is whiter this is because the subject participates more in that particular accidental form which inheres more fully or deeply in the subject.

Yet another characteristic of the second mode of participation is that it involves composition. For Aquinas says that in every case of predication of real participation there must be some existing thing in addition to what is participated,[20] and in the second mode these separate things have to unite in a composition. According to the second mode of participation Aquinas tells us that a subject is presupposed for an accident.[21] This subject enters into a real ontological composition with the accident, that is, a nonsubstantial *esse aliquid* of some sort. In this case, the subject is the potency principle and the accident is the act principle. For the accidental form determines some potency to this or that kind of accidental being, for example, being white or being virtuous.[22]

If the second mode signifies composition while implying an efficient cause of that composition, the third mode signifies an efficient cause of that composition while implying some composition resulting from the efficient cause. The emphasis of the third mode of participation is first and foremost on causality, specifically, equivocal efficient causality; but composition is necessarily implied if the participated and efficient-

---

19. Furthermore (to add matter and form, the other part of the second mode of participation), prime matter cannot exist without form.

20. *Quodl.* II, q. 2, a. 1 [Leonine 25.2:214.44–46].

21. *De ebd.*, l. 2. See also te Velde's discussion of this mode of participation in *Participation and Substantiality*, 36–40.

22. In the line of existence, the soul is the act principle and an accident is the potency principle, for accidental being participates in being through substance's causing the accidental being. That is, being is predicated *per prius* and of substance and *per posterius* of accidents. But this is not what he has in mind in the second kind of participation.

ly caused perfection is to belong to the one participating.[23] The second mode of participation, on the other hand, names formal causality, substantial and accidental, but it does not signify what causes the substantial or accidental form itself. In the case of substance participating in an accident, participation tells us of composition, degrees of inherence, and its mode of existing (*inesse*); but it does not, as does the third mode of participation, name or even point to the cause of the accidental composition or its intensification. There obviously must be such a cause. Aquinas does not think it can be a Platonic separate version of the participated form. Furthermore, the accidental form itself cannot be the cause, as it cannot reduce itself from potency to act, and if it could it would have to be separate.

In particular, we can say that a person has temperance and can have it to a greater or lesser extent. In this way we could say that a temperate person (substance) participates in temperance (an accident). What I am interested in, however, is that temperance itself is a participation in reason. It seems that this participation cannot be understood according to the second mode of participation. For temperance cannot enter into composition with reason, as temperance is not a substance. Although one accident may inhere in a subject via another accident,[24] it is obviously nonsense to say that reason inheres in a person by way of temperance. Temperance, of course, inheres in the sense appetite.

Aquinas says, over and over again, that the sense appetites participate in reason insofar as they obey the command of reason. We might intuitively guess, at this point, that the command of reason is an equivocal efficient cause, in other words, that Aquinas here means the third mode of participation. But the *De hebdomadibus* is supposedly a late text (1271–72) and he may very well have developed his thinking on participation. Indeed, in Aquinas's commentary on the *Sentences*, as we shall see, his account of how the sense appetites participate in reason is couched in a formal language that seems far more suited to the second mode of participation. And although it is highly unlikely, perhaps, we have still not ruled out the possibility that he means it as the first kind of

23. See, for example, *QSC*, q. 1 [Leonine 24.2:13–14.363–85], in chapter 1, 31n35.

24. One accident may inhere in a subject by way of another. The example Aquinas usually uses is of whiteness (quality) inhering in the surface (quantity) of a substance. *In III Sent.*, d. 33, q. 2, a. 4, sol. 1 [Moos 1062].

participation, that is, as a kind of logical participation. But there is a still more important interpretation and serious objection. Perhaps Aquinas does not mean participation here in any particularly specific way at all. Aristotle's text was simply translated into Latin as *participans quidem aliqualiter rationem*.[25] When one reads enough of Aquinas's treatments of this topic one cannot help but notice that these exact words were permanently burned into Aquinas's memory. The phrase (*participat aliqualiter rationem*) immediately rolls right off his tongue (or pen, or his scribe's quill) verbatim as soon as the question of moral virtue arises in early, middle, and late texts.[26] Perhaps we are being misled by the accidental use of the same word, participation, in both his metaphysics and ethics. Perhaps one is better off abandoning the superficial similarity by translating the phrase *participat aliqualiter rationem* as "somehow shares in reason"; we ought perhaps even to emphasize the vagueness of the adverb (*aliqualiter*), which was permanently attached to the phrase. The sense appetites *somehow* share in reason—leave it at that. At least then we will not be tempted to overcomplicate and overburden his ethics, that is, we will not be using the wrong kind of precision for the subject matter at hand.

In order to answer these questions, we must delve into the texts themselves to see if we can find sufficient support for one kind of participation rather than another, or whether we ought to conclude that

---

25. See chapter 1, n00 above. The earlier *Ethica Vetus* only contains books II and III (thus not this passage), but the *Ethica Nova* contains this and added fragments of books I, VII, and VIII translated by Burgundio of Pisa and was made available in Paris around 1217 or 1220. See R. Durling, "The Anonymous Translation of Aristotle's *De generatione et corruptione (Translatio Vetus)*," *Traditio* 49 (1994): 320–30. See also Gudrun Vuillemin-Diem and Marwan Rashed, "Burgundio de Pise et ses manuscrits grecs d'Aristote: Laur. 87.7 et Laur. 81.18," *Recherches de Théologie et Philosophie médiévales* 64, no. 1 (1997): 136–98. That Moerbeke was indeed the reviser of Grosseteste's text see Jozef Brams, "The Revised Version of Grosseteste's Translation of the Nicomachean Ethics," *Bulletin de philosophie médiévale* 36 (1994): 45–55. The critical edition is found in *Ethica Nicomachea. Translatio Antiquissima libr. II-III sive 'Ethica Vetus,' Translationis Antiquioris quae supersunt sive 'Ethica Nova,' 'Hoferiana,' 'Borghesiana,' Translatio Roberti Grosseteste Lincolniensis sive 'Liber Ethicorum' (Recensio Pura et Recensio Recognita)*, ed. R. A. Gauthier, Aristoteles Latinus 26/1–3 (Brill / Brussels: Leiden / Desclée De Brouwer, 1972–74). The revised text used by Aquinas is printed at the beginning of each *lectio* in the Leonine edition of his commentary.

26. *In II Sent.*, d. 41, q. 2, a. 2, ad 2; *In III Sent.*, d. 27, q. 2, a. 3, ad 5; d. 33, q. 1, a. 1, qc. 2; a. 2, qc. 3, ad 3; q. 2, a. 4 qc. 2, ad 2; qc. 3, ad 1; q. 3, a. 1, qc. 2, ad 3; *QDV*, q. 14, a. 4; q. 15, a. 4, ad 6; q. 25, a. 5, ad 4; *QSC*, a. 9; *ST* I, q. 57, a. 4, ad 3; *ST* I-II, q. 24, a. 1, ad 2; q. 58, a. 2; q. 68, a. 3; *ST* II-II, q. 156, a. 4; *DM* 7.1 ad 14; etc.

Aquinas simply means participation in some generic sense, and that he was really only using it because the very important Aristotelian phrase was permanently burned into his memory. Of course, the permanence of the phrase does not necessarily exclude the possibility that he may also have had in mind one or another kind of participation. We must also consider the possibility that Aquinas's thinking on the topic matured in the course of his roughly twenty-year career. Let us now turn to the texts themselves and see how Aquinas answers these questions. I will most fully resolve them in chapter 11, the conclusion of the second part.

6

POWERS AND PASSIONS IN AQUINAS'S *SENTENCES* COMMENTARY

Tripartite Division

Aquinas clearly accepts Aristotle's broad tripartite division of the soul in his early commentary on the *Sentences*. One part of the soul is essentially rational and another part (the sensitive part) is rational by participation;[1] however, the vegetative part does not participate in reason.[2] Aquinas does not speak of all of the powers of the sensitive part as participating in reason, but only of the concupiscible and the irascible powers.[3] Thus two parts of the tripartite division seem quite clear: the vegetative part, which in no way participates in reason, and the sensitive part (the concupiscible and irascible powers), which participates in reason.

Aquinas does say, however, that universally all appetite participates

---

1. *In III Sent.*, d. 23, q. 1, a. 3 [Moos 707]: "Cum autem homo ex hoc sit homo quod habet rationem et intellectum, illae potentiae humanae sunt quae aliqualiter rationales sunt, vel per essentiam, sicut quae sunt in parte intellectiva, vel per participationem, sicut quae in parte sensitiva sunt rationi obedientes."

2. *In II Sent.*, d. 25, q. 1, a. 3, ad 3 [Mand 652–53]; *In III Sent.*, d. 33, q. 2, a. 4, sol. 2 [Moos 1063].

3. See, e.g., *In III Sent.*, d. 33, q. 1, a. 2, sol. 3 [Moos 1030]; *In II Sent.*, d. 41, q. 2, a. 2, ad 2 [Mand 1043]: "virtus non est in concupiscibili nisi secundum quod aliqualiter participat rationem, inquantum est rationi obediens." In fact, Aquinas claims that reason, as it needs phantasms, participates in the other sense powers; *In III Sent.*, d. 33, q. 2, a. 4, sol. 2, ad 6 [Moos 1064].

129

in reason.[4] Because the will is an appetite, it too somehow participates in reason.[5] In this context Aquinas has in mind the moral virtue of justice, which is a virtue of the will. To fit justice into Aristotle's tripartite division of the soul in which moral virtue must be "placed" in the middle part, Aquinas allows for there to be a way in which the will can habitually participate in reason through the moral virtue of justice. Thus, in the context of justice, the will participates in reason, but in the context of the moral virtues of temperance and courage, the will is essentially in the rational part.[6]

As our topic concerns the sense appetites and their passions and moral virtues, it is worth noting that the very word *moral* implies a necessary relation to the will. In fact, it is really only the acts of the will that are moral *per se*; all other acts are moral *per accidens*.[7] Choice (*electio*) is the principle of virtue, and thus virtue can only be in choice or in those acts that are commanded by choice.[8] Thus acts of moral virtue involving the sense appetites are only moral as they are related to or commanded by the will.

But what is moral is also, of course, necessarily related to reason. In explaining Augustine's view that virtue is a good quality of the mind, Aquinas says that even if some virtue inheres in some power which is not the mind, nevertheless as a subject is posited in the definition of an accident so is the mind (*mens*) posited as the subject of moral virtue, for moral virtue is not virtue except insofar as it participates in mind or reason. In this way, reason is the subject of virtue whether essentially or by participation.[9]

Furthermore, in the context of discussing Christ's two wills (i.e.,

4. *In III Sent.*, d. 33, q. 2, a. 4, sol. 3, ad 1 [Moos 1065]: "rationale per participationem non solum dicitur irascibilis et concupiscibilis, sed universaliter appetitus, ut ibidem dicit."

5. Ibid., "Et ideo voluntas quamvis per essentiam sit in parte intellectiva, tamen quantum ad actum aliqualiter ratione participat."

6. Ibid., ad 2: "rationale comprehendit non solum rationem cognitivam, sed etiam voluntatem; et sic justitia est in rationali sicut in subjecto." *In III Sent.*, d. 33, q. 2, a. 1, sol. 3, ad 2 [Moos 1048]: "ratio quandoque comprehendit duas potentias, scilicet vim cognitivam in qua est prudentia, et vim affectivam quae voluntas dicitur in qua est justitia."

7. *In II Sent.*, d. 42, q. 1, a. 1 [Mand 1053]; d. 24, q. 3, a. 2 [Mand 621]; d. 40, q. 1, a. 1 [Mand 1011].

8. *In II Sent.*, d. 24, q. 3, a. 2 [Mand 621]. He even goes so far as saying that acts which are commanded by the will are not moral in their species, but only in their use as they are commanded by the will: *In III Sent.*, d. 23, q. 1, a. 4, sol. 2 [Moos 713–14].

9. *In II Sent.*, d. 27, q. 1, a. 2, ad 3 [Mand 299].

"not my will, but thine, be done," in Lk 22:42), Aquinas says that sense appetite can be called will by participation, for insofar as it obeys reason (he cites *Nic.* I.13) it participates in reason and in that manner it also somehow participates in the freedom of the will.[10] Thus when Aquinas says that the sense appetites participate in reason he also means that they participate, as he here says, in the freedom of the will.

Therefore, in thinking about how the sense appetites participate in reason, we must not only consider the sense appetites and reason, but also the will and free decision, which involves both reason and will. Because the sense appetites do not have their perfections except insofar as they participate in the perfection of a higher power,[11] we should consider what role reason plays here and also how he means to include will.

Will and Intellect

We have seen Aquinas lump will and reason together under the name reason and we have seen that this couplet is related to moral virtue in some crucial way. Let us break apart the couplet and examine each part to see what role it plays in moral virtue.

In Aquinas's commentary on the *Sentences* the will follows intellect; the operation of the will begins wherever the intellect leaves off.[12] The will is an appetite and appetite is a passive power: it is a moved mover.[13] In fact, he calls the act of the will the motion of reason (*motus rationis*).[14] Or, as he says, the will follows reason, and the process of the will is proportioned to the process of the intellect.[15]

Aquinas divides the will in two: will as nature and will as reason. This division of the will is not a division of the will into two powers.

10. *In III Sent.*, d. 17, a. 1, sol. 2 [Moos 531]; cf. ad 3 [Moos 532].

11. *In III Sent.*, d. 27, q. 3, a. 4 [Moos 889].

12. *In III Sent.*, d. 27, q. 2 [Moos 895]: "Unde cum ad intellectum affectus sequatur, ubi terminatur operatio intellectus ibi incipit operatio affectus sivi voluntatis."

13. *In III Sent.*, d. 27, q. 1, a. 1 [Mand 854]: "Appetitus autem est virtus passiva. Unde in III De anima, dicit philosophus, quod *appetibile movet sicut movens non motum, appetitus autem sicut movens motum.*" Ibid., ad 6 [Moos 858]: "Ad sextum dicendum, quod appetitus, ut dictum est, movet motus." See 186n17, chapter 9, for some secondary literature on this point.

14. *In II Sent.*, d. 24, q. 3, a. 1 [Mand 617]: "Appetitus autem rationalis est qui consequitur apprehensionem rationis, et hic dicitur motus rationis, qui est actus voluntatis."

15. *In III Sent.*, d. 17, a. 2, sol. 1 [Moos 536–37]: "cum voluntas sequatur rationem, processus voluntatis proportionatur processui rationis."

In fact, the division is entirely accidental to the will itself,[16] that is, it is completely dependent on and posterior to the act of reason, which he also divides in two. Thus the twofold acts of the will simply follow the twofold acts of reason.[17]

These two acts of reason, although at first they might seem to be, are *not* the two acts of the intellect, that is, (1) abstraction (dematerialization) and understanding of a quiddity and (2) judgment that often involves a returning to phantasms and the forming of propositions.[18] The

---

16. *In II Sent.*, d. 39, q. 2, a. 2, ad 2 [Mand 994]: "voluntas ut deliberata et ut natura non differunt secundum essentiam potentiae: quia naturale et deliberatorium non sunt differentiae voluntatis secundum se, sed secundum quod sequitur judicium rationis: quia in ratione est aliquid naturaliter cognitum quasi principium indemonstrabile in operabilibus, quod se habet per modum finis, quia in operabilibus finis habet locum principii, ut in VI *Ethicorum*, cap. 11, dicitur. Unde illud quod finis est hominis est naturaliter in ratione cognitum esse bonum et appetendum, et voluntas consequens istam cognitionem dicitur voluntas ut natura. Aliquid vero est cognitum in ratione per inquisitionem ita in operativis sicut in speculativis; et utrobique, scilicet tam in speculativis quam in operativis, contingit inquirentem rationem errare; unde voluntas quae talem cognitionem rationis sequitur, deliberata dicitur, et in bonum et malum tendere potest, sed non ab eodem inclinante, ut dictum est." *In III Sent.*, d. 17, q. 1, sol. 3, ad 1 [Moos 532–33]: "Ad primum ergo dicendum, quod *thelesis* secundum Damascenum est voluntas naturalis, quae scilicet in modum naturae movetur in aliquid secundum bonitatem absolutam in ipso consideratam; *bulesis* autem est appetitus rationalis qui movetur in aliquod bonum ex ordine alterius. Et haec duo aliis nominibus a Magistro dicuntur voluntas ut ratio et voluntas ut natura: secundum quae tamen non diversificatur potentia voluntatis, quia ipsa diversitas est ex eo quod movemur [one manuscript says movetur] in aliquid sine collatione vel cum collatione. Conferre autem non est per se voluntatis, sed rationis. Unde illa divisio voluntatis non est per essentialia ipsius, sed *per accidentalia*. Et propter hoc non sunt diversae potentiae, sed una differens secundum respectum ipsius ad apprehensionem praecedentem, quae potest esse cum collatione vel sine collatione." Aquinas's texts on Christ's two wills, of which this is one, are particularly helpful. The two wills refers to Christ's famous statement in the garden of Gethsemane, "not my will, but thine, be done." Christ's paradoxical willing against his own will prompted speculation on what exactly these two volitions were. For a book which is invaluable for its trove of historical information on the medieval discussion of the two wills see Corey L. Barnes, *Christ's Two Wills in Scholastic Thought: The Christology of Aquinas and Its Historical Context* (Toronto: Pontifical Institute of Mediaeval Studies, 2012). For his discussion of these passages in the *Sentences* see 132–53. Although I quibble, Barnes cites Aquinas's distinction between the will as potency and the will as act as a major development in Aquinas's thought from the *Sentences* to the *tertia pars* (139, 148, 158, 161), but I would like to point out that the distinction is also present in the *Sentences*, just not in the passages on Christology; see *In II Sent.*, d. 39, q. 1, a. 1 [Mand 985].

17. *In II Sent.*, d. 24, q. 3, a. 1 [Mand 617]: "Appetitus autem rationalis est qui consequitur apprehensionem rationis, et hic dicitur motus rationis, qui est actus voluntatis. Sed rationis apprehensio dupliciter esse potest. Una simplex et absoluta, quando scilicet statim sine discussione apprehensum dijudicat, et talem apprehensionem sequitur voluntas quae dicitur non deliberata. Alia est inquisitiva, quando scilicet ratiocinando, bonum vel malum, conveniens vel nocivum investigat, et talem apprehensionem sequitur voluntas deliberata."

18. For the twofold operation of the intellect see *In I Sent.*, d. 19, q. 5, a. 1, ad 7 [Mand

two acts of reason at stake here are two kinds of the latter, that is, of judgment, which concern the forming of propositions and their truth.

In judgments concerning individual material beings, the intellect judges the truth of a proposition by returning to the phantasms (which includes materially conditioned singulars) and somehow knows a quiddity as it exists in matter. Aquinas uses the famous word *adequatio* between the intellect and thing to explain truth, that is, an equaling, comparing, checking or verifying—it is by returning to a phantasm that the intellect judges that this or that is true.[19] But in the case of practical reasoning there is no phantasm by which the intellect can check or verify that something is or is not true. Rather than checking the validity of its thinking against apprehended sensible forms, it reduces them (or brings them back) to what Aquinas describes as naturally or habitually known first principles. In the case of speculative matters (and hence in the theoretical sciences) this is called understanding (*intellectus*), but in our case, that of practical reasoning, it is called synderesis.[20] This habit of first principles is in some way illumined by the agent intellect.[21] These infallible and general habitual principles are always present and always murmuring at evil and enjoining toward good.[22]

He describes the first kind of judgment as a simple and absolute (*simplex et absoluta*) apprehension that judges without discursion; he describes the second kind of judgment as an inquisitive consideration of good and bad, and suitable or harmful. A nondeliberative volition follows the former and a deliberative volition follows the latter.[23] Examples of what is grasped by this first kind of absolute and simple cognition are knowledge, virtue, health, happiness, and death.[24] What is characteristic

---

489], and d. 38, q. 1, a. 3 [Mand 903]. See also the relatively early (1257–58) but very developed *In De trin.*, p. 3, q. 5, a. 3 [Leonine 50:146–49].

19. See *In De trin.*, p. 3, q. 6, a. 3 [Leonine 50:159–60] for the difference between logic, mathematics, and physics with respect to the terminus of their distinctive kinds of judgments.

20. *In II Sent.*, d. 39, q. 3, a. 1 [Mand 996].

21. *In II Sent.*, d. 24, q. 2, a. 4 [Mand 610]; note this passage *vis-à-vis* the practical syllogism mentioned in this text, ibid. [Mand 613]: "synderesis in hoc syllogismo majorem ministrat."

22. *In II Sent.*, d. 39, q. 3, a. 1 [Mand 997], and ad 1; and a. 2 [Mand 999].

23. *In II Sent.*, d. 24, q. 3, a. 1 [Mand 617]. See text, 131n14.

24. *In I Sent.*, d. 48, q. 1, a. 4 [Mand 1089]: "Est et quaedam voluntas in nobis spiritualis naturalis qua appetimus id quod secundum se bonum est homini, inquantum est homo; et hoc sequitur apprehensionem rationis, prout est aliquid absolute considerans : sicut vult

of these simple and absolute judgments is the nondiscursive[25] or natural grasp of the goodness or badness of whatever is being understood. For example, when one thinks of happiness one immediately grasps that it is good and when one thinks of death one immediately grasps that it is evil. No one really needs to think about whether or not happiness is good or death is evil, for their attractiveness or repulsiveness are intuitively grasped without discursion.

Because this first kind of simple cognition reduces to synderesis[26] the volition that follows it (will as nature) is characterized as natural as it follows the naturally known first principles of the mind. When the intellect considers these first principles it cannot but assent to them.[27] When reason presents something to the will, grasped as good in light of these principles, the will naturally follows suit. For example, as soon as one considers health, one wishes for it. Whether or not health is actually willed as the end of some particular action depends on deliberation.[28]

But if humans necessarily will things like happiness, following the

---

homo scientiam, virtutem, sanitatem et hujusmodi." Death is the example often given in the Christological context.

25. *In II Sent.*, d. 39, q. 3, a. 1 [Mand 996].

26. *In II Sent.*, d. 39, q. 2, a. 2 [Mand 993].

27. *In II Sent.*, d. 25, q. 1, a. 2 [Mand 649].

28. For more details on this see *In III Sent.*, d. 17, a. 2, sol. 1 [Moos 536–37]: "cum voluntas sequatur rationem, processus voluntatis proportionatur processui rationis. Ratio autem habet aliquod principium per se notum, ad quod resolvendo [cf. *In De trin.*, q. 6, a. 3 (Leonine 50:159–60)] reducit illud cujus cognitionem quaerit; et quando ad illud reducere potuerit, habet certitudinem de re et sententiat quod ita est. Sed antequam ad illud principium reducere possit, movetur aliquibus verisimilitudinibus; et si quidem illis detineatur tamquam certis, decipitur et errat quandoque; si autem illis non detineatur, tunc habet opinionem unius partis cum formidine alterius. Finis autem, ut dicit Philosophus, VII *Eth.* [1154a16], se habet in voluntariis sicut principium in speculativis. Unde quando voluntas reducit aliquid consiliabile in finem in quo totaliter quiescit, sententialiter acceptat illud; si autem reducat in finem in quo non totaliter quiescit, trepidat inter utrumque. Sed si consideretur hoc quod est ad finem sine ordine ad finem, movetur voluntas in ipsum secundum bonitatem vel malitiam quam absolute in eo inveniet. Sed quia voluntas non sistit in motu quem habet circa hujusmodi, cum non feratur in ipsum sicut in finem; ideo non sententiat finaliter secundum praedictum motum suum de illo, quousque finem in quem illud ordinat, non consideret; unde voluntas non simpliciter vult illud, sed vellet, si nil inveniretur repugnans. Voluntas autem ut natura movetur in aliquid absolute, ut dictum est (art. praeced. sol. 3). Unde si per rationem non ordinetur in aliquid aliud acceptabit illud absolute, et erit illius tamquam finis; si autem ordinet in finem, non acceptabit aliquid absolute circa hoc, quousque perveniat ad considerationem finis quod facit voluntas ut ratio. Patet igitur quod *voluntas ut natura* imperfecte vult aliquid, et sub conditione, nisi feratur in ipsum sicut in finem; sed eorum quae ordinantur ad finem, habet *voluntas ut ratio* ultimum judicium et perfectum."

intellect's necessary assenting to first principles, how are humans free? Freedom for Aquinas is primarily a question about choice (*electio*) and Aquinas accounts for free choice here by distinguishing between the compulsion of a power by way of a subject and its compulsion by way of an object. A power may be compelled by its subject if it is bound to a material organ, but because the will is immaterial it cannot be so compelled. A power not attached to a material organ cannot be compelled by way of its subject, but it may be compelled by its object, as the intellect is compelled by the force of a demonstration.[29] The will is indeed compelled along the line of the object concerning volitions following the intellect's natural and simple judgment of what is good. When the will presents something to the intellect that cannot be considered bad or harmful in some way, for example, happiness, the will cannot but will that object. In this sense we are not free. However, nothing that can be chosen here is so good that it cannot be considered bad in some way, and nothing is so bad that it cannot be considered good in some way.[30] We

29. *In II Sent.*, d. 25, q. 1, a. 2 [Mand 649]: "in partibus animae quaedam sunt quae compelli possunt: sed dupliciter. Quaedam enim compelluntur ex subjecto, sicut illae vires quae sunt organis affixae: cum enim sine organis operationes habere non possint, compulsis organis, ipsae virtutes prohibentur vel compelluntur, earum actibus violenter extortis. Quaedam vero sunt quae quidem subjecto non compelluntur, quia organis affixae non sunt; compelluntur tamen objecto, sicut intellectus: ipse enim non est actus alicujus partis corporis, ut Philosophus dicit in III *De anima*, et tamen demonstrationis vi cogitur. Voluntas autem neque subjecto cogi potest, cum non sit organo affixa, neque objecto; quantumcumque enim aliquid ostendatur esse bonum, in potestate ejus remanet eligere illud vel non eligere." Note that although the subject/object distinction also appears in later texts, there the distinction is not exactly the same; in the later texts subject/object is cast in terms of exercise/specification. There is no discussion of exercise or efficient causality in these texts; it is only a question of whether the materiality of the subject can compel the power of the soul, or more specifically whether or not the organ of the power of the soul can compel the power. In the case of the will it cannot (in the case of the sense appetites it can, e.g., a very vehement passion), and I do not think one should read back into these texts the later discussions of freedom of exercise and infer that Aquinas really means that the will can move the intellect. I shall discuss this further in chapter 9, below.

30. *In II Sent.*, d. 25, q. 1, a. 2 [Mand 649]: "Similiter etiam si proponatur voluntati aliquod bonum quod completam boni rationem habeat, ut ultimus finis, propter quem omnia appetuntur, non potest voluntas hoc non velle; unde nullus non potest non velle esse felix, aut velle esse miser. In his autem quae ad finem ultimum ordinantur, nihil invenitur adeo malum quin aliquod bonum admixtum habeat, nec aliquod adeo bonum quod in omnibus sufficiat: unde quantumcumque ostendatur bonum vel malum, semper potest adhaerere et fugere in contrarium, ratione alterius quod in ipso est, ex quo accipitur, si malum est simpliciter, ut apparens bonum, et si bonum est simpliciter, ut apparens malum; et inde est quod in omnibus quae sub electione cadunt, voluntas libera manet, in hoc solo determinationem habens quod felicitatem naturaliter appetit, et non determinate in hoc vel illo." For another text on the two acts of the will and reason see *In II Sent.*, d. 38, q. 1, a. 4 [Mand 976–77].

can think about things that we cannot help but will, for example, health and happiness, but they are not what are chosen even if they may serve as the ends of choice. Thus, in this life, we make free choices.

More broadly, to understand the rational appetite in the *Sentences* one ultimately looks to reason: as the appetite of reason, the will is an appetite that follows reason. It is reason that accounts for the will's volitions, both as nature and as reason. Moreover, natural aspects of volition are traced back to reason's natural understanding of first principles. The motion is quite unidirectional from intellect to will.

However, I must qualify this claim a little. There are a few more "voluntaristic" passages scattered here and there in the *Sentences* commentary. For instance, in one passage he argues that reason operates rather deterministically, but only the will is truly self-determining.[31] In other passages he argues that the will wills itself to act or not to act,[32] it even determines itself to will this rather than that,[33] and it moves reason to consider or not consider something.[34] Aquinas does seem anxious in the *Sentences* to avoid the charges of intellectual determinism. It is the will, he vehemently says, that is "most free,"[35] but nevertheless in the commentary on the *Sentences* he most often traces the will's freedom back to the fact that it follows reason.[36] So although his treatment of volition in the commentary on the *Sentences* leans toward granting reason primacy of place in free choice, there are some notable exceptions. For the most part, he overwhelmingly argues that the will's volitions are traceable to reason.[37] After I have ex-

31. *In II Sent.*, d. 39, q. 1, a. 2 [Mand 988].

32. *In II Sent.*, d. 35, q. 1, a. 3, ad 5 [Mand 907]: "in voluntatis potestate est actum non facere, sicut et facere."

33. *In II Sent.*, d. 34, q. 1, a. 3, ad 4 [Mand 882]: "voluntas autem non est determinata ad unum, sed seipsam determinat secundum quod huic vel illi adhaeret."

34. *In II Sent.*, d. 35, q. 1, a. 4 [Mand 909]: "potest enim intellectus considerare et non considerare, prout a voluntate est motus."

35. *In II Sent.*, d. 39, q. 1, a. 1, ad 3 [Mand 986]: "voluntas liberrima est."

36. *In II Sent.*, d. 7, q. 1, a. 1 [Mand 181]: "Electio autem non est de fine, sed de his quae sunt ad finem: et haec non eliguntur nisi secundum regulam finis quae est in aestimatione." See *In III Sent.*, d. 33, q. 2, a. 5, sol. 4 [Moos 1066].

37. For some more texts from the commentary on the *Sentences*, other than the ones already cited in the notes above, see the following: *In I Sent.*, d. 40, q. 1, a. 2, ad 2 [Mand 946]: "actum voluntatis, sed praesupponit actum cognitionis ostendentis finem in quem voluntas tendit." *In I Sent.*, d. 45, q. 1, a. 2, ad 2 [Mand 1035]: "illud quod est volitum sicut finis, est movens voluntatem." *In I Sent.*, d. 41, q. 1, a. 3 [Mand 971]: "causa eliciens actum voluntatis non est nisi finis eius." This is the dominant line of thinking: the intellect gives the will the final cause, and the final cause (the *causa causarum*) is the ultimate cause of willing, i.e., the

amined his treatment of volition in the also early *De veritate* as well as his full mature treatment of the topic in the *De malo* and the *Summa*, I will be able to evaluate how he alters his position on free choice. Concerning Aquinas's account of volition in the commentary on the *Sentences* as a whole, and in light of the treatment of volition that I will shortly examine in the early *De veritate*, I am willing to generalize and claim that free decision in Aquinas's early texts is primarily accounted for by looking to reason's role in providing the end and the means to this end. There is no question that free decision requires reason in both early and late texts, but as his thinking on will and causality matures in his later texts, this affects his thinking on moral virtue, as we shall see.

To return to my initial question concerning how the sense appetites participate in reason: as moral virtue is necessarily tied to the will, which itself follows reason, when it is said that the sense appetites are virtuous insofar as they participate in reason and obey the command of the will, there is no real need to distinguish between what comes from the will or what comes from reason, as the will follows reason. Let us now turn to the sense appetites and their passions.

Passions

In this section I will first introduce the passions and then move on to the sense powers in the following section, so that we have a good sense of the working relationship between the parts of the sensitive soul, that is, this particular cluster of sensitive powers and their relevant acts. This section, although taken from Aquinas's commentary on the *Sentences*, will also serve as a general introduction to this topic because Aquinas

---

intellect is the real cause of the volitions. *In II Sent.*, d. 24, q. 2, a. 1 [Mand 603]: "aestimativa proprie se habet ad eam sicut ratio practica ad liberum arbitrium, quae etiam est movens." *In II Sent.*, q. 25, q. 1, a. 1 [Mand 645]: "Determinatio autem agentis ad aliquam actionem, oportet quod sit ab aliqua cognitione praestituente finem illi actioni. Sed cognitio determinans actionem et praestituens finem, in quibusdam quidem conjuncta est, sicut homo finem suae actionis sibi praestituit." Cf. *In III Sent.*, d. 26, q. 2, a. 4 [Moos 842]. See *In II Sent.*, d. 39, q. 3, a. 3 [Mand 1002]: "Voluntas autem non movetur in aliquid appetendum, nisi praesupposita aliqua apprehension; objectum enim voluntatis est bonum vel malum, secundum quod est imaginatum vel intellectum. Intentionem autem boni vel mali ratio ipsa demonstrat." *In III Sent.*, d. 23, q. 2, a. 5, ad 5 [Moos 740]: "non potest affectus firmari in aliquo per amorem in quo intellectus firmatus non est per assensum; sicut etiam non potest tendere in aliquod per desiderium quod prius intellectus non apprehendit." See *In III Sent.*, d. 26, q. 1, a. 2, ad 2 [Moos 818], and a. 3, sol. 1 [Moos 838–39].

does not develop his thinking on this topic too much. I will, however, note in my treatment of the *De veritate* and his late texts the places where he develops his thinking on the sensitive powers.

In the most generic sense, a passion is simply the passive reception of motion from an agent. It is simply motion, but from the perspective of the passive power receiving it rather than from the perspective of the active power causing it. In another more specific sense, however, a passion is a particular kind or motion, namely, an alteration. An alteration is an accidental change involving the destruction of one material quality of the third species and its replacement with another quality of the third species. Thus we may consider the motion itself as simultaneously destroying one quality and generating a new one, but we may also consider the old quality and the new quality, which are described as the *terms* of the alteration. In other words, we can distinguish between the alteration itself of *becoming* tan, and the terms of this accidental generation, that is, the quality of *being* pale and then the quality of *being* tan. The motion itself, however, is not in the category of quality, but it is in the category of passion. Because this motion is first and foremost understood from the perspective of the passive-receiving end of the motion, it is relegated to the predicamental category of passion rather than of action. Nevertheless, an action from some active agent is, of course, presupposed to actively cause the passion in the patient. Thus the active power of the sun causes the alteration from pale to tan in the passive power of skin. The skin (or, the person lounging on the beach) suffers this passion.[38]

Furthermore, Aquinas insists that properly speaking passions cannot be perfections for they must actually harm the patient in some way. Strictly speaking a passion requires an external agent that "conquers" the patient, that is, the active power of an external quality conquers and destroys a natural passive quality. For everything conquered, he says, is drawn from its own term to the term of another, that is, the subject is dragged or yanked beyond its own nature (*extra suam naturam trahi*).[39] Presumably this is because Aquinas thinks we are naturally good (we might say that we are good by default), at least with respect to our bodily natures, and any external active cause altering some natural quality

38. *In III Sent.*, d. 15, q. 2, a. 1, sol. 1 [Moos 483–84].
39. Ibid.

of the body is destroying a naturally good quality. As Aquinas points out, becoming sick is more properly a passion than becoming healthy.[40] In the proper sense, passions are always contrary to our natures, that is, there is an implied reference here to human teleology.[41] However, it is worth noting that although this is the proper *ratio* of *passio*, Aquinas nevertheless uses the word without all of these conditions being fulfilled.

From the ethical perspective, the relevant question is how a person, or more particularly, the soul, is affected by passions. Because the soul is immaterial, and alterations only concern changes in material qualities, the soul itself cannot be directly altered, but it can suffer passion *per accidens* in two ways corresponding to the soul's twofold role as form and as motor. The soul as form suffers corporeal passions (*passiones corporales*) and the soul as mover suffers psychic passions (*passiones animales*), which he sometimes calls the passions of the soul (*passiones animae*). Let us start with corporeal passions.

Corporeal passions, most simply, immediately affect the body. These are pure passions (*purae passiones*), as Aquinas puts it.[42] Examples of these are being externally struck, cut, burnt, etc., or suffering from more internal[43] material causes, such as fever, madness, mental illness, etc. For instance, he mentions sleep (I gather he means falling asleep) as such a corporeal passion.[44] We would hardly characterize such a corporeal passion as destroying some good natural quality, in fact, he says that "it is a passion pertaining to the perfection of the whole animal."[45] Likewise, when sick the power of medicine alters some qualities which then cause and constitute health. This motion from sickness to health,

40. Ibid. Note that sickness and health are not the terms of the alteration. Sickness and health are dispositions of the body, as discussed in chapter 4. But these dispositions are partly composed of sensible qualities and thus the change from one disposition to another presupposes a real alteration of the sensible qualities that underlie that disposition. Thus Aquinas admits that heat properly belongs to the third genus of quality, but it can also belong to the first, when it is considered as a part of (or cause of) health.

41. This does not put pressure on the division of the category of quality by reference to the end of nature, as I discussed in chapter 4, for a passion is not a quality; it is in the category passion (see 103n58, chapter 4).

42. *In II Sent.*, d. 36, q. 1, a. 2 [Moos 926–27].

43. These are not, of course, caused by altogether internal causes; these internal maladies may have external causes, but not of the sort that can be perceived by touch.

44. *In IV Sent.*, d. 33, q. 3, a. 1 [Busa].

45. *In II Sent.*, d. 19, q. 1, a. 3, ad 3 [Mand 489].

passively received from the active power of medicine, is a corporeal passion, although imperfectly so because it is ordered to restoring our natural health which is a perfection.[46] Thus corporeal passions may involve both the destruction of good and bad qualities, even if they are first and foremost understood as destroying naturally good qualities and replacing them with adventitious harmful ones.

Aquinas insists that corporeal passion "follows the action of nature: when, namely, the species of the agent is received in the patient according to material existence [*esse material*] as when water is heated by fire."[47] In other words, corporeal passion happens to all material substances as they are directly moved by material efficient causes. Water, stones, plants, and all animals can be affected by such passions. It is not the soul that is directly corrupted by such passions, but via the body the whole composite is corrupted, and because the soul is the form of the body, corporeal passions *per accidens* affect the soul.[48] Furthermore, as the powers of the soul are rooted in the soul itself, this bodily motion indirectly moves the soul, which in turn somehow extends to the powers.[49] In other words, a corporeal passion affects the body and corrupts the composite, which somehow moves the soul, which in turn follows the causal chain out to the powers of the soul.

If corporeal passions pertain to the soul as it is the form of the body, animate passions (*passiones animales*) pertain to the soul as the mover of the body, that is, as the soul is the principle of action through its powers. Concerning the three clusters of powers (rational, sensitive, and nutritive), Aquinas argues that because passion requires material alteration, animate passions cannot happen in the immaterial rational powers. And because nutritive powers are active powers, but passion demands a passive reception of a quality, nor do animate passions happen in the nutri-

---

46. Health, as discussed, is in the first species of quality. But health itself is composed of qualities of the third species, and thus heat can be considered simply as a quality of the third species or included in the first, if one considers that it is part of health. When the body moves from sickness to health there is undoubtedly bodily alteration happening, some qualities are being replaced with others. Thus moving from sickness to health is not strictly speaking a passion, although it does involve corporeal passions. See chapter 4.

47. *In II Sent.*, d. 19, q. 1, a. 3, ad 1 [Mand 489].

48. *In II Sent.*, d. 15, q. 2, a. 1, sol. 2 [Mand 484].

49. Ibid., a. 3, sol. 2 [Mand 484]. Aquinas, however, does not spell out what this entails in his commentary on the *Sentences*.

tive powers. Therefore, by default, they properly belong to the sensitive powers. These powers, which are the forms of their corporeal organs, are the proper subject of animate passions, and insofar as the powers of the soul suffer passions, the soul does so *per accidens*.[50]

But there are two kinds of sensitive powers, namely, apprehensive and appetitive powers. The apprehensive sense powers are passive in the sense that they receive what is apprehended by way of a species or intention, and in this way, as Aristotle said in the *De anima* 424a, to sense is in a way to suffer (*pati*). These apprehensive powers, however, are not moved by the material existence (*esse materiale*) of the sensible object, but by the spiritual existence (*esse spirituale*) as apprehended in the sense power by a species or intention, and for this reason there is no material destruction of a natural quality in the sense power and its organ, but the reception of the spiritual form is rather its perfection and actualization. And even though the external senses have material organs, these material organs are always perfected by their being actualized in apprehension—in normal sense cognition there is simply no natural contrariness.[51] Thus we may describe sense cognition as a passion, loosely speaking, but not properly so.

The appetitive powers, however, are moved movers, moved by the object itself via sense cognition. Unlike the apprehensive powers, the appetitive powers are moved by and toward things according to the reality of the things themselves. That is, they seek the extra-mental things themselves, not simply their apprehension. Because passion, by definition, means being moved passively by something else, and because the sense appetites are more fully moved by the things themselves, they are more fully passions. It is true that apprehension involves the passive reception of an intelligible form from the object, but this terminates in apprehension. In the appetitive sense powers, however, Aquinas thinks that we are really *passively moved* by the object itself in a more powerful way than mere apprehension. For instance, we perceive the delectable cookie through apprehension, but it is through the sense appetites that we are actually *moved* or drawn toward the cookie itself. It is through

---

50. *In II Sent.*, d. 15, q. 2, a. 1 [Mand 484–85].

51. Ibid. [Mand 485–86]. However, he goes on to point out that if the apprehended object is beyond the sense power there will be the reception of a contrary quality, e.g., staring at the sun. This would be a proper passion as it would destroy the qualities of the eye's organ.

such passions that we are really moved by the sensible objects around us.[52]

Because the sense appetites are the forms of their bodily organs, these powers are the immediate cause of corporal alteration in these organs.[53] And, of course, the motions of the sense appetites are passions more so when the soul is moved by something unsuitable than suitable, for in that case a suitable quality is destroyed and the soul is dragged beyond the mode of its own nature (*trahitur anima extra modum suum naturalem*),[54] albeit *per accidens*. Thus pain is more properly a passion of the soul than pleasure, as pleasure is more of a perfection than a destruction.

In corporeal passions, it is *esse materiale* that directly causes the alteration. In animate passions, however, *esse spirituale* must be partly causally responsible.[55] This is important. The causal chain of animate passions partly comes from externally apprehended material objects but also and crucially they are partly caused by the active power of the soul itself via sense cognition. Sense cognition, for Aquinas, requires a kind of active abstraction on the part of the soul, namely, a stripping away of matter, which must occur in order for sensible and rational creatures to apprehend the forms of material beings without the matter in which they exist in themselves. Aquinas insists that even if sense cognition is not as completely an immaterial act as intellectual apprehension, it is nevertheless necessarily partly immaterial and involves *esse spirituale*. Even touch, which is the most material of the external senses, involves a partly immaterial act.[56] For instance, when we touch a hot stove, in order for apprehension to occur, the form of heat must be apprehended without the material which it has in the stove. Thus animate passions are always partly caused by the soul itself through its apprehensive powers in the dematerializing action required by sense cognition. That is why animate passions require the soul's active causal role as mover through its apprehensive powers, but corporal passions affect the body immediately and thus affect the soul as form.

---

52. These objects need not exactly be immediately extra-mentally present, for passions can follow memory and imagination. I will discuss this in a few pages.

53. *In IV Sent.*, d. 49, q. 3, a. 1, qc. 1 [Busa].

54. *In III Sent.*, d. 15, q. 2, a. 1, sol. 1 [Moos 483–84].

55. *In II Sent.*, d. 19, q. 1, a. 3, ad 1 [Mand 489].

56. *In III Sent.*, d. 21, q. 2, a. 4, sol. 2, ad 5 [Moos 655]; *In IV Sent.*, d. 44, q. 2, a. 1, qc. 4, ad 1, and qc. 3 [Busa].

When Aquinas considers corporeal passions, he abstracts from the powers of the soul and focuses on the immediate bodily harm. But bodily harm may, of course, be perceptible. We might step on a flower, which would cause a *passio corporalis* for that flower, but step on an animal and the animal will apprehend and sense the *passio corporalis*, which must also cause a *passio animales*. In other words, one can consider any particular bodily harm (if it is perceptible) either as immediately harming the body, or as it passes through the various sensitive powers of the soul. Of course, some corporeal passions may not be immediately perceptible, such as brain disease or certain poisons, etc. Furthermore, many corporeal passions would always be perceived by touch (e.g., a punch) and thus would be perceptible.[57]

Although perception grants us a sort of minimum threshold to distinguish animate from corporeal passions, I would not want to go so far as to say that perception is what essentially constitutes animate passions. We can say this: there is certainly no animate passion without perception, but what Aquinas means by animate passion is broader than that: it is meant to signify the fact that many powers of the soul are involved in multifaceted ways. These are the passions of the soul as it moves itself, often in highly complex ways involving many powers in suffering or perceiving something. And this suffering or perceiving moves or causes a passion or motion in the sense appetites. Thus an animate passion can be either the relatively simple pain suffered upon being slapped, or it can be the quite complex emotion of anger that we feel on perceiving an insult from someone else. Although both of these cases involve some sort of external event (the slap or the insult) and perception, the former is perceived in a more bodily fashion while the latter (the perception of an insult) requires intellectual perception, but both of these perceptions cause a motion in the sense appetite and its corresponding bodily alteration. Animate passions need not be directly caused by something external; we may, for instance, imagine ourselves saying the perfect joke at exactly the right time and that may cause the passion of pleasure in us, but even in that case the sense appetites "suffer" this passion through our imag-

57. My reading of the texts thus differs from Daniel De Haan's, who argues that all corporeal passions are accompanied by apprehension. See "Aquinas's Doctrine of Antecedent and Consequent Passions," *Documenti e studi sulla tradizione filosofica medievale* 25 (2014): 318.

ination. An animate passion can have a whole host of co-causes as the various powers of the soul (the potential whole) may contribute to the passion itself (I will discuss this in greater detail below), but at the very least perception of some sort or other is always necessary.

For the most part, corporeal passions happen to us out of our control, and therefore they are not the most relevant kinds of passions for ethics. Animate passions, however, as we will see, always affect reason and will and thus are brought into the realm of the moral and as such they are crucial to Aquinas's ethics. For instance, while it may not be up to us whether or not we feel the emotion of anger (say when someone says something incredibly obnoxious), the emotion of anger certainly puts a kind of pressure on our choices, and how we choose to react to that anger is certainly voluntary and thus within the realm of what is moral. There are exceptions, of course, for instance, there are cases where an animate passion may be so strong that one's act is rendered completely involuntary, as in so-called crimes of passion (e.g., catching a spouse in the act of committing adultery). There may be cases in which we voluntarily afflict ourselves with corporeal passions, for example, corporeal penance.[58] Or corporeal passions may be brought into the moral realm in the way that one may choose to suffer disease with dignity, etc.[59] Although there are some exceptions, from the ethical perspective, it is animate passions, which concern the soul as mover, that are of primary concern. Indeed, this is why Aquinas's so-called treatise on the passions in *ST* I-II, qq. 22–48, is silent about corporeal passions, namely, because as he says in the prologue to the *prima secundae*, he is considering man as he is the principle of his own acts, which is, of course, as the soul is a mover.[60] However, this distinction between corporeal passions and the passions of the soul are highly emphasized in the *De veritate* and briefly

58. See *In IV Sent.*, d. 14, q. 1, a. 1, qc. 6, ad 2 [Moos 591].

59. *In II Sent.*, d. 36, q. 1, a. 2 [Moos 926–27].

60. Aquinas is silent about corporeal passions in the second part of *ST*, which is devoted to ethics. His massive "treatise on the passions" in *ST* I-II, qq. 22–48, is almost exclusively devoted to the passions of the soul, and one is hard pressed to find a single clear reference to corporeal passions there. But as the prologue to the second part says, Aquinas is now considering man as he is the principle of his own acts, i.e., man qua self-mover, and from this perspective it is obvious why he would gloss over corporeal passions. Of course, they become highly relevant again in his Christology, the third part of *ST*, in which much of Christ's suffering is through corporeal passions.

in the *tertia pars* of the *Summa*, as these texts discuss Christ's suffering of corporeal passions.[61]

The Sense Powers

Let us now turn to these animate passions and consider them more fully while also giving a brief introduction to the sense powers. A passion of the soul, as I just discussed, is a motion of the sense appetites following upon some cognition from the five external senses, which perceive sensible qualities. When someone smells and sees a peach, however, there is an internal sense power, the common sense, that perceives that it is sensing and can distinguish between sensible qualities, such as the peaches' smell and color. The external senses and the common sense help us to grasp the material object (i.e., the peach itself), but we still must seek what accounts for the formal aspect under which it is sought, that is, why the object is grasped as attractive or repulsive.[62]

As the will does not move toward anything unless it is apprehended under the intelligibility of the good (*sub ratione boni*), neither does the sense appetite move toward anything unless it is apprehended as suitable or unsuitable (*sub ratione convenientis vel inconvenientis*),[63] that is, as attractive or repulsive. This apprehension of suitability or lack thereof is the formal object of the passion. In *In II Sent.*, d. 24, q. 2, a. 1, he offers two possible origins for this apprehension.

The power that apprehends suitability seems to be (*videtur*) the aestimative power. This is the power by which a sheep flees a wolf and follows its mother. The aestimative power is related to the sense appetite as the practical intellect is related to the will.[64] Here the aestimative power seems to be accounting for the whole formal object of the passion,[65] but

---

61. *QDV*, q. 26, a. 2 [Leonine 22.3:752.70–107], a. 3 [755–56.169–230], a. 9 [779–80.94–133], and a. 1 [749.312–28]. See *ST* III, q. 15, a. 4 [St. Paul 1944]; on this last text see Lombardo, *Logic of Desire*, 45–46.

62. See Mark Drost, "Intentionality in Aquinas's Theory of Emotions," *International Philosophical Quarterly* 31 (1991): 449–60, for a discussion of this.

63. *In II Sent.*, d. 24, q. 2, a. 1 [Mand 601–2].

64. Ibid. [602].

65. For another, perhaps stronger (notice the *movens*) restatement of the analogy see *In II Sent.*, d. 24, q. 2, a. 1, ad 2 [Mand 603]: "vires apprehensivae sensitivae pertinent ad sensualitatem, licet secundum quemdam ordinem: quia aestimativa proprie se habet ad eam sicut ratio practica ad liberum arbitrium, quae etiam est movens." However, in the remainder of this passage he also allows imagination and the other powers to play a role, albeit a more remote one.

another immediately following analogy qualifies the role of the aestimative power: the sense appetite is to the internal and external senses as will is to intellect.[66] Here Aquinas seems to grant that the other internal and external senses can also play a role in determining the apprehension of suitability.[67]

This suitability (*conveniens ... aut ratio suae convenientiae*) that moves sense appetite is either apprehended by sense, as are delectable things according to singular senses; or it is not apprehended by sense, as the enmity of wolf, which the sheep perceives neither by seeing or hearing, but only by estimation.[68] Thus the formal object of a passion may either be determined by the external senses themselves or by the aestimative power, or perhaps by some combination.

Aquinas posits the aestimative power in animals to account for those complex apprehensions (e.g., something harmful, *nocivum*) that cannot be fully accounted for by their external sense powers. When a sheep senses a wolf, it also immediately senses danger or harm. The apprehension of danger cannot be explained, according to Aquinas, by the external senses, but is caused by a certain natural instinct. Aquinas seems to restrict the use of the aestimative power to relatively complex apprehensions. For example, I do not think he would want to say that an animal needs the aestimative power to judge that this food is appetible or suitable—he seems to allow for such cognition below the level of the

---

66. *In II Sent.*, d. 24, q. 2, a. 1 [Mand 601–2]: "hoc modo se habeat sensualitas ad partem sensitivam, sicut se habet voluntas et liberum arbitrium ad partem intellectivam." He had explained these terms a few lines above: "sensibilitas enim omnes vires sensitivae partis comprehendit, tam apprehensivas de foris, quam apprehensivas de intus, quam etiam appetitivas; sensualitas autem magis proprie illam tantum partem nominat per quam movetur animal in aliquod appetendum vel fugiendum." Note the distinction he makes between *sensualitas* and *sensibilitas*; cf. Klubertanz, *The Discursive Power*, 154.

67. For a somewhat later passage (1265–68) explicitly saying this see *In III De an.*, l. 11 [Leonine 45.1:256.226–28]: "Et ideo, nisi animal haberet sensum tactus per quem discerneret conueniencia a corruptiuis, non posset haec fugere et illa accipere." He says the same about taste (ll. 232–36).

68. Ibid. "Hoc autem conveniens quod sensualitatem movet, aut ratio suae convenientiae, aut est apprehensa a sensu, sicut sunt delectabilia secundum singulos sensus, quae animalia persequuntur: aut est non apprehensa a sensu; sicut inimicitiam lupi neque videndo neque audiendo ovis percipit, sed aestimando tantum: et ideo motus sensualitatis in duo tendit: in ea scilicet quae secundum exteriores sensus delectabilia sunt, et hoc est quod dicitur, quod ex sensualitate est motus qui intenditur in corporis sensus; aut ad ea quae nociva vel convenientia corpori secundum solam aestimationem cognoscuntur, et sic ex sensualitate dicitur esse appetitus rerum ad corpus pertinentium."

aestimative power.[69] There is a limit to the apprehension of the other sense powers; the aestimative power accounts for what goes beyond this limit. One would have wanted Aquinas to say more about exactly where to draw this line, or even about how the lower sense powers judge something as suitable.

The aestimative power in humans, however, is quite different than it is in animals. It has various names: cogitative power, passive intellect, and particular reason.[70] In humans it does not operate by a natural instinct, but rather is bound to reason and operates through it.[71] This internal sense power in humans operates as a kind of bridge between thought and sense, between the universal and the particular. There is no need to rely on instinct, as the aestimative power along with reason performs some kind of a comparison (*collatio*) of intentions, by which the person determines that this or that is dangerous or harmful.[72] A sheep perceives a wolf, apprehends danger, and runs. Man, however, perceives the same wolf, but first apprehends that it is a wolf, then judges that it is dangerous, and then runs. Humans apprehend suitability or harm by way of a kind of collation with the intellect, that is, the universal quiddity of the wolf is involved, with a whole series of judgments that involve returning to phantasms. The cogitative power is involved in this process of practical reasoning.[73] This process involves complex interactions between material and immaterial powers, but again, here it seems to me that Aquinas simply did not say enough for us to say exactly how this

69. See previous note.

70. For a discussion of this power and a full reference to the literature see Daniel De Haan, "Perception and the *Vis Cogitativa*: A Thomistic Analysis of Aspectual, Actional, and Affectional Percepts," *American Catholic Philosophical Quarterly* 88 (2014): 397–437.

71. *In II Sent.*, d. 24, q. 2, a. 2 [Mand 605]: "nullus appetitus movetur in suum objectum nisi fiat apprehensio alicujus sub ratione boni vel mali, convenientis vel nocivi. Hanc autem rationem convenientis et boni aliter homo percipit, aliter brutum: brutum enim non conferendo, sed quodam naturali instinctu sibi conveniens vel nocivum, cognoscit; homo autem per investigationem quamdam et collationem hujusmodi rationes considerat; et ideo vis illa per quam in hujusmodi rationum cognitionem venit consequenter ratio dicitur, quae investigativa est et deductiva unius in alterum." That this is indeed refering to the cogitative power see *In II Sent.*, d. 24, q. 2, a. 1, ad 3 [Mand 603]: "unde et quaedam pars sensitiva, scilicet cogitatione, alio nomine ratio dicitur, propter confinium ejus ad rationem."

72. *In II Sent.*, d. 25, q. 1, a. 2 [Mand 647]: "animalia non apprehendunt rationem convenientis per collationem, sed per quemdam naturalem instinctum; et ideo animalia habent aestimationem, sed non cognitionem."

73. The cogitative power itself does not grasp universals; it shares in intellect because it compares particular intentions. See Klubertanz, *The Discursive Power*, chap. 6, esp. 175.

collatio works.[74] Nevertheless, we can say that the formal object of certain passions may be taken directly from the senses or it may come from the cogitative power, and thus be somewhat rational, or it may involve some kind of combination of both.

To complicate matters slightly, Aquinas suggests that passion may also follow upon imagination.[75] The imagination is the power that stores in a phantasm what has been sensed by the external senses and organized by the common sense. We may as well add the memorative power, which recognizes as past what has been stored in a phantasm and recognized as helpful or harmful by the aestimative or cogitative power; for I may think of a snake or a worm-filled apple and experience fear or disgust without the material object actually being present. Thus all of the internal sense powers as well as the external senses may play some part in the determination of the formal object of a passion.

Before ending this section I would like to briefly consider the particular passion called love, *amor*. Love, as I mentioned, is the principle and root of all of the ten other passions.[76] That is, all of the other passions either begin from love or its privation, namely, hatred or dislike. For we only hate or dislike things because they deprive us of what we love and like—love, for Aquinas, is first no matter how you cut the cake. The English word love, I should note, is often not quite the best translation, it is often better to translate *amor* as some kind of liking or fondness. For instance, in English we would more often say that we like this apple rather than that we love it.

In any case, love, for Aquinas, is determined by these external and internal senses. The internal and external senses move the sense appetite by presenting their apprehended form to the sense appetites. The terminus of this presenting motion is a kind of rest in the beloved object. This reception of and rest in the apprehended form in the concupiscible ap-

---

74. Some may object that this is serious weakness in Aquinas's position. For my part, I think that, in the long run, Aquinas's vagueness here is an advantage. I would rather leave it to contemporary scientists to figure out the details of this. We can say of Aquinas's position, in general, that animals are capable of remarkably complex perceptions that far surpass basic sense cognition without being fully rational. Human sense perception may be animalistic, in this sophisticated sense, but it can also involve reason. I think this is a quite plausible position to hold.

75. *In II Sent.*, d. 24, q. 3, a. 2 [Mand 617].

76. For a brief discussion of the eleven passions see 71–72 in chapter 3.

petite is called love. Here Aquinas is very explicit that appetite is a passive moved mover, passively moved by the imparted form of the agent.[77] When the form of something suitable is received in the appetite, the moved appetite rests in it and then takes delight in it. In simpler words, we like and take pleasure in what we have apprehended. As Aquinas explains it, love is a formal likeness between the lover and beloved, and sensitive love is determined by the exigency (*exigentiam*) of the received form of the beloved.[78] As Michael Sherwin has noted, love in Aquinas's *Sentences* commentary is ultimately formal and passive.[79] This is, of course, very similar to the manner in which the will receives its form from the intellect in the *Sentences* commentary, and I am willing to say that his account of passion, insofar as it is formal and passive, mirrors his treatment of volition here. Just as the will follows whatever the intellect understands as good, so passion follows whatever sense cognition (via the external and internal senses) perceives as suitable.

From the moral perspective, what is important here is the degree to which these animate emotions are voluntary. For choice, as I discussed, is primary in virtue, and all acts of virtue proceed from choice.[80] Depending on a passion's causes, it may or may not be voluntary. As attached to a material organ, the sense appetite can be compelled to some motion or passion by an alteration in its organ.[81] Such passions are not caused by imagination (which is open to the influence of the will and cogitative power), but by natural active causes. All of this is to say that sometimes the passions of the soul can be caused by physical changes that are completely out of our control—sickness, a drop in air pressure, hormonal changes, etc. Nevertheless, Aquinas thinks that although such

---

77. *In III Sent.*, d. 27, q. 1, a. 1 [Moos 854–55]: "amor ad appetitum pertinent. Appetitus autem est virtus passive. Unde in III *De anima*, dicit philosophus quod appetibile movet sicut movens non motum, appetitus autem sicut movens motum. Omne autem passivum perficitur secundum quod formatur per formam sui activi et in hoc motus ejus terminatur et quiescit…. Unde amor nihil aliud est quam quaedam transformatio affectus in rem amatam."

78. Ibid., ad 3 [Moos 856]: "amoris radix, per se loquendo, est similitudo amati ad amantem, quia sic est ei bonum et conveniens." See also ad 2: "amor dicitur virtus unitiva formaliter … convenientia est secundum quod ab uno participatur id quod est alterius; et sic amans quodammodo habet amatum," as well as ad 6: "appetitus, ut dictum est, movet motus: unde passio, quia movetur ab amato, est ulterius movens secundum exigentiam amati." Cf. *In III Sent.*, d. 27, q. 1, a. 1 [Moos 855].

79. See Sherwin, *Knowledge and Love*, 64–70 and 80–81.

80. See *In II Sent.*, d. 24, q. 3, a. 2 [Mand 620].

81. *In II Sent.*, d. 39, q. 1, a. 2 [Mand 989]; cf. *In IV Sent.*, d. 4, q. 49, a. 3, ad 1, sol. 1 [Busa].

passions are not caused by the will's command, because the will can impede or not impede them, they almost immediately become subject to the will and drawn into the realm of the voluntary and thus into the moral.[82] It is here, in the realm where the partly material passions interact with immaterial volition, that moral virtue can play its role in helping them participate in reason.

82. See *In II Sent.*, d. 24, q. 3, a. 2 [Mand 620].

7

PARTICIPATION AND VIRTUE IN AQUINAS'S *SENTENCES* COMMENTARY

Moral Virtue

Aquinas suggests that there are many answers to the question: "What is virtue?" This is because definitions must include all of a thing's causes and in this case there are too many causes to neatly bundle them up in one simple definition.[1] If nothing else, this highlights the complexity of virtue—there are multiple causes, all of which must be taken into account if one is to grasp what (which is what a definition signifies) virtue is. We have already seen this causal complexity in the discussion of habits in chapter 4. But let us consider his treatment of moral virtue in his *Sentences* commentary.

Moral virtue is bound to appetite, and appetite is an inclination toward something.[2] In some respects appetite is naturally right, as with respect to an ultimate end, for example, as everyone desires happiness, but in respect to other things the rightness (*rectitudo*) of the appetite is "caused by reason, insofar as appetite in some way participates in reason, as Aristotle said."[3] And so one may ask: where does the rightness (or

1. *In II Sent.*, d. 27, q. 1, a. 2 [Mand 700].
2. For the claim that appetite is an inclination see *In III Sent.*, d. 27, q. 1, a. 2 [Moos 861]. For the claim that appetite is an inclination toward something see *In III Sent.*, d. 26, q. 1, a. 5, ad 4 [Moos 830–31]; see also *In II Sent.*, d. 24, q. 2, a. 1, ad 5 [Mand 604].
3. *In III Sent.*, d. 33, q. 1, a. 1 [Moos 1020–21].

rectitudo) of appetite come from, and is it always (as it seems from this passage) from reason?

In *In III Sent.*, d. 23, q. 1, a. 1, Aquinas notes that in all things that have a rule and measure, their goodness consists in a conformity to their rule or measure and their badness consists in a falling away from it; divine wisdom, however, is the first measure and rule of all things. Then Aquinas distinguishes between two kinds of powers. Some powers are limited to determined actions or passions and as such are conformed to their rule as ordered by divine wisdom and therefore naturally have their own rectitude and goodness. But higher and more universal powers (such as those which are rational) are not limited to some one object or mode of operation (*modum operandi*) as they can have their rectitude according to diverse objects and in diverse ways. Such powers do not naturally have this rectitude, but must receive it from elsewhere.[4] In other words, their received rectitude must be caused by something else. This perfection is received in the manner of an inhering quality and as such the rectitude of the rule inheres in the regulated power.[5] Because of this inhering quality the power does what is right or suitable to its form with ease and pleasure. When this quality is imperfect it is called a disposition, but when it is perfected it is called a habit—we may also then call it a second nature as it inclines to one (*ad unum inclinant*).[6]

Using this distinction, Aquinas points out which powers cannot have habits, namely, those that are naturally determined *ad unum*: the apprehensive sense powers are already perfect in their operation, as is the will by way of its object (the ultimate end), and so is the agent intellect by its own determinate action. The possible intellect, however, which is indeterminate, needs habits by which it can participate in the rectitude of its own rule. These habits may be natural, as those that are immediately illuminated by the light of the agent intellect, that is, the first

---

4. *In III Sent.*, d. 23, q. 1, a. 1 [Moos 697–98].

5. Powers are not perfected simply by being acted on (*per modum passionis*); see *In III Sent.*, d. 23, q. 1, a. 1 [Moos 698].

6. Ibid., 698–99: "Oportet ergo ut alio modo recipiatur, scilicet per modum qualitatis inhaerentis, scilicet ut rectitudo regulae efficiatur forma potentiae regulatae; sic enim faciliter et delectabiliter quod rectum est operabitur, sicut id quod est conveniens suae formae. Et haec quidem qualitas sive forma, dum adhuc est imperfecta, dispositio dicitur; cum autem jam consummata est et quasi in naturam versa, habitus nominatur, qui, ut ex II *Eth.* [1105b25] et V *Meta.* [1022b10] accipitur, est secundum quem nos habemus ad aliquid bene vel male."

principles (which are understood only by the possible intellect). Or they may be acquired, as are those that are educed from these first principles, or they may be infused, as those that participate in things that exceed the agent intellect. It is the same with the will and the sense appetites. Concerning those things toward which it is not already naturally determined *ad unum*, habits are needed that participate in the rectitude of reason, which is their rule.[7]

This passage makes it quite clear that in the *Sentences* when Aquinas says that the sense appetites participate in reason he really means the power of reason itself. The first principle in the acquired moral virtues is the agent intellect, by whose illuminating power the possible intellect understands, and from this are educed (*educi*) the virtues for the will and sense appetites. The scope of the agent intellect is the line by which Aquinas distinguishes between the acquired and the infused virtues. If the action falls under the power or purview of the agent intellect, then we are in the realm of acquired intellectual and moral virtues. If, however, the action requires cognition that is beyond the range of the agent intellect, then we are in the realm of the infused virtues.

It is reason that ultimately causes the form that is received in the sense appetites. We can also see this if we consider his argument (elsewhere) against what he considers to be Avicenna's view that virtue comes from the *dator formarum*, that is, a separate substance. Man's actions, according to this line of thought, merely dispose him to receive virtues from this separate substance. Aquinas replies as follows:

This position, however, destroys a natural power [*virtus*], which is in each natural principle to producing like itself, insofar as the matter on which it acts is receptive of its own similitude. Which indeed is necessary from this that everything which acts, acts from this that it is in act. Whence it is necessary that anything which is something in act, in some way can be the active cause of that. And so every natural principle naturally introduces its own similitude through its own act. Since therefore the principles of the sciences and virtues are naturally placed in us, as was said, it is necessary that through actions

---

7. Ibid. Here are the last few lines of this text: "Similiter etiam in voluntate quantum ad illa ad quae ex natura non determinatur, et in irascibili et in concupiscibili, indigemus habitibus, secundum quod participant rectitudinem rationis, quae est eorum regula, vel rectitudinem primae mensurae in his quae humanam naturam excedunt, quantum ad habitus infusos."

proceeding from those principles, the habits of virtues and sciences are completed.[8]

It is thus from the naturally known first principles of the intellect and the actions proceeding from the understanding of these principles that the moral virtues are acquired.[9] Aquinas is critical of Avicenna's position because it seems to deny that humans are the active principle of their own virtue. This active principle, according to Aquinas, is the agent intellect, which is always fully in act and by which the content of the naturally known first principles is illumined. Reasoning from his two axioms that every agent produces something like itself and that every agent acts insofar as it is in act, he explains that the virtues are caused by reason as it is actual and a likeness is communicated when this act actualizes something in potency, that is, the power in need of being perfected by, or participating in, reason.

Mode and Exemplarity

Let us further hone in on this causality and communication of similitude by considering an important passage that discusses prudence. The rectitude of appetite is caused by reason as it participates in reason, but reason itself is made right by prudence (the virtue of deliberation).[10] Because right reason (prudence) is required for moral virtue, when the sense appetites participate in reason through the moral virtues this means they are participating in reason informed by the habit of prudence. Prudence rules the moral virtues and they participate in

---

8. *In III Sent.*, d. 33, q. 1, a. 2, sol. 2 [Moos 1028–29].

9. Ibid. and ad 2 [Moos 1029]: "in operibus animae est quidam gradus, secundum quod una potentia alteri subjacet. Et in eadem potentia est inveniri superius et inferius, secundum quod ad diversa objecta comparatur. Inferius autem natum est recipere a superiori ; et ideo per operationes egredientes a ratione naturali et voluntate, in quibus praeexistunt seminaria virtutum, acquiritur habitus in irascibili et concupiscibili." Remember that the natural will here follows the intellect, as discussed above, and that the distinction between natural and rational movements is accidental to the will itself and is dependent on the two kinds of acts of the intellect.

10. See also *In III Sent.*, d. 33, q. 1, a. 1, sol. 2 [Moos 1020–21]: "rectitudo appetitus ex ratione causatur, secundum quod appetitus aliqualiter ratione participat, ut in II *Eth.* dicitur. Et quia prudentia facit rationem rectam, ideo praeter prudentiam requiruntur aliae virtutes morales quae faciunt appetitum rectum in his in quibus naturaliter rectus non est. Et quia bonum rationis non eodem modo invenitur in ipsa ratione et in his quae rectitudinem rationis participative habent."

prudence as they participate in reason.[11] Here is the passage I wish to highlight:

For an inferior power does not have the perfection of virtue except insofar as it participates in the perfection of a superior power; as a habit which is in the irascible appetite does not have the nature [*rationem*] of virtue, as is said in VI *Eth.* 1144b1, except insofar as it receives understanding and discretion from reason, which prudence perfects, and according to this prudence posits form and mode in all of the other moral virtues.[12]

This last line illustrates what I consider to be the most peculiar facet of Aquinas's account of virtue in the *Sentences*: when the moral virtues, temperance and fortitude, are said to participate in reason Aquinas explains it in terms of form and mode. The kind of formal causality he means is exemplar causality.[13]

There are two kinds of exemplar forms. One according to whose representation something comes to be, and for this similitude alone is required, as we say that true things are the exemplar forms of their depictions. In another way an exemplar form is said to be that according to whose similitude something comes to be and through participation in it has *esse*, as the divine goodness is the exemplar form of every goodness, and divine wisdom of every wisdom. And such an exemplar form need not be one in species with its effects, since those participating do not always participate through the mode of the participated. And in this way prudence is the form of the other moral virtues, insofar as a certain sealed or stamped [*sigillatus*] order of prudence in the lower powers grants to habits, which are there, the intelligibility of virtue [*rationem virtutis*].[14]

The exemplar causality between reason and the sense appetites is explained by way of analogy to the manner in which God is the exemplar cause of *esse*, goodness, and wisdom. This requires a little explanation. Aquinas distinguishes between two kinds of exemplarity in the *Sentences* and in later texts. An idea is an exemplar cause of its effect. For ex-

---

11. *In III Sent.*, d. 33, q. 3, a. 1, sol. 2, ad 3 [Moos 1075]: "prudentia regulat omnes alias virtutes, ideo omnes participant aliquid prudentiae ; sicut irascibilis et concupiscibilis participant aliqualiter rationem. Unde illud quod ad alias virtutes pertinet participative, cautio scilicet, ad prudentiam pertinet essentialiter."

12. *In III Sent.*, d. 27, q. 2, a. 4, sol. 3 [Moos 889].

13. That exemplarity is indeed a kind of formal cause see the section "Exemplarism and the Four Causes" in Doolan, *Divine Ideas*, 33–43.

14. *In III Sent.*, d. 27, q. 2, a. 4, sol. 3, ad 1 [Moos 889–90].

ample, a carpenter has an idea for a cabinet that he builds, or God has a divine idea for a person whom he creates. This is not, however, the kind of exemplarity Aquinas has in mind in the case of reason and the moral virtues. Here he means a kind of exemplar causality that is rather explained by way of analogy to nature in the way that man generates man, that is, man produces a form that is similar to himself. In a similar way, God as *ipsum esse* produces *esse*, or God as good produces things that are good. Aquinas is not emphasizing the exact formal likeness between God's divine idea and its created effect, but rather the communication of a diminished likeness from the cause's nature (God's nature) and its effect (a creature), an analogical likeness.[15]

There are, however, two different ways that causes can be like to their effects. (1) They may be univocally like one another, as a human generates a human or heat causes heat, that is, both the causes and effect can be said to be exactly like one another, at least insofar as they are both human or both heat. This must be denied of God as there is no univocal formal communication between God and creatures.[16] In a similar but different way, participations in reason, the moral virtues, do not have the full nature of the power of reason itself. Thus (2) there are non-univocal causes, which are equivocally like their effects.[17] In this case the form exists in the cause in a more eminent way than it does in its effect.[18] Thus God and created beings are good, but goodness exists in God supereminently. Aquinas, however, further distinguishes between two kinds of equivocal causes. The communicated form may exist in the cause according to the same form or not according to the same form. In the latter case the cause has the form virtually, that is, in its power (*virtus*). For example, the sun, which is not hot (to use his outdated medieval example) causes heat; the sun is not formally hot itself but it has the power to cause the form of heat.[19] This is not the kind of causality he means in

---

15. *In I Sent.*, d. 19, q. 5, a. 2, ad 4 [Mand 493].

16. *In I Sent.*, d. 8, q. 1, a. 2 [Mand 198].

17. Previously I discussed things which are equivocally predicated of one another, such as a dog and a star. In such a case there is no real likeness at all; they just accidentally happen to share the same name. This is not the case with what is called "equivocal causality." See the text referred to in the previous note.

18. *In II Sent.*, d. 14, q. 1, a. 2, ad 3 [Mand 351], and d. 15, q. 1, a. 2, ad 4 [Mand 372].

19. *In II Sent.*, d. 14, q. 1, a. 2, ad 3 [Mand 351]; *In I Sent.*, d. 2, q. 1, a. 2 [Mand 62–63], and d. 8, q. 1, a. 2 [Mand 198].

our case: he means to point to a communication of the same form. God truly is *esse*, good and wise, and he communicates these in causing creatures, albeit in a diminished fashion. In a similar way the sense appetites participate in reason. Reason, of course, is the very form of reason, and it communicates this form, albeit in a diminished fashion, to the sense appetites in the form of the moral virtues.

There is a likeness between sense appetite and reason, indeed a formal exemplar likeness, an impression of reason, but not the exact same form. What is clear from this passage is that when Aquinas says that the moral virtues participate in reason he has in mind formal causality, specifically the kind of analogical/equivocal-exemplar causality in which the cause possesses the form that it communicates to its effect.[20] The way he sometimes puts it is that there is a formal likeness, but a difference according to *mode*.

But what does he mean by using the term mode so frequently in the *Sentences* commentary? And what is its connection to formal causality? For example, he says that "reason posits mode in all the powers which are under it,"[21] and he says that the "inferior powers participate in the perfections of the superior powers according to their own mode."[22] I take this to be a variation of his axiom that everything that is received is received according to the mode of the receiver. For he does say that the "participations are determined in the ones participating by the capacities and natures of the ones participating."[23] The lower powers have or receive a form from a higher power, as they are able to receive them. In other words, it depends on the nature of the potency insofar as this kind of potency can receive a form and be actualized in some particular manner or mode:

And so each virtue which is in an inferior power has a certain form which is a virtue from participation in the perfection of a superior power; but it has the form, which is this virtue, from the nature of its own power through the determination to its proper object, and each virtue posits this form and mode which it has with respect to [*circam*] its own act, and again, that form and mode from

---

20. *In III Sent.*, d. 27, q. 2, a. 4, sol. 3, ad 2 [Moos 890].
21. Ibid., ad 3.
22. Ibid., ad 5 [Moos 891].
23. Ibid.

a higher power; thus temperance in its own act posits its proper mode and that of prudence, charity, and grace.[24]

It is clear enough that a virtue has something from its natural power, that is, determination to its proper object, but it also has something from its participation in a higher power, that is, a form or mode concerning a relation to its proper object, which the virtue adds over and above the natural relation to this object. The English translation of *modus* as "way" is perfectly suitable. One could say that virtue adds a way of being related to the object, a kind of *modus operandi*. For example, the sense appetites are naturally related to pleasurable objects, but when a virtuous habit is added to the sense appetites, they are related to a pleasurable object in a different *way*. Aquinas does not seem to want to distinguish between form (*forma*) and way (*modus*); it seems to me that what the form does as a formal cause in the sense appetites is to change the *way* that the sense appetites operate. I offer this as an interpretation of how to take Aquinas's peculiar use of the term *modus*, but it still seems to me to be somewhat obscure, and I will not insist on this interpretation, especially because in his late texts he does not lean on *modus* to explain the moral virtues.

However we might interpret Aquinas's use of *modus* here, we may still ask exactly in what way (*modus*) the sense appetites of the virtuous operate. This discussion so far has been highly abstract. I have discussed exemplar causality, form, mode, etc., but let us now turn to examine this participation more concretely.

What Moral Virtue Does to the Sense Appetites

Aquinas grants a few different roles to moral virtue. One is facility. A power, he says, is a principle of simply acting, but a habit is a principle of acting quickly and with ease.[25] This certainly counts as a way of operating, namely, with a kind of quickness and ease. Aquinas also notes that all moral virtues are distinguished by their end; virtues are according to their end and vices fall short of it. The proximate good to which the moral virtues are ordered is the good of reason, but because the good of reason is not found in the same way in all moral matters there are specif-

24. Ibid.
25. *In III Sent.*, d. 33, q. 1, a. 1 [Moos 1019].

ically different kinds of moral virtue.[26] "What is of reason and intellect is not participated in the same way in the matters of all moral virtues, since the medium of reason is rightly found in diverse matters in diverse ways. And so such diversity of matter causes diversity of form and species; as also happens in natural things, when diverse matters are not proportionate to receiving the form of one kind [*rationis*]."[27]

Note again the language of formal causality and the likeness to the reception of form in matter. But also notice that what moral virtues receive is the mean as determined by reason. It is the role of deliberation and of prudence to determine the mean, that is, to find what is right in moral actions which necessarily concern contingents,[28] and it is the role of moral virtue to participate in reason by receiving this mean. Thus, whatever else this participation may entail, Aquinas does want to say that the sense appetites receive, in some way, reason's prudential and practical considerations of what should be done here and now.

In a helpful passage, Aquinas outlines three ways that this can happen. Moral virtues, he says, are distinguished from the good of reason which consists essentially (*essentialiter*) in the judgment of reason, which belongs to prudence; but in these matters that are disposed by reason, by participation (*participative*), they pertain to moral virtues. Reason disposes or orders these moral matters, passions and actions, in three ways.[29]

First by ordering the passions themselves through actions according to themselves insofar as reason reduces them to a medium according to a certain measure; and so it is said to posit a *mode* in them, since mode implies measure. Second by ordering the subject to the very actions and passions ordered in the first way, namely, so that a man might firmly inhere in these things which reason orders. Third, in a relation to something external to which our acts need to be proportioned, whether this is the end, or some other man, or something extrinsic; and according to this, rectitude or equality is caused in virtue.[30]

Although there is a general way in which all three are applicable to all of the moral virtues, because the entire force (*intensio*) of reason and

---

26. Ibid.

27. Ibid., ad 2 [Moos 1020].

28. Ibid.: "quod in omnibus moralibus invenitur una ratio veri, quod est verum contingens in hominis actione consistens; et ideo ad unum actum cognoscitivum pertinent."

29. *In III Sent.*, d. 33, q. 1, a. 1, sol 3 [Moos 1021–22].

30. Ibid.

virtue is to make up for nature's shortcomings and because our natures usually fall short in regularly particular ways, each virtue corresponds to one of these roles: temperance, courage, or justice. Temperance, he says, whose matter is connatural bodily pleasures, is concerned with the most difficult business of keeping the mode (*difficillimum est modum tenere*), and this is why temperance particularly concerns mode.[31] I would like to point out one difference from a passage that we examined in chapter 5 (*ST* I-II, q. 49, a. 2), in which he discusses mode (*modus*) and measure with respect to habits.[32] In that passage Aquinas does not mean it to signify a *way* that the power operates in which the habit inheres, but rather its *modus essendi*, that is, the way it has existence as a predicamental accident. In any case, here in the *Sentences* fortitude concerns firmly holding onto what reason has ordained in the most difficult matters, namely the fear of death, and justice concerns rightness in one's dealings with others. Insofar as nature fails in these three respects (in holding onto mode, or moderation, in firmness in holding onto mode, and in one's dealings with others and external things), we apparently need moral virtues, which participate in reason, to remedy nature's shortcomings.

Let us consider what this "having of mode" (*modum tenere*) might mean, as it is common to both temperance and courage, which inhere in the sense appetites. He often describes this mode as facility. At times he seems to mean a kind of general facility of action in moral matters, but at times he seems to mean that the sense appetites easily *obey* reason. In this sense reason is not dragged around by passion because the virtues of the sense appetites repress vehement passions, which leaves reason unperturbed and also enables the sense appetites to more easily obey reason's command.[33] This makes the moral virtues, in a sense, utterly passive— their role is to lower the force of passion so that reason's command is more easily obeyed. And the person needs these habits so that his choices can be executed without trouble and difficulty from the passions.[34]

But this is only part of the story of moral virtue according to Aquinas. For the moral virtues in the sense appetite incline toward virtuous action—there is a forward thrust of sorts toward acting virtuously. Thus

---

31. Ibid.
32. See chapter 4, above.
33. *In III Sent.*, d. 33, q. 2, a. 4, sol 2 [Mand 1063].
34. *In III Sent.*, d. 23, q. 1, a. 1, ad 3 [Mand 700].

there is a twofold role of the moral virtues, (1) a kind of passive obedience to reason, and (2) a kind of active inclination toward virtuous acts. Let us consider this latter aspect.

Virtue, Aquinas says citing Cicero "moves in the mode of nature, namely, through a certain inclination of affect [*inclinationem affectus*]," in other words, it is a kind of appetitive motion (in contrast to an apprehensive motion).[35] Another way he puts this is to say that habits incline to doing something (*inclinare ad agendum aliquid*).[36] We are inclined and impelled by habits, but we are not compelled by them. This distinction is important for it means that free decision is not nullified by habits; however, as habits draw or impel agents to chose certain things over others there is a kind of quasi-diminished freedom, at least in those with vices. He calls lack of vice freedom from impulsion or dispositions.[37]

But to what exactly is the habit inclined and how did the habit become so inclined? The answer to the first question is quite simple, almost too simple. The virtuous habit is inclined to virtuous acts:

However, in the act of virtue not only should the substance of the act itself be considered, but also the mode of acting [*modus agendi*]: for not he who acts chastely in any way is chaste, but he who acts with ease and delight, as is stated in book I, c. 13 of the Ethics. Delight, however, is caused by suitableness [*convenientia*], as also in sensibles it is obvious that the conjunction of the suitable thing with the one to whom it is suitable produces delight. Therefore it is necessary that the act of virtue proceed from a power adapted and assimilated to this act. The rational power, however, does not have this from itself, since it is indeterminately related to many [*ad utrumlibet*]. It is therefore necessary that something be superadded to the power, as its perfection, through which it produces such an act, from wherever it is caused: and this we say is a habit of virtue; and so the Philosopher in II Ethics says that a sign of a generated habit must be that delight be taken in its act. Hence it is also that a power perfected by a habit of virtue tends to a similar act through the mode of a certain nature: on account of which Cicero says (prooem. *Rhet.*) that virtue is a habit in the mode of nature, in agreement with reason. As gravity tends downwards, so does chastity produce chaste deeds.[38]

---

35. *In III Sent.*, d. 33, q. 2, a. 4 [Moos 1068].
36. *In II Sent.*, d. 25, q. 1, a. 2 [Mand 649–50].
37. Ibid., q. 1, a. 4 [Mand 654]; a. 5 [Mand 656]; d. 27, q. 1, a. 1, ad 3 [Mand 696–97].
38. *In II Sent.*, d. 27, q. 1, a. 1 [Mand 695].

In this passage we see that the sense appetites become conformed or likened to the virtuous act. Because pleasure is caused by likeness, the habituated power takes delight in its act, and this pleasure undoubtedly adds to the act's ease. This likening of the power to the virtuous act is also described as making the act connatural to the power,[39] that is, the habit is a second nature, which is acting quite naturally according to itself. Whereas the power is indeterminately related to virtuous acts, the habit is determinately related to virtuous ones. Aquinas pushes this quite far in the *Sentences*; he goes so far as saying that chastity acts like the force of gravity pulling downwards, and the will perfected by justice acts like fire, naturally rising upwards.[40] This likening of virtue to natural causality in the particular sense of nonrational actions is risky because it seems to put pressure on the voluntary nature of moral virtue. Aquinas is emphasizing that moral virtue has a kind of natural gravity by which it tends or draws one to acts of virtue in a rather deterministic way or mode. But the sense appetites, of course, may act deterministically without determining choice.

The inclining power of habit also seems to involve some kind of judgment. For example, because of the inclination of his habit an intemperate person will judge incorrectly, namely, that "to delight in a woman," is a *per se* good, and "according to that which is from habit, the end seems to someone to be such as that person is; for example, to him who has the habit of voluptuousness or intemperance, sexual pleasures will seem to be the best, which is according to his own habit."[41]

But toward what, exactly, is the inclination of temperance drawn? In the case of vice it seems that one could be directed toward rather concrete objects, for example, sexual pleasures, etc. But temperance is much more complex. The temperate person neither simply rejects nor desires

---

39. *In IV Sent.*, d. 49, q. 3, a. 2 [Busa].

40. *In II Sent.*, d. 25, q. 1, a. 2 [Mand 649–50]; *In I Sent.*, d. 39, q. 2, a. 2, ad 4 [Mand 934–35].

41. *In II Sent.*, d. 25, q. 1, a. 1, ad 5 [Mand 646–47]. Indeed in vice the form of the habit enables the agent to perform bad actions without any shame or regret, and because of the vice, which is like to vicious acts, the agent takes pleasure in his own vicious acts. This is why Aquinas says that a just person cannot instantaneously become unjust, for he would be tormented by the murmur of synderesis, at least for a while, until his habit managed to obscure and utterly obstruct it; see *In II Sent.*, d. 25, q. 1, a. 4 [Mand 655]. I will take up this "seeming" in chapter 12.

all naturally pleasurable objects, but he must find the mean which is in accord with prudence in each contingent situation, taking into account all of the complex and particular circumstances. In the case of moral virtue, it is reason perfected by prudence that determines or prescribes the means of the moral virtues. Thus prudence is included in the definition of moral virtue simply because definitions must include causes.[42] Prudence is the exemplar cause of virtue, and this causality is then articulated in the language of participation:

When some things are distinguished from one another, with each equally receiving a predication of something common, then one is not included in the definition of another; but when the common term is predicated of them *per prius* and *per posterius*, then the first is included in the definition of the others, as substance is included in the definition of accidents. This is why prudence is included in the definition of the other virtues, in which the good of reason is found *per prius* and the intelligibility of virtue [*ratio virtutis*] *per consequens*; since what is essentially [*per essentiam*] is prior to what is by participation [*per participationem*].[43]

Virtue, he says, is an inclination, and every inclination requires some cognition by which it is ordered and inclined.[44] But, once again, if moral virtue (habitually, qua second nature) is inclined to something or some kind of thing, to what can this be if prudence must always be free to hit a moving contingent target? Whereas the end of vice seems intelligible: say, to take delight in a woman; the end of temperance, the temperate act itself, seems more obscure. How is the habit inclined to this act by prudence? I will return to this question in great detail in chapter 11.

---

42. *In III Sent.*, d. 27, q. 2, a. 4 [Moos 887].

43. *In III Sent.*, d. 33, q. 1, a. 1, sol. 2, ad 1 [Moos 1021]. Cf. *In III Sent.*, d. 33, q. 2, a. 1, sol. 1, ad 2 [Moos 1046]: "ea quae dividunt aliquod commune univocum, simul sunt quantum ad intentionem generis, quamvis unum possit esse causa alterius quantum ad esse, sicut motus localis est causa aliorum motuum contra quos dividitur. Sed ea quae dividunt aliquod commune analogum se habent secundum prius et posterius, etiam quantum ad intentionem communis quod dividitur, sicut patet de substantia et accidente. Unde ex hoc quod una virtus condividitur alteri, non oportet quod una non sit altera principalior." This last claim is worth emphasizing, namely that because one virtue is divided from another it does not follow that one is not more principal than another.

44. *In III Sent.*, d. 33, q. 2, a. 4 [Moos 1068–69].

Summary

Aquinas's account of reason and will in the *Sentences* gives primacy of place to reason. The sense appetites participate in reason according to exemplar analogical causality in which reason formally possesses that which it communicates to the sense appetites. It is important to point out that such causality also implies efficient causality as an exemplar cause cannot cause anything unless there is an efficient cause that actually causes the effect.[45] The emphasis, however, is nevertheless on the formal nature of exemplarity, which is consistent with his metaphysics of participation when writing the *Sentences*.[46] At this point, if we were to choose among the three kinds of participation outlined in the *De hebdomadibus*,[47] we might waffle between the second kind, which includes formal causality, or the third kind, which explicitly refers to efficient causality. For on the one hand, an exemplar cause is a kind of formal cause, but on the other hand there is no exemplar causality without efficient causality. As Aquinas so heavily emphasizes the formal aspects of this exemplar causality, we might be tempted to lean toward the second kind, but I will leave this as an open question for the time being.

I am willing to conclude, however, that he does not simply mean participation here in some loose or vague sense because he so explicitly binds it to exemplar causality. Nor can he mean the first kind of participation—that is, logical participation—because that kind of participation involves the univocal communication of formal content, but this participation clearly involves the analogical communication of formal content. I will have more to say on this after we have examined his mature texts, and I will most fully resolve this in chapter 11.

Be that as it may, the sense appetites receive this exemplar causality and this reception causes a mode in the sense appetite.[48] This mode

---

45. See *In I Sent.*, d. 19, q. 5, a. 2 [Mand 492–93]. There he refers to God as the efficient-exemplar cause (*principio effectivo exemplari*) of the *esse*, the truth, and the goodness of all else, see also ibid., ad 2–3.

46. See Montagnes, *Analogy*, 34–39. I will discuss this further in chapters 10–11.

47. For this discussion, see chapter 5; see text, 122n7.

48. The modal nature of the virtues is particularly interesting and it should also be noted that his account of the gifts of the Holy Spirit in the *Sentences* are also explained in the language of modes. On the gifts see *In III Sent.*, d. 34, q. 1, a. 1, [Moos 1114] and ad 5, as well as a. 2 [Moos 1117–21] and a. 3 [Moos 1123]. It seems to me that some thinkers trying to grasp

then seems to describe the *way* in which the sense appetites operate. The way virtue acts in the sense appetites is by lowering the vehemence of passion, by rendering them docile to reason, and by granting a connatural inclination toward the virtuous act, which produces some kind of judgment. But there is something strange about the account. On the one hand the moral virtues are diminished participations or forms of reason, but on the other hand this diminished form of reason is meant to account for all of these phenomena. How is granting ease and facility, rendering the passions less vehement, making the sense appetites obedient, being an inclination to virtue, and causing a kind of "judgment" to be understood formally in the sense of being the effect of some kind of diminished form of reason? Perhaps an argument could be made for the "judgment" facet, but in my opinion Aquinas would have had to spell this out in far greater detail. Let us now turn to the *De veritate* and see how he tinkers with the details.

---

what Aquinas says about the gifts in the second part of the *ST* turned to the *Sentences* to find some help, and were mistakenly drawn to explain the latter in the modal language of the former. For a discussion including the relevant literature see Angela McKay, "The Infused and Acquired Virtues in Aquinas' Moral Philosophy" (PhD diss., University of Notre Dame, 2004), 42–51. Aquinas does not use this modal language in the late texts to do the work that it does in the *Sentences*.

8

PARTICIPATION IN REASON IN THE *DE VERITATE*

For our purposes, the salient feature of the disputed questions *De veritate* is Aquinas's enormous discussion of volition (qq. 21–24 discuss volition in some detail) and his more developed account (q. 26) of the passions and sensuality (q. 25). The text offers us far more detail on the relation between reason, will, and passion. The *De veritate* does not have any questions or articles directly on moral virtue, but it nevertheless has enough material hidden in various places to let us offer a rather complete account of his views. This chapter will try to mirror the last; hence I will begin with reason and will before moving to the sense appetites and to a discussion of how they may participate in the former.

Will and Intellect

The relation between will and reason in the *De veritate* is quite similar to that of the *Sentences*; however, it is considerably more developed. Aquinas here also divides reason between reason as nature and reason as reason. The former concerns reason's relation to what it naturally knows; the latter concerns reason insofar as it compares.[1] The will, in turn, follows the twofold kinds of judgment.[2] The will as nature natural-

1. *QDV*, q. 26, a. 9 [Leonine 22.3:781.211–18], and ad 4 [Leonine 22.3:782.306–9].
2. *QDV*, q. 22, a. 12 [Leonine 22.3:645.196–207]. See also ll. 177–89, which are interesting

ly follows the first kind of cognition, and will as reason follows reason's indeterminate consideration.[3] The first kind of judgment is absolute or universal and pertains to synderesis, and the second kind of judgment concerns particular actions that pertain to choice.[4]

In general, the apprehended good moves appetite.[5] The intellect directs and rules the will,[6] and it does so by "showing" the will what it should seek.[7] This showing is crucial, for the will cannot will anything without the intellect "showing" it what to will. The simple and absolute judgment provides the end that spurs the remainder of volition. A person, for example, by a simple judgment recognizes that health is good, and thus wills health. From this simple willing of health, a person then wills to deliberate about how to attain health. She then chooses the best way to achieve that end (health) here and now. Thus what is chosen (freely) is for the sake of what is naturally (not-freely) understood to be naturally good.[8]

The intellect by itself is indeterminately related to good and bad, but by the habit of synderesis it is determined as a nature to one, namely, to the good.[9] It is thus that the intellect provides or "shows" the end to the

---

because Aquinas discusses the will's natural tending to its own object apart from any discussion of cognition. But the remainder of the passage shows that he means that this natural motion of the will is precisely to follow the intellect's cognition, that is, the first kind of judgment we have been discussing. For further support of this point see *QDV*, q. 24, a. 1, ad 20 [Leonine 22.3:684.557–67].

3. *QDV*, q. 22, a. 5, ad s.c. 5 [Leonine 22.3:626.357–63].

4. *QDV*, q. 16, a. 2, ad 15 [Leonine 22.2:507.430–34].

5. *QDV*, q. 22, a. 4 [Leonine 22.3:619.96–98].

6. *QDV*, q. 32, a. 6 [Leonine 22.3:667.59–62]: "Voluntas autem non habet rationem primae regulae, sed est regula regulata; dirigitur enim per rationem et intellectum."

7. *QDV*, q. 22, a. 11, ad 5 [Leonine 22.3:640.226–29]: "intellectus regit voluntatem non quasi inclinans eam in id in quod tendit, sed sicut ostendens ei quo tendere debeat."

8. *QDV*, q. 23, a. 4 [Leonine 22.3:662.159–75]: "Sciendum est igitur quod cuiuslibet voluntatis est duplex volitum: unum quidem principale et aliud quasi secundarium. Principale quidem volitum est in quod voluntas fertur secundum suam naturam, eo quod et ipsa voluntas natura quaedam est et naturalem ordinem ad aliquid habet; hoc autem est quod naturaliter voluntas vult, sicut humana voluntas naturaliter appetit beatitudinem, et respectu huius voliti voluntas necessitatem habet cum in ipsum tendat per modum naturae; non enim potest homo velle non esse beatus, aut esse miser. Secundaria vero volita sunt quae ad hoc principale volitum ordinantur sicut in finem. Et ad haec duo volita hoc modo se habet voluntas diversimode, sicut intellectus ad principia quae naturaliter novit, et ad conclusiones quas ex eis elicit." See *QDV*, q. 22, a. 5 [Leonine 22.3:624.193–201].

9. *QDV*, q. 16, a. 3, ad 4 [Leonine 22.2:509.132–37]. On its inclination to the good see ibid., a. 1, ad 7 [Leonine 22.2:505.316–18]. See also ibid., a. 1, ad 11 [Leonine 22.2:506.357–61].

will.[10] In the *De veritate*, the intellect moves the will in the line of final causality by "showing" or "presenting" the end, but the will moves the intellect in the line of efficient causality.[11] Granting this, one immediately wonders how to avoid the problem of circularity, for the will efficiently moves the intellect, which in turn moves the will by presenting to the will what it should efficiently will.[12]

Aquinas answers that the infinite regress stops "in the natural appetite by which the intellect is inclined to its own act."[13] Aquinas is quite explicit in the *De veritate* that every power of the soul is a nature and is inclined to something by a natural appetite,[14] which means that the intellect has its own natural appetite. Furthermore, he says that the natural habit of synderesis always "inclines to the good."[15] As he does say that the apprehended good *moves* the will,[16] Aquinas traces the regress back to the intellect as first in the series of movers.[17]

10. *QDV*, q. 22, a. 12 [Leonine 22.3:642.67–79]: "Ratio autem agendi est forma agentis per quam agit; unde oportet quod insit agenti ad hoc quod agat. Non autem inest secundum esse naturae perfectum, quia hoc habito quiescit motus; sed inest agenti per modum intentionis, nam finis est prior in intentione sed posterior in esse, et ideo finis praeexistit in movente proprie secundum intellectum, cuius est recipere aliquid per modum intentionis et non secundum esse naturae. Unde intellectus movet voluntatem per modum quo finis movere dicitur, in quantum scilicet praeconcipit rationem finis et eam voluntati proponit."

11. See the entirety of ibid., ll. 56–117. For the same view see *SCG* I.72 [Leonine manualis 70]; *SCG* III.26 [Leonine manualis 256].

12. See *QDV*, q. 22, a. 12, obj. 2 [Leonine 22.3:641.8–18].

13. *QDV*, q. 22, a. 12, ad 2 [Leonine 22.3:642.127–30]: "Ad secundum dicendum quod non est procedere in infinitum; statur enim in appetitu naturali quo inclinatur intellectus in suum actum."

14. *QDV*, q. 25, a. 2, ad 8 [Leonine 22.3:734.237–44]: "sed concupiscere appetitu naturali pertinet ad quamlibet potentiam; nam quaelibet potentia animae natura quaedam est et naturaliter in aliquid inclinatur."

15. *QDV*, q. 16, a. 1, ad 7 [Leonine 22.2:505.312–17].

16. *QDV*, q. 22, a. 3 [Leonine 22.3:619.96–98]: "bonum apprehensum est movens appetitum." *QDV*, q. 22, a. 12 [Leonine 22.3:645.196–207]: "Cum enim voluntas moveatur in suum obiectum sibi propositum a ratione, diversimode movetur, secundum quod diversimode sibi proponitur. Unde cum ratio proponit sibi aliquid ut absolute bonum, voluntas movetur in illud absolute, et hoc est velle; cum autem proponit sibi aliquid sub ratione boni ad quod alia ordinentur ut ad finem, tunc tendit in illud cum quodam ordine, qui invenitur in actu voluntatis non secundum propriam naturam sed secundum exigentiam rationis."

17. In the late texts God moves the will directly as the first cause in this context. On God and the will see *QDV*, q. 22, a. 8 [Leonine 22.3:631.67–73], and on God and the agent intellect and synderesis see *QDV*, q. 16, a. 3 [Leonine 22.3:510.44–56]. Neither of these texts (nor *QDP*, q. 3, a. 7, for that matter) speak of God's moving of the will with respect to intellect or his moving the agent intellect with respect to will—neither settles the problem of the infinite regress. I am not firmly committed to this interpretation that I have laid out, but in light of the *Sentences*, where reason seems to be the first mover, I think these texts can at least be read

Also, in the *De veritate*, Aquinas is quite emphatic that man is free because of cognition and reason. His explanation of freedom is primarily that man *knows* the end and can *consider* what can be ordered to this end, and further, that man can judge or consider his own judgments.[18] In either case, the cause of freedom in the *De veritate* is first and foremost cognition and its indetermination.[19] The distinction between the two kinds of volitions, that is, between willing the end absolutely and the means to this end is, as in the *Sentences*, entirely dependent on the operation of reason and is accidental to the will itself.[20] The root of all freedom is reason (*totius libertatis radix est in ratione constituta*),[21] and as such it should not be too surprising that the first principle of motion is intellect.

Moreover, the end is the cause of causes (*causa causarum*), and it is the final cause that is ultimately the cause of efficient causality and not the other way around.[22] Even if they are mutually reinforcing causes, which they undoubtedly are,[23] one is primary. Efficient causality without final causality would be utterly unintelligible and arbitrary for there would be no reason why something efficiently caused this rather than that; in other words, it would not be efficient causality. This is why I think it is fair to say that the buck ultimately stops with the intellect, for the intellect is responsible for the end. This is also why it is highly significant that Aquinas later shifts the *causa causarum* from intellect to will. I will have more to say on this in the next chapter.

After my discussion of reason and will in the commentary on the

---

as consistent with the those texts. The *De veritate* is, of course, chronologically closer to the *Sentences* than to the late texts. But I nevertheless grant that they can be interpreted along the lines of the later texts in which God directly moves the will. I am more committed to the change from the *Sentences* to the later texts than from the *De veritate* to the later texts. For the secondary literature on the question of whether Aquinas changed his mind on free choice see 185n15 in chapter 9.

18. *QDV*, q. 22, a. 4 [Leonine 22.3:620.94–98]: "Quod autem aliquid determinet sibi inclinationem in finem, non potest contingere nisi cognoscat finem, et habitudinem finis in ea quae sunt ad finem: quod est tantum rationis." On judging one's own judgments see *QDV*, q. 24, a. 1 [Leonine 22.3:681.286–93].

19. *QDV*, q. 24, a. 3 [Leonine 22.3:685.69–72]: "tota ratio libertatis ex modo cognitionis dependet. Appetitus enim cognitionem sequitur, cum appetitus non sit nisi boni, quod sibi per vim cognitivam proponitur."

20. *QDV*, q. 24, a. 6 [Leonine 22.3:695.77–83].

21. *QDV*, q. 24, a. 2 [Leonine 22.3:685–86.92–101].

22. *QDV*, q. 28, a. 7 [Leonine 22.3:840.150–60], and q. 22, a. 5 [Leonine 22.3:624.193–96].

23. *QDV*, q. 24, a. 6, ad 5 [Leonine 22.3:696.135–40].

Sentences, I pointed out that there are more a few voluntaristic sounding passages in that text. Because these two texts were written so close together, we should expect to find similar passages in the *De veritate*—and they are there.[24] On the one hand, he wants choices to be rational and thus causally traceable to reason, but on the other hand he seems to recognize that freedom demands that the will cannot be utterly moved or caused by reason without falling into some kind of intellectual determinism. As I see it, Aquinas had not yet fully made up his mind about how to resolve this tension.

Sense and Sensuality

Aquinas's account of the sense appetites is rather similar to the account in the commentary on the *Sentences*, but there are important new details. The entire discussion is framed, as the title of q. 25 suggests, around sensuality, *De sensualitate*. This is helpful because sensuality names the sense appetites precisely insofar as they do *not* participate in reason; it names these powers according to their natural inclination, which is contrary to reason.[25] The forces at work are stark: sensuality always inclines to evil (*ex corruptione fomitis*); synderesis always inclines to good.[26] The *fomes* or sensuality is part of the inheritance of original sin and moral virtue seeks to repair some of this damage, even if it can never be fully repaired.[27]

The fourth article of question 25 asks whether sensuality obeys reason. The sense appetites, he says, are subject to reason in three ways. The first is from the side of reason itself. For reason can consider something under diverse aspects, for example, as pleasurable or repugnant. In this way reason opposes sensuality by means of imagining things as pleasurable or painful depending on how it seems to reason. This is what Aristotle meant when he said that reason persuades "to the best" in *Nic.* I.13.[28] Thus we see here the important role of the internal sense power

---

24. See, e.g., *QDV*, q. 11, a. 3, ad 11 [Leonine 22.2:360.370–82].

25. *QDV*, q. 25, a. 5 [Leonine 22.3:740.164–67], in particular: "sensualitas nominat has vires quantum ad inclinationem naturalem sensui, quae est in contrarium rationi, et non secundum quod participant rationem." See also ibid., a. 4 [Leonine 22.3:737.82–85], and ad 2 [ll. 94–96].

26. *QDV*, q. 16, a. 1, ad 7 [Leonine 22.2:505.313–17].

27. *QDV*, q. 25, a. 7 [Leonine 22.3:743.54–60].

28. *QDV*, q. 25, a. 4 [Leonine 22.3:737.52–62]: "Subduntur autem appetitivae inferiores,

imagination, which stores and puts together sensible images in different combinations. In a few other places Aquinas offers us a helpful example of how this works: "that which is understood by the intellect universally, is formed in the imagination particularly, and thus the inferior appetite is moved, as when the understanding of a believer intellectually grasps future punishments and forms phantasms of them by imagining burning fire and gnawing worms and other things of this sort, from which the passion of fear follows in the sensitive appetite."[29]

Thus reason controls the imagination, which in turn can alter the passion. In other words, whenever you are in the throes of some temptation (and grant intellectually the existence of eternal punishment), just imagine gnawing worms and burning fire and perhaps you will be less inclined toward whatever seems so attractive. There is undoubtedly something true about this, and there are, of course, other things than hell for us to imagine when tempted, for example, the queen of England. It is worth noting that most of what we loosely call "thinking" in fact occurs with phantasms and involves imagination, and for the most part the very act of thinking will shape and alter our passions. In sum, reason can oppose sensuality by imagining something from a different perspective or by simply imagining something else. This is one of the ways that our sense appetites are said to participate in reason. Aquinas will not modify his position on this point.

The second way that sensuality obeys reason is from the side of the will. Aquinas says that the will moves the lower powers by overflowing (*redundat*) upon them. He explains that in powers ordered and connected to one another, they are so related that an intense motion in one of them, especially in a superior power, overflows to a lower power. When the will moves toward something chosen, by way of a kind of overflow, the motion of the sense powers follows suit.[30] Thus when someone wills

---

scilicet irascibilis et concupiscibilis, rationi tripliciter: primo quidem ex parte ipsius rationis: cum enim eadem res sub diversis conditionibus considerari possit et delectabilis et horribilis reddi, ratio opponit sensualitati mediante imaginatione rem aliquam sub ratione delectabilis vel tristabilis secundum quod ei videtur, et sic sensualitas movetur ad gaudium vel tristitiam; et ideo dici Philosophus in I Ethicorum [1102b15] quod ratio persuadet 'ad optima.'"

29. *QDV*, q. 26, a. 3, ad 13 [Leonine 22.3:758–59.444–51]. See also *QDV*, q. 26, a. 6, ad 13 [Leonine 22.3:770.366–72].

30. *QDV*, q. 25, a. 4 [Leonine 22.3:737.62–72]. Cf. *QDV*, q. 26, a. 3, ad 13 [Leonine 22.3:758–59.442–56], and a. 6, ad 13 [Leonine 22.3:770.363–74].

something intensely, the intensity of this volitional motion spills over and causes a motion in our sense appetites, a passion, which we feel sensibly.

The third way that sense appetites are subject to reason is from the side of the motive power executing the act. The motive power does not move the members except at the command of reason. Thus reason prevents or represses (*reprimit*) the sense appetites so that they do not proceed to an exterior act.[31] In other words, here we have a case where it seems that reason and will have not succeeded in altering the passions in the sense appetites—perhaps they are too powerful. Someone experiencing a strong passion for something can simply turn and walk in the other direction, that is, reason can simply (but not easily) command one's bodily members to do something else. In such a case one simply overrides and bypasses the sense appetites altogether. This seems to be what he means by preventing or repressing one's passions.[32] A passion may be powerful, but it does not last long, and not long after moving away, the vehemence of a passion will die down.

In sum, there are three ways that the sense appetites are subject to, or participate in, reason. The last option simply bypasses the sense appetites altogether and thus reason is able to frustrate or repress its passions. But in the first two reason seems to have a direct role in shaping them, either by way of the imagination or by way of an overflow of the will's intensity.

Passions and Merit: Antecedent and Consequent Passions

QDV, q. 25, a. 4, considers whether sensuality obeys reason at all, and Aquinas notes these three ways that it can. The problem is that sensuality by itself names the sense appetites precisely as they do not obey reason, namely, as they are somehow beyond our control. If so, is there any way that they can be controlled? One of the great virtues and developments of the *De veritate* is that Aquinas precisely delineates how passions are and are not moral and voluntary. Merit, for Aquinas, requires that the meritorious (or blameworthy) act is voluntary, simply because

31. *QDV*, q. 25, a. 4 [Leonine 22.3:737.72–80]. For another use of this *reprimere* see ad 2.
32. Cf. ibid., ad 2 [ll. 94–96].

he thinks that we cannot praise or blame acts that are not freely chosen. The question about how the passions can be meritorious is thus the question of how they can be voluntary. Corporal passions are obviously not voluntary, as they are caused by external efficient causes. Animate passions, however, sometimes seem to be voluntary, but sometimes seem not to be so. To put this in its most simple terms, sometimes we seem to be responsible for our passions, but sometimes we seem not to be. Thus, for Aquinas to explain how passions may or may not be meritorious, he has to explain exactly how they are voluntary.

In q. 26, a. 6, he outlines three different ways that passions are related to the will. The first way is as the object of the will, and in such a case passions are meritorious because they are willed or loved. It is not the passion that causes the merit *per se*, but the will of that passion.[33] It would have been helpful if he had spelled this out a bit, but he seems to mean that we can think about a passion and will it. What he means here is unclear, but we need not dwell on it for he leaves it out when he revisits the same question in latter texts.

In the second way, passion is a principle of volition; in the third way, it is the effect of volition.[34] A passion can be a principle of volition by exciting or inclining the will, and this can happen either *per se* or *per accidens*: *per se*, when the passion inclines the will to what is similar to itself, for example, when the passion of concupiscence inclines the will to consent to an attractive object; *per accidens*, when the passion inclines the will to what is contrary to itself, for example, when the passion of concupiscence in a chaste person causes the will to resist that passion.[35]

The third way outlining the relation between will and passion is as an effect of the will. This, as I discussed above, happens through the *redundantia* of the will. Aquinas gives the example of feeling shame.[36] Fear in the will of moral depravity redounds into the sense appetites. Blushing is the somatic effect of this overflow.

Although passion may be either a principle or an effect of the vo-

---

33. *QDV*, q. 26, a. 6 [Leonine 22.3:769.198–203]. See also ll. 224–31, where he notes that passions as the object of the will are meritorious just as gold can be meritorious as an object of the will. For another reference, see ibid., ad 7, ll. 291–97.

34. *QDV*, q. 26, a. 2 [Leonine 22.3:769.224–27].

35. Ibid. [768.203–14].

36. Ibid. [769.217–24].

lition, it is nevertheless first and foremost volition that is meritorious, in particular, free decision. In the following article, a. 7, he explains that passions can be related to free decision in two ways, as preceding or as consequent. Passions are preceding or antecedent when they impel the will to choose something; they are consequent to the will as they redound from it, or even insofar as the will "arouses and brings about these passions of its own accord."[37]

Antecedent passions diminish the meritorious nature of human acts because acts are praiseworthy as they are ordered by reason (not by passion) to the good.[38] Consequent passions, however, do not diminish the meritorious nature of the acts, but rather add to their praiseworthiness, as they have been moderated by the judgment of reason. One cannot help but wonder about the consequent passions of vicious or incontinent acts, but Aquinas here only seems to be thinking of good choices. The more general and important point is that antecedent passions are always dangerous because they distort the discretion of reason,[39] that is, they distort deliberation, which should judge things to be as they are and not on the basis of the impulsion of the sense appetites. Thus sensuality is always naturally opposed to reason, for it distorts reason's deliberation.

This is why Aquinas insists that one of the roles of moral virtue is to lower the vehemence of antecedent passions. Even the virtuous have passions, good and bad ones, foreseen and unforeseen, but they are weak (*debiles*). Moral virtue restrains (*refrenare*) the inferior powers by lowering the vehemence of antecedent passions.[40] This is why sinners are "followers of passion" as Aristotle said (*Nic.* I.3, 1095a4), but the just are never led by passions.[41]

37. Ibid., a. 7 [773.103–11].
38. Ibid., ll. 114–16.
39. Ibid. [Leonine 22.3:773.112–20]: "Secundum igitur quod sunt praecedentes voluntatem, sic diminuunt de ratione laudabilis, quia laudabilis est actus voluntatis secundum quod est per rationem ordinatus in bonum secundum debitam mensuram et modum. Qui quidem modus et mensura non servatur nisi cum actio ex discretione fit; quae quidem discretio non servatur cum homo ex impetu passionis ad aliquid volendum etiamsi sit bonum, provocatur."
40. *QDV*, q. 26, a. 8 [Leonine 22.3:776.146–65]. Aquinas explains a few lines later (175–77) that in Eden there was nothing which could be apprehended as harmful, so there were no bad passions like fear, pain, or anger. Adam would have been attracted to the forbidden fruit prior to his decision to eat it, as it must have been very attractive indeed, but there were undoubtedly many other attractive things to eat and the passion would not have been so vehement that it could have distorted his judgment.
41. See ibid. and *QDV*, q. 25, a. 7, ad 4 [Leonine 22.3:744.91–94]: "temperatus, secundum

Making the Bad Seem Good

Perhaps the best passage discussing the role of passion, moral virtue, and judgment is hidden away in a discussion on whether free decision in the damned can be immutably fixed in evil (q. 24, a. 10). In the case of humans, he notes, as their natural appetite is for the good, no one sins except because of some species of an apparent good. For example, the fornicator knows in general that fornication is bad, but he nevertheless does it because he deems it to be good for him right now.[42] Thus one must find some kind of cause for the appearance (*species*) which makes this *particular* action seem to be good and choiceworthy. Here he offers three such causes which make something that should not be chosen seem to be good.

The first such cause is a passion. It is passion's impetus that cuts off the judgment of reason from judging in particular what it holds universally and habitually. Thus a person follows the passion's momentum and chooses what that passion inclines toward as if it were a *per se* good.[43] In other words, passions somehow make things seem to be good in themselves and choiceworthy. But because Aquinas thinks that choosing in this way is a sin, he explains how it is possible not to make such a choice. He argues that a person is not determined by passion to so choose because he has right understanding of the end, and because he is so disposed toward the end, he can resist the impetus of the passion.[44] In other words, because an agent knows universally or habitually (by means of synderesis) that fornication is wrong, it is possible to recognize that this particular act is an act of fornication and thus resist the temptation to fornicate. Aquinas wants to emphasize that because we have such universal knowledge of our ends (with which can also know that fornication is incompatible), it is at least possible to avoid acting according to a passion's particular thrust.

In *QDV*, q. 22, a. 9, he approaches the same problem from a different angle. He explains that passion only moves the will from the side of an object, that is, as what is presented to the will by the intellect. Because

---

philosophum, non caret omnino concupiscentiis, sed concupiscentiis vehementibus, quales possunt inesse continenti."

42. *QDV*, q. 24, a. 10 [Leonine 22.3:706.232–39].

43. Ibid., ll. 240–46. For the point that even a fornicator seeks a *per se* good, albeit according to sense, see *QDV*, q. 22, a. 1, ad 6 [Leonine 22.3:615.286–92].

44. Ibid., ll. 264–77.

all actions concern particulars, a good apprehended by universal reason cannot move except by means of some particular apprehensions. In simpler terms, understanding something universally will not help us do particular things here and now, we also must grasp at least some particulars to help us apply universal considerations to particular actions. And it is in the realm of particular apprehension that the passions wreak havoc. Sometimes passions are so strong that they completely bind the particular apprehensions and as a result the will is moved by them and sets aside or simply misses the good that universal reason presents.[45] The passions here seem to so consume the acts of the inferior powers[46] that higher considerations are simply tabled or ignored. In other words, it is difficult not to think about fornication when this particular sexual pleasure is beckoning. It is difficult, Aquinas thinks, but not impossible.

The second cause of the appearance (*species*) that makes something appear good is the inclination of a habit. For a habit is a kind of nature for the one possessing it; according to Aristotle custom is a second nature, and according to Cicero virtue consents to reason (*consentit rationi*) as a nature. The habit of vice inclines as a kind of nature to what is suitable or fitting to itself (*sibi conveniens*), and thus to the one who has the habit of voluptuousness, the good seems to be that which agrees with that habit (*luxuriae convenit*) and is as it were connatural to it. That is why Aristotle said "as each person is, so does the end appear to him," *qualis unusquisque est talis et finis videtur ei.*[47] In other words, vices also make things which should not be chosen seem to be good.

But once again, because vice is a sin, he has to explain how it is possible to act otherwise. Free choices, Aquinas argues, are not compelled by a habit because no matter how corrupt by vice any particular power may be, there will remain some rectitude in another power by which a person can consider and do what is contrary to the corrupted power. For example, someone whose concupiscible appetite is corrupted by voluptuousness may be incited by the irascible appetite to doing some arduous good opposed to this soft vice.[48] Perhaps Aquinas is here thinking about the

---

45. *QDV*, q. 22, a. 9, ad 6 [Leonine 22.3:634.184–209].

46. *QDV*, q. 24, a. 1 [Leonine 22.3:700.117–27].

47. *QDV*, q. 24, a. 10 [Leonine 22.3:706.246–58]. Cf. *QDV*, q. 5, a. 1 [Leonine 22.1:139.137–47].

48. *QDV*, q. 24, a. 10 [Leonine 22.3:706.277–90].

possibility of moral progress from vice, for instance, when overcoming one's intemperance is an arduous good requiring great irascible effort, or perhaps he means a more occurrent good act, say when an intemperate person forgoes having a drink in order to help someone.[49] One could think of all kinds of scenarios, but the general point is that even though vice causes something to seem to be better than it is, because this happens in one part of the soul, the other parts are not completely consumed by it and can overcome it.

Thus we see that both habit and passion can make things seem to be otherwise than they are in particular and this obstructs and deflects synderesis, which always inclines to the good but in a general and universal way.[50] And furthermore, although this may happen in one part of the soul, and although this drains the soul's resources from the other parts of the soul, there is still enough power, so to speak, in the other powers of the soul to overcome the trouble.

The third cause of this appearance (*species*) is a false judgment of reason about some particular thing one might choose. This can happen either from passion or the inclination of habit, that is, the two just discussed; or, again, from an ignorance of a universal precept, for example, that fornication is not a sin.[51] But it is always possible to avoid this error, says Aquinas, because a person grasps this rationally, that is, by way of deliberation (*per viam inquisitionis et collationis*), and thus it is possible to think contrary thoughts and not sin.[52] In other words, the non-deterministic nature of reason's deliberation means that we can always consider something from a different perspective and that we can even consider our own considerations and thus we are not bound to choose according to a false consideration of reason.

In q. 24, a. 12, Aquinas further elaborates on the second of these

---

49. For a discussion of the arduous progress from intemperance see Tobias Hoffmann, "Aquinas on the Moral Progress of the Weak Willed," in *Das Problem der Willensschwäche im mittelalterlichen Denken / The Problem of Weakness of Will in Medieval Thought*, ed. Tobias Hofmann, Jörn Müller, and Matthias Perkams, Recherches de Théologie et Philosophie médiévales Bibliotheca 8 (Leuven: Peeters, 2006), 241–43.

50. See also *QDV*, q. 16, a. 3 [Leonine 22.2:510.65–73], and ad 1 [510–11.79–82].

51. *QDV*, q. 24, a. 10 [Leonine 22.3:706.258–63]. See Hoffmann, *Conscience and Synderesis*, 256–58, for a discussion about this. For Aquinas, synderesis is very general and universal, and one can reason from it to the conclusion that fornication is evil, but it follows from the first principles and so mistakes can be made.

52. *QDV*, q. 24, a. 10 [Leonine 22.3:707.290–96].

three, namely, how habits, in particular the moral virtues, influence our choices. Aquinas here distinguishes between the role of a passion and a habit prior to choice. Both can be prior to choice and both can incite someone toward sin. He makes Aristotle's point that courage is seen more clearly when a person is fearless and unperturbed by sudden threats than by foreseen threats. The more an action follows from preparation, the less it follows from habit. For when something is known beforehand, someone may choose it without a habit simply by thinking; but things that happen suddenly occur only according to habit. This does not mean, however, that an action that is by habit is altogether without deliberation, as virtue is a habit of choice (*habitus electivus*), but it means that the person who has the habit already somehow has the determined end of his choice. Thus whenever something happens which is suitable to that end (*conveniens illi fini*), it is immediately chosen, unless it is impeded by some better and more attentive deliberation.[53]

This is very interesting because the habit of moral virtue already somehow has the end of choice present in it. But the passage almost makes it seems that in the case of a sudden threat the courageous man acts by habit apart from deliberation. The problem with such an interpretation is that it makes the sense appetites essentially rational and not rational by participation, that is, it makes it seem like the habit actually has some kind of rational faculty of choice by itself. But the sense power's role in choice and deliberation need not be limited to what the sense powers themselves can do, for habits can transcend their powers. In other words, whatever Aquinas may mean here (see chapter 12 for detailed analysis of this topic), sense powers and habits are capable of more than sense powers by themselves, and thus there is no reason to limit the role of the virtues to what the sense powers are capable of doing by themselves.

For further corroboration of this point we can turn to q. 24, a. 4, ad 9, in which Aquinas explains that there are two reasons that powers need habits. Either it is because the operation of a power exceeds the power of that potency (*vim potentiae*), or because the operation exceeds the power of the whole nature. The latter kind of operation is supernatural and requires the habit of grace. The former kind of operations are not

53. *QDV*, q. 24, a. 12 [Leonine 22.3:716.335–51].

beyond the power of human nature, but only of a particular power or potency. These perfections, namely the acquired virtues, do not exceed human nature, but they exceed the power of the sense appetites. "Thus it is necessary that that which belongs to the superior power, namely reason, is impressed in them and that the very stamp of reason formally perfects the moral virtues in the lower powers."[54]

Summary

Note that as in the commentary on the *Sentences* the emphasis in the *De veritate* is on the power of *reason*. But unlike the *Sentences*, there is hardly any discussion of moral virtue as a mode.[55] In the last passage mentioned above he says that reason is formally impressed in the sense appetites, and while we can certainly read this as being compatible with the more detailed account of exemplarity in the *Sentences*, there simply is not enough to explicitly connect the dots. Aquinas uses the language of formal causality to mean all kinds of things in many different contexts, and I will not try to force the connection without more evidence.

But the details of how reason, will, and emotion are related to each other add much to Aquinas's *Sentences* commentary. Sensuality names the sense powers as they are naturally, that is, as they do not participate in reason and are contrary to reason. He explains in far greater detail how sensuality can obey reason, and within this context he develops more fully how passion, habit, and false judgments make things which should not be chosen seem good, and how such seemings put pressure on choices. The distinction between antecedent and consequent passions is particularly important for it enables us to see how passion is related to merit and morality, and it also enables us to explain with much more precision what exactly Aquinas thinks moral virtue does to passion. Vehement antecedent passions are contrary to reason because they obscure deliberation. Moral virtue lowers the vehemence of antecedent passion so that reason informed by prudence may properly do its work. After the judgment of reason has run its course, consequent passions may follow

---

54. *QDV*, q. 24, a. 4, ad 9 [Leonine 22.3:691.236–60].

55. What little discussion there is in *QDV*, q. 26, a. 7, co., and ad 2 [Leonine 22.3:773–74] means rather that that someone without virtue may do some good act, but he does not do it in the *way* that a virtuous agent does. But then again, Aquinas did not say too much about moral virtue in the *De veritate*.

reason's determination and make the execution prompt, pleasurable, and passionate (whatever passion may be appropriate).[56] Moral virtue thus both "orders and represses" passion, as he puts it.[57] But where his *Sentences* commentary offers a rather metaphysical explanation of this participation, the *De veritate* is silent. This is not an oversight on Aquinas's part—it's simply that the *De veritate* is shorter and covers a more limited range of topics.

56. See, e.g., *QDV*, q. 26, a. 7 [Leonine 22.3:774.193–200].
57. *QDV*, q. 25, a. 7, ad 2 [Leonine 22.3:744.80–84]. The following is a helpful summarizing passage: *QDV*, q. 14, a. 4 [Leonine 22.2:450.128–48].

9

PARTICIPATING PARTS
IN LATE TEXTS

After having considered Aquinas's position on my topic in his commentary on Peter Lombard's *Sentences* (1251–56) and the *De veritate* (1256–59), let us now turn to consider his thought from the later period, primarily in the second part of the *Summa* (1268–72), the *De malo* (1266–72), and *De virtutibus in communi* (1271–72). As I mentioned, I will sparingly use his commentary on the *Nicomachean Ethics* (1271–72), and only when there is evidence that he is speaking in his own voice and not simply explaining Aristotle's position. Granting the great bulk of these texts, the large scholarly attention they have received, and the fact that they represent Aquinas's mature thought, I will devote two chapters to them. I begin by discussing the relevant participating parts, and then in chapter 10 I will consider this participation from a metaphysical and ethical perspective.

Will and Intellect

As the rational appetite, the will always follows reason. Everything willed is first understood, but it is crucial to appreciate the precise nature of this following. Aquinas explains this by noting that a power can be moved in two ways. It can either be moved on the part of the subject or on the part of the object. On the part of the subject, an agent can exercise the power of sight by opening and closing his eyes, for example. On the part of the object, however, the thing seen specifies or determines

181

the form of the object, for example, one sees something black or white.[1] It is in this latter way, on the part of the object, that everything willed is first understood.

Reason is the first principle of choice by way of specifying the formal content of the object of the will; however, the will is the first principle not only in the line of efficient causality, but also in the line of final causality.[2] Thus reason and will move each other along different but mutually reinforcing causal lines: reason moves the will by presenting the formal content of volition, but the will simultaneously moves reason in the line of efficient and final causality.

In the case of specification (the intellect's role in specifying the object willed), the object understood that moves the will is the good apprehended as suitable (*bonum conveniens apprehensum*). If the intellect proposes something to the will which is good but not suitable (for that person), then that object will not necessarily move the will. Because deliberation and choice only concern particulars, the good apprehended must also be good and suitable in particular (not only universally good). If, however, the intellect understands something as good and suitable in every possible way that it can consider the object, then the will is necessarily moved in the line of specification, although it is still free in the line of exercise as it may simply not will this good. If, however, the object is not good in every possible way that it can be considered, then the will will not necessarily be moved by it in the order of specification, for one could always consider the object in some less favorable light, which would make it less choiceworthy.[3] As far as I understand this, the only possible particular object of choice that is so good that it cannot be considered bad or deficient in some way is the beatific vision of God himself, and because this is not something we can choose in this life, human choice is always free along the lines of specification. In simpler terms, the understanding of something that can be chosen never compels choice.

---

1. *QDM*, q. 6 [Leonine 23:148.308–19]. Cf. *ST* I-II, q. 9, a. 1 [St. Paul 600].

2. *QDM*, q. 6 [Leonine 23.148:326–31]: "Si autem consideremus obiecta voluntatis et intellectus, inveniemus quod obiectum intellectus est primum et precipuum in genere cause formalis, est enim eius obiectum ens et verum; set obiectum voluntatis est primum et precipuum in genere causae finalis, nam eius obiectum est bonum." Cf. *ST* I-II, q. 9, a. 3, co., and ad 3 [St. Paul 601–2].

3. *QDM*, q. 6 [Leonine 23:149–50.418–49]; *ST* I-II, q. 10, a. 2 [St. Paul 606].

Of course, what is presupposed here is that the will can and does efficiently will and move the intellect to consider an object from different perspectives.[4]

This brings us to the will's role in efficient and final causality. Aquinas argues that because the end pertains to the will, it moves all other things that are for the sake of the end; in this way the will moves itself and all of the other powers.[5] For example, the will moves the intellect to think.[6] Concerned to show that the motion of the will does not violate the act/potency axiom (everything that is moved is moved by another), Aquinas explains that when it is said that the will moves itself, this does not mean that the will is in potency and act at the same time and in the same respect.[7] He offers a concrete example. From the desire for health, the will begins to deliberate about how best to attain health. When the person has concluded that he ought to take medicine, he then wills to take medicine. The problem of the infinite regress arises at the level of deliberation. If the will wills the intellect to deliberate, does the will to deliberate require a prior deliberation of the intellect? In other words, if one must deliberate in order to will to deliberate, we are trapped in an infinite series where the will moves the intellect which in turn moves the will, *ad infinitum*.[8]

---

4. *QDM*, q. 6, ad 15 [Leonine 23:152.604–19]: "illa causa que facit voluntatem aliquid velle [i.e., the object from reason], non oportet quod ex necessitate hoc faciat, quia potest per ipsam voluntatem impedimentum praestari, vel removendo talem considerationem que inducit eum ad volendum, vel considerando oppositum, scilicet quod hoc quod proponitur ut bonum secundum aliquid non est bonum." Cf. *ST* I-II, q. 9, a. 1 [St. Paul 600].

5. *QDM*, q. 6 [Leonine 23:149.343–52]: "Si autem consideremus motus potentiarum animae ex parte exercitii actus, sic principium motionis est ex voluntate. Nam semper potentia ad quam pertinet finis principalis movet ad actum potentiam ad quam pertinet id quod est ad finem, sicut militaris movet frenorum factricem ad operandum. Et hoc modo voluntas movet se ipsam et omnes alias potentias." Cf. *ST* I-II, q. 9, a. 1 [St. Paul 600].

6. *QDM*, q. 6 [Leonine 23:149.343–52].

7. Ibid., ll. 360–65: "Quantum ergo ad exercitium actus, primo quidem manifestum est quod voluntas movetur a seipsa: sicut enim movet alias potentias, ita et se ipsam movet. Nec propter hoc sequitur quod voluntas secundum idem sit in potentia et in actu." Cf. *ST* I-II, q. 9, a. 4, ad 1 [St. Paul 602].

8. *QDM*, q. 6 [Leonine 23:149.370–86]: "Sicut per hoc quod vult sanitatem, movet se ad volendum sumere potionem: ex hoc enim quod vult sanitatem, incipit consiliari de his quae conferunt ad sanitatem, et tandem determinato consilio vult accipere potionem; sic igitur voluntatem accipiendi potionem precedit consilium, quod quidem procedit ex voluntate volentis consiliari. Cum igitur voluntas se consilio moveat, consilium autem est inquisitio quedam non demonstrativa set ad opposita viam habens, non ex necessitate voluntas se ipsam movet. Sed cum voluntas non semper voluerit consiliari, necesse est quod ab aliquo moveatur ad hoc quod

Aquinas's solution to this problem is that in the line of exercise or efficient causality the will is first moved efficiently by an exterior (i.e., not the intellect) impulse or instinct (*instinctus*) from God.[9] Thus God moves the will by an instinct, which is the same as saying that the will is naturally moved to will health—that is the first moment of volition along the lines of exercise and finality.[10] This reduction of the will from potency to act or whether or not the will actually wills is reduced to God and nature, as I discussed in chapter 4.[11] This first motion of the will, which is natural and caused by God, is not present in his earlier texts. His first explicit statement of God's role here is in *SCG* III (1263–65).[12]

velit consiliari; et si quidem a seipsa, necesse est iterum quod motum voluntatis precedat consilium et consilium praecedat actus voluntatis." See *ST* I-II, q. 9, a. 4 [St. Paul 602].

9. *QDM*, q. 6 [Leonine 23:149.386–91]: "et cum hoc in infinitum procedere non possit, necesse est ponere quod quantum ad primum motum voluntatis moveatur voluntas cuiuscumque non semper actu volentis ab aliquo exteriori, cuius instinctu voluntas velle incipiat." And ll. 406–10: "Relinquitur ergo, … quod id quod primo movet voluntatem et intellectum sit aliquid supra voluntatem et intellectum, scilicet Deus." See also *QDM*, q. 16, a. 8 [Leonine 23:321.235–38]; *ST* I-II, q. 9, a. 4 [St. Paul 602], and q. 17, a. 5, ad 3 [St. Paul 629]. For a discussion of how to translate *instinctus* see n12 below.

10. *ST* I-II, q. 9, a. 4 [St. Paul 602]: "Sed quia non semper sanitatem actu voluit, necesse est quod inciperet velle sanari, aliquo movente."

11. On the connection between God and nature see 88–97, *ST* I-II, q. 9, a. 6 [St. Paul 604], and a. 4, ad 1 [St. Paul 602].

12. *SCG* III.89 [Leonine manualis 331–32], written in 1260–65. Cf. also *SCG* III.67 and I.68, as well as *QDP*, q. 3, a. 7, ad 13–14 [Marietti 452], written in 1265–66. Around this time a translation of the *Liber de bona fortuna* became available; this text includes an important part of Aristotle's *Eudemian Ethics* VII.14, 1248a25–32 (this edition of the *Aristoteles Latinus* is still in progress), which is a crucial text on this topic of how God moves the will. For the dating of this chapter in the *SCG* see Torrell, *Person and Work*, 102. For the importance of these texts see Fabro, "Le '*Liber de bona fortuna*' de l' '*Ethique à Eudème*' d'Aristote et la dialectique de la divine Providence chez Saint Thomas," *Revue Thomiste* 88 (1988): 556–72; *Participation et Causalité*, 377–409 and 488–508. See also especially Brian J. Shanley, "Divine Causation and Human Freedom in Aquinas," *American Catholic Philosophical Quarterly* 72 (1998): 113 and n40. Shanley argues that it was only after reading this text from the *Eudemian Ethics* in the *Liber de bona fortuna* (which took place after *SCG* III.9) that Aquinas solves the problem of the infinite regress between will and intellect by appealing to God as cause. See also Wippel, *Metaphysical Themes in Thomas Aquinas*, 258–62, and *Metaphysical Thought*, 449–52. See the key texts in *QDP*, q. 3, a. 7, and *ST* I, q. 105, a. 5, and note the distinction between primary and secondary causality; see Shanley's discussion of this point in "Divine Causation." See also Garrigou-Lagrange, *God: His Existence and His Nature*, trans. Dom Bede Rose (St. Louis, Mo.: Herder, 1934), 1:268–69. The Latin term Aquinas uses (*instinctus*) can be translated into English as instinct or impulse. Garrigou-Lagrange and Wippel translate this term as impulse (see the passages just referred to), Shanley ("Divine Causation," 113) translates it as impulse or instinct. One reason to translate it as impulse is to avoid excessively implying animal instinctual motions. There are undoubtedly many passages in which Aquinas contrasts the natural *instinctus* of animals with man's free and rational motion, e.g., *In I*

The subject/object distinction in the *Sentences* is different.[13] In that text the question of how the subject moves is strictly a question of materiality or immateriality—efficient and final causality are not brought up.

If granting efficient causality to the will is a development on Aquinas's part, what is also new is that he places final causality on the side of the will rather than the intellect, which he had done in the *De veritate*.[14] One might ask whether there is any real difference between granting the will causal efficacy in the realm of final causality and granting reason causal efficacy in the line of formal causality. Is it not the intellect, which understands health to be good (in the light of its naturally known first principles of practical reasoning), that in fact "presents" or gives the final cause to the will? Is it not precisely the exact same "form" or idea that reason grasps as good that becomes the end of the will? This is clearly the teaching of the *De veritate*. But how are these latter texts different?[15]

Sent., d. 9, q. 2, a. 2; *In II Sent.*, d. 20, q. 2, a. 2, ad 5; *ST* I, q. 83, a. 1, etc. When God moves the will efficiently by his *instinctus* this is a strictly immaterial motion (as the will is immaterial) and in that sense it is not animal; cf. *ST* I, q. 115, a. 4. However, his use of *instinctus* in these two contexts (of certain animal motions and of God's moving of the will) nevertheless have much in common, namely, that both are motions or efficient causes (*ad unum*) caused by an external source; see *ST* I-II, q. 50, a. 3, and *ST* I, q. 19, a. 10. Although they are on different levels, i.e., the material (or at least partly material) and immaterial, they both describe being efficiently moved by an external source. It seems to me that an animal's instinctual motion is the first and primary use of the word, but that it is perfectly legitimate to use the same word for these natural (not as material but as determined by nature or God) movements of the will. Aquinas even uses the word in the highly theological and spiritual context of the gifts of the Holy Spirit, which are precisely dispositions by which a person is made able to follow the *instinctus* of the Holy Spirit. See *ST* I-II, q. 68, a. 1 (and ad 3), a. 2, a. 4; *In III Sent.*, d. 35, q. 2, a. 4, qc. 1. In any case, when I translate it as instinct, I do not mean it in exactly the same way as an animal instinct. I would rather keep the same word, as it is in Latin, although it means somewhat different things in different contexts.

13. See *In II Sent.*, d. 25, q. 1, a. 2 (see text, 135n29 in chapter 6).

14. *QDV*, q. 22, a. 12 [Leonine 22.3:642.76–79]: "Unde intellectus movet voluntatem per modum quo finis movere dicitur, in quantum scilicet praeconcipit rationem finis et eam voluntati proponit." See 168n10 in chapter 8.

15. For a helpful summary of the debate about whether or not Aquinas developed his thinking on will see Daniel Westberg, "Did Aquinas Change His Mind about the Will?," *The Thomist* 58 (1994): 41–60; Yul Kim, "A Change in Thomas Aquinas's Theory of the Will," *American Catholic Philosophical Quarterly* 82 (2008): 221–36. See also Gallagher, "Thomas Aquinas on the Causes of Human Choice" (PhD diss., The Catholic University of America, 1989), 193–207; Kent, *Virtues of the Will*, 121. Lottin originally argued that Aquinas radically moved from an intellectualist to a voluntarist position; see Lottin, "Libre arbitre et liberté depuis saint Anselme jusqu'à la fin du XIIIe siècle," in *Psychologie et morale aux XIIe et XIIIe siècles* (Brussels: Gembloux, 1957) 1:260–61 and n4. See also Westberg's critique of Lottin in *Right Practical Reason: Aristotle, Action, and Prudence in Aquinas* (Oxford: Oxford University Press, 1994), 59.

The object of the will is the good apprehended as suitable, that is, as it is apprehended by *reason* as suitable or good.[16] Such apprehensive causality, we might say, provides the formal content of volition, but neither the efficient nor the final causality for it. Although the will is a moved mover, moved by the understood object, Aquinas nevertheless insists that the will is an active rather than a passive power.[17]

As I previously mentioned, for Aquinas, there is no such thing as efficient causality without final causality, for without a final cause there is no way to explain why this rather than that was efficiently caused, that is, without an intention or a final cause, efficient causality would be entirely arbitrary or *per accidens*.[18] Thus if God is truly the first efficient cause of a volition then he must also provide the final cause.[19]

I would like to make the simple and related point that not all of the will's volitions are free,[20] but some are natural. Let us consider why he calls them natural. The general rule is quite simple: natural motion is *per se*, that is, it is not by chance but by some intention, and thus it is intelligible because it comes from some intellect. If an agent's own intellect cannot account for the intelligibility of the motion, it must come from another intellect. For Aquinas, the fact that natural things lacking

16. See for example *ST* I, q. 82, a. 2, ad 1 [St. Paul 393]; q. 8, a. 1 [St. Paul 598]; q. 9, aa. 1–2 [St. Paul 600–601]; *QDM*, q. 6 [Leonine 23:149.418–21]; etc.

17. The will is an active principle; *ST* I-II, q. 10, a. 4 [St. Paul 607]; *QDM*, q. 6 [Leonine 23:148.272–74]. It was very important for Aquinas to distance himself from the position that the will was simply a moved mover (*QDM*, q. 6, a. 7), as it appears to be in Aristotle's *De anima*. For then sin is simply an intellectual mistake. Most recently he has been accused of holding this by Thomas Williams, "The Libertarian Foundations of Scotus's Moral Philosophy," *The Thomist* 62 (1998): 199–200. Of course, he was accused of this a few years after his death as well. See Wippel, "Thomas Aquinas and the Condemnation of 1277," *The Modern Schoolman* 72 (1995): 255–61; Kent, *Virtues of the Will*, 110–29. The will is a moved mover along two different lines. On the one had the will is moved by the object apprehended as good and on the other hand the will is moved directly by God/nature as the unmoved mover. These two kinds of passivity are not the same, as reason's apprehension of health as good does not always move us to will to deliberate.

18. *ST* I-II, q. 1, a. 2 [St. Paul 557]. Cf. *SCG* III.2 [Leonine manualis 228]. For a helpful discussion of the need for final causality see also *De princ.* 3 [Leonine 43:41.120–42]. Of course, it is presupposed that "natura est causa agens per se" (*In IX Metaph.* 6 [Marietti 440]). Also see Klubertanz, "St. Thomas' treatment of the Axiom *omne agens agit propter finem*," in *An Etienne Gilson Tribute*, ed. C. J. O'Neill (Milwaukee, Wis.: Marquette University Press, 1959), 101–17.

19. This does not mean that there are no created final causes. All final causes qua created are caused by God in some way, but these are directly caused by God in a different way than the others. See *QDP*, q. 3, a. 7 [Marietti 57–58].

20. *ST* I-II, q. 13, a. 3 [St. Paul 615], and ad 1; q. 14, a. 2 [St. Paul 619].

cognition act for the sake of an end (always or for the most part) implies that they do not act by chance but by some intention or intelligence.[21] This intentionality or natural inclination comes from the first cause of that nature, namely, God, who efficiently impresses this order or inclination upon it (in the manner of a natural appetite that follows such a nature or form).[22] Thus irrational animals can act in rational or prudent[23] ways because God efficiently causes their natures and natural inclinations by which they act for the sake of a final cause. Thus the end for the sake of which they act is caused by God's intelligence and will, and natural motions are not rational in the sense that they need to be traced back to the created agent's own reason. Man is free because choice always requires his own cognition, but it does not follow that the entirety of man's choice or volition must be fully explained by his own cognition. Some of man's volitions, according to Aquinas, are natural in the sense that they are not causally reducible to his own cognitions.

Because efficient causality without final causality would be arbitrary, volitions that are traced to God as the first efficient cause must have some kind of finality or intentionality that is also ultimately caused by God. In other words, these natural or instinctual volitions carry an intelligible content that has not been provided by the reason of the individual acting person. Thus it seems to me that one could call this first natural motion or efficient cause of the will instinctual rather than intellectual (granting that one is mindful of the disanalogy).[24] This motion is

21. This is Aquinas's fifth way of *ST* I, q. 2, a. 3 [St. Paul 14]. There is a more developed version of this argument in *QDV*, q. 5, a. 2 [Leonine 22.1:143–44.120–84]. For a discussion of the latter text see Wippel, *Metaphysical Thought*, 410–13, and for the former see 480–85. See also *SCG* II.63 [Leonine manualis 296] (the fourth argument).

22. *ST* I-II, q. 27, a. 2, ad 3 [St. Paul 673]: "amor naturalis, qui est in omnibus rebus, causatur ex aliqua cognitione, non quidem in ipsis rebus naturalibus existente, sed in eo qui naturam instituit, ut supra dictum est." *In I Physic.* 15 [Marietti 68]: "Sciendum est enim quod omne quod appetit aliquid, vel cognoscit ipsum et se ordinat in illud; vel tendit in ipsum ex ordinatione et directione alicuius cognoscentis, sicut sagitta tendit in determinatum signum ex directione et ordinatione sagittantis. Nihil est igitur aliud appetitus naturalis quam ordinatio aliquorum secundum propriam naturam in suum finem." At times he traces the cause of the natural inclinatio back to the cause of generation, but if one follows the causal chain backwards up through the heavenly bodies the cause of generation is ultimately reduced back to God. As secondary causes, of course, one can attribute the cause of the inclination to the *causa generans*. For more texts on God as the cause of natural appetite see *ST* I, q. 60, a. 1, ad 3 [St. Paul 283]; *ST* I-II, q. 26, a. 1 [St. Paul 670]; *In I Ethic.* 1 [Leonine 47:5.165–73] and 2 [Leonine 47:8.44–47].

23. *ST* I-II, q. 13, a. 2, ad 3 [St. Paul 615].

24. For a discussion of this disanalogy see 184n12. That this movement is caused by an

analogous to the manner in which animals cannot give a reason for their intentional and intelligible action, but it occurs on a spiritual plane.

It should be no surprise that the intellect understands everything to be good that the will naturally wills as good.[25] God, of course, is the author of both the will's nature and is the first cause of its instinctual movements and synderesis, and so it would be unthinkable that there be any contradiction between the two. Furthermore the priority of this natural inclining need not be temporally prior; the priority concerns the kind of causality. Thus, in some texts, Aquinas describes the apprehension of reason as being temporally first,[26] but this does not preclude that God by a natural priority along the lines of final and efficient causality moves the will toward what was apprehended as good.

As the *causa causarum* is the final cause, and in particular the final cause is the cause of the efficient cause's action, to claim that the intellect's formal causality provides the final causality is to place final causality on the side of intellect, as it was in the *De veritate*. Moreover, if one says that the intellect provides the final cause and if the final cause is the cause of the efficient cause's action, then the intellect is ultimately the cause of the efficient cause of the will as well. That is, in the exercise-specification distinction, the intellect's specification ultimately causes the will's exercise. But in the later texts Aquinas does not grant this, as by squarely placing final causality in the will and by saying that the will is efficiently moved by an external source, he has cut off reason from causing the will's exercise and from providing the final cause in free decision. Thus the exercise-specification distinction is somewhat different in the *De veritate* than it is in the later texts.

The way I understand this distinction in the later texts is as follows:

---

instinctus; see *ST* I-II, q. 9, a. 4 [St. Paul 602]: "Et si quidem ipsa moveret seipsam ad volendum, oportuisset quod mediante consilio hoc ageret, ex aliqua voluntate praesupposita. Hoc autem non est procedere in infinitum. Unde necesse est ponere quod in primum motum voluntatis voluntas prodeat ex instinctu alicuius exterioris moventis, ut Aristoteles concludit in quodam capitulo Ethicae Eudemicae." See also *ST* I-II, q. 9, a. 5, ad 2 [St. Paul 603]; q. 17, a. 5, ad 3 [St. Paul 629]; q. 6, a. 1, ad 2 [St. Paul 589]. On his use of this in animals see q. 12, a. 5, and ad 3 [St. Paul 613].

25. *ST* I-II, q. 94, a. 2 [St. Paul 955]: "omnia illa ad quae homo habet naturalem inclinationem, ratio naturaliter apprehendit ut bona." For a full-length article on this passage see Steven Brock, "Natural Inclination and The Intelligibility of the Good in Thomistic Natural Law," *Vera Lex* 6, nos. 1–2 (2005): 57–78.

26. For example, *ST* I-II, q. 15, a. 1 [St. Paul 623].

reason is ultimately responsible for specifying the object willed, that is, *what* is willed, but the will (not the intellect) is ultimately responsible for the end or *why* it is willed. For example, I choose to take medicine (*what* I will, which I have deliberated about) because I will health (*why* I will it, the end of choice).[27] If someone asks why I wish to be healthy, I can answer that it is because I understand health to be good, and this is undoubtedly true; without some knowledge of the end we cannot be said to cause our own actions.[28] But there is also something more natural and instinctual about my attraction to health and happiness than intellectual understanding. There are many things that we understand to be good, but not all of them start the process of deliberation (in other words, not all understood goods reduce deliberation from potency to act). Moreover, sometimes the same understood good (e.g., health) begins deliberation and sometimes it does not. The answer or cause, according to Aquinas, is not to be found in understanding or reason, but in the will and, in particular, God's efficiently moving it by way of *instinctus*.[29] Thus, compared to the *Sentences*, the will has a certain spontaneity or increased causal role *vis-à-vis* the intellect. In the *Sentences* the will's natural volitions are entirely accidental to the will itself and reducible to reason. In the *Summa* and the *De malo* the will's natural volitions are grounded in the will's rootedness in man's nature and are not simply traceable to reason.[30]

27. See *ST* I-II, q. 9, a. 6, ad 3 [St. Paul 604]. Here it is argued that God moves the will universally to the good and through reason man determines himself to will this or that particular good. Ultimately, the question *why* can always be answered because it is good. But the will does not only naturally will the good in general; it also wills certain less universal goods without which this general good cannot be had, e.g., happiness, health, existence, life, etc. See *ST* I-II, q. 10, a. 2, ad 3 [St. Paul 606], and a. 1 [St. Paul 605], as well as q. 13, a. 6, ad 1 [St. Paul 617]. These things (e.g., health) are universal. No one can simply choose health, we still have to deliberate about how to obtain health. In any case, the end of the will is not the transcendental good which is convertible with all being, but rather the general good for the person, which necessarily includes happiness, wisdom, health, life, etc.

28. *ST* I-II, q. 6, aa. 1–2 [St. Paul 588–89]. In q. 94, a. 2 [St. Paul 955], he says that the first principles of moral reasoning, synderesis, perfectly correspond to our natural inclinations, and that the order of the rational principles of natural law follows the order of the natural inclinations.

29. *ST* I-II, q. 9, a. 4 [St. Paul 602]. In the case in which reason's deliberation discovers that a naturally willed end cannot be obtained, say one wills health but one discovers that one has a rapidly deteriorating terminal disease, in such a case reason is the cause of one ceasing to will the end, or more precisely, of ceasing to find a means to that end. *ST* I-II, q. 13, a. 5 [St. Paul 616]. But the first cause of willing health was nevertheless God and nature.

30. In *ST* I-II, q. 10, a. 1, ad 1 [St. Paul 605], he clearly roots these natural volitions in man's nature.

Concerning our topic, Aquinas is quite clear that the sense appetites participate in reason insofar as they obey reason's command. Aquinas is also quite explicit that even if command is an act of reason, it is nevertheless not fully reducible to reason: "Since command is an act of reason, that act is commanded, which is subject to reason. The first act of the will, however, is not from the ordering of reason, but from the instinct of nature or of a superior cause."[31] Thus when we say that the sense appetites participate in reason, we must grant that the will has something to contribute to this command that is not simply caused by reason.

Consent

Granting the medieval faculty psychology (I examined Aquinas's position in chapters 1–4) it was hotly disputed in the high Middle Ages whether one ought to give primacy of place to reason (the intellectualist position) or to will (the voluntarist position) in accounting for free human actions.[32] Tobias Hoffmann argues for a somewhat voluntaristic (relative to more intellectualistic-leaning Thomists) reading of Aquinas based on God's direct moving of the will; Bonnie Kent, however, also argues for a similar position based on Aquinas's theory of consent.[33] I think both pieces of evidence are quite strong.

Consent is an act of the will.[34] In order to begin discussing consent, we should distinguish it from choice.[35] First one wills the end, say health, which is general and universal, and then one deliberates about the best way to attain that health in the concrete particular circumstances. After having considered the best possible way to become healthy here and now, one then chooses to do this particular thing that one has deliberated about. Choice is always about a particular means to some end,

---

31. *ST* I-II, q. 17, a. 5, ad 3 [St. Paul 629]: "imperium sit actus rationis, ille actus imperatur, qui rationi subditur. Primus autem voluntatis actus non est ex rationis ordinatione, sed ex instinctu naturae, aut superioris causae, ut supra dictum est. Et ideo non oportet quod in infinitum procedatur."

32. For a helpful overview of the medieval debate see Hoffmann, "Intellectualism and Voluntarism," in *Cambridge Companion for Medieval Philosophy*, ed. Robert Pasnau (Cambridge: Cambridge University Press, 2010), 414–27.

33. Hoffmann, *Angelic Sin*, 122–56; Kent, *Virtues of the Will*, 122.

34. *ST* I-II, q. 15, a. 1, and ad 3 [St. Paul 622].

35. For a helpful discussion of the historical use of consent see Judith Barad, *Consent: The Means to an Active Faith according to St. Thomas Aquinas* (New York: Peter Lang, 1992), 13–17.

but not about the end itself. But before one chooses to do this particular action one consents to it.[36] Consent is thus distinguishable from choice and is causally between deliberation and choice, even if they happen simultaneously.[37] Choice and consent are thus both at the level of particular contingents that can actually be done by us, for example, how I might, in these particular circumstances, become healthy.

Consent is an act of the will. Consent does not concern the willing of the end, but rather the willing of means to the end.[38] It is the "application" of the "appetitive motion" to the determination of what has been deliberated,[39] and it is in man's power to "apply or not to apply to this or that."[40] It is the deliberation of reason that determines a means to an end. We may call this means to an end the practical judgment of reason.[41] But in order for a person to actually choose a practical judgment, the will must consent to it. And this consent is not determined by that very deliberation, for when it is uncertain whether or not practical reason has reasoned correctly from its first principles, it is not the judgment of reason that has the final say, but it is the will that has the final say (*finalis sententia*) in consent.[42]

36. *ST* I-II, q. 15, a. 3, ad 3 [St. Paul 623]: "post consensum, adhuc remanet electio."

37. Ibid.: "Sed si inveniatur unum solum quod placeat, non differunt re consensus et electio, sed ratione tantum, ut consensus dicatur secundum quod placet ad agendum; electio autem, secundum quod praefertur his quae non placent."

38. Ibid.

39. Ibid. "consensus nominat applicationem appetitivi motus ad aliquid praeexistens in potestate applicantis. In ordine autem agibilium, primo quidem oportet sumere apprehensionem finis; deinde appetitum finis; deinde consilium de his quae sunt ad finem; deinde appetitum eorum quae sunt ad finem. Appetitus autem in ultimum finem tendit naturaliter: unde et applicatio motus appetitivi in finem apprehensum, non habet rationem consensus, sed simplicis voluntatis. De his autem quae sunt post ultimum finem, inquantum sunt ad finem, sub consilio cadunt: et sic potest esse de eis consensus, inquantum motus appetitivus applicatur ad id quod ex consilio iudicatum est. Motus vero appetitivus in finem, non applicatur consilio: sed magis consilium ipsi, quia consilium praesupponit appetitum finis. Sed appetitus eorum quae sunt ad finem, praesupponit determinationem consilii. Et ideo applicatio appetitivi motus ad determinationem consilii, proprie est consensus. Unde, cum consilium non sit nisi de his quae sunt ad finem, consensus, proprie loquendo, non est nisi de his quae sunt ad finem."

40. *ST* I-II, q. 15, a. 2 [St. Paul 622]: "Unde brutum animal appetit quidem, sed non applicat appetitivum motum ad aliquid. Et propter hoc non proprie dicitur consentire, sed solum rationalis natura, quae habet in potestate sua appetitivum motum, et potest ipsum applicare vel non applicare ad hoc vel ad illud."

41. In *De veritate* the practical judgment is emphasized, but in the later texts, *ST* I-II and *QDM*, deliberation is emphasized. Some hold that this amounts to a significant change in position, but I am not persuaded as *what* is chosen out of the process of deliberation is precisely a practical judgment of the intellect. See David Gallagher, "Free Choice and Free Judgement in Thomas Aquinas," *Archiv für Geschichte der Philosophie* 76 (1994): 268–69 and n57.

42. *ST* I-II, q. 15, a. 4 [St. Paul 623]: "Manifestum est autem quod superior ratio est quae

Bonnie Kent has rephrased this in a helpful way: "The will cannot specify or determine the judgment, but it can at least veto various means presented by the intellect as suitable to the end."[43] I would add that not only does it have this veto power, but consent also has a kind of affirmative role. We might say that the will approves of or votes for the practical judgment when it consents to it. This "approval" is not the sole cause of choice, but there is certainly no choice without it. Aquinas explains this "approval" or "veto" by noting that the act of consent involves the will being pleased (*placet*) or not pleased (*non placet*) with the practical judgment of reason.[44] It involves a certain "taking pleasure for itself in that" (*complacet sibi in ea*).[45]

Now pleasure involves the presence of a connatural good,[46] and each thing has a kind of connaturality to what is suitable according to its nature.[47] Aquinas notes that the fact that something seems suitable and good (*bonum et conveniens*) depends on two things, namely, the condi-

---

habet de omnibus iudicare: quia de sensibilibus per rationem iudicamus; de his vero quae ad rationes humanas pertinent, iudicamus secundum rationes divinas, quae pertinent ad rationem superiorem. Et ideo quandiu incertum est an secundum rationes divinas resistatur vel non, nullum iudicium rationis habet rationem finalis sententiae. Finalis autem sententia de agendis est consensus in actum. Et ideo consensus in actum pertinet ad rationem superiorem: secundum tamen quod in ratione voluntas includitur, sicut supra dictum est."

43. Kent, *Virtues of the Will*, 120.

44. *ST* I-II, q. 15, a. 3, ad 3 [St. Paul 623]: "electio addit supra consensum quandam relationem respectu eius cui aliquid praeeligitur, et ideo post consensum, adhuc remanet electio. Potest enim contingere quod per consilium inveniantur plura ducentia ad finem, quorum dum quodlibet *placet*, in quodlibet eorum consentitur, sed ex multis quae *placent*, praeaccipimus unum eligendo. Sed si inveniatur unum solum quod *placeat*, non differunt re consensus et electio, sed ratione tantum, ut consensus dicatur secundum quod *placet* ad agendum; electio autem, secundum quod praefertur his quae *non placent*." Emphasis added. Kevin White pointed out to me that *non placet* means to veto, even in English. Thus we could say that the will somehow vetos or votes for some practical judgment in consent.

45. *ST* I-II, q. 15, a. 1 [St. Paul 622].

46. *ST* I-II, q. 31, a. 1 [St. Paul 686]: "causa delectationis, scilicet praesentia connaturalis boni." This is also applicable to *complacentia*: see *ST* I-II, q. 26, a. 4 [St. Paul 672]: "amor importat quandam connaturalitatem vel complacentiam amantis ad amatum; unicuique autem est bonum id quod est sibi connaturale et proportionatum." For more on this see also ibid., aa. 1–2 [St. Paul 697–70]; and *ST* I-II, q. 11, a. 1, ad 3 [St. Paul 608]. For Aquinas on pleasure see *ST* I-II, qq. 31–34, and for a definition see q. 31, a. 1 [St. Paul 686]. For Aquinas, pleasure presupposes the presence of a connatural good and the sensation of this presence. Although Aquinas's treatment of pleasure in the *prima secundae* is primarily concerned with pleasure as a passion, he is explicit that there is also pleasure in the will; see *ST* I-II, q. 31, a. 4 [St. Paul 688].

47. *ST* I-II, q. 26, a. 1, ad 3 [St. Paul 670]: "unaquaeque res habeat connaturalitatem ad id quod est sibi conveniens secundum suam naturam."

tion of what is proposed and that to which it is proposed.[48] This means that the intellect's proposal of the suitable good (in some particular practical judgment) has to fit, so to speak, the condition, nature, natural appetite, or potency of the will.[49] If it does, then the will takes delight in it, for likeness causes love and pleasure,[50] and it consents.[51] If it does not, then the will vetoes, that is, it does not consent.

Here is how I understand this. After our deliberation has reached its term and has proposed this particular thing which should be done, we are either somehow attracted to this or somehow not. When we are attracted to the conclusion of our deliberation, we have a *reason* for the attraction, namely, the practical judgment itself. This is why choice is rational, for one can always point to the practical judgment that has been chosen. But when we are not attracted to the practical judgment, we have no such reason to point to.[52] Rather we have a sense (we are displeased with it) that something is not quite right, and rather than choose that practical judgment we will to reconsider in the hope of coming up with a better plan of action. We reject the proposal and go back to the drawing board, so to speak. When we do not consent, we will to redeliberate; when we consent, we will to follow whatever reason has determined, and then we choose it. The rejection of a practical judgment is not a choice, so it need not be rational in the same way that choices

48. *ST* I-II, q. 9, a. 2 [St. Paul 601]: "Quod autem aliquid videatur bonum et conveniens, ex duobus contingit: scilicet ex conditione eius quod proponitur, et eius cui proponitur. Conveniens enim secundum relationem dicitur, unde ex utroque extremorum dependet."

49. See, e.g., *ST* I-II, q. 6, a. 7, ad 1 [St. Paul 593]: "Malum autem secundum se contrariatur voluntati, sed bonum est voluntati consonum." See also *ST* I-II, q. 6, a. 4, obj. 2, and ad 2 [St. Paul 590–91].

50. *ST* I-II, q. 27, a. 3 [St. Paul 673–74], and q. 32, a. 7 [St. Paul 695–96].

51. This does not mean that the person chooses what the will consents to, as one can consent to multiple practical judgments simultaneously. See *ST* I-II, q. 15, a. 3, ad 3 [St. Paul 623].

52. This cannot be traced to another better reason, as this would already be included in the practical judgment. That is, if there were some other known (or habitually known) reason, then the intellect would not present that particular practical judgment as something to will—the person would still be deliberating toward the best practical judgment that he could. See also Hoffmann, *Angelic Sin*, 149: "The passage from inactivity to activity of the will requires an antecedent cause, a reason that makes the will want to start to consider a certain object. Yet when the object is already habitually present in one's intellect, the focus on one rather than another characteristic of the object does not seem to require an antecedent cause in addition to the object that receives special attention. Indeed Aquinas nowhere posits a chain of motives to consider a specific aspect of an object. The efficacy of a specific motive is in fact not to be traced to ever more specific reasons, but rather to the inclination of the will to the ultimate end." See also ibid., 150–51.

are, but the will to reconsider nevertheless compels us to ask how a non-rational power (as will is distinct from reason) can "veto" or "approve" a practical judgment of reason. Does this not compel us to paradoxically make the will the ultimate *judging* power?

In a way yes, and in a way no. It does not because free human actions are always chosen, and choice always follows the practical judgment of reason which judges that something is suitable and good. But if the will is understood to be an entirely blank slate that only follows the dictates of reason, and if reason, which sometimes makes mistakes, is determined by the way things appear, then human choices are determined by the appearances of things, just as sense appetite is determined by sense cognition. This kind of intellectual determinism would destroy moral responsibility and true freedom. What is required, as has been persuasively argued by David Gallagher and Tobias Hoffmann, is that humans have control over the way things appear, and this control must be reduced to the will as its cause; as Hoffmann rightly points out this makes human freedom somewhat irrational.[53] But what is also added by consent is that the will seems to have some sense of when practical reasoning derails, for in the case of a

53. Gallagher, "Free Choice," 247–77, esp. 277. In *ST* I-II, q. 74, a. 1, and ad 2 [St. Paul 870], this objection notes that the will wills the good or the apparent good. There is no sin in willing the good, but nor is there in willing the apparent good, as the defect is in the apprehensive powers rather than the will. In other words, we are not responsible for how things appear to us. In his response he simply notes that the defect of the apprehensive power is subject to the will, i.e., the will has control over how things appear to it—and this is why we are responsible when we choose something that seems good to us even when it is not. Hoffmann rightly notes that the advantage of delegating this role to the will is that it safeguards human freedom from intellectual determinism; the disadvantage is that it renders choice somewhat irrational. Hoffmann, *Angelic Sin*, 152–53: "In short: Aquinas's account of free decision is not determinist. This is at the same time a fortunate and a troubling result. If the good or evil choice of the angels had not depended on them, it would be hard to see how they could have earned eternal satisfaction or eternal frustration from something that did not lie in their power to do or to avoid. On the other hand, the contingent aspect of their choice poses a challenge with regard to its rationality. Angelic choice, and acts of free decision in general, seem to be rational up to a point, but not intelligible through and through .... Even if Thomas is free from the charge of intellectual determinism, matters are far from being solved. Contingent choices can be described, but not fully explained. At most it is possible to say *post eventum* that one person acted for this reason and another for that reason. Any attempt to give an a priori account of an individual act of free decision is destined to fail. Hence the decision of the good angels cannot be fully illuminated any more than the evil decision of the demons: even with regard to the good angels it cannot be said in the last analysis why they acted for an adequate reason; only in retrospect can it be said that they did so. To say that it is because of their will that good or bad angels decided the way they did surely means to indicate a cause, but not a reason why some chose in one way and others in a different way. The

faulty practical judgment it is somehow the responsibility of the will not to consent to a bad idea. Again, the will cannot come up with a practical judgment or a reason for the rejection itself, but it somehow affectively "judges," or discriminates between practical judgments by way or being "pleased" or "displeased" with whatever reason has determined.[54]

Here it will be helpful to briefly discuss Aquinas's earlier account of consent. Consent in the commentary on the *Sentences* and the *De veritate* is quite different than in the *Summa*. In the early texts consent is an act of will following reason.[55] Consent always follows reason as it has deliberated, but there are two kinds of consent following upon two kinds of deliberative reason. Consent which follows inferior reason is said to *consentire in delectationem* and consent which follows superior reason is called *consensus in executionem operis*.[56] Inferior reason and superior reason are not two distinct powers: they are distinguished by whatever object is being considered, that is, deliberations concerned with God and man's ultimate end belong to superior reason and those concerned with more secular and earthly matters belong to inferior reason.[57] As ruled by the eternal reasons (*rationibus aeternis*), superior reason considers man's ultimate end and can judge whatever inferior reason judges in light of this ultimate end. Thus the consent that follows superior reason (*consensus in executionem operis*) is the ultimate consent (*ultimus consensus*).[58]

In the early texts the ultimate consent follows the divine reasons, but

---

fact that natural inclination decreases the probability of sinning does not help to explain the individual choice. In the last analysis, the dilemma to reconcile the non-deterministic and the rational character of free decision remains unsolved."

54. Although I do not have space to pursue this here, it seems to me that the will's affective natural inclination has its own intelligible content (as it naturally inclines to something) that somehow "discriminates" by way of likeness or unlikeness in this non discursive manner along these lines. See *ST* I-II, q. 29, a. 1 [St. Paul 679]: "unumquodque habet naturalem consonantiam vel aptitudinem ad id quod sibi convenit, quae est amor naturalis; ita ad id quod est ei repugnans et corruptivum, habet dissonantiam naturalem, quae est odium naturale. Sic igitur et in appetitu animali, seu in intellectivo, amor est consonantia quaedam appetitus ad id quod apprehenditur ut conveniens: odium vero est dissonantia quaedam appetitus ad id quod apprehenditur ut repugnans et nocivum."

55. *In III Sent.*, d. 23, q. 2, a. 2, qc. 1, ad 1 [Moos 726]; *In IV Sent.*, d. 30, q. 1, a. 1.

56. *In II Sent.*, d. 24, q. 3, a. 2. This terminology is taken from Peter Lombard's *Sentences* II, d. 24, cc. 9–12, and is originally from Augustine's *De trinitate* XII, c. 12 (PL 42:1007). Aquinas does not use this terminology too often in his later texts. For a later use see *ST* I-II, q. 74, aa. 7–10.

57. *QDV*, q. 14, aa. 2–3.

58. *In II Sent.*, d. 24, q. 3, a. 1 [Mand 618], and ad 4–5. See also *QDV*, q. 15, a. 3 [Leonine 22.2:491.109–37].

this is not so in *ST* I-II, q. 15. There, Aquinas is explicit that it is precisely when we are not sure whether we have deliberated correctly *vis-à-vis* the eternal reasons that consent has the final or ultimate say.[59] In other words, the ultimate or final consent is not reducible to the deliberations of superior reason and it does not simply follow deliberations that take the highest things into consideration. The will is granted a far larger role in the late texts. In these texts the volition of consent can either rightly approve or veto the practical judgment of reason—there is nothing like this in his early texts. Consent in the late texts offers a kind of appetitive ballast to our deliberations.

In the early texts, consent is good if it follows reason, it is bad if it does not. This seems to me to be true in general of the volitional independence of the will *vis-à-vis* reason in the *Sentences* and the *De veritate*. The will is independent from reason because it can will against it, thus the will's independence from reason only fully arises in the context of evil. In other words, the will seems to be free because it can act irrationally and thus will evil. But when the will acts as it ought, it simply follows and is moved by reason. In the latter texts, however, this is not exactly true, for the will is sometimes right to act against reason, by vetoing when reason has gone wrong. It is undoubtedly true that good choices always follow good deliberations, but in the late texts the will also has a far more powerful active causality for the good which is independent of reason, both in its efficiently moving reason to start deliberating and in its consenting to or vetoing practical judgments.

Let us summarize Aquinas's volitional development from the commentary on the *Sentences* to the later texts. Although there are early texts in which Aquinas says that God moves the will as a primary cause moves a secondary cause, there is no explanation of what this is meant to account for in the various moments of volition. Furthermore, what is rejected in the *Sentences* is the claim that the will is moved instinctually—natural instinctual motion is restricted to the realm of animality. In the late texts, after Morebeke's translation of the Aristotle's *Eudemian Ethics*, Aquinas is very clear that God moves the will precisely in this sense, namely by efficient causality as an *instinctus*. Furthermore, he explains exactly what role this plays in volition, that is, actively spurring deliberation. It is also worth

59. *ST* I-II, q. 15, a. 4. See text, 191–92n42.

considering that the condemnation of the position (from Aristotle's *De anima* III) that the will is a passive power simply moved by the intellect undoubtedly put some pressure on Aquinas. If all we had to go by was Aquinas's commentary on the *Sentences* and the *De veritate*, it seems to me that he could be fairly labeled an intellectualist insofar as reason provides the end, along the lines of final and formal causality, and granting that the final cause is the cause of the efficient cause it follows that reason is the active/efficient cause that moves the will as a passive power. In the late texts, however, the end ultimately comes from God by way of *instinctus* and thus the efficient cause of the will's first motion is not fully traceable to reason. Aquinas thus uses Aristotle's passage in the *Eudemian Ethics* to counter the charges leveled against Aristotle's *De anima*.

Furthermore, Aquinas's thinking on consent is another important part of his volitional development. In the early texts consent simply follows the practical judgment of reason when it is right; when consent is bad, it departs from reason and is moved by passion or vice. However, in the late texts, consent has a far more powerful role in vetoing bad practical judgments and in approving good ones.

My goal here is simply to point out that in Aquinas's later texts the will looms larger—it is more muscular and spontaneous. Unlike the earlier texts, Aquinas is quite clear that command includes not only the intelligible content provided by reason but also that which comes from God's natural moving of the will as the first cause; in other words, the will does not simply follow the intelligible content of reason. God and nature provide some of it.[60] It is important to point out that this does not destroy human freedom, for as Aquinas says, God moves created agents in accord with their nature, and hence moves free agents to act

---

60. *Vis-à-vis* natural law, Aquinas says in *ST* I-II, q. 94, a. 2 [St. Paul 955]: "omnia illa ad quae homo habet naturalem inclinationem, ratio naturaliter apprehendit ut bona, … secundum igitur ordinem inclinationum naturalium, est ordo praeceptorum legis naturae." Thus when practical reason derails (in conscience), the natural inclinations are still there in the will, and through the act of consent we can somehow sense a dissonance between these inclinations and the practical judgment and thus veto. In other words, we are to revise our erring conscience (*Quodl.* III, q. 12, a. 2, ad 2), and to reconsider the matter more carefully in the light of the naturally known first principles of synderesis, which correspond perfectly with our natural inclinations. Alternately, when practical reason reasons correctly, this pleases the will, i.e., it somehow feels right, and we consent and choose. Moral-practical reasoning thus requires a kind of volitional sensitivity or attentiveness to our natural inclinations. Virtue, of course, is particularly helpful insofar as it further inclines us to the good.

freely.[61] Beyond God's moving of the will directly, consent, which is also not fully reducible to reason is involved in reason's command of the lower powers,[62] for there is no choice without consent and there is no command without choice.[63] Thus when the sense appetites are said to participate in reason insofar as they obey reason's command in the later texts, the formal exemplar causality of the *Sentences* in which reason communicates its form to the sense appetites will not sit quite as easily.

Amor

Because his treatment of the operations of the sensitive soul, that is, of the internal and external sense powers, is largely the same in early and late texts, I will not canvas Aquinas's mature texts on the matter. Nor for that matter, have I discovered much relevant difference in his treatment of the passions, except, of course, for the fact that Aquinas's so-called treatise on the passions (*ST* I-II, qq. 22–48) is a massive expansion on his earlier writing. There is, however, one important difference that I wish to highlight. Aquinas's mature treatment of love is somewhat different than his treatment in the commentary on the *Sentences*. Rather than explaining that love is completely determined by the exigency of the apprehended form,[64] the sense appetites themselves have a greater role in the determination of the attractiveness or repulsiveness of the apprehended object. Love is now recast as a *complacentia*, a taking pleasure in (note that this is the same language used in consent in the *Summa*), or as a *coaptatio*—that is, an adaptation, a kinship, a quality of being suited for something, etc.—between the sense appetite and the sensed object.[65] The object must be "connatural" (*connaturalis*). The word connatural is synonymous with natural, but the prefix *co-* means together with or along with. Something is connatural because it is suitable to that nature, which means that it is precisely the kind of a thing that is actually

---

61. *QDM*, q. 6 [Leonine 23:149.407–18]. See also *SCG* III.70.

62. *ST* I, q. 81, a. 3 [St. Paul 391].

63. *ST* I-II, q. 17, a. 3, ad 1 [St. Paul 628].

64. See 149n78 in chapter 6.

65. *ST* I-II, q. 26, a. 1 [St. Paul 670]: "coaptatio appetitus sensitivi, vel voluntatis, ad aliquod bonum, idest ipsa complacentia boni, dicitur amor sensitivus, vel intellectivus seu rationalis." See also a. 2: "appetibile dat appetitui, primo quidem, quandam coaptationem ad ipsum, quae est complacentia appetibilis; ex qua sequitur motus ad appetibile."

suitable and good for that particular nature.[66] Thus although the apprehension of the object as suitable is necessary and crucial, the object itself must also be the kind of thing that is naturally suitable to the nature (or natural inclination) of the sense appetite.

One way to put this is simply to say that we are already naturally disposed to or inclined to certain kinds of goods. The concupiscible appetite as a nature is a particular form that is naturally ordered to or disposed to bodily goods, and thus bodily goods are connatural to the sense appetite itself. In other words, the object is apprehended, but this apprehended object has to be like (*connaturalis*) to the sense appetite itself if there is going to be an inclination to or *complacentia* in the object itself. After this likeness happens, that is, after we are pleasurably inclined toward a perceived suitable object, then the actual motion of desire follows from this initial attraction caused by likeness.[67]

Formal likeness is extremely important in both texts, but what the later texts clarify and add to the formal likeness between the apprehended form and the thing loved is that there must *also* be a likeness or harmony between the apprehended object and the natural inclination of the sense appetite itself. If there is no such likeness or harmony, there is unlikeness and dissonance, and thus rather than causing desire, the dissonance causes a repulsion or aversion from the apprehended object.[68] The likeness between the apprehended good and the sense appetite causes a kind of pleasure, a *complacentia*, and pleasure, for Aquinas, is caused by the possession of a connatural good and the perception of that pos-

---

66. *ST* I-II, q. 26, a. 1, ad 3 [St. Paul 670]: "amor naturalis non solum est in viribus animae vegetativae, sed in omnibus potentiis animae, … cum unaquaeque res habeat connaturalitatem ad id quod est sibi conveniens secundum suam naturam." *ST* I-II, q. 62, a. 3 [St. Paul 808]: "Appetitus enim uniuscuiusque rei naturaliter movetur et tendit in finem sibi connaturalem: et iste motus provenit ex quadam conformitate rei ad suum finem."

67. *ST* I-II, q. 26, a. 2 [St. Paul 670]: "Prima ergo immutatio appetitus ab appetibili vocatur amor, qui nihil est aliud quam complacentia appetibilis; et ex hac complacentia sequitur motus in appetibile, qui est desiderium."

68. *ST* I-II, q. 29, a. 1 [St. Paul 679]: "unumquodque habet naturalem consonantiam vel aptitudinem ad id quod sibi convenit, quae est amor naturalis; ita ad id quod est ei repugnans et corruptivum, habet dissonantiam naturalem, quae est odium naturale. Sic igitur et in appetitu animali, seu in intellectivo, amor est consonantia quaedam appetitus ad id quod apprehenditur ut conveniens: odium vero est dissonantia quaedam appetitus ad id quod apprehenditur ut repugnans et nocivum." See also *In I De an.*, c. 7 [Leonine 45.1:34.158–62]; *ST* II-II, q. 141, a. 4 [St. Paul 1635].

session.[69] In this case, the good thing itself is not yet fully possessed, but it is possessed as apprehended and presented to the sense appetite, that is, it is a "union of affect," in which the beloved thing is really absent, but it is nevertheless also in this peculiar way present in the sense appetite.[70] This causes a kind of first and weaker pleasure in that good—this is love or *amor*. For example, when we apprehend a perfect low-hanging apple on a tree, this causes a kind of initial attracting pleasure (*complacentia*) toward the delightful apple, which leads to the actual desire (*desiderium*) for the apple, which, if all goes well, ultimately culminates in the more complete pleasure (*placentia* or *delectatio*) taken in eating the real apple.

Aquinas is quite explicit in the *Summa* that this also happens at the level of the will.[71] The additional clarification of the role of the nature of the appetitive power itself seems to me to parallel his mature treatment of volition, but along the lines of sense appetition. For the naturalness of the inclination to connatural goods must ultimately come from God via nature.[72] In other words, our passions or emotions are not completely determined by the exigency of the apprehended form, but the nature of the appetite itself is a co-cause in explaining why appetite is attracted to this rather than that as good.

Translating this into metaphysical terms is helpful. The concupiscible appetite is a power of the soul, and as a power (*potentia*) it is in potency, and as a particular kind of potency it is actualized by particular objects, for example, sensible bodily goods. Thus prior to the reception of any particular material good, it is already inclined to such things simply by being the kind of potency it is. It is in a way already like to such

69. *ST* I-II, q. 31, a. 1 [St. Paul 686]: "causa delectationis, scilicet praesentia connaturalis boni." See also a. 5 [St. Paul 689]: "delectatio provenit ex coniunctione convenientis quae sentitur vel cognoscitur."

70. *ST* I-II, q. 28, a. 1 [St. Paul 675]: "duplex est unio amantis ad amatum. Una quidem secundum rem: puta cum amatum praesentialiter adest amanti. – Alia vero secundum affectum. Quae quidem unio consideranda est ex apprehensione praecedente: nam motus appetitivus sequitur apprehensionem." See also ibid., ad 1–2; and q. 32, a. 3, ad 3 [St. Paul 693].

71. *ST* I-II, q. 26, a. 1 [St. Paul 670].

72. *ST* I-II, q. 41, a. 3 [St. Paul 728]: "aliquis motus dicitur naturalis, quia ad ipsum inclinat natura. Sed hoc contingit dupliciter. Uno modo, quod totum perficitur a natura, absque aliqua operatione apprehensivae virtutis; sicut moveri sursum est motus naturalis ignis, et augeri est motus naturalis animalium et plantarum. – Alio modo dicitur motus naturalis, ad quem natura inclinat, licet non perficiatur nisi per apprehensionem: quia, sicut supra dictum est, motus cognitivae et appetitivae virtutis reducuntur in naturam, sicut in principium primum."

objects as it is disposed to or in potency toward them. Once any such object is perceived we are further inclined or actualized toward it. Of course, there is no actualization of a potency unless there is some actualizing cause, that is, there is no actual inclination or motion toward any particular sensible good until it is apprehended by the other sense powers. But prior to apprehension the concupiscible appetite is already in potency to these goods and not to others. Thus it is already somehow like them, in the way that potency is like its actualizing cause. Most generally, potency is always and only intelligible by way of act, and once any potency has been distinguished from any other, we have already made a claim about what kind of thing actualizes it, that is, what the potency is like and what it is not. These are simply active and passive powers that are proportionate and connatural to each other, as one naturally actualizes another. As a passive power, the concupiscible appetite is naturally in potency to be actualized by these kinds of objects, and thus their actualizing or moving the concupiscible appetite via apprehension is a perfection of its nature or potency.[73]

73. See text in previous note and *ST* I-II, q. 27, a. 1 [St. Paul 672]. Sherwin makes two salient points. Love in the *Sentences* is primarily if not exclusively portrayed in the language of formal causality; it is the terminus of another motion, i.e., the exigency of the form of the apprehended object informs the appetite and the appetite then rests. In the later texts, however, the emphasis is on *complacentia* as a *principle*, as an *inclination* to act, in other words, love is a principle of action rather than simply a passive resting in a form received; see *By Knowledge and Love*, 80–81. That seems right to me, but I wish to add to this that the likeness at stake in the late texts is also between the appetite itself and its connatural goods, which is an crucial aspect of the sense appetites active inclination toward perceived goods.

10

PARTICIPATION AND
VIRTUE IN LATE TEXTS

Participation in Reason

In Aquinas's later texts, the use of the phrase "to participate in reason" within the tripartite division of the soul is quite similar to the earlier texts.[1] Most generally all appetite is said to obey reason and to participate in reason.[2] There are four subjects of the cardinal virtues, namely,
what is essentially rational, which prudence perfects, and what is rational by participation, which is divided into three: (1) the will, which is the
subject of justice, (2) the concupiscible appetite, which is the subject of
temperance, and (3) the irascible appetite, which is the subject of courage.[3] Thus the three powers of the soul that can participate in reason are
the will and the irascible and sensitive appetites.

When Aquinas speaks of moral virtue generally, including justice,
courage, and temperance, he sometimes emphasizes that appetitive powers participate in the apprehensive power of reason itself.[4] But when he
is discussing the sense appetites in particular, will is generally included

---

1. Perhaps the most unusual late use is in *ST* I-II, q. 17, a. 6, ad 2 [St. Paul 630], in which
he speaks of reason as participating in itself, as its cognition of conclusions participates in its
cognition of principles because of the diversity of its objects.

2. *ST* I-II, q. 56, a. 6, ad 2 [St. Paul 782]. See also *ST* II-II, q. 58, a. 4, ad 3 [St. Paul 1334].

3. *ST* I-II, q. 61, a. 2 [St. Paul 802]. See also q. 59, a. 4, ad 2 [St. Paul 796].

4. *ST* I-II, q. 66, a. 1 [St. Paul 821]: "causa et radix humani boni est ratio. Et ideo prudentia, quae perficit rationem, praefertur in bonitate aliis virtutibus moralibus, perficientibus
vim appetitivam inquantum participat rationem." See also q. 63, a. 2, ad 3 [St. Paul 811]; q. 58,
a. 2 [St. Paul 790]; and *In II Ethic.* 1 [Leonine 47:77.98–114].

in reason.[5] In one passage he even says that sense appetite can have virtue and vice "insofar as they participate in will and reason."[6] In another passage he explains that the passions can be moral "insofar as they participate in something of the voluntary and of the judgment of reason."[7] We have seen passages like this in the *Sentences*.[8]

Although his use of the phrase *participare rationem* is quite stable when compared to earlier texts, his explanation of the kind of causality evolves. As we saw in the *Sentences*, he argued that the sense appetites participate in reason by way of exemplar causality,[9] but his description of it in *ST* I-II, q. 60, a. 1, is somewhat different:

Moral virtues are certain habits of the appetitive part. Habits, however, differ in species according to specific differences of objects, as was said above. The species, however, of the appetible object, as of anything, is taken according to the specific form, which is from the agent. But it must be considered that the matter of a recipient is related to an agent in two ways. For sometimes the patient receives the form of the agent according to the same intelligible content [*rationem*] as it is in the agent, as is in all univocal agents. And so it is necessary that if the agent is one in species, the matter receives the form of one species, as from fire there is generated univocally only something existing in the species of fire. But sometimes matter receives form from an agent not according to the same intelligible content as is in the agent, as is obvious in non-univocal generating agents, as an animal is generated by the sun. And then the forms received in matter from the same agent are not of one species, but they are diversified according to a diverse proportion of matter to receiving the influx of the agent, as we see that from one action of the sun, through putrefaction, animals of diverse species are generated, according to a diverse proportion of matter. It is manifest, however, that in moral things reason is involved as commanding and as moving; but the appetitive power is as commanded and moved. Appetite, however, does not receive the impression of reason, as if, univocally, since it

5. *ST* III, q. 18, a. 2 [St. Paul 1964]: "Sciendum est autem quod sensualitas, sive sensualis appetitus, inquantum est natus obedire rationi, dicitur rationale per participationem, ut patet per philosophum, in I Ethic. Et quia voluntas est in ratione, ut dictum est, pari ratione potest dici quod sensualitas sit voluntas per participationem." As far as I can tell he only calls sensuality will by participation in his Christology; see also *ST* III, q. 18, a. 5 [St. Paul 1966]. For the point that will is in reason (not as inhering) see *ST* III, q. 18, a. 2, ad 1 and 3 [St. Paul 1964].

6. *ST* I-II, q. 74, a. 2, ad 2 [St. Paul 871].

7. *ST* I-II, q. 24, a. 4 [St. Paul 665].

8. See chapter 6 above.

9. See chapter 7 above.

does not come to be rational essentially [*per essentiam*] but by participation [*per participationem*], as is said in I *Ethic.* Whence appetible things are constituted according to the motion of reason in diverse species, insofar as they are related to reason in diverse ways. And so it follows that moral virtues are diverse in species, and not only one.[10]

As in his commentary on the *Sentences*, Aquinas explains that the sense appetites' participation in reason must be understood in the context of univocal, analogical, and equivocal likeness. He explicitly here rejects univocal predication of reason to the sense appetites, and also by implication equivocal predication. The intelligible content of reason as it is predicated of the sense appetites is neither identical (univocal) to reason itself, but nor is it so foreign that it shares no intelligible likeness (equivocal) as *canis* can signify dog or a constellation. There is enough likeness—enough to merit predication by participation. The only alternative left is analogical likeness. Although he does not explicitly mention it here, he does so in *ST* I-II, q. 61, a. 1, ad 1:

When a univocal genus is divided in its own species, then the parts of the division are equally related according to the intelligible content of the genus; .... But when there is a division of something analogous, which is predicated of many according to the prior and posterior [*secundum prius et posterius*], then nothing prohibits one from being more principal than another, even according to a common meaning [*rationem*], as a substance is more principally said to be a being than an accident. And such is the division of the virtues into the diverse genera of virtues, that the good of reason is not found in all virtues according to the same order.[11]

Although this statement concerns the division of the virtues, Aquinas clearly holds that the ground for this division, which is an analogical predication of reason, is the rectitude of appetite (*rectitudinem appetitus*) (q. 61, a. 1), or the manner in which appetite receives the impression of reason (*appetitus recipit impressionem rationis*) (q. 60, a. 1). In other words, the predication of reason of the sense appetites is analogical, and conversely, the participation of reason by the sense appetites is analogical.

The emphasis here is not on exemplar causality, as it was in the com-

---

10. *ST* I-II, q. 60, a. 1 [St. Paul 797].
11. *ST* I-II, q. 61, a. 1, ad 1 [St. Paul 802].

mentary on the *Sentences*, but rather on agent or efficient causality. In q. 60, a. 1, he explains that the agent cause (*agens*) is reason as commanding and moving and the receiving or patient cause is appetite as commanded and moved (*ratio est sicut imperans et movens; vis autem appetitiva est sicut imperata et mota*). It is the "motion of reason" which causes the participation by appetite in reason, and reason, as we discussed, only commands or moves by way of will. This is why the very meaning (*ratio*) of habits includes an order to the will,[12] that is, these participations are essentially related to the command of reason, which necessarily also includes the will.

Although he does not bring up the so-called transcendentals as he did in the commentary on the *Sentences*, the example of generation and the sun is enough to conclude that he means equivocal efficient causality, the basis for the third kind of participation outlined in *In De hebdomadibus* c. 2.[13] Concerning these three kinds of participation, this one cannot be the first kind, logical participation, as he clearly points to a cause (reason's command) and its distinct participated effect in the sense appetites (moral virtue). Nor can it be either of the second kinds of participation, as cause and effect do not enter into hylomorphic composition of matter and form and nor do they enter into accidental composition as substance and accident. Furthermore, the fact that this participation involves analogical communication of formal content militates against the first two kinds of participation, which involve univocal communication of formal content. Rather, we clearly have a relation between an agent or efficient analogical cause and its effect, as the sun causes quite diverse effects which are consequently analogically like their cause, the sun. I will compare this with his earlier thinking in the following chapter, but for now I will consider what this means on a more concrete ethical plane.

---

12. *ST* I-II, q. 50, a. 5 [St. Paul 760]: "Ex ipsa etiam ratione habitus apparet quod habet quendam principalem ordinem ad voluntatem, prout habitus est quo quis utitur cum voluerit, ut supra dictum est." See also *ST* I-II, q. 56, a. 3 [St. Paul 779]: "Subiectum vero habitus qui simpliciter dicitur virtus, non potest esse nisi voluntas; vel aliqua potentia secundum quod est mota a voluntate."

13. See 122n7 in chapter 5; he uses the same example there.

Command

Because Aquinas repeatedly tells us that the sense appetites participate in reason insofar as they obey reason's command,[14] it must be the case that this command is the relevant efficient cause discussed above. Sometimes he speaks quite generally and simply says that the sense appetites participate in reason insofar as they are *obedient* to reason.[15] Nevertheless, this is obedience to the command of reason: "reason is as commanding and moving, the sense appetites are commanded and moved."[16]

Let us consider command which, it is worth pointing out, is utterly absent from Aristotle. Most broadly Aquinas distinguishes between acts, which are immediately elicited by the will, and acts by which the will commands other powers to their acts.[17] We are primarily concerned with the latter. Elicited acts, however, are acts of the will that are not necessarily related to other powers. Here we may speak of the natural willing of the ends, intention, choice, and consent. The commanded acts of the will, however, follow upon choice as the will moves the whole person through his powers to execute what he has chosen to do. Aquinas uses the phrases "command of the will" and "command of reason" interchangeably.[18] Most precisely, however, Aquinas argues that command is an act of reason because command involves ordering and advocating or

14. See, e.g., *QDM*, q. 8, a. 3, ad 18 [Leonine 23:205.350–55]: "uirtutes morales sunt in ui appetitiua, que est rationalis per participationem in quantum movetur per imperium rationis." See *ST* I, q. 57, a. 4, ad 3 [St. Paul 273]: "secundum quod moventur a voluntate et ratione: quia etiam inferior pars animae participat aliqualiter rationem, sicut obediens imperanti, ut dicitur in *I Ethic.*" See also *ST* I-II, q. 68, a. 3 [St. Paul 835]: "virtutes morales perficiunt vim appetitivam secundum quod participat aliqualiter rationem, inquantum scilicet nata est moveri per imperium rationis," and *In I Ethic.* 20 [Leonine 47:72.126].

15. *ST* I-II, q. 56, a. 4 [St. Paul 780]: "Alio modo [the sense appetites] possunt considerari inquantum participant rationem, per hoc quod natae sunt rationi obedire." See also *ST* I, q. 79, a. 2, ad 2 [St. Paul 376]; *ST* I-II, q. 26, a. 1 [St. Paul 672]; q. 56, a. 4, ad 1 [St. Paul 781]; q. 58, a. 2 [St. Paul 790]; *ST* II-II, q. 58, a. 4, ad 3 [St. Paul 1334]; *ST* III, q. 18, a. 2 [St. Paul 1964], and ad 1; q. 19, a. 2 [St. Paul 1970]; *In I Ethic.* 20 [Leonine 47:72.126, 140–46, 171–77]; *In II Ethic.* 1 [Leonine 47:77.107–9]; and *QDA*, q. 11, ad 15 [Leonine 24.1:103.366–74].

16. *ST* I-II, q. 60, a. 1 [St. Paul 797]: "Manifestum est autem quod in moralibus ratio est sicut imperans et movens; vis autem appetitiva est sicut imperata et mota. Non autem appetitus recipit impressionem rationis quasi univoce: quia non fit rationale per essentiam, sed per participationem, ut dicitur in I *Ethic.*"

17. *ST* I-II, q. 6, prol. [St. Paul 588]; see also a. 4 [St. Paul 590].

18. To be exact, a search with the online *Index Thomisticus* shows that he used some verion of the phrase *imperium voluntatis* 83 times in 71 different places and he used some version of the phrase *imperium rationis* 85 times in 64 places.

announcing (*intimando vel denuntiando*), but it nevertheless presupposes the will's act in the order of exercise and finality, which I have already discussed,[19] and thus we may trace the first cause of the motion back through choice and ultimately to God.[20] To summarize, after a person has made a choice, the person must will the action and this means willing that the powers of the soul act—that is what command is.

When Aquinas says that reason commands and the sense appetites are commanded, he does not mean that reason commands the sense appetites directly. More precisely, he does not mean that we can immediately command our sense appetites to feel something. For example, if I am experiencing some uncomfortable emotion, I cannot simply will it to go away as I can will my hand to move however I please. Command, as the execution of what has been deliberated upon, is generally about particular actions that are to be done. We almost never try to change our emotions directly. Usually, when we are affected by some passion the struggle is not directly with the passion itself, but rather whether or not we succumb to the object of the passion. For example, when faced with a freshly baked plate of cookies that should not be eaten, one does not command the desire for the cookies to go away; rather one commands oneself not to eat the cookies.

19. *ST* I-II, q. 17, a. 1 [St. Paul 626–27]: "Respondeo dicendum quod imperare est actus rationis, praesupposito tamen actu voluntatis. Ad cuius evidentiam, considerandum est quod, quia actus voluntatis et rationis supra se invicem possunt ferri, prout scilicet ratio ratiocinatur de volendo, et voluntas vult ratiocinari; contingit actum voluntatis praeveniri ab actu rationis, et e converso. Et quia virtus prioris actus remanet in actu sequenti, contingit quandoque quod est aliquis actus voluntatis, secundum quod manet virtute in ipso aliquid de actu rationis, ut dictum est de usu et de electione; et e converso aliquis est actus rationis, secundum quod virtute manet in ipso aliquid de actu voluntatis. Imperare autem est quidem essentialiter actus rationis: imperans enim ordinat eum cui imperat, ad aliquid agendum, intimando vel denuntiando; sic autem ordinare per modum cuiusdam intimationis, est rationis. Sed ratio potest aliquid intimare vel denuntiare dupliciter. Uno modo, absolute: quae quidem intimatio exprimitur per verbum indicativi modi; sicut si aliquis alicui dicat, *Hoc est tibi faciendum*. Aliquando autem ratio intimat aliquid alicui, movendo ipsum ad hoc: et talis intimatio exprimitur per verbum imperativi modi; puta cum alicui dicitur, *Fac hoc*. Primum autem movens in viribus animae ad exercitium actus, est voluntas, ut supra dictum est. Cum ergo secundum movens non moveat nisi in virtute primi moventis, sequitur quod hoc ipsum quod ratio movet imperando, sit ei ex virtute voluntatis. Unde relinquitur quod imperare sit actus rationis, praesupposito actu voluntatis, in cuius virtute ratio movet per imperium ad exercitium actus."

20. Thus the first cause of motion in the line of efficient and final causality is traced back to God, from the "instinct of nature," as I have discussed. *ST* I-II, q. 17, a. 6, ad 3 [St. Paul 629]: "cum imperium sit actus rationis, ille actus imperatur, qui rationi subditur. Primus autem voluntatis actus non est ex rationis ordinatione, sed ex instinctu naturae, aut superioris causae, ut supra dictum est. Et ideo non oportet quod in infinitum procedatur."

There are three main passages in Aquinas's corpus that discuss how the sense appetites are subject to reason: *QDV* q. 25, a. 4; *ST* I, q. 81, a. 3; and *ST* I-II, q. 17, a. 7. The *QDV* passage, which we have already examined, argues that the sense appetites are subject to reason in three ways: (1) on behalf of reason as it controls the imagination and thus how things appear attractive or repulsive; (2) on behalf of the will as the intensity of the will's motion redounds upon the sense appetite; and (3) on behalf of the motive power, which follows the command of reason despite whatever passions there may be.[21] In *ST* I, q. 81, a. 3, he drops (2) and rather presents the will's role with respect to the sense appetite as executing the motive power. On the side of the intellect, reason is now presented as moving the cogitative power rather than the imagination. Whereas in *De veritate* reason controlled the sense appetites by directing the imagination to imagine objects differently and thus make them appear attractive or repulsive, in *ST* reason's role rather is to supply the universal premise in the practical syllogism, enabling one to move from universal principles to particular actions—and the cogitative power somehow plays a role in this.[22]

But in *ST* I-II, q. 17, a. 7, he does not distinguish between what comes from will and what comes from reason, nor is there is there any mention of redounding or the motive power. Reason now commands the sense appetite through imagination (he reverts back to the imagination from the cogitative power). Some think that this latter passage simply follows from the earlier passages,[23] as if there is no significant difference between the two, but I am not so sure.

The role of reason is significantly different in the two prior passages. In the *De veritate* it is that of deliberation, that is, of imagining something from different perspectives. Deliberation is always and only about particulars that can be done by us, and particulars are almost always con-

---

21. For the text and discussion, see chapter 8 above.

22. I am not going to make too much of the cogitative power because Aquinas himself said rather little about it, at least with respect to my topic. See Cates, *Emotions*, 116. For some late passages on the *vis aestimativa* see *ST* I, q. 81, a. 2, ad 2 [St. Paul 393]; *ST* I-II, q. 6, a. 2 [St. Paul 589]. On the *vis cogitativa* see *ST* I, q. 78, a. 4 [St. Paul 373–74], and q. 81, a. 3 [St. Paul 390–91]. On the *intellectus passivus* see *ST* I, q. 79, a. 2, ad 2 [St. Paul 367]. On the *ratio particularis* see *ST* I, q. 20, a. 1, ad 1 [St. Paul 113]; q. 78, a. 4 [St. Paul 373–74]; q. 79, a. 2, ad 2 [St. Paul 367]; q. 81, a. 2, ad 3 [St. Paul 393]; *ST* I-II, q. 30, a. 3, ad 3 [St. Paul 684–85]; q. 51, a. 3 [St. Paul 763].

23. G. Butera, "Thomas Aquinas on Reason's Control of the Passions in the Virtue of Temperance" (PhD diss., The Catholic University of America, 2001), 150–52.

sidered with the imagination. When we deliberate about eating a ripe apple it is not surprising if our imagining it causes us to desire it. If we wish to change this emotional response to disgust we can simply command ourselves to imagine a worm in the apple. The role of reason in *ST*, however, is to provide the universal first principles from which our practical reasoning proceeds or to which it is reduced. Here the desire for my neighbor's delectable apple is tempered by my universal knowledge that I should not steal. Of course, these two accounts of reason's role in controlling the sense appetites are in no way incompatible, and both require the use of the internal sense powers, but they are quite different.

If one considers the role of the will, it appears that it has dropped out altogether by the time of *ST* I-II. First the will's role consisted in redounding on the sense appetites (*QDV*), then in executing the motive power (*ST* I), but finally it is not mentioned at all (*ST* I-II), and all that is apparently left is reason's role via the imagination or cogitative power. Perhaps the will's redounding is too indirect and vague. And perhaps moving the motive power is not really moving the sense appetites at all, for in such a case a person moves themselves to do something despite whatever may be happening in their sense appetites. So perhaps he means to drop the will from the equation.

I think that the context in the questions on human volition and acts (*ST* I-II, qq. 6–21) strongly implies that will is already included in any command of the sense appetites. For this article comes on the heels of his explanation that command is an act of reason which necessarily also involves an act of the will. Thus this discussion on command must also include will.

There is also ample textual evidence to show that Aquinas was still firmly committed to the will's redounding or overflowing into the sense appetites.[24] For example, later in the *prima secundae* he says that any intense volition will necessarily redound in the sense appetite.[25] And this brings us to the role of the will in moving the external motive power.

---

24. *ST* I-II, q. 24, a. 3, ad 1 [St. Paul 664]; q. 30, a. 1, ad 1 [St. Paul 683]; q. 31, a. 5 [St. Paul 689]; q. 38, a. 4, ad 3 [St. Paul 718]; q. 59, a. 5 [St. Paul 796]; q. 61, a. 4, ad 1 [St. Paul 804]; q. 77, a. 6 [St. Paul 889]; *ST* II-II, q. 58, a. 8, ad 1 [St. Paul 1337]; *QDM*, q. 7, a. 2, ad 17 [Leonine 23:165.410–12]. I should note that the redounding can also move from the sense appetite to the will; see *ST* I-II, q. 9, a. 5 [St. Paul 603].

25. *ST* I-II, q. 77, a. 6 [St. Paul 889].

There is a way in which we have control over our sense appetites because we can move our motive power, which moves our muscles to do things without or even despite our passions. In other words, if I am experiencing an obviously inordinate passion for something, getting up and walking away will often do much good. If the object was before me, now it no longer is. Moreover, even if the object was not right before me but only imagined, now I have an entirely new set of sensory inputs, which are now affecting my sense appetites and causing new passions. This is one of the ways that we repress (*reprimere*) our emotions, as he often puts it. But any such action against some passion requires a great effort of command and thus it will also directly redound upon the sense appetites. Thus the action of commanding oneself to turn away affects the sense appetites in two ways: (1) by offering new sensory inputs to the sense appetites, and (2) by the will's redounding to the lower sense powers.

But if one actually performs such an action, one must have chosen this action, and this presupposes deliberation, which includes both considering the first principles of practical reasoning and thinking about some appetible thing from different perspectives, that is, one is using both imagination and the cogitative power.[26] In any such action, we are in fact affecting the sense appetites along many different causal lines: (1) new sensory inputs, (2) redounding, (3) imagination, and (4) cogitation.

Moreover, reason can only move the imagination and the cogitative power because it wills to, for it is only through the will that the other powers of the soul are moved.[27] In other words, the acts that Aquinas attributes to reason are imbued with will and the acts that he attributes to will are imbued with reason. As he has already explained that both reason and will are included in command (*ST* I-II, q. 17, a. 1), I prefer the formulation in a. 7, which does not distinguish between the role of reason or will, but rather emphasizes the connection between freedom and immateriality.[28]

---

26. The application of universal principles to particular cases involves the cogitative power, but intellectual awareness of something as individual need not.

27. See, e.g., *QDM*, q. 6 [Leonine 23:149.349–52].

28. The whole article works on the distinction between materiality and immateriality. What is immaterial is in our control, while what is material is not strictly in our control. The sense appetites, as powers of the soul are in our control, but as they are affixed to a material organ they are not in our control. Thus will and intellect are completely in our control, the sense appetites are not completely in our control, and the more material vegetative powers are

Command affects the sense appetite in the four ways just mentioned. Any particular command can have some of these and not others, or more of one and less of others. For example, sometimes when angry, the consideration of mitigating circumstances can quiet the anger, but sometimes it is best to go for a short walk. It entirely depends on the circumstances and the judgment of prudence.

When reason has successfully commanded the sense appetite, the motion of the sense appetite accompanies or follows reason.[29] When reason has not successfully commanded the sense appetite, that sense appetite does not accompany reason, but pulls in a contrary direction. A great role, perhaps the greatest role, of courage and temperance is thus simply to render the sense appetites obedient or docile to reason's command so that it follows along with reason's command.

Moral Virtue and Passion

In a certain sense this is all quite simple: either I can do what I want or my passions make it very difficult, if not impossible, for me to do so. The sense appetites can be considered insofar as they follow their own natural inclinations or they may be considered insofar as they obey reason's command, that is, insofar as they participate in reason.[30] Moral virtue makes the sense appetites docile and obedient to the command of reason[31] and thus it helps us to do what we will. But how exactly does moral virtue do this?

---

utterly out of our control. It offers a principle for control and lack of control, for freedom and the lack thereof, but within the sense powers there is tremendous difference in the degree of control. The motive power is almost completely in our control, so long as we are not injured.

29. *ST* I-II, q. 30, a. 1, ad 1 [St. Paul 683].

30. *ST* I-II, q. 56, a. 4 [St. Paul 780]: "Alio modo [the sense appetites] possunt considerari inquantum participant rationem, per hoc quod natae sunt rationi obedire"; *ST* I, q. 79, a. 2, ad 2 [St. Paul 376]: "appetitus sensitivus, in quo sunt animae passiones; qui etiam in I *Ethic.* dicitur rationalis per participationem, quia obedit rationi"; *ST* I-II, q. 26, a. 1 [St. Paul 669]: "Et talis est appetitus sensitivus in brutis: qui tamen in hominibus aliquid libertatis participat, inquantum obedit rationi"; *ST* III, q. 18, a. 2 [St. Paul 1964]: "Sciendum est autem quod sensualitas, sive sensualis appetitus, inquantum est natus obedire rationi, dicitur rationale per participationem: ut patet per philosophum, in *I Ethic.*"; ibid., ad 1: "Sed voluntas participative dicta potest esse in parte sensitiva, inquantum obedit rationi" (see discussion on parallel use in *Sentences*); *In I Ethic.* 20 [Leonine 47.1:72.126, 140–46, 171–77]; *In II Ethic.* 1 [Leonine 47.1:77.107–9]; and cf. the slightly earlier (1266–67) *QDA*, q. 11, ad 15 [Leonine 24.1:103.366–74].

31. *ST* I-II, q. 56, a. 4, ad 1 [St. Paul 781]; q. 67, a. 1, ad 3 [St. Paul 827]: "Unde et poterit in irascibili esse fortitudo, et in concupiscibili temperantia: inquantum utraque vis perfecte erit disposita ad obediendum rationi."

In order to address this, I would like to start with the general point that there is no distinctly human goodness without free choice, for human actions can be neither meritorious nor culpable if compelled. In one passage Aquinas points out that what is voluntary is deeply internal to the agent, but passions are external, that is, they are exterior principles of human actions, and thus are neither meritorious nor blameworthy.[32] In fact, they diminish the voluntariness of an action and thus make it less praiseworthy or blameworthy. The strength of a passion thus diminishes the praise or blame owed to an action, but to the extent that they have been freely chosen and commanded, some passions are in our control and thus meritorious. Thus passions that are consequent to free choice increase the praiseworthiness or blame due to an action. For we freely choose to act in accordance with them, and we may incite or repress them as we see fit. In sum, antecedent passions diminish and consequent passions increase the merit or culpability of human actions.[33]

It would seem that antecedent passions should be morally neutral, as their effect can be equally for good or bad, but if anything at all, antecedent passions are troublesome because they obstruct free decision, a crucial human good. Passions cloud and bind the judgment of reason.

---

32. *QDM*, q. 3, a. 11, ad 3 [Leonine 23:90.62–73]: "Ad tertium dicendum quod de ratione peccati est quod sit uoluntarium. Voluntarium autem dicitur cuius principium est in ipso agente. Et ideo, quanto principium interius magis augetur, tanto et peccatum fit gravius; quanto autem principium exterius magis augetur, tanto peccatum fit levius. Passio autem est principium extrinsecum voluntatis, motus autem voluntatis est principium intrinsecum. Et ideo, quanto motus voluntatis fuerit fortior ad peccandum, tanto peccatum est maius; set quanto passio fuerit fortior impellens ad peccandum, tanto peccatum fit minus."

33. The following is a good summarizing passage: *ST* I-II, q. 77, a. 6 [St. Paul 889]: "peccatum essentialiter consistit in actu liberi arbitrii, quod est *facultas voluntatis et rationis*. Passio autem est motus appetitus sensitivi. Appetitus autem sensitivus potest se habere ad liberum arbitrium et antecedenter, et consequenter. Antecedenter quidem, secundum quod passio appetitus sensitivi trahit vel inclinat rationem et voluntatem, ut supra dictum est. Consequenter autem, secundum quod motus superiorum virium, si sint vehementes, redundant in inferiores: non enim potest voluntas intense moveri in aliquid, quin excitetur aliqua passio in appetitu sensitivo. Si igitur accipiatur passio secundum quod praecedit actum peccati, sic necesse est quod diminuat peccatum. Actus enim intantum est peccatum, inquantum est voluntarium et in nobis existens. In nobis autem aliquid esse dicitur per rationem et voluntatem. Unde quanto ratio et voluntas ex se aliquid agunt, non ex impulsu passionis, magis est voluntarium et in nobis existens. Et secundum hoc passio minuit peccatum, inquantum minuit voluntarium. Passio autem consequens non diminuit peccatum, sed magis auget: vel potius est signum magnitudinis eius, inquantum scilicet demonstrat intensionem voluntatis ad actum peccati. Et sic verum est quod quanto aliquis maiori libidine vel concupiscentia peccat, tanto magis peccat." See also ad 2 and q. 74, a. 6 [St. Paul 873].

Without passion a person can judge more clearly and with greater per-spicacity.[34] But why such a negative view on the passions?

Aquinas offers a few reasons. First, he explains that passions distract from the higher operations of the soul. The intensity of a passion in the sense appetite detracts the other powers from their operations. Because our powers are rooted in one soul, and because the soul's concentration or attention applies each power to its own act, when someone is concen-trating on the act of one power, the attention granted to another power is necessarily diminished and at times utterly impeded. He offers the helpful example of someone listening intensely who does not notice an-other person passing by.[35] It is the vehemence of the passion that has this effect; it has nothing to do with the object of the passion.

Vehement passions also clog up the normal operations of the imag-ination and cogitative powers, which are crucial for deliberation. He notes that lovers have a very difficult time turning their imagination to-ward something else.[36] This will, of course, cause great trouble in delib-eration, which must be able to consider and imagine a particular object from different perspectives. Presumably reason will request a phantasm that will not be produced by the imagination.[37] In other words, reason will not be able to consider its object in a free and disinterested manner because it cannot conjure up the right phantasm at will.

The other great effect of passion is that it makes things seem to be other than they truly are.[38] My desire for this cookie makes it seem to be better than that piece of broccoli next to it. Here there is a conflict or contrariness between the "seeming" of the sense appetite, and the "seem-

---

34. *ST* I-II, q. 59, a. 2, ad 3 [St. Paul 794]; *QDM*, q. 3, a. 11 [Leonine 23:90.28–59].

35. *QDM*, q. 3, a. 9 [Leonine 23:86–87.180–92]; *ST* I-II, q. 33, a. 3 [St. Paul 699]; q. 77, a. 1 [St. Paul 885].

36. *ST* I-II, q. 77, a. 1 [St. Paul 885].

37. This is Baker's idea (*Passions*, 118) and I have not found Aquinas saying it, but it seems correct: "But in the grip of a passion which has transfixed the imagination and the estimative sense exclusively upon the delectable object, the contrary phantasm needed by the intellect to actualize the habitual knowledge, by which the sensible object would be judged in a rational way, cannot be produced."

38. *ST* I-II, q. 44, a. 2 [St. Paul 736]: "Alio modo dicitur aliquis consiliativus, a facultate bene consiliandi. Et sic nec timor, nec aliqua passio consiliativos facit. Quia homini affecto secundum aliquam passionem, videtur aliquid vel maius vel minus quam sit secundum rei veritatem: sicut amanti videntur ea quae amat, meliora; et timenti, ea quae timet, terribiliora. Et sic ex defectu rectitudinis iudicii, quaelibet passio, quantum est de se, impedit facultatem bene consiliandi."

ing" of reason,[39] between my attraction to the cookie and my knowledge that I ought rather to eat something healthy. These two "seemings" or appearances cause the powers of the soul to move contrary to one another,[40] one toward the broccoli and the other toward the cookie. Aquinas often speaks of this as the "contrariness" of passions.[41] Because reason cannot simultaneously choose both, and because choice always follows the practical judgment of reason, at the very moment that I choose to eat the cookie, my reason's judgment is in accord with that passion. In this way passion moves the will, namely, insofar as it affects the object that reason presents to the will.[42] And lastly, if the passion is vehement enough, its corporeal aspect can utterly bind free decision and render the act involuntary.[43] I would like to point out that this way that passion "binds" is not simply black or white, free or not, it seems to be a question of degrees.[44] In other words, the material aspect of the passion seems to diminish freedom in proportion to the degree of its vehemence.[45]

Thus we can note four ways that passion harms reason's judgment: (1) by distracting the soul's attention away from reason and will, (2) by clogging imagination and cogitation which are crucial to reason's deliberation, (3) by making things seem to be otherwise than they are, and (4) very powerful bodily dispositions can bind reason altogether, but less powerful dispositions can also diminish freedom to a certain extent. As the root of human goodness is free decision, one can see the troublesome nature of passion and the reason why Aquinas is at times willing to speak of passion as naturally contrary to reason.[46] From a theological

39. *ST* I-II, q. 10, a. 3, ad 2 [St. Paul 607].

40. *ST* I-II, q. 9, a. 2, ad 3 [St. Paul 601].

41. *QDM*, q. 3, a. 9 [Leonine 23:87.193–207]. See also *ST* I-II, q. 33. a. 3 [St. Paul 699]; q. 77, a. 2 [St. Paul 886].

42. *ST* I-II, q. 9, a. 2 [St. Paul 601]; q. 10, a. 3 [St. Paul 606].

43. *QDM*, q. 3, a. 9 [Leonine 23:87.193–207]; *ST* I-II, q. 33. a. 3 [St. Paul 699].

44. *ST* I-II, q. 10, a. 3 [St. Paul 607].

45. Cf. *ST* I-II, q. 17, a. 7 [St. Paul 630], mentioned above. There he says that we have control over powers to the degree that they are immaterial or not affixed to material organs.

46. Richard Baker notes that the chief kind of ignorance caused by passion is the "ignorance which results from not *actually* considering what should be considered in the deliberation proceeding a moral choice." Baker, *Passions*, 114. Failure to pay attention to what one should have at the moment of choice is the cause (or, more precisely, the noncause) of sin. For two very good discussions of nonconsideration as a cause of sin see Hoffmann, *Angelic Sin*, 122–53, and Matthews S. Grant, "God, The Sinner, and The Act of Sin" *The Thomist* 73 (2009): 455–96. It is not difficult to see that force of passions makes us prone to not consider something as one should (whether by distraction, by causing a false "seeming" or by clogging

perspective, this natural disorder is part of the punishment of original sin, as discussed in chapter 3. And as I also mentioned, moral virtue cannot remove this problem altogether, for original sin is permanent, but such virtue can mitigate its effects to a limited extent.

Reason (including will) has some power over the sense appetite (in the other four ways mentioned above), and the sense appetites have some power over reason (in the four ways just mentioned). There is a kind of cycle here that can easily become vicious: passion affects deliberation, which affects command, which affects passion, *ad infinitum*. The more vehement the passions, the more pressure they put on reason, and the less reason is able to judge clearly and control that passion. One can see how this often spirals out of control in a kind of snowball effect. There is a kind of gravity to the passions drawing us away from reason toward evil.

For our purposes, because Aquinas says that the sense appetites participate in reason insofar as they obey its command, this can be understood in two ways: (1) properly, as describing the sense appetites' actual reception of command, or (2) very loosely, as describing the habitual way in which the sense appetites are rendered docile to that command. Concerning the latter, the sense appetites in the virtuous agent have become habitually docile and obedient to the command of reason. In particular, this means that the agent's antecedent passions are not very vehement. It should be recalled that Aquinas argued that passions are neither morally good nor bad prior to choice, but vehement antecedent passions are inherently disordered because they obstruct lucid thinking required for free decision and they make it very difficult for reason to command the sense appetites, and they make good consequent passions very difficult. Thus the only kind of good passions are consequent passions, and it is only possible to have these kinds of passions habitually if one's antecedent passions are mild, which requires moral virtue.

The lowering of the intensity of antecedent passions has very powerful effects: it leaves reason clear-sighted, enables commands to be followed

---

the internal senses) and thus is a cause of defective practical judgments. Baker notes (*Passions*, 114): "The ignorance arising from a passion, therefore, is the temporary ignorance existing here and now which the reason suffers because of the fact that the passion has distracted it from the consideration of everything else except the object of the passion. We might say that that the net result of the various influences which a passion exerts on the reason is that the latter does not actually consider the good points of that which is contrary to the passion."

promptly, and allows for the proper emotional response to follow effort-lessly. None of these things is possible with strong antecedent passions. But, properly speaking, this is not what Aquinas means by participation.

In this cycle in which reason affects passion and passion affects reason,[47] participation in reason concerns the motion from reason to passion. Consider the following passage in which Aquinas is asking whether the sense appetites are the subject of virtue.

The irascible and concupiscible can be considered in two ways. In one way according to themselves, insofar as they are parts of the sensitive appetite. And in this way it does not belong to them to be the subject of virtue. In another way they can be considered insofar as they participate in reason, because they naturally obey reason. And so the irascible and concupiscible can be the subject of human virtue, for thus it is the principle of human acts, insofar as it participates in reason. And in these powers it is necessary to posit virtues. For it is evident that there are some virtues in the irascible and concupiscible appetites. For an act which progresses from one power insofar as it is moved by another cannot be perfect unless each power is well disposed to the act, as the act of a craftsman cannot be suitable unless both the craftsman and also the tool itself are well disposed to act. Therefore in these things concerning which the irascible and concupiscible powers operate insofar as they are moved by reason, it is necessary that there be some habit perfecting them to act well, not only in reason, but also in the irascible and concupiscible powers. And because the good disposition of a power moved by a mover is attained according to its conformity to the moving power, therefore the virtue, which is in the irascible and concupiscible, is nothing else than a certain habitual conformity of those powers to reason.[48]

This passage brings out the passive nature of the kind of participation at stake when Aquinas says that the sense appetites participate in reason. They participate in reason by the virtue or disposition by which the sense appetites are well disposed to being *moved* by reason. This, as I previously discussed, makes the sense appetites a little more like slaves, making them more subject to reason. He describes this as habitual conformity (*habitualis conformitas*) of the sense appetites to reason.[49]

---

47. Cf. *ST* I-II, q. 59, a. 1 [St. Paul 793]: "motus passionis, inquantum passio est, principium habet in ipso appetitu, et terminum in ratione, in cuius conformitatem appetitus tendit. Motus autem virtutis est e converso, principium habens in ratione et terminum in appetitu, secundum quod a ratione movetur."

48. *ST* I-II, q. 56, a. 4 [St. Paul 780].

49. For another important passage which says the same, see *ST* I-II, q. 58, a. 2 [St. Paul

In the *prima pars*, Aquinas had said that anything that is participated in is related to the participant as its act.[50] In this case the sense appetites participate in reason insofar as they are moved or actualized by reason, and hence they are in potency to the act they receive from the command of reason. The more they are habitually disposed or conformed to be so moved or actualized, the better or more virtuous they are. This happens, as we have seen, not by making the sense appetites essentially rational—that is, by making the sense appetites judge and decide what should and should not be sought in this particular circumstance (the proper role of deliberation and prudence)—but rather by lowering the vehemence of the antecedent passions and thereby letting reason informed by prudence operate with clear vision and swift execution. In fact, any virtuous act, which involves the sense appetites participating in reason, must include the full and complete operation of reason and will. There is no need to make the sense appetites take over the role of reason and will.

This is evident in two very important articles (*ST* III, q. 19, aa. 1–2) on the unity and plurality of operations in Christ. In a. 1 he explains:

The action of that which is moved by another is twofold: one indeed which it has according to its own form; another, however, which it has insofar as it is moved by another. As the operation of an axe according to its form is to cut; however, insofar as it is moved by the artisan, its operation is to make a bench. Therefore the operation which belongs to something according to its own form is its own, and it does not pertain to the mover except insofar as it uses a thing of this sort for its own operation: thus to heat is the proper operation of fire, but not of the blacksmith, except insofar as he uses fire to heat iron. But that operation which pertains to a thing as moved by another, is not another operation beyond the operation of the one moving it: as in the case of making a bench, the operation of cutting is not an operation of the axe separate from the operation of the artisan. And so, wherever a mover and moved have diverse forms or operative powers, there it is necessary that there is some proper operation of the mover, and another proper operation of the moved, although what

---

790]. But see also *ST* I-II, q. 59, a. 2 [St. Paul 794], in which he speaks of passion trying to conform reason to itself. See also a. 4 [St. Paul 795] and *In II Ethic.*, l. 1 [Leonine 47.1:77.98–114].

50. *ST* I, q. 75, a. 5, ad 4 [St. Paul 347]: "omne participatum comparatur ad participans ut actus eius." This does not refer to logical participation, i.e., the first of the threefold division of participation in *De ebd.* 2.

is moved participates in the operation of the mover, and the mover uses the operation of what is moved, and so each acts in communion with the other.[51]

In the next article (a. 2) he explicitly connects this framework to the manner in which the sense appetites participate in reason:

Since man is that which he is according to reason, that operation is said to be human in the unqualified sense which proceeds from reason through will, which is the appetite of reason. If, however, there is some operation in man which does not proceed from reason and will, it is not a human operation in the absolute sense, but it is suitable to man according to some part of human nature: sometimes indeed according to the very nature of a corporeal element, as to be borne downwards; sometimes according to the power of the vegetative soul, as to be nourished and to grow; but sometimes according to the sensitive part, as to see and to hear, to imagine and to remember, to desire and to be angry. Among these operations there is a difference. For the operations of the sensitive soul are somehow obedient to reason [*aliqualiter obedientes rationi*]: and so they are somehow rational and human, insofar as they obey reason, as is apparent from the Philosopher in I *Ethic*. But the operations that follow the vegetative soul, or also the nature of elemental body, are not subject to reason: whence in no way are they rational, nor are they human in the absolute sense, but only according to a part of human nature. It was said above [in a. 1, translated above] that when an inferior agent acts through its own form, then the operation of the inferior agent is other than the operation of the superior agent; but when the inferior agent does not act except as it is moved by the superior agent, then the operation of the superior agent and the inferior are one and the same. So therefore in each pure man [that is, not Christ] the operation of the elements and of the vegetative soul are different from the operation of the will, which is properly human. Likewise also the operation of the sensitive soul with respect to that which is not moved by reason; but with respect to that which is moved by reason, the operation of the sensitive and rational part is one and the same. There is one operation of the rational soul itself, if we attend to the principle itself of operation, which is reason and will. They are diversified, however, with respect to diverse objects.[52]

The sense appetites only participate in reason to the extent that reason is actually actualizing them. Reason is the cause or the act, which is received in the potency of the sense appetites. The act of the sense appe-

---

51. *ST* III, q. 19, a. 1 [St. Paul 1968].
52. *ST* III, q. 19, a. 2 [St. Paul 1970].

tites can be somewhat (*aliqualiter*) rational when reason is causing or commanding them to be so—in this sense they participate in reason. But it is as the artisan uses fire to make the sword. By no means can he make a sword without fire, nor can fire make the sword without the artisan—both are required. Here cause and command are identical. Command and being commanded are a necessary part of any action of moral virtue. In fact, Aquinas explains that in any act of moral virtue, the act of prudence and the act of the moral virtue operate together as form and matter,[53] that is, they are inextricable and moral virtue is unintelligible without both. The very virtue of being commanded needs the very virtue of command, namely, prudence.[54] This is why Aquinas will say that we only use our habits when we *will* to do so.[55] There cannot be an act of moral virtue without the prudential free choice that actualizes the moral virtues. This actualization or command is precisely the equivocal efficient cause of the third kind of participation that I discussed at the beginning of this chapter. Let us now turn to consider this within the context of Aquinas's evolving metaphysical and ethical thought.

53. For this hylomorphic description of prudence and moral virtue, where prudence is referred to as form and moral virtue as matter, see *ST* I-II, q. 66, a. 2 [St. Paul 822–23].

54. *ST* II-I, q. 47, a. 8 [St. Paul 1295].

55. *QDM*, q. 6 [Leonine 23:149.352–54]; *ST* I-II, q. 71, a. 4 [St. Paul 851]. Bonnie Kent has pointed out that although Aquinas attributes this to Averroes, it is not in Averroes, or at least not in this way. Averroes (*Commentarium Magnum in Aristotelis De anima* 3.18 [Crawford 439]) discusses intellect and Aristotle's claim that the agent intellect is a *hexis* (*De anima* 430a14–17). See Kent, "Losable Virtue," 107–8.

11

CONCLUSION OF PART 2

This chapter summarizes and ties together the main points of the second part of this book by returning to its beginning, namely, participation. Now that I have examined the evolution of Aquinas's thought on how the sense appetites participate in reason (chapters 6–10), it is worth returning to his more metaphysical account of participation (chapter 5), and seeing more precisely how these two accounts fit together. I will argue that Aquinas's evolving thought on how the sense appetites participate in reason dovetails with his simultaneously evolving metaphysical thought on participation. While I will turn away from these more anthropological/metaphysical issues in the third part of this book, I will nevertheless use these conclusions in the third part of the book to engage contemporary Thomists and other philosophers along more straightforward ethical lines.

As discussed in chapter 5, in c. 2 of *In De hebdomadibus* Aquinas begins his discussion of participation by noting that to participate is, in a way, to take a part (*quasi partem capere*); it is to receive in a particular fashion what pertains to another universally. He then outlines three kinds of participation: (1) what may be called logical participation as an individual participates in a species or as a species participates in its genus, (2) as matter participates in form and substance participates in an accident, and (3) that based on efficient causality, especially as an effect participates in a higher-level cause.[1]

---

1. *De ebd.* 2 [Leonine 50:271.69–85]; see text, 122n7. For a fuller discussion of this issue see chapter 5.

One way of having in particular what belongs to another universally, according to the first kind of participation, is the manner in which we might say that the idea of this man participates in the idea of animal, for a man is an animal, or the idea of a species such as man participates in a genus (animal). As there is no separate form of animality that causes all animals to be animals, we are speaking of a logical participation of one less extended idea or concept in another that is more extended. Because this involves the relationship between ideas or concepts, rather than between really distinct things or principles of being, it is called logical participation.

When we say, however, that the sense appetites participate in reason, we signify really distinct forms, which I established in the discussion of the distinction between the soul and its powers in chapters 1–4. Because the powers of reason and will are really distinct from the sense appetites, this is obviously not a case of the first kind of participation, that is, logical participation.

Concerning the second mode of participation there is a real distinction and composition between participant and what is participated, whether between matter and form or between substance and accident. But sense appetites and reason enter into no such composition, neither as substance participates in an accidental form nor as matter participates in substantial form. Furthermore, both the first and second kinds of participation involve the univocal communication of formalities, whereas the third kind involves an analogical communication of formal content. And Aquinas is very explicit that when the sense appetites participate in reason there is an analogical communication of reason to the sense appetites. Thus, by a process of elimination we can see that the sense appetites can participate in reason only according to the third mode of participation, namely, that of an effect participating in an equivocal efficient cause, where reason is analogically predicated of the sense appetites.

Before saying anything positive about this kind of participation, I wish to mention briefly Fabro's division of participation, and the place of the sense appetite's participation in reason within it. Fabro distinguishes between transcendental and predicamental participation.[2] By predica-

2. See Fabro, "The Intensive Hermeneutics of Thomistic Philosophy," *Review of Metaphysics* 27 (1974): 471–76. See also Wippel, *Metaphysical Thought*, 125, and Mitchell, *Being and Participation*, 164–73 and 472–85.

mental participation Fabro means the communication of a univocal formality wherein the participated perfection does not exist separately in itself apart from the participant(s).[3] By transcendental participation he means the analogical communication of a formality where the participated perfection does exist separately, as in the case of *esse*, in God himself.[4] Broadly speaking, Fabro is interested in understanding Aquinas's unique reconciliation of Platonic vertical participation (i.e., transcendental) with the more horizontal Aristotelian immanence of forms (i.e., predicamental).[5] For Fabro the first and second kinds of participation in c. 2 of *In De hebdomadibus* are predicamental participations.[6] The third kind of participation seems to be divided into predicamental-univocal participation, that is, *fieri*, and transcendental-analogical participation, that is, God's creating *esse*.[7]

Fabro himself suggests that the case of the sense appetites participating in reason is "closely connected with the predicamental order."[8] I

3. For a definition of predicamental univocal participation, see Fabro: "All the participants have in themselves, the same formality, according to all its essential content, and the participated does not exist in itself, but only in the participants (Aristotelian moment of Thomistic participation)." *La nozione metafisica di partecipazione secondo san Tommaso d'Aquino, Opere Complete* (Segni: Editrice del Verbo Incarnato, 2005), 3:305, translated with some adjustments by Mitchell, in *Being and Participation*, 168. Mitchell cites the incorrect page number in referring back to Fabro's text.

4. For a definition of transcendental analogical participation, see Fabro: "The participants only have in themselves a 'degraded similitude' of the participated which subsists in itself, outside of these, either as a property of a superior subsistent, or, without anything else, as a pure and subsistent formality in the full possession of itself" (ibid., translation modified).

5. Fabro, *Participation et causalité selon s. Thomas d'Aquin* (Louvain: Publications Universitaires de Louvain, 1961), 320 and 335. All vertical transcendental participation is tied to *esse* (in which similitude is analogically communicated between God and creation) and all predicamental participation is tied to essence (from the immanence or *energeia* of Aristotelian form). He seems to be taking this distinction from an important text: *Quodl.* II, q. 2, a. 1 [Leonine 25.2:214–15].

6. Fabro, *Intensive Hermeneutics*, 472 and 481–82.

7. This is how Jason Mitchell takes the division; see his "Being and Participation: The Method and Structure of Metaphysical Reflection according to Cornelio Fabro" (PhD diss., Pontifical Athenaeum Regina Apostolorum, 2013), 461. This seems to have a textual warrant in Fabro, *Intensive Hermeneutics*, 474. Aquinas himself says that the third kind of participation happens especially (*praecipue*) when the effect does not equal the power of its cause, which suggests that there are cases in which the effect does equal the power of its cause (see text, 122n7). Generation would be such a case in which the cause does equal the power of its effect and in which effect and cause are univocally like one another, as man generates man. On this see *CT* II, c. 9 [Leonine 42:201.145–54] in which Aquinas clarifies that a son does not participate in his father, but that in generation the father induces the son to participate in the essence of the species, i.e., man. This text is cited in Fabro, *La Nozione*, 306.

8. Fabro, *Intensive Hermeneutics*, 478.

have shown, however, that this kind of participation clearly involves an analogical communication of formality. But according to Fabro's general division, a predicamental-analogical participation should be impossible, as predicamental participation is always univocal. Furthermore, this case of the sense appetites participating in reason cannot be grasped as transcendental participation, at least not in the way Fabro understands such participation as immediately related to the divine.[9] In other words, my conclusion, if it is correct, may pose a kind of exception to Fabro's division between predicamental and transcendental participation. I will leave this as an open question. As Wippel has observed, this distinction between predicamental and transcendental participation is not Aquinas's own but Fabro's; I will simply follow Aquinas's threefold division.

Perhaps the best discussion of this third kind of participation is in Bernard Montagnes's monograph *The Doctrine of the Analogy of Being according to Thomas Aquinas*. Montagnes praises Fabro for his groundbreaking work in uncovering the metaphysical underpinning of participation and analogy, but he also criticizes Fabro for not taking into account the manner in which Aquinas developed his thinking on this point.[10]

Let us briefly consider Aquinas's development in thinking on the third kind of participation at the level of God and creation. One of the

9. Ibid., 477–80, and "Elementi per una dottrina tomistica della partecipazione" in his *Esegesi tomistica* (Rome: Libreria editrice della Pontificia Universita Lateranense, 1969), 421–48, esp. 440–42. In these texts, Fabro seems to connect this case of participation to the so-called principle of contiguity or continuity. I say that he *seems* to connect it, as in *Intensive Hermeneutic*, 478, he notes that it is "closely connected" with the predicamental order (in *Elementi*, 441, he notes that it is "quasi di ordine predicamentale"), and concerning the sensitive appetites participating in reason he notes his explanation "may explain" why the sense appetites participate in reason. I mention these qualifications because I think we can fairly read Fabro as leaving this somewhat open. In any case, the reasoning he lays out follows Dionysius the Areopagite's understanding that the lower participates in the higher by a kind of affinity or contiguity (*QDV*, q. 16, a. 1 [Leonine 22.2:504.189–210]). See, e.g., *In X Ethic.*, l. 11: "quod quidem perfectissime invenitur in substantiis superioribus, in homine autem imperfecte et quasi participative," cited in *Elementi*, 441. I would like to point out, however, that this kind of participation and this line of thinking is applicable to all humans qua rational. It is different from the one we are discussing, as that kind of participation is applicable to all humans, but our case (when the sense appetites participate in reason) is only in some, and only very rarely (as virtue is rare). We might correctly say that all sense appetites *can* participate in reason qua human, but not that all do so, which is true of the kind of participation that follows from the principle of continuity or contiguity.

10. Montagnes, *Analogy*, 10.

characteristics of this kind of participation is that it involves analogical predication. The first two kinds of participation, as Fabro points out, involve the predication of univocal formalities.[11] When we predicate animal of a man and a donkey, we mean animal in the exact same way, that is, univocally.[12] When we say that a substance participates in whiteness, or even when we speak of more of less whiteness (i.e., the intension and remission of accidental forms), we are predicating that formality of a subject univocally, for it is one and same meaning (*ratio*) of whiteness that we mean.[13]

What is distinct about this third kind of participation, however, is that it involves a communication of a formality that is not exactly the same (unvocal) but nor is it entirely different (equivocal). As Aquinas puts it, something is predicated analogically when it is applied to things which have different intelligible contents (*rationes*), or which are partly the same and partly different, but these *rationes* are ordered to one and the same thing.[14] This one and the same thing, in turn, is the cause of these secondary analogates. These secondary analogates are like the prime analogate because they are effects that are like their cause (the prime analogate). This is how we say that an effect (a secondary analogate) participates in its cause (the prime analogate).[15]

Montagnes shows how Aquinas's thinking on the third kind of participation evolves in the context of the relation between divine and cre-

11. Fabro, *Intensive Hermeneutics*, 471–72, 481–82. As he puts it, "Predicamental participation is therefore, strictly speaking, confined to univocity" (484).

12. *De princip.* 6 [Leonine 43:46:27–29].

13. *De ente* 5 [Leonine 43.379:113–20]. See Montagnes, *Analogy*, 30–31.

14. *De princip.* 6 [Leonine 43:46.33–35]: "Analogice dicitur predicari quod predicatur de pluribus quorum rationes diverse sunt, sed attribuuntur uni alicui eidem." *In IV Metaph.*, c. 2 [Marietti 151]: "Sed sciendum quod aliquid praedicatur de diversis multipliciter: quandoque quidem secundum rationem omnino eamdem, et tunc dicitur de eis univoce praedicari, sicut animal de equo et bove. – Quandoque vero secundum rationes omnino diversas; et tunc dicitur de eis aequivoce praedicari, sicut canis de sidere et animali. – Quandoque vero secundum rationes quae partim sunt diversae et partim non diversae: diversae quidem secundum quod diversas habitudines important, unae autem secundum quod ad unum aliquid et idem istae diversae habitudines referuntur; et illud dicitur analogice praedicari." For a comparison of these texts see Wippel, *Metaphysical Thought*, 81–82.

15. See Montagnes, *Analogy*, 40. The relation of causality undergirding participation and analogical predication is apparent when one considers that participating and participant are related as act and potency: see *ST* I, q. 75, a. 5, ad 4 [St. Paul 347]; *SCG* II.54 [Leonine manualis 146–47]. In other words, they are related causally; see *SCG* II.15 [Leonine manualis 101]: "Quod per essentiam dicitur, est causa omnium quae per participationem dicuntur."

ated being.[16] In the *Sentences*, it is clear that likeness is said of two things which possess the same form.[17] In the case of analogy, however, the form is in one fully (*per essentiam*) and in another according to participation (*per participationem*) by some imitation and diminished likeness.[18] Created being is an imperfect and inadequate imitation or representation of its divine exemplar, God, who is the exemplar form that created beings imitate by participation (*omne ens, quantumcumque imperfectum, a primo ente exemplariter deducitur*).[19]

God is an exemplar cause in two ways: (1) according to his nature and (2) according to his ideas. These two kinds of exemplarism correspond to two kinds of equivocal causes, (1) as the effect is formally present in its cause and (2) as the effect is virtually present in its cause. According to (1) the form by which the agent acts is communicated to its effect, which then resembles its cause by an intrinsic formal participation, for exam-

16. See Montagnes, *Analogy*, 34–43. I have cited some of the texts below, but see his footnotes for a more comprehensive list. At the level of analogy of being on the transcendental plane, Aquinas's thinking developed in a nonlinear threefold manner, corresponding to three sets of texts—his commentary on the *Sentences*, his *De veritate*, and his mature position beginning from the *Summa Contra Gentiles*. Although I will only outline the first and last of these three, the middle position is crucial, as it explains his unhappiness with his first solution in the *Sentences*, and his recognition that his somewhat formalist early conception of being or "formalist ontology" as Montagnes calls it (74–75) tended toward univocity. This he rejects in the *De veritate* with his famous analogy of *proportionalitas*, found in q. 2, a. 11. As I skip this middle step in Aquinas's development in my very brief sketch, it may seem that Aquinas simply tinkered with or slightly modified his solution in the *Sentences* to arrive at his mature solution, but as Montagnes shows that is not entirely the case.

17. *In I Sent.*, d. 48, q. 1, a. 2 [Mand 1080]: "conformitas est convenientia in forma una, et sic idem est quod similitudo quam causat unitas qualitatis, ut in V Metaph. dicitur. Unde hoc modo aliquid Deo conformatur quod sibi assimilatur. Contingit autem aliqua dici similia dupliciter. Vel ex eo quod participant unam formam, sicut duo albi albedinem; et sic omne simile oportet esse compositum ex eo in quo convenit cum alio simili, et ex eo in quo differt ab ipso, cum similitudo non sit nisi differentium, secundum Boetium. Unde sic Deo nihil potest esse simile nec conveniens nec conforme, ut frequenter a philosophis dictum invenitur. Vel ex eo quod unum quod participative habet formam, imitatur illud quod essentialiter habet. Sicut si corpus album diceretur simile albedini separatae, vel corpus mixtum igneitate ipsi igni. Et talis similitudo quae ponit compositionem in uno et simplicitatem in alio, potest esse creaturae ad Deum participantis bonitatem vel sapientiam vel aliquid hujusmodi, quorum unumquodque in Deo est essentia ejus." This last statement is important, as it is the same way that the sense appetites participate in reason as creatures participate in God's goodness.

18. Montagnes cites (*Analogy*, 35) the following two texts: *In I Sent.*, d. 48, q. 1, a. 1 [Mand 1080]: "unum quod participative habet formam, imitatur illud quod essentialiter habet," and *In II Sent.*, d. 16, q. 1, a. 1, ad 3 [Mand 398]: "unum per se est simpliciter, et alterum participat de similitudine ejus quantum potest."

19. *In II Sent.*, d. 3, q. 3, a. 3, ad 2 [Mand 122]; *In I Sent.*, d. 3, q. 1, a. 3 [Mand 96]: "creatura exemplariter procedat a Deo sicut a causa quodammodo simili."

ple, because God is good we are good, because God is wise we are wise, etc. Thus the effect is present *formaliter* in God. In the case of (2) the effect is only present *effective secundum virtutem* in the cause, because the cause has the power to produce an effect which is not formally present in the cause, for example, the sun which is not hot produces heat.[20] The sun has the power to produce heat, but heat (as they understood it) is not a formal attribute of the sun. In this manner, God creates beings through his divine ideas, which include essence, form, matter, separable and inseparable accidents, among other things.[21] The predominant language of this third kind of participation in Aquinas's commentary on the *Sentences* is that of formal likeness, in particular, a diminished formal likeness explained in the language of exemplar causality. Montagnes points out that this implies a somewhat "formalist ontology" and a "formalistic conception of causality and being."[22]

In the latter texts, however, the emphasis is on act and potency and reduction of potency to act by way of efficient causality. The participated perfection is related to the participant as act to potency.[23] In the case of God and the analogy of being, the emphasis is now on *esse* as act, and *ipsum esse per se subsistens* acts insofar as it is pure act and brings new beings into existence. "In sum, participation is presented as the communication of act to a subject in potency. The act is communicated by a productive causality that assimilates the effect to the agent."[24]

According to Montagnes, the crucial shift "is the substitution of the notion of act for that of form."[25] As he puts it:

20. *In II Sent.*, d. 14, q. 1, a. 2, ad 3 [Mand 351]: "et tamen non oportet eodem modo inveniri aliquid in causa quo est in effectu, sed eminentiori: et ita etiam calor aliquo modo est in sole, non quidem denominans ipsum, ut dicatur calidus formaliter, sed effective secundum virtutem calefaciendi, quae in eo est." See also *In I Sent.*, d. 2, q. 1, a. 2 [Mand 62–63], and d. 8, q. 1, a. 2 [Mand 198].

21. For the distinction between the two kinds of exemplarity see *In I Sent.*, d. 19, q. 5, a. 2, ad 4 [Mand 493], and d. 2, q. 1, a. 2 [Mand 62–63]. See texts, 156nn15–16. See also Doolan, *Divine Ideas*, 77. I was surprised to find that Aquinas held that some separable accidents are included in the divine idea of a substance; see his account of time in *In I Sent.*, d. 38, q. 1, a. 3, ad 1 [Mand 904]. However, he denies that they are included in his *QDV*, q. 3, a. 7 [Leonine 22.1:114.66–89].

22. Montagnes, *Analogy*, 74 and 79.

23. *ST* I, q. 75, a. 5, ad 4 [St. Paul 347]: "Omne participatum comparatur ad participans ut actus eius." *SCG* II.54 [Leonine 13:391]: "Omne participans aliquid comparatur ad ipsum quod participatur ut potentia ad actum: per id enim quod participatur fit participans actu tale."

24. Montagnes, *Analogy*, 40.

25. Ibid., 80.

Causality is presented as the communication of a form, whereas subsequently it is that of an act. According to the first perspective, the agent acts in virtue of its form, and causality consists in imprinting its likeness; according to the second, the agent acts in as much as it is in act and does so in order to bring a new being into existence. Correlatively, the perfection received by the effect is limited either owing to its imperfect likeness or as an act received by a potency.[26]

On the other hand, exemplar causality in the *Sentences* also implies efficient causality.[27] Moreover, equivocal efficient causality necessarily also involves communication of formal content, as otherwise there would be no analogical likeness between cause and effect. Montagnes suggests that the later formal communication arises out of Aquinas's axiom that "every agent produces something like itself," which in turn is grounded in the more fundamental axiom that "every agent acts insofar as it is in act."[28]

The problem with the earlier and more formalist account is that it tends toward univocity,[29] as it is the same form that is possessed in a

26. Ibid., 42.

27. *In I Sent.*, d. 38, q. 1, a. 1 [Mand 899]. Furthermore, Aquinas does speak of the exemplar causality of the divine nature in later texts; see *ST* I, q. 47, a. 1, ad 2 [St. Paul 235]. Cf. *QDP*, q. 3, a. 4, ad 9 [Marietti 48]: *Quodl.* IV, q. 1, a. 1 [Leonine 25.2:319.34–60].

28. Montagnes cites *QDP*, q. 7, a. 5 [Marietti 198], and *SCG* I.29 [Leonine manualis 31]. Note the linking of this causality with equivocal and efficient causality using the example of the sun.

29. Montagnes describes the general problem this way: "There [in the *Sentences*] Thomas accepts the same formalist conception according to which the principal relation of being to God is that of imitation, but he grasps the danger that it presents: more or less to confuse the creature with the creator and to succumb to the univocity to which our conceptual process inclines us. There is only one means to eliminate this danger: to accentuate the distance, to deny all direct likeness, to refuse every sort of determinate relation. At what price, then, does one safeguard the divine transcendence? By radically separating beings from God, by accentuating the distance to the point of rupture, by running the risk of equivocity and agnosticism. Neither theologically nor philosophically is this a satisfactory solution: it annihilates our knowledge of God; it eliminates the unity of being. The cause of this is the underlying metaphysics which inspires this solution. To escape the impasse, one had to conceive being no longer as form but as act, and causality no longer as the likeness of the copy to the model but as the dependence of one being on another being which produces it. Now this is exactly what efficient causality implies: exercised by a being in act, it makes a new being exist in act, which being is not confounded with the first, as the effect and the cause each exist on its own account, but which communicates with it in the act, as the act of the agent becomes that of the patient. Thus it is by a veritable communication of being that God produces creatures and creative causality establishes between beings and God the indispensable bond of participation so that there might be an analogy of relation between them." Montagnes, *Analogy*, 78. Cf. Fabro, *Participation et Causalite*, 525, cited in ibid., 43.

diminished fashion *per participationem*. Granting the formal nature of exemplar causality, it is as if our minds gravitate toward imagining this participation using the example of the form of whiteness, for example, something participates in whiteness as it is more or less perfectly white. But such participation is nevertheless univocal.[30]

Concerning the nature of this development, Montagnes himself warns against both exaggerating and downplaying its significance. Exemplarism in the *Sentences* commentary involves efficient causality, as an exemplar cause cannot cause anything unless an agent also efficiently causes it, and Aquinas certainly does not abandon these two forms of divine exemplarism in his late texts. But the emphasis in the early texts is first and foremost on formal communication (with efficient causality implied), but in the later texts the emphasis is on efficient causality (with formal communication implied).[31]

Equivocal Causality and Participation in Reason

As the kind of participation at stake when Aquinas says the sense appetites participate in reason is the third kind, it is not surprising that we have found Aquinas explaining this participation in the early texts in terms of exemplar causality and in the late texts in terms of efficient causality. In the *Sentences* commentary, the sense appetites participate in reason (their exemplar cause) through the moral virtues; in fact, the moral virtues themselves are, as it were, participations in reason. Moreover, their exemplar cause is not only reason itself, but reason informed by prudence. Aquinas is explicit that the kind of exemplarism is that of nature, that is, as the effect is formally present in its cause and as the form by which the agent acts is communicated to its effect, which then resembles its cause by an intrinsic formal participation. This participat-

---

30. Montagnes, *Analogy*, 76.

31. Ibid., 40 and 43. For more details on Aquinas's metaphysical shift see ibid., chaps. 1–2. Concerning moral virtue, there is no need to account for something like *QDV*, q. 2, a. 11, i.e., the disputes about the analogy of proportion and the analogy of proportionality. The development in Aquinas's thinking on participation of the sense appetites in reason is a much simpler story to tell than that of his metaphysics. For a recent challenge to Montagnes's account of Aquinas's progression, especially concerning the *De veritate*, see Steven Long's *Analogia Entis* (Notre Dame, Ind.: University of Notre Dame Press, 2012). But Long does not offer nearly the same wealth of detailed textual support as Montagnes, nor does he offer a historically based interpretation of analogy in Aquinas.

ing form, either temperance or fortitude, is in fact a diminished likeness of reason (informed by prudence) impressed upon the sense appetites. This participating form then causes a mode (*modus*) which can be understood either as a way of operating (facility, lowered vehemence of passion, obedience, connaturality) or as the formal receiving of the habit in the sense appetites along the lines of the axiom that everything that is received is received according to the mode (*modus*) of the receiver.[32]

The emphasis in exemplar causality, as the name exemplar signifies, is clearly formal. However, one wonders what exactly this natural exemplarism is meant to explain. It is tempting to grasp this likeness as the exemplarism of ideas, as our ideas are obviously from reason, and reason does exercise such exemplarism when making external things (e.g., building houses). But it is not as if an agent thinks of moral virtue and tries to make himself virtuous in the manner in which a man builds a house: that is clearly not what Aquinas means, because the natural exemplarism named is explicitly contrasted with exemplarism of ideas.[33] Rather by placing this exemplarism on a natural level it seems to suggest that the sense appetites are deficient likenesses of reason itself. But if the participated effect exists formally in the cause, what exactly is the formal similarity between the two forms (moral virtues and reason informed by prudence)? Should one explain this similarity in terms of the decreased vehemence of passion, or of the increased pleasure, or of the facility of action, or of the connatural inclination? Are these quasi-rational actions of a quasi-rational form?

In the later texts, however, the emphasis of Aquinas's appeal to participation is rather on efficient causality. What is now emphasized is that the sense appetites participate in reason by the act of *command*, and the sense appetites participate as they *obey* this command. Participation is now cast in the language of act/potency and movers/moved. Participated and participant are related as act and potency, as moving and moved. Unlike the earlier exemplarism, which implies that sense appetites (via moral virtue) themselves formally possess reason in some diminished fashion, now all that is required is that the sense appetites receive the

---

32. See chapter 7.

33. See, e.g., *In I Sent.*, d. 19, q. 5, a. 2, ad 4 [Mand 493]; *In I Sent.*, d. 2, q. 1, a. 2 [Mand 62–63]. See also Doolan, *Divine Ideas*, 77.

act of reason from reason itself. When the sense appetites are actually being commanded, they participate. When they are not actually being commanded, they do not. This is helpful because it allows one to explain how, in the case of a continent act, a person's sense appetite may also be said to participate in reason. Likewise, habits of the sense appetite, temperance and fortitude, are only actualized when we will to use them. That is, although they exist as accidents when they are not being used, they do not participate in reason as "first acts" but only as "second acts," that is, as actually actualized by reason. Moral virtues are a particular kind of potency that can only be actualized by a particular cause, namely, reason's command.[34]

When it is said that the sense appetites participate in reason, this means that they quite literally "have reason," albeit in a partial manner through receiving reason's actual causality in command. Thus, as the passages in the *tertia pars* show, these are not two acts, namely first the command of reason and then that of sense appetites, but one act of sense appetite qua actualized as commanded and moved by reason.[35] The habit of moral virtue helps this act to come about habitually by lowering the vehemence of antecedent passion and by causing facility and delight in action.[36] It is true that the habit connaturally inclines toward this act, for this inclination follows upon the habit's first act as an accidental quality, but Aquinas does not describe this inclination as a participation in reason because the unactualized habit is not actually participating in reason's command. It is only inclining toward it.[37]

It is worth pointing out that in equivocal causality (of the third kind of participation) one may distinguish between analogical formal communication and efficient causality even if these are not separable in reality. There is no question but that in the line of efficient causality it is the will that is causally efficacious. This is true of early and late texts. But in the *Sentences* commentary and in the *De veritate*, it is reason that provides both the formal content and the end of volition, that is, what (the object) is willed and why (the final cause) it is willed. That is, practically all of the formal intelligible content comes from reason, and the will

34. Chapter 10.
35. See chapter 10, 218nn51–52.
36. See chapter 10 and chapter 12.
37. See chapter 12.

simply executes whatever that may be along the lines of efficient causality; we can think of the will in the early texts as a bridge between reason and moral virtues, over which reason must pass to cause its likeness (the moral virtues) in the sense appetites. The caused habit or moral virtue is simply a likeness of reason itself, its natural exemplar cause.[38]

In the late texts, however, reason no longer has a monopoly on formal content, but the will, in fact, provides some of it; this is evident from our discussion of the will's natural inclination, God's *instinctus*, and consent. There is thus a significant change here. Command, which presupposes choice, is no longer reducible to reason as it was in the *Sentences*. When it is said that the sense appetites participate in reason, here it no longer means the power of reason itself, but rather the rational part of the soul, that is, reason and will acting together in unison along different causal lines, neither reducible to the other. The act of command in both the *Sentences* and the later texts, includes reason and will, but in the late texts the will contributes substantially more (by way of *instinctus*, consent, and final causality in choice) to the choice itself and thus makes its own contribution to command that far surpasses what Aquinas grants to the will in the *Sentences*. This means that the intelligible content analogically communicated to the sense appetites in command is no longer solely the domain of reason, but includes some content also provided by the will. With Aquinas's later strengthening of the role of the will, free choices are no longer causally reducible to reason as they were in the early texts, and participation is no longer grasped as a likeness between two forms, for example, between reason and moral virtue, but rather as the actualization of the sense appetites by reason's and will's *act* of command.[39]

In order to distinguish efficient causality from formal communication, we must thus try to pick apart command. Command, as we have seen in chapter 10, is highly complex. Whether or not this act affects the sense appetites by redounding, by causing new external sense inputs, through the imagination or through the cogitative power in a certain sense makes no difference. Prior to this one must grasp that what is commanded is first of all chosen, as command is the execution of choice

38. See chapters 6–8.
39. See chapters 9–10.

vis-à-vis the lower powers of the soul. Distinguishing the efficient cause from its formal content must thus occur at a prior and higher level in the causal chain, namely, that of choice.[40]

Reason and will are now, in a different way, understood as included in reason (taken more broadly as the rational part of the soul) as co-causes in reason's act of choice and command. Efficient causality, and this can only be grasped as *per se* efficient causality, is now a better way of understanding the causal foundation of this relation of participation between the sense appetites and reason. By definition all *per se* efficient causes are intelligible. When I speak of the formal content of an efficient cause, I do not mean a formal cause as one of the four Aristotelian causes. What is meant is the formal content of the final cause, namely, the "that for the sake of which," the *causa causarum*, which is the reason for the efficient cause. Without such a cause, according to Aquinas, an efficient cause is not an efficient cause, but only a *per accidens* efficient cause. Efficient causes always convey and are bound to intelligible content. In the case of free decisions, this intelligible content is partly provided by reason (what is willed, the object) and partly provided by the will (the end of volition). However, in a series of *per se* efficient causes, the lower movers need not themselves be able to account for the intelligibility of their action—for example, a saw cannot say what it is making or why it is making it—but the action itself is, nevertheless, perfectly intelligible. In the case of free human action, it seems, we are partly like saws, on the one hand efficiently moved by God's *instinctus*, but on the other hand we simultaneously have reasons for choosing what we do. Both our own reasons and God's efficiently moving us are included in free choice and command, and thus the action is partly intelligible and partly unintelligible to us. While God's efficiently moving our wills is unintelligible to us, it is not unintelligible *in se*, as it is caused by God's reason and will.

Granting this, we cannot really say that our own reason is the exemplar cause that is participated in, as the participated form is no longer simply a deficient imitation of reason itself, understood as some sort of formal lessening. Rather once one takes the strengthened will into consideration and all that it brings into the picture, efficiency has far superior explanatory power. Efficiency can explain both what moves and

40. See chapters 9–10.

what is moved (act and potency, participated and participant), but also the conveying of an intelligible content which need not and cannot be fully reduced to the agent's own reason and which must remain partially obscure to us as caused by God's reason. It is this rational act that is participated in by the sense appetites.

There is much opposition to explaining the relation of participation between the sense appetites and reason in terms of efficient causality, as it seems inevitably to lead to a Cartesian understanding where the only relation between soul and body is that of an efficient cause. But once one introduces the distinction between the soul as a mover (*motor*) and the soul as form (*forma*), one sees that this account of how the parts of the soul are related to one another, and in our case how some of these parts are related to others by way of efficient causality, in no way contradicts or conflicts with the manner in which the soul is the form (*forma*) of the body.

Furthermore, when I consider the soul as a potential whole, I am considering it teleologically as a complex group of operative powers which are ordered to that being's end. In the case of a human being, this complex group is ordered to the person's end, ultimately, to happiness. When these parts are out of order the whole cannot act as it should. Consider a car, which in some sense is a highly complex group of parts that function together to take us places. When some part of the engine does not work, the car cannot properly drive. The soul as a potential whole is something like this, but it is a complex group of material and immaterial parts, rooted in one substance, with its own intrinsic principle of motion and rest. When the sense appetites participate in reason, these parts work together in a better, more seamless way than they otherwise would have. It is far from guaranteeing happiness, but Aquinas does think that we will live better and more happily than we would have otherwise.

To what degree one should emphasize Aquinas's development on how the sense appetites participates in reason, I am unwilling to say. On the one hand, one can find many of the elements of his later thought scattered here and there in his earlier works, and on the other hand exemplarity is undoubtedly part of his later thinking on participation as well. Be that as it may, his shift of emphasis from exemplarity to efficiency in this particular context seems fully warranted by an abundance of texts. He does not return to explaining the participatory relation between reason and the sense appetites in the language of exemplarity, but he does speak of moral virtue in the sense appetites as a "habitual conformity" of those powers to reason, understood as a disposition (or habit) of a potency toward what actualizes or moves it.[41] Moreover, this shift of emphasis aligns perfectly with the shift from Aquinas's exemplarist and quasi-formalist ontology in his earlier texts to his later emphasis on *esse* as *actus* and efficient causality in his account of creation, as Montagnes has pointed out. On the ethical plane, his earlier accounts of free decision shift from being somewhat intellectualist to being somewhat more voluntarist, and this aligns with his shift in reason's relation to the sense appetites along the lines of exemplarism and then in terms of efficient causality. To be clear, I would never go so far to claim that Aquinas went from being an intellectualist to being a voluntarist, as others have done.[42] It is rather a question of degrees, and of explaining exactly what causal roles reason and will each bring to choice, and then exactly how the execution of this choice is participated in by the sense appetites.

41. He does discuss the habitual conformity of the sense appetites to reason as caused by reason's command: *ST* I-II, q. 56, a. 4 [St. Paul 780]: "Et quia bona dispositio potentiae moventis motae, attenditur secundum conformitatem ad potentiam moventem; ideo virtus quae est in irascibili et concupiscibili, nihil aliud est quam quaedam habitualis conformitas istarum potentiarum ad rationem." Cf. *ST* I-II, q. 61, a. 5 [St. Paul 805].

42. See chapter 9, 185n15, for the literature and a discussion of this debate.

PART 3

THE PLAUSIBILITY OF AQUINAS'S POSITION

12

WHAT MORAL VIRTUE DOES AND DOES NOT DO

In part 3, I will build on the material from the first two parts and apply it to the question of the relation between reason and emotion in virtue ethics. One classical position holds that virtue grants humans spontaneously good passions. Chapter 12 will engage contemporary Thomists and argue that Aquinas does not believe that virtues have the power to do this, and I will explain what exactly Aquinas does think the moral virtues can do. I gather that many people will not be satisfied with what Aquinas offers in place of spontaneously good passions, and chapter 13 will address these concerns and explain why I think Aquinas's position is plausible. I will begin to address these concerns by contrasting Aquinas with both Kant and Aristotle, and I will end by contextualizing Aquinas in the contemporary challenge to virtue ethics posed by some philosophers interested in social psychology.

Choice and Habituation: The Medieval Problem

I will begin framing the issue of spontaneous passions by contextualizing it in the high medieval problem of the role of habits in moral virtue. Bonnie Kent depicts the problem as follows: all the masters generally agreed that actions are good and meritorious because they are free, but they disagreed on how to incorporate two Aristotelian elements of moral virtue into their particular accounts of freedom. On the one hand, Aristotle emphasizes that a habit is a *habitus electivus*,[1] that is, it is always bound to choice, which is indeterministic; but on the other hand habits, as second natures, act in a natural and deterministic way. These two elements, *prima facie*, seem to be intrinsically in conflict, for if the *habitus electivus* compels an agent to act deterministically, then virtue or vice destroys the voluntary act itself and hence the meritorious or blameworthy nature of virtue or vice.[2]

There were two broad explanations of moral virtue corresponding to one's views on the relation between intellect and will. For those who offered a voluntaristic account of the will's freedom over and against reason, the role of moral virtue was to help the will accord with reason's dictates in spite of contrary passions. The business of moral virtue was first and foremost about making good choices. The main concern of the voluntarists, and a very important one, was to safeguard the free nature of virtuous acts. Although they had many good arguments for positing all of the moral virtues in the will, their main line of thought seems to have been this: only the will is free, as a *habitus electivus* free choice is an essential part of moral virtue, and thus moral virtues are in the will.[3]

If, however, one takes the will in an intellectualist sense, then the role of the virtues will be concomitantly altered and placed in the sense appetites. Consider Godfrey of Fontaines, who held that the will is efficiently moved by the intellect (in Aquinas's terms, both in the line of specification and of exercise).[4] As he saw it, because the will is the kind of thing that is determined by the intellect, there is no need for virtue to help it do what it already naturally does. Godfrey thus argued that *all* of the moral virtues are in the sense appetites.[5] He notes that the inferior appetite naturally should obey the superior appetite, but this does not always hap-

---

1. *Nic.* VI, 1106b36.

2. Kent, *Virtues of the Will*, 226.

3. E.g., Scotus, *Lectura* III, d. 33, ll. 40–45 (ed. Vat. XXI, 269): "Contra: II *Ethicorum:* <<Virtus est habitus electivus>>; <<electio aut est appetitus consiliativus aut consilium>>, 'appetitus qui saltem est appetitus consiliativus aut consilium'; ergo praesupponit rationem. Igitur est voluntatis"; ll. 54–55: "Item, bonum huiusmodi est laudabile, igitur in potestate est nostra; igitur in voluntate." See also ll. 282–94 (ed. Vat. XXI, 282); Henricus, *Quodl.* IV, q. 22 (ed. Badius, f. 138vQ–139rR); Petri Ioannis Olivi, *QQ. de virtutibus*, q. 4 (ed. Grottaferrata, XXIV:227).

4. *Quodl.* VI, q. 7 (*Philosophes Belges* 163); VIII, q. 16 (169, 176); X, q. 13 (375–76).

5. *Quodl.* XIV, q. 3 (5:343): "Est ergo iustitia et omnis virtus moralis ponenda in appetitu sensitivo."

pen because the intellect is sometimes enticed by the sense appetites. The problem, as he saw it, is not between intellect and will, but between flesh and spirit, that is, between the sense appetite and the intellect/will.[6] In other words, for Godfrey, the moral virtues exist in the sense appetites to modify the passions before they can obstruct reason and will.

Both sides agree that the moral virtues are concerned with not letting passion hinder the right use of reason and will, but the voluntarists placed their efficacy in the will (emphasizing their voluntary nature), whereas the intellectualists placed their efficacy in the sense appetites (emphasizing their role as a second nature in moderating passion). For the intellectualists the first role of moral virtue is to order passion; for the voluntarists it is to enable good choice. For Aquinas the moral virtues are in the sense appetites and thus they moderate passions, but as they are only used when willed they are also strictly voluntary.

Aquinas's position is unique because he can accommodate the concerns of both the intellectualists and the voluntarists: on the one hand, accounting for the free nature of moral virtue; on the other hand, accounting for how moral virtues temper the passions, which is precisely what the voluntarists neglect. The moral virtues as habits or natures are determinate in the sense that they incline to reason's command, which is itself indeterminate as bound to free choice. In other words, moral virtue itself is *ad unum* to something which is *ad utrumlibet*. What distinguishes his position from the others is that his "psychological division of labor,"[7] to use Kent's phrase, neither has to grant excessively heavy roles to intellect, will, or the sense appetites. Scotus's will, for example, has to do all of the heavy lifting: it must account for both the free and virtuous nature of human acts.

In Aquinas, however, moral virtue plays a smaller role. As I discussed when considering habits and their role *vis-à-vis* the human soul, we are considering the soul not as form but as mover, as it is composed of parts. Moral virtue helps to make the parts of the potential whole work to-

---

6. Ibid., 342: "Sed quia in homine isti duo appetitus sunt coniuncti et inferior natus est oboedire superiori, non tamen prompte propter hoc quod frequenter alliciendo trahit contra illud quod apprehenditur a ratione per aliquid apprehensum a sensu et sic est ibi repugnantia non voluntatis ad intellectum, sed carnis, id est carnalis affectionis appetitus sensitivi ad spiritum quae non contingit ex parte appetitus rationalis, sed ipsius appetitus sensitivi."

7. Kent, *Virtues of the Will*, 223–24.

gether more seamlessly. For Aquinas, both the intellectualist and the voluntarist positions involve distortions of the psychological division of labor. Because the sense appetites are only virtuous to the extent that they participate in reason or are commanded by reason, in any particular virtuous act one has the full force of reason, will, and sense appetites simultaneously operating along different causal lines. Reason and will actualize the potency and virtues of the sense appetites. This is precisely what it means for the sense appetites to operate as they ought.

Scotus's position that the will was always free to choose against the practical judgment of reason severed the connection between the virtues and the parts of the soul. Because prudence is in the intellect, Scotus correctly saw that it is quite possible (although highly unlikely) to have prudence without the moral virtues in the will.[8] For Aquinas, however, insofar as choice always follows the practical judgment of reason and moral virtue is bound to choice through command, moral virtue is inseparably bound to prudence, the habit of good choice. This is not to say that for Aquinas the free agent always chooses according to prudence. As mentioned above, Aquinas thinks that we are always free to act against our habits, for we only use our habits when we will to do so. Nevertheless, Aquinas does hold that any act of moral virtue is always according to the judgment of prudence. This is because any act of temperance is necessarily bound to prudence via command, for the habit of temperance is only actualized by the prudential judgment and command of reason.

However, there are some contemporary Thomists who imply that this is not the case, namely, that it is possible to have virtuous passions prior to prudential judgment.[9] They claim that the emotions may participate in reason prior to reason's command. If these Thomists are right, this poses a serious challenge to my argument. Before we delve into the current debates, however, I want to emphasize that this is not simply a

***

8. For a discussion of this see Stephen Dumont, "The Necessary Connection of Moral Virtue to Prudence according to John Duns Scotus—Revisited," *Recherches de théologie et philosophie médiévales* 55 (1988): 184–206.

9. See, e.g., Cates, Aquinas on the Emotions, 218 and 228–29, and "The Virtue of Temperance (IIa–IIae, qq. 141–170)," in Ethics of Aquinas, ed. Pope, 327; Jean Porter, The Recovery of Virtue: The Relevance of Aquinas for Christian Ethics (Louisville, Ky.: Westminster John Knox Press, 1990), 103; Harak, Virtuous Passions, 4, 10, 21, 91, 96; Titus, "Passions in Christ." For a non-Thomist perspective, see Robert C. Roberts, "Temperance," in Virtues and Their Vices, ed. Kevin Timpe and Craig A. Boyd (Oxford: Oxford University Press, 2014), 93–114.

live debate among Thomists, but is also central to the history of Western moral thought and has perdured up to the present.

Virtuous Emotional Spontaneity

The debate concerns whether or not there is such a thing as a virtuous antecedent passion. It strikes at the very heart of the role of moral virtue. Advocates of the existence of these kinds of passions argue that the virtuous habituation of the sense appetites makes them feel the right passions concerning the right objects spontaneously. By spontaneously they mean apart from (or antecedent to) reason's command. In other words, like any other habit, once the emotional faculties (the sense appetites) have been properly habituated by many acts over a long period of time they will by themselves be automatically or spontaneously attracted to the right things at the right time in the right way prior to reason's command. They argue that having good emotional responses prior to prudence's deliberation and choice is an essential aspect of moral virtue. The temperate agent, for example, simply has the right spontaneous emotional responses before he has to think about them.

Indeed, Aristotle repeatedly claims that the virtuous agent always has the right passions, in the sense of being toward the right object, in the right amount, at the right time, and in the right circumstances.[10] In fact, any agent who does not experience such emotions is simply not fully virtuous. For Aristotle's virtuous man, there is no conflict between the sensitive part of the soul and the rational part of the soul.[11] Aristotle is, of course, both the father of virtue ethics and of hylomorphism, and many thinkers believe these two topics are inextricably linked. The unarticulated thought goes something like this: as matter and form are united in one substance, so are reason and sensibility united in the virtuous man. Virtue is a kind of mirror-image of hylomorphism, reason and passion working together harmoniously as matter and form: a full life is a passionate life, in which there is no need to suppress and repress our passions in some kind of a Kantian manner; reason and passion, in the virtuous agent, seamlessly help each other out.

Furthermore, they usually hold some form of this argument: the ear-

---

10. *Nic.* 1115b11–20, 1119a11–18, 1146a10–12, 1151b34–1152a4, etc.
11. *Nic.* 1102b27–28.

ly modern rejection of Aristotelian hylomorphism leads to some version of Cartesian dualism, where *res cogitans* and *res extensa* are utterly separate from one another, and where they are certainly not united in any Aristotelian hylomorphic sense. Fast-forward to Kant's division between phenomenal and noumenal reality, where passions are part of the natural phenomenal a posteriori reality and reason is part of the rational noumenal a priori reality, and you have something resembling Cartesian dualism, where reason, *res cogitans*, must control and rule over passion, which inhabits the a posteriori phenomenal natural world of *res extensa*.

Indeed, in the *Groundwork*, Kant is adamant that passions have no real moral worth; if anything at all they are simply troublesome. It is only in pure reason that there is moral worth at all, and hence the moral project consists in conquering and ruling our troublesome sensible inclinations. The only good thing is the good will, and everything else is only derivatively good.[12] Thus the rejection of hylomorphism and virtue ethics go hand in hand. Reject hylomorphism and you fall into dualism, which in virtue ethics means radically sundering the rational from the sensible and ultimately in reason unnaturally suppressing the sensible. Descartes is, after all, quite adamant in *Discourses* VI that nature is something to be conquered and used by us. Of course, many will rightly object that this is unfair and terribly simplistic (I agree). But let us nevertheless indulge this popular line of thought a little more by considering Schiller's criticisms of Kant.

Schiller argues that there are three possible ways reason can relate to sensibility: by suppression, by indulgence, or by harmony.[13] Suppression amounts to tyranny or oppression, a heavy-handed quashing of sensibility by reason. He attributes this position to Kant. The second model, indulgence, is cast as a kind of anarchy or ochlocracy, where reason has abandoned its independence and nature rules willy nilly. The third model, harmony, is different: because humans are both rational and sensible, when the two are in harmony, "a human being is at one with himself."[14]

---

12. Kant, *Groundwork*, 4:393–402 (9–17).

13. Schiller, "On Grace and Dignity," *The Complete Works of Friedrich Schiller*, vol. III: *Aesthetical and Philosophical Essays* (New York: P. F. Collier and Sons, 1902), 202–4. See also Baxley, *Kant's Theory*, 89–90.

14. Schiller, "Grace," 202; this is Baxley's translation in *Kant's Theory*, 90.

Indeed, the oppression of one part of us to another can never constitute a victory. Schiller writes:

It is only when he gathers *his entire humanity* together, and his way of moral thinking becomes the result of the united action of both principles, when morality has become second nature for him, it is then only that it is secure; for, as long as the moral mind still exerts *force*, natural impulse must still have the *power* to resist it. The enemy that is merely *overturned* can rise up again, but that enemy that is *reconciled* is truly vanquished.[15]

Schiller characterizes such a harmonious soul as a beautiful soul (*schöne Seele*), much like Aristotle's use of the term *kalon* (beautiful) to describe the same phenomenon. Such a soul has become fully human and acts with grace (*Anmut*, in a nontheological sense) and ease, and need not even think before acting but can "abandon herself with a certain security to instinct."[16] In other words, Schiller argues that real moral virtue cannot mean that reason voluntarily has to control sensibility; that is simply not what virtue is. Virtue must so habituate sensibility that there is no battle between these parts of the soul. The troublesome parts are not vanquished by virtue in the sense of being controlled by some kind of compulsion, rather they are vanquished because they now play on the same team, and reason, without thought, can happily abandon itself to them much like one trusts other players on a highly trained team to execute their own roles.

Consider Kant's infamous sympathetic man from the *Groundwork*. Because the sympathetic man helps others from his feeling of sympathy, he fails to show moral worth; however, the unsympathetic, cold, and indifferent person, who acts beneficently from duty alone, "even though no inclination moves him any longer, he nevertheless tears himself from this deadly insensibility and performs the action without any inclination at all, but solely from duty—then for the first time his action has genuine moral worth."[17] Indeed, Kant writes that "the sublimity and in-

15. Ibid., 206 (91).

16. Ibid., 209 (92). To explain this, Schiller contrasts the children of the house with the servants of the house. According to Schiller, such children do not experience the moral law as an obligation or an imperative. See Baxley, *Kant's Theory*, 91–92, for a discussion of this. "On Grace and Dignity" was published in 1793, the year in which his first son was born, and I cannot help but wonder if he changed his mind as his four children were growing up.

17. Kant, *Groundwork*, 4:398 (13).

ner worth of the command are so much the more evident in a duty, the fewer subjective causes [inclinations] there are for it and the more they oppose it,"[18] and thus everyone wishes "to be free from such inclinations which are a burden."[19]

Thus Schiller penned this incisive joke, directed at Kant:

I like to serve my friends, but unfortunately I do it by inclination.
And so often am I bothered by the thought that I am not a virtuous person.

Decision:
There is no other way but this! You must seek to despise them
And do with repugnance what duty bids you.[20]

Schiller's point, of course, is that we should spontaneously love our friends apart from the command of reason. A great part of virtue, for Schiller and Aristotle (and others),[21] is the insight that when we say that sensibility can become virtuous, what we mean is precisely that we can have spontaneous passions for good objects, and what we mean by spontaneous is precisely that these passions need not be voluntarily and explicitly commanded. Many Thomists today argue along precisely these lines, and in fact, to deny the existence of these spontaneously virtuous passions is apparently to be no different than Kant, namely, cold, dry, rationalistic, and voluntaristic. All reason, no passion. I will return to Kant in the next chapter to give him his due. For now I wish to turn to the debates among Aquinas scholars as they strike this nerve.

Like Schiller, many Thomists currently argue that it is precisely the role of moral virtue to so habituate sensibility that it can be trusted without voluntary thought.[22] In other words, virtue works as an emotional autopilot, ensuring that one will always, in Aristotle's words, have

18. Ibid., 4:425 (33).
19. Ibid., 4:454 (55); cf. Kant, *Critique of Practical Reason*, trans. Mary Gregor (Cambridge: Cambridge University Press, 1997), 5:118 (99).
20. Johann Wolfgang von Goethe and Friedrich Schiller, *Xenien*, "The Philosophers," in Goethe, *Werke*, vol. 1, ed. Erich Trunz (Munich: Beck, 1982). This translation is by Allen Wood, *Kant's Ethical Thought* (Cambridge: Cambridge University Press, 1999), 28.
21. For an excellent broad overview of the many different philosophers who have argued that habits should cause spontaneously good emotions, see Clare Carlisle, *On Habit* (New York: Routledge, 2014).
22. See, e.g., Pinkaers, *The Sources of Christian Ethics* and *The Pinkaers Reader*. See also Gondreau, "The Passions and the Moral Life"; Titus, "Passions in Christ"; and Harak, *Virtuous Passions*.

the right passions for the right objects, in the right ways, and at the right times. If there is struggle between reason and emotion, then there is no virtue, as Aristotle suggests in *Nic.* I.13. Where there is struggle, there is continence, incontinence, or something else, but certainly not virtue. Aquinas, they say, is firmly Aristotelian in this respect.

Aquinas's thinking on emotions, however, is far more developed and detailed than Aristotle's and it enables him to more clearly discuss what exactly might be meant by a spontaneous passion.[23] As I discussed above,[24] he distinguishes between antecedent and consequent passions. To briefly summarize, antecedent passions precede the judgment of reason and consequent passions come afterwards. When people speak of spontaneously good passions, what they generally mean is that they are spontaneous precisely with respect to thinking or willing. Spontaneously good passions, if they exist, would have to be virtuous antecedent passions ordered to some good object by moral virtue prior to reason's judgment. Consequent passions would not fit the bill, because as consequent to and caused by the judgment of reason, they would not count as spontaneous.

However, Giuseppe Butera has powerfully challenged the common view that Aquinas allows for virtuous ordered antecedent passions, that is, spontaneously good passions. Butera argues against this position for five main reasons. First, he points out that Aquinas nowhere in his corpus says there are virtuous antecedent passions. Second, because Aquinas argues that antecedent passion decreases merit (by obscuring practical reason)[25] whereas virtue increases merit, it is contradictory to hold that there is a passion that is both antecedent and virtuous; for it would simultaneously increase and decrease merit. Third, virtuous antecedent passions would displace the role of prudence. If there were passions that were reliably good prior to the command of reason, it would mean that the sense appetites could judge exactly what and to what degree some particular thing was worth pursuing, in other words, they would determine the mean, which is precisely the role of prudence. It follows, I

---

23. There is nothing like Aquinas's massive so-called treatise on the passions (*ST* I-II, qq. 22–48) in Aristotle.

24. In chapter 10, above.

25. For an earlier and very clear account of this point see Richard K. Mansfield, "Antecedent Passion and the Moral Quality of Human Acts According to St. Thomas," *Proceedings of the American Catholic Philosophical Association* 71 (1997): 221–31.

would add, that such passions would also sever the connection between the virtues. For if it were the case that the sense appetites could desire the virtuous thing or act before prudence had determined what that was, then temperance, for instance, would not need prudence. Fourth, he points out that antecedent passions in usual situations would lead to opposing commands. For instance, an antecedent passion for a healthy breakfast of eggs, fruit, and toast would be insufficient on a day when someone was going to climb a mountain; on that day, such a person would have to command himself or herself to eat more than he or she desires. Fifth, he argues that the goal of temperance is despotic or slavish control of the sense appetites, that is, no antecedent passions at all (even though this is unattainable). Butera is right to point out that in all of the passages in which Aquinas discusses the political analogy, that is, whether we should have despotic or democratic control of the passions, the goal is always despotic control. Along these lines, Butera also points out that in Christ, Adam, and Mary, who were free from the *fomes peccati*, there were no antecedent passions at all. Granting these four reasons, which all have strong textual support in Aquinas, Butera concludes that there is no such thing for Aquinas as virtuous antecedent passions. Butera's arguments are hard to gainsay and the textual support is abundant.[26] There have been no serious criticisms of his argument to date.

Steven Jensen, however, who basically agrees with Butera, offers a

26. Butera, "Thomas Aquinas on Reason's Control of the Passions." In the first four chapters he develops this theory that temperance only affects the vehemence of antecedent passions, but not their ordination. See also Butera, "On Reason's Control of the Passions in Aquinas's Theory of Temperance," *Mediaeval Studies* 68 (2006): 133–60, esp. 159. The latter is an article version of his dissertation. Mansfield implicitly seems to agree with Butera simply because he insists that antecedent passions always diminish merit and hence moral goodness. See Mansfield, *Antecedent Passion*, 229. Claudia Eisen Murphy, "Aquinas on Our Responsibility for Our Emotions," *Medieval Philosophy and Theology* 8 (1999): 163–205, and Leonard Ferry, "Sorting Our Reason's Relation to the Passions in the Moral Theory of Aquinas," *Proceedings of the American Catholic Philosophical Association* 88 (2016): 227–44, also seem to hold positions similar to Butera. Paul Gondreau, in his *The Passions of Christ's Soul in the Theology of St. Thomas Aquinas* (Scranton, Penn.: University of Scranton Press, 2008), previously published as Gondreau, *The Passions of Christ's Soul in the Theology of St. Thomas Aquinas*, Beiträge zur Geschichte der Philosophie und Theologie des Mittelalters–Neue Folge 61 (Münster: Aschendorff, 2002), and "The Passions and the Moral Life: Appreciating the Originality of Aquinas," *The Thomist* 71 (2007): 419–50, obviously disagrees with Butera's thesis, but he does not provide much evidence for taking a stand one way or another. Jeffrey Hause, "Aquinas on the Function of Moral Virtue," *American Catholic Philosophical Quarterly* 81 (2007): 1–20, also disagrees, but he argues for a position that he admits has no textual support in Aquinas. None of these clearly hone in on the problem as Butera does.

slightly different interpretation of antecedent and consequent passion. First, he points out that the distinction between antecedent and consequent is not really a temporal distinction of before and after, but rather a causal distinction between causing and being caused.[27] Second, he points out that antecedent and consequent passions do not pivot around choice but rather "the judgment of reason," which is not limited to choice.[28] There are many "judgments of reason" within the various moments leading up to the final judgment of reason, namely, choice, and Aquinas simply does not mean the final one. Thus an antecedent passion is a passion that has a causal influence on our judgments and a consequent passion is caused by our judgments. Jensen's main point is that a virtuous judgment can cause a virtuous consequent passion which in turn can causally function as a virtuous antecedent passion for the next virtuous judgment. In other words, a virtuous judgment J can cause passion P, which causes another virtuous judgment J2, etc. P is both consequent to J and antecedent to J2. So why not consider P to be a virtuous antecedent passion if it was caused by a prior virtuous judgment? Jensen is careful not to use the term virtuous antecedent passion, for he agrees with Butera that Aquinas never puts it this way, but he thinks this is a charitable and helpful interpretation that is compatible with Aquinas's thought.

Jensen is right to highlight the important causal element in the antecedent/consequent distinction. He is also right to draw our attention to the phenomena of reason-produced intra-deliberation passions, namely, that deliberative judgments can cause passions which will help us focus on making further judgments. I do, however, think his depiction misses something crucial about the big picture. Textually, Aquinas does often say that the judgment around which the antecedent/consequent pivot hinges is choice,[29] and in those passages in which he is vague,

---

27. Steven J. Jensen, "Virtuous Deliberation and the Passions," *The Thomist* 77 (2013): 199. Jensen was here partly influenced by Lombardo's *Logic of Desire*, 109 and 186n208, and Murphy, who also offers a causal account of antecedent and consequent passions in "Responsibility for Our Emotions," *Medieval Philosophy and Theology* 8 (1999): 182–84 and 190.

28. Jensen, *Virtuous Deliberation*, 214–17.

29. *QDV*, q. 26, a. 7, ad 1 [Leonine 22.3:774.157–67]: "perfecta ratio laudabilis et vituperabilis consistit in voluntario; unde id quod minuit de ratione voluntarii, diminuit rationem laudabilis in bono et vituperabilis in malo. Passio autem praecedens electionem diminuit rationem voluntarii, et ideo laudem boni actus et vituperium mali diminuit; sed passio sequens est signum magnitudinis voluntarii, ut dictum est, [in the resp.] unde sicut in bono addit ad laudem ita in malo ad vituperium."

I hold that he means it.[30] This must be so because the whole point of Aquinas's antecedent/consequent distinction is to explain how passions can be good or meritorious, and something is only meritorious to the extent that it is freely chosen. Most simply, if something is not freely chosen, then someone can hardly be praised or blamed for it. We are not praised or blamed for our deliberations or our antecedent passions, but we are praised or blamed for our choices and our consequent passions as they reflect these choices, and thus the hinge around which antecedent and consequent passions pivot must nevertheless be choice.[31] Furthermore, I will also point out that choice does indeed happen at a moment in time.[32] Thus the antecedent/consequent distinction is both temporal and causal, and it pivots around choice. At this point we may provisionally say that if passions are temporally prior to choice and causally affect our choices, then they are antecedent, but if they are caused by our choices and thus also come afterwards, then they are consequent.

30. *In IV Sent.*, d. 50, q. 2, a. 4, qc. 2: "Ad secundam quaestionem dicendum, quod misericordia vel compassio potest inveniri in aliquo dupliciter: uno modo per modum passionis; alio modo per modum *electionis*. In beatis autem non erit aliqua passio in parte inferiori, nisi consequens *electionem* rationis; unde non erit in eis compassio vel misericordia, nisi secundum rationis *electionem*. Hoc autem modo ex electione misericordia vel compassio nascitur, prout scilicet aliquis vult malum alterius repelli; unde in illis quae non volumus secundum judicium rationis repelli." Emphasis added, but see the next few lines of this text as well in which he clearly means electio in the phrase *quae non volumus secundum judicium rationis repelli*. Jensen argues that because Aquinas uses the phrase judgment of reason in different ways (he cites *ST* I-II, q. 15, a. 4; q. 14, a. 1; II-II, q. 47, a. 8; *QDV*, q. 17, a. 1, ad 4), all of these passages on antecedent and consequent passions are ambiguous. It is true that Aquinas will use the phrase to mean different things in different contexts, but I think it is very clear that in this context (and the parallel texts) he means choice, both because he often expressly uses the word *electio*, and because he sometimes uses the phrase to mean choice and as the argument about merit only makes sense because he means choice. It seems to me that Jensen is rather criticizing Aquinas's account of choice and all its various "moments" as too rigid and fixed, especially the difference between deliberation, choice, and execution. For another example where he is clearly using *iudicium rationis* to mean the act of *liberum arbitrium*; see *ST* I-II, q. 77, a. 6, ad 2 [St. Paul 889], and its clarification in q. 77, a. 6 [St. Paul 889]; see also *QDM*, q. 3, a. 11 [Leonine 23.90:28–59]. Aquinas's use of *electionis* in *ST* I-II, q. 24, a. 3, ad 1 [St. Paul 664], refers to deliberately and self-consciously willing to feel a particular emotion; both this and the *redundantia* there mentioned are consequent to free choice. See *ST* I-II, q. 77, a. 6 [St. Paul 889].

31. Jensen speaks of "virtuous deliberations," which Aquinas does not. For an excellent discussion of the nonculpability of deliberations see Hoffmann, *Angelic Sin*, 122–56.

32. The best descriptions of this are in the questions about whether angels sinned in the first instant of their creation. Granting that angelic time is different, there is nevertheless a real temporal before and after in their choice; see *QDM*, q. 16, a. 4 [Leonine 23:298–300.343–45]. The point is that choice happens in an instant: before we have not sinned and afterwards we have, but we are not culpable until that very moment.

Granting this reading of Aquinas, one might still wonder about Jensen's point. Why cannot such intra-deliberation passions be virtuous, or something quite close to being virtuous? I think the reason is relatively straightforward: for something to be virtuous it can only be good. Consider fear; it may help cause us to deliberate, but it may also be quite unhelpful. Fear may be about the wrong thing, or we may have too much or too little fear, and more often than not we waste energy worrying about things, that in hindsight really were not worth worrying about. There are times when we get it right, and often this fear will carry over to the next choice that we have to make. For instance, perhaps one is rightly fearful/anxious about something at work, but this anxiety does not translate well when we come home to our children. I do not want to make it seem like the passions of one moment will have nothing to do with the next, as if moments are schizophrenic and the passions appropriate to one would not be appropriate to the next. It is obviously the case that they often are appropriate, but then again they often are not, and the passions as sensible motions with their own bodily momentum carrying them forward to the next moment simply have no way of tracking the difference without reason.[33]

Because the antecedent/consequent distinction must pivot around choice, and because deliberation is the thinking leading up to the moment of choice, such passions within deliberation must be antecedent passions of some sort. If they are vehement, they will obscure our deliberation, if they are not, then they simply are not problematic and may at times be helpful in focusing our deliberations on certain aspects of what is being considered.

But while antecedent passions may be helpful at times, they cannot be virtuous and ordered. This is because deliberation itself is an indeter-

---

33. Jensen asks: "Why could not a person's fear make him evaluate the danger just as it should be evaluated, especially if that fear is consequent upon a judgment of reason?" (*Virtuous Deliberation*, 213). Jensen of course thinks that it could, and I think Aquinas would agree. But then again, depending on all kinds of other circumstances, that fear may be wrong. What also carries through, from one moment to the next in deliberation, is not only the bodily passion of fear, but also, of course, the reason that went into causing the fear in the first place. That is, it is not simply the passions that perdure from one moment to the next that help us keep our deliberations on track, but, of course, certainly also our previous rational judgments. The nondeterminate discursive practical deliberation builds upon what was previously considered, and it is far more nimble and adaptable to the various factors which need to be taken into consideration than the bodily momentum of passions.

minate rational process that has not yet settled on anything fixed. Consider a general's fear at seeing the approach of an enemy army. His fear of the approaching army will fluctuate depending on all kinds of further considerations, for example, what kind of an army he has himself, how long they can withstand a siege, whether they have the better position and weapons, etc. There is nothing virtuous about such fear, of course, for the person experiencing it may just as well be virtuous, vicious, or something else. Furthermore, because for Aquinas a virtuous person can act against his virtue, he may very well be considering a cowardly flight, even if he would probably not act upon such thoughts. Briefly considering all of one's options, good ones and bad ones, and figuring out which ones are better than others, will produce all kinds of passions, none of which are morally good or bad until the actual choice is made. This antecedent fear is ordered by many different principles: by the approaching army, by the external and internal senses, and even by reason; and while this fear may be useful in spurring deliberation, it is hardly virtuous.

Overlapping Distinctions: Propassions/Perfect Passions and Antecedent/Consequent Passions

To further hone in on this issue—namely, why antecedent passions cannot be morally good or virtuous—let us consider Aquinas's distinction between perfect and imperfect passion. Perfect passion has four characteristics: (1) it comes from some external source, (2) it is quite vehement, (3) it affects man's highest part, reason, and not only the sense appetite, and (4) it affects reason adversely.[34] The full *ratio* of passion means suffering something external, something relatively powerful, and something that adversely affects us all the way to our highest part. It is felt with some magnitude and we are moved by it, that is, it drags our reason down toward it.[35] The causal chain must at least partially have its origin from outside of the person, rooted in some external object or event beyond one's control. Mild passions are not perfect passions, as we are not really suffering them, but a perfect passion affects our

---

34. The best passage on perfect passion is *QDV*, q. 26, a. 8 [Leonine 22.3:775–76.93–145], but see also *ST* III, q. 15, a. 4 [St. Paul 1944]; a. 6, ad 1 [St. Paul 1946]; a. 7, ad 1 [St. Paul 1947] and ad 3 [St. Paul 2096].

35. This vocabulary of "yanking" and "dragging" as a way of translating *trahere* comes from Kevin White, "The Passions of the Soul (IaIIae, qq.22–48)," in *The Ethics of Aquinas* (ed. Pope).

reason quite vehemently and thus adversely destroys its equanimity.[36]

Aquinas distinguishes these perfect passions from imperfect passions or propassions that do not fully meet these criteria but are also temporally prior to choice. Propassions are not consequent passions, for their main impetus also comes from without rather than the manner in which consequent passions are caused by us, and they also temporally precede choice. Thus perfect passions and propassions are not consequent passions, but they are some sort of antecedent passions. However, while the temporal or external factor causes propassions to seem to fall on the antecedent side of the distinction, because they are not causally efficacious on our choices they do not decrease merit and therefore they are not fully antecedent passions. All of this is to say that there is a kind of imperfect "antecedent passion" that is mild, that does not skew our deliberations and choices, and as such, it also does not decrease merit. For the same reason that they do not decrease merit (because they arise externally), they of course, certainly do not increase it either. And for Aquinas it is axiomatic that what is virtuous always increases merit.

For our purposes, propassions are important because Aquinas says that the virtuous have propassions. Jensen argues, using the example of Christ, that these propassions can be quite vehement in humans.[37] I think this is misguided, partly because vehemence is one of the factors that distinguishes propassions from perfect passions. The reason Aquinas makes the distinction between propassions and perfect passions is to explain how Christ could suffer passions that in no way incline him to sinning mortally or venially. The basic question is this: how can Christ be

---

36. *In III Sent.*, d. 15, q. 2, a. 3, sol. 3 expos. [Moos 504–5]: "Et dicendum quod passio importat immutationem patientis. Non autem dicitur aliquis immutari simpliciter, quando id quod est principale in ipso immutatum permanet. Et ideo simpliciter loquendo, quando ratio non immutatur a sui aequalitate vel aequitate, non dicitur passio, sed propassio, quasi imperfecta passio. Et hoc modo fuit in Christo. Et ideo dicendum ad primum quod propassio proprie loquendo, est immutatio inferioris partis tantum; et ideo quando talis immutatio in nobis accidit, non praeordinatur a ratione, ideo Glossa [L. 114, 94] secundum statum potentiarum in nobis loquens, dicit propassionem subitum motum. In Christo autem aliter fuit, ut ex dictis patet. Nec tamen est verum quod omnis subitus motus sensualitatis sit peccatum veniale; sed tunc tantum quando est in illicitum tendens: quod in Christo nullatenus fuit. Ad secundum dicendum quod dicitur non esse passio quia non est perfecta passio, quamvis sit de genere passionis; sicut ea quae parva sunt, quasi pro nihilo reputantur; sicut dicit Damascenus, 'passio proprie est, quando habet aliquam magnitudinem perceptibilem.'"

37. Jensen, *Virtuous Deliberation*, 215–17. For Aquinas's claim that the virtuous have propassions, see *QDV*, q. 26, a.8 [Leonine 22.3:775. 145–59].

fully human and suffer passion if passions as a result of original sin and by their very *ratio* incline reason away from good judgment? Aquinas's answer is that Christ does not have perfect passions but imperfect passions, that is, propassions, whose defining characteristic is that they do not adversely affect reason, but remain inchoate in the sense appetites.[38]

However, Christ's propassions are quite different than the propassions of the virtuous, for Christ could suffer far more powerful propassions than virtuous humans. Aquinas says that a propassion does not adversely affect reason either on the strength of the higher powers or on account of a passion's low vehemence. Being untouched by original sin and full of grace, and experiencing the beatific vision,[39] the strength of Christ's higher powers could and did suffer very vehement passions that did not disturb or affect his reason, for example, he could sweat blood from fear of death without it affecting his choice. The passion vehemently affected him, but not his choice. We could have vehement propassions if we had the strength of Christ's reason and were experiencing the beatific vision, but this is probably not going to happen. For us,[40]

38. See *QDV*, q. 26, a. 8 [Leonine 22.3:776.131–38]: "Tunc autem totaliter homo per huiusmodi affectus transmutatur quando non solum sistunt in appetitu inferiori, sed trahunt ad se etiam superiorem; quando vero in solo appetitu inferiori sunt, tunc homo immutatur eis quasi secundum partem, unde sic dicuntur propassiones, primo autem modo passiones." *ST* III, q. 15, a. 4 [St. Paul 1944]: "Quia in nobis quandoque huiusmodi motus non sistunt in appetitu sensitivo, sed trahunt rationem. Quod in Christo non fuit: quia motus naturaliter humanae carni convenientes sic ex eius dispositione in appetitu sensitivo manebant quod ratio ex his nullo modo impediebatur facere quae conveniebant.... ut passio perfecta intelligatur quando animo, idest rationi, dominatur; propassio autem, quando est inchoata in appetitu sensitivo, sed ulterius non se extendit." On the historical precedents of propassion see Gondreau, *The Passions of Christ's Soul*, 67–70 and 366–72.

39. *CT* I.232 [Leonine 42:181.26–30]: "Iam enim supra dictum est quod anima Christi perfecta Dei visione fruebatur. Superior igitur ratio animae Christi, que rebus eternis contemplandis et consulendis inheret, nichil habebat adversum aut repugnans ex quo aliqua nocumenti passio in ea locum haberet." To see that the higher powers in Chirst were not affected by the lower, see *ST* III, q. 46, aa. 7–8 [St. Paul 2096–97]. This kind of passage makes one wonder if propassions are at all applicable to virtuous humans, were it not for the fact that Aquinas explicitly says that they are in other passages.

40. The propassions of Adam, Eve, and Mary are also different than the propassions of the virtuous. Untouched by original sin, their reason was supernaturally united to God, by whose power the sense appetites were despotically controlled. Because of the graced power of their reason and will there was no possibility of the inferior dragging around the superior. Moreover, many passions that commonly have this effect, e.g., fear and anger, were simply absent in paradise; see *ST* I, q. 95, a. 2 [St. Paul 462]; *QDV*, q. 26, a. 8 [Leonine 22.3:775–77.86–185]. Mary is an interesting case, as Aquinas both wants to grant her the inheritance of original sin (so that she can be saved by Christ) but also free her from the *fomes*, which inseparably follow upon original

or at least for those who are virtuous, propassions will be mild.[41]

Let me summarize and bring together these two overlapping distinctions, namely, antecedent/consequent and pro-/perfect passions. Antecedent passions cause and are temporally prior to choice, while consequent passions are caused by and are temporally posterior to choice. Perfect passions are caused by something external, are vehement, and thus detrimentally affect our choices. Propassions in normal humans are also caused by something external, but because they are mild they do not detrimentally affect our choices. Both perfect and propassions are antecedent passions as they are caused by something external and are temporally prior to choice. However, as the whole point of the antecedent/consequent distinction is to show how passions affect human merit, and as the only way that antecedent passions decrease merit is by being vehement, what Aquinas means by an antecedent passion is therefore a perfect passion. Thus we may call propassions imperfect antecedent passions because their mildness does not decrease merit. Propassions are imperfect in the sense that they are not fully and completely what perfect/antecedent passions are.

Aquinas is offering a rather general framework for thinking about how the passions can be moral or nonmoral and thus related to merit. Passions may be considered to be nonmoral for two reasons: (1) insofar as they are caused by something external and (2) insofar as they are causally and temporally prior to our choices. Concerning (1), passion, in the fullest sense of the word, namely, a perfect passion, involves us sensibly suffering the world around us in rather powerful ways—a slight, which causes anger; a cookie, which causes us to want it; a threatening stranger, which causes fear; etc. The basic point of the external/internal distinction is that insofar as a passion is caused by something else beyond a per-

----

sin. What Aquinas does in her case is argue that grace completely and utterly binds her sense appetites so that she simply does not feel them (*non sensit*) and with the help of divine providence God insures that nothing illicit draws her (analogous to the manner in which there simply are no evils in Eden); *CT* I.224 [Leonine 42:175–76.48–97]. See esp. ll. 55–62.

41. *QDV*, q. 26, a. 8 [Leonine 22.3:776.146–59]: "Sciendum est ergo quod in hominibus in statu viae, si sunt peccatores, sunt passiones respectu boni et respectu mali, quandoque quidem non solum praevisae sed etiam subitae et intensae et frequenter etiam perfectae; unde dicuntur 'passionum sectatores' in I Ethicorum. In iustis vero nunquam sunt perfectae, quia ratio in eis nunquam deducitur a passionibus; sunt tamen vehementes in imperfectis, sed in perfectis sunt debiles, inferioribus viribus per habitum virtutum moralium refrenatis; habent tamen passiones non solum praevisas sed etiam subitas, et non solum respectu boni sed etiam respectu mali."

son's control, we do not hold that person morally accountable. What is voluntary comes from within as agents cause such an action, but what is involuntary comes from without as we are not causally responsible, that is, as the principle of the motion is external (*ST* I-II, q. 6, a. 1).

However, while everything moral is voluntary, not everything voluntary is moral. For the voluntary is itself divided into what is natural and nonmoral, and what is chosen and moral. For instance, our natural desire for sex or health is voluntary as it comes from an internal and natural principle, but it is not chosen. Moral acts require a more perfectly voluntary cause of motion, namely, the causality of free choice. And free choice requires deliberation, which is itself indetermined (*ad utrumlibet*), whereas natural motions are determined (*ad unum*). That is, we must be free to consider something from different perspectives, to judge our own judgments, and to sift through the various means and ends. Even though such considerations may cause passions, because such passions are not chosen (as they are part of the deliberation leading up to choice), they are not moral. We are not praised or blamed for our deliberations and the passions that we feel while thinking through things, but for our choices and the actions and passions that they cause. The general point here is that something is only fully moral to the degree that it is freely chosen.[42]

One might be tempted to think that there is something intrinsic

---

42. One might object to the way I am using "moral" here. If merit is precisely what makes actions moral, then it would seem to be the case that passions that decrease merit would be essentially immoral in the sense that they take away the very principle of morality. I think this is correct, and I think Aquinas would be fine with formulating it in that way, but this is taking morality in a different sense, namely, as signifying a necessary condition or principle of morality rather than as the morally good or bad things themselves. For if we wish to say whether any passion is good or bad or somewhere in between, Aquinas thinks one can only ultimately label them as such if we ourselves are causally responsible for them by way of our choices. An anonymous reviewer of this manuscript suggested that most propassions are venial sins, but Aquinas is quite clear that it is only those movements toward illicit things that count as venial sins; see *In III Sent.*, d. 15, q. 2, a. 3, sol. 3 expos. [Moos 504–5]: "Nec tamen est verum quod omnis subitus motus sensualitatis sit peccatum veniale; sed tunc tantum quando est in illicitum tendens." However, Aquinas also points out that such passions may be for licit objects, e.g., the desire to help someone in need or the fear of an approaching threat. This is why I still hold that they are neutral, in a general way. In *QDV*, q. 24, a. 12, Aquinas points out that if we say that we can avoid all sin, then we are Pelagian, but we hardly want to say that the sense appetites always tend to sin (albeit venial sin), for that would lead to a form of Manicheanism.

The other way that Aquinas speaks of venial sin is the manner in which I discussed his "negative view of the passions" in chapter 10 and the effects of the Fall in chapter 3.

about the antecedent passions of the virtuous and vicious that make them respectively morally good and bad, but it is rather the case for Aquinas that habits (good ones as well as bad ones) lower the vehemence of the passions across the board,[43] thus rendering virtue and vice more voluntary and free. In other words, the lowered vehemence of antecedent passions makes the vicious act more culpable and the virtuous act more meritorious.

In any case, Aquinas thus offers two broad ways of understanding when passions are moral. The first and rougher distinction is simply between passions that are externally caused, and those that are internally caused. Secondly, among those that are internally caused, we may distinguish between those that are freely chosen and those that are not.

Butera's arguments still stand on firm ground. The antecedent passions of the virtuous person will be mild, and these passions do not become actually virtuous until they are temporally and causally consequent to prudential choices—it is only then that they are fully virtuous in the sense that they increase merit and are ordered to the right objects. As far as I see it, for someone to say that there are virtuous antecedent passions implies that the sense appetites are essentially rational rather than rational by participation. The benefit of simply saying that temperance lowers the vehemence of antecedent passion is that the virtuous sense appetites do not need to discriminate between complicated contingents that prudential reason may or may not judge to be good for the person. Granting virtue the power to order antecedent passions requires that these sensible motions toward sensible bodily goods are somehow ordered to the spiritual and bodily good of the whole person in this particular contingent context. How the virtues of the sense appetites could make this judgment before prudential reasoning has run its course is utterly mysterious, and if they could, there would be no need for prudence. Lowering the vehemence of every antecedent passion requires no discrimination. It makes no rational kinds of judgments of any sort. Rather it lets prudence and the judgment of reason perform their task and it enables the sense appetites to follow whatever reason has chosen.[44]

43. Besides the passages I have already considered, cf. *In IV Sent.*, d. 31, q. 2, a. 1, ad 3: "superabundantia passionis quae vitium facit, non attenditur secundum intensionem quantitativam ipsius, sed secundum proportionem ad rationem."

44. Butera himself once attempted to argue for the existence of something like virtuous

Virtuous Affectivity

There are some scholars who resist making the sense appetites' perfection consist in obedience, as this seems to destroy the sense appetites' own causality. But to emphasize the despotic control of reason over the emotions is not to take away from the sense appetites' own causal role. This would follow if the sense appetites were really free, that is, fully rational beings, but they are not and their virtue lies precisely in being made docile and subject to reason's command, that is to say, in participating in reason. Consider the following passage, which describes the moral virtues in reference to the gifts of the Holy Spirit:

The gifts are certain perfections of man by which man is disposed to this, namely, that he follows well the instinct of the Holy Spirit. It is manifest, however, from what has already been said, that the moral virtues perfect the appe-

---

antecedent passions by appealing to the habituation of the cogitative power, the most rational of the internal sense powers (*Thomas Aquinas*, 357–65). Daniel De Haan has recently tried to take a similar route, also avoiding the term "virtuous antecedent passion" but arguing that the antecedent passions are ordered to a good object through the habituated cogitative power in "Moral Perception and the Function of the Vis Cogitativa in Thomas Aquinas's Doctrine of Antecedent and Consequent Passions," *Documenti e studi sulla tradizione filosofica medievale* 25 (2014): 289–330. As far as I see it, while he avoids calling them virtuous, such passions would nevertheless be so. One still must ask how the cogitative power could make "rational judgments" about the formal object of the passion before reason itself has judged. If the habituated cogitative power could make these judgments without reason, then the cogitative power would not be working with reason, which Aquinas apparently thinks it always is, and one would still have to wonder to what exactly these habitual inclinations would be toward. De Haan (327) says that the temperate person would immediately feel disgusted by pornography. Presumably the habituated cogitative power knows it when it sees it. But arriving at a precise definition of pornography is very difficult, as surely it comes in all kinds of degrees and types, etc. As Michael Gorman pointed out to Butera (*Thomas Aquinas*, 339n122), let us grant that temperance was inclined to be disgusted by naked (or scantily clad) sexually suggestive people. What about on a temperate person's wedding night? Is he supposed to then act against his virtue? De Haan also suggests that perhaps the cogitative power's habitual role is really part of prudence rather than temperance (317, 322–29), but if so, Aquinas is quite adamant that prudence is a habit inhering in reason and not in the sensitive part of the soul, the cluster of powers to which the cogitative power belongs. If it is in prudence by participation then prudence is still doing the heavy lifting, and thus these passions cannot be antecedent in the sense of being ordered before the act of prudence so orders it (I have no problem in granting that the cogitative power is always used by prudence in an act of deliberation). Furthermore, there is simply no textual evidence in Aquinas that the cogitative power plays such a role. It seems to me that what is motivating the discussion is the wish that Aquinas had said that there are such things as ordered propassions, the wish to rescue Aquinas because these commentators are convinced that lowering the vehemence of passion simply does not go far enough in habituating sensibility.

titive power insofar as it somehow participates in reason [*participat aliqualiter rationem*], insofar as it naturally is moved by the command of reason. In this way the gifts of the Holy Spirit are related to man in comparison to the Holy Spirit, as the moral virtues are related to the appetitive power in comparison to reason. Moral virtues, however, are certain habits by which the appetitive powers are disposed to promptly obey reason. Whence also the gifts of the Holy Spirit are certain habits by which man is perfected to promptly obey the Holy Spirit.[45]

Clearly it is natural for the sense appetites' potency to obey reason, and moral virtue perfects this. The whole point of the gifts as habits in the powers of the soul is to make man able to follow the promptings of the Holy Spirit. Just as a gift could never be actualized without the Holy Spirit's actual instinctual movement, neither could a moral virtue be actualized without reason's actual command or motion. These are their perfections, not their destructions. To say that virtues are commanded is not to take away from their causal role or that of the sense appetites. In fact, they act as efficient causes of action,[46] but secondary ones in an ordered series of *per se* causes. They are "naturally" the kinds of things that can and ought to obey or be commanded by reason.

However, this is only part of the story of moral virtue. For Aquinas, the role of the habits of the sense appetites is not simply limited to passively receiving and lowering the vehemence of antecedent passions; he grants them an active role as well. For the habit, in an appetitive way, also inclines to an action like the one that caused it. Habits are forms, and all forms qua forms incline to something.[47] I will argue that these habits incline to virtuous acts, and that means that they incline to the act of prudence, namely, the prudential command. In other words, they are inclined toward participating in reason.

A courageous habit, for instance, is caused (acquired) by courageous acts and it appetitively inclines back to those same acts. Or as Aquinas puts it, the proximate end of the courageous person is to express a likeness of his habit in act; he intends to act according to what is suitable (*secundum convenientiam*) to his habit.[48] As the attainment of what is

---

45. *ST* I-II, q. 68, a. 3 [St. Paul 835]; see also a. 4 [St. Paul 836].

46. *ST* I-II, q. 71, a. 3, ad 3 [St. Paul 851].

47. See chapter 4, 91n14.

48. *ST* II-II, q. 123, a. 7 [St. Paul 1584]: "Finis autem proximus uniuscuiusque agentis est

suitable to something causes pleasure, when the courageous person acts courageously he takes pleasure in that.[49]

Aquinas recasts this in the language of Aristotle's famous statement, which we have already seen a few times, "however each man is, such seems the end to him."[50] By the first part of the phrase, "however each man is," Aquinas means however each man is disposed, and he usually means however each man's appetite is disposed.[51] As appetite is ordered to something as an end, the dispositional cause disposes the appetite to some end rather than another, and thus the disposition is like to the thing to which it is now disposed.[52] But it is worth pointing out that this "seeming" is not essentially cognitional,[53] even though it must ultimate-

---

ut similitudinem suae formae in alterum inducat … fortis sicut finem proximum intendit ut similitudinem sui habitus exprimat in actu: intendit enim agere secundum convenientiam sui habitus." See also *ST* I-II, q. 7, a. 3, ad 3 [St. Paul 596]: "fortis fortiter agat propter bonum fortitudinis," and *QDV*, q. 5, a. 1 [Leonine 22.1:139.136–47]: "Sed finis agibilium praeexistit in nobis dupliciter: scilicet per cognitionem naturalem de fine hominis, quae quidem naturalis cognitio ad intellectum pertinet, secundum Philosophum in VI Ethicorum [1143a35], qui est principiorum operabilium sicut et speculabilium; principia autem operabilium sunt fines, ut in eodem libro dicitur; *alio modo quantum ad affectionem, et sic fines agibilium sunt in nobis per virtutes morales*, per quas homo afficitur ad iuste vivendum vel fortiter vel temperate, quod est quasi finis proximus agibilium" (emphasis added).

49. The problem with courage, however, is that courageous actions usually also involve a fair amount of pain, and this pain tends to drown out the pleasure that connaturally accompanies the act. *ST* II-II, q. 123, a. 8 [St. Paul 1584–85], and *In Ethic.* III.18 [Leonine 47.1:177.55–59].

50. *Nic.* III.13, 1114a32-b1.

51. *In Ethic.* III.13 [Leonine 47.1:156.18–20]: "sed qualis est unusquisque, talis finis videtur ei: id est tale aliquid videtur ei appetendum quasi bonum et finis." This is in an articulation of an argument, which he refutes, but he does not refute this point, and he later in the same *lectio* affirms it; see ibid., ll. 59–73. *QDM*, q. 2, a. 3, ad 9 [Leonine 23:37.165–73]: "qualis enim est unusquisque, talis et finis videtur ei, ut dicitur III Ethicorum [1114a32-b1]: experimento enim cognoscimus quod aliter videtur nobis bonum aliquid vel malum circa ea quae amamus et ea quae odimus. Et ideo cum aliquis est inordinate affectus ad aliquid, impeditur iudicium intellectus in particulari eligibili ex inordinata affectione." See the following note as well.

52. *ST* I-II, q. 88, a. 3 [St. Paul 931]: "disponens est quodammodo causa…. Est enim causa quaedam movens directe ad effectum: sicut calidum calefacit…. et sic disponit ad actum similem secundum speciem…. nam unicuique habenti habitum, inquantum huiusmodi, finis est operatio secundum habitum."

53. Thomas Ryan, "Revisiting Affective Knowledge and Connaturality in Aquinas," *Theological Studies* 66 (2005): 52–53, and Taki Suto, "Virtue and Knowledge: Connatural Knowledge According to Thomas Aquinas," *Review of Metaphysics* 58 (2004): 61–79, both claim that this connaturality is a kind of cognition. What is often referred to as connatural knowledge, I put squarely on the side of appetite. When Aquinas discusses it in cognitive terms it is always qualified, it is quasi-knowing or like knowing. For another discussion see Hoffmann, *Prudence and Practical Principles*, 165–84.

ly be caused by cognition of some sort.[54] It can, however, be described in cognitional language. Being attracted to something does make that thing *seem* to us to be good, regardless of whether or not it is good.

Aquinas uses this particular Aristotelian statement to explain four different seemings concerning: (1) will, (2) habits, (3) passions, and (4) bodily dispositions. My concern is primarily with (2), but I would like to briefly say something about the others. Passion (3) is perhaps the most obvious one; those freshly baked cookies that we know we should not eat *seem* very attractive to us. It is not simply the smell, or the look, or our knowledge that they will taste delicious that does this; it is rather the fact that we are being drawn or yanked toward them with a kind of momentum that makes them seem so good.[55] In any passion there can be many co-causes of its disposition, as we have discussed: the object itself, the inner and outer senses, and intellect and will. The will's movements (1), like the sense appetites, are likewise appetitive inclinations that can also be described as a kind of seeming. In the will this disposition can refer to the intellect's formal presentation of the object to the will, or the will's natural disposition to its end.[56] In either case the seeming refers to the will desiring or being repulsed by this or that, which is caused by what disposes the will to this or that. The bodily dispositions (4) are quite straightforward. For example, to a sick person something may taste repulsive which

54. For Aquinas all three kinds of appetite (rational, sensitive, and natural) are caused by cognition of some sort or other, as we have discussed. See chapters 4 and 9.

55. *ST* I-II, q. 9, a. 2 [St. Paul 601]: "id quod apprehenditur sub ratione boni et convenientis, movet voluntatem per modum obiecti. Quod autem aliquid videatur bonum et conveniens, ex duobus contingit: scilicet ex conditione eius quod proponitur, et eius cui proponitur. Conveniens enim secundum relationem dicitur, unde ex utroque extremorum dependet. Et inde est quod gustus diversimode dispositus, non eodem modo accipit aliquid ut conveniens et ut non conveniens. Unde, ut Philosophus dicit in III Ethic. qualis unusquisque est, talis finis videtur ei. Manifestum est autem quod secundum passionem appetitus sensitivi, immutatur homo ad aliquam dispositionem. Unde secundum quod homo est in passione aliqua, videtur sibi aliquid conveniens, quod non videtur extra passionem existenti, sicut irato videtur bonum, quod non videtur quieto. Et per hunc modum, ex parte obiecti, appetitus sensitivus movet voluntatem." Cf. *ST* I-II, q. 10, a. 3, ad 2 [St. Paul 607]. Aquinas argues that passions, in general, make things seem otherwise than they really are; *ST* I-II, q. 44, a. 2 [St. Paul 736]: "Quia homini affecto secundum aliquam passionem, videtur aliquid vel maius vel minus quam sit secundum rei veritatem: sicut amanti videntur ea quae amat, meliora; et timenti, ea quae timet, terribiliora. Et sic ex defectu rectitudinis iudicii, quaelibet passio, quantum est de se, impedit facultatem bene consiliandi."

56. *SCG* IV.95 [Leonine manualis 565]; *QDM*, q. 2, a. 3, ad 9 [Leonine 23:37.156–76]; see also *QDM*, q. 6 [Leonine 23:150.461–72].

would have tasted good when healthy; the difference is a bodily dispositional alteration, which makes things seem to be in a certain way.[57]

Habits (2) have this same effect; they make things seem to be good.
As appetitive inclinations ordered to ends, they make the ends seem to
be such by inclining to such ends. There is no real difference between the
final causality of appetitive motion and the "seeming"; they are two different ways of describing the exact same thing. This is why he sometimes
speaks of this appetitive inclination as a kind of judgment or knowledge
(sometimes connatural knowledge) of the end, namely, the virtuous act.[58]
This appetitive judgment[59] is instinctual or intuitive and is experienced
somewhat like the manner in which our intellects assent to first principles.[60] In other words, there is nothing discursive about it. This connatural inclination to virtuous acts exists prior to choice and independently of

57. See *ST* I-II, q. 9, a. 2, 193n48, and *ST* I, q. 83, a. 1, ad 5 [St. Paul 397]. Notice how his
position has slightly shifted; in *ST* the corporeal disposition makes things seem to be in a
certain way, but not so in this earlier passage: *In II Sent.*, d. 25, q. 1, a. 1, ad 5 [Mand 646–47].

58. *Quaestio disputata de caritate* (hereafter, *QDC*), q. 12 [Marietti 787]; *QDVC*, q. 2
[Marietti 819]. Jacques Maritain has emphasized this theme of knowledge by connaturality
in *The Range of Reason* (New York: Charles Scribner's Sons, 1952), 22–29. This inclination is
sometimes described as the end or principle of prudence. In some texts moral virtue provides
the ends that prudence reasons toward; see *ST* I-II, q. 56, a. 4, ad 4 [St. Paul 781]; *In VI Ethic.*
10 [Leonine 47.2:373.153]; *ST* I-II, q. 65, a. 1 [St. Paul 817], but in other texts reason provides
the ends that prudence reasons toward. See *ST* I-II, q. 66, a. 3, ad 3 [St. Paul 824]; *ST* II-II,
q. 47, a. 6 [St. Paul 1294]. In *ST* I-II, q. 58, a. 5 [St. Paul 792], Thomas clarifies or distinguishes
between two principles or ends: particular principles (moral virtues) and universal principles (synderesis). He notes that the universal principles are not sufficient by themselves for
us to reason about particulars because sometimes our universal understanding is corrupted
in particular by some passion. For example, to someone overcome by desire, the object lusted
for trumps the universal judgment of reason. We might conclude that what is needed then is
simply docile sense appetites, lowering antecedent passions allowing reason to judge clearly.
While this is undoubtedly important, Aquinas goes further and says that the moral virtues
perfect man so that "it comes to be in a certain way connatural to man that he rightly judge
about the end." For an interesting passage see *In VII Ethic.* 3 [Leonine 47.2:392.204–20], in
which he says that the incontinent person knows that it is not good to eat sweets, but does
not feel it in his heart (*sentit in corde*). Although I am not sure whether Aquinas is speaking
in his own voice here, nevertheless I think it is perfectly compatible with my position that one
somehow "feels like doing the right thing," namely, the virtuous act. Furthermore, to connect
this to prudence, being inclined to virtuous acts (which are inseparably bound to prudence)
without strong distracting passions will tremendously help one deliberate clearly and judge
what one should do in the here and now.

59. *ST* I, q. 1, a. 6, ad 3 [St. Paul 7]. To see that this judgment by connaturality is in fact
an appetitive inclining see the use of *affectus* in *In librum Beati Dionysii De divinis nominibus
exposito* 2.4 [Marietti 59].

60. *ST* II-II, q. 2, a. 3, ad 2 [St. Paul 1102].

any particular choices.[61] For example, the act of fortitude is connatural to the "exigency" of the habit of fortitude,[62] it is suitable (*conveniens*) to the habit,[63] and thus it seems good to the one who has the virtue because he is drawn toward it or inclined to it.[64] Thus any habit is simply inclined to producing acts of a particular sort, and this inclination makes such acts seem good and attractive.

But I must emphasize here that the seeming of a habit is simply not the same as the seeming of a passion: Aquinas clearly distinguishes between them.[65] Passions are always ordered to particulars, for instance, toward a cookie. The habit of temperance cannot be ordered to such particulars, for as we have discussed, there are no particulars which are always good for a person. Temperance cannot even be ordered to healthy food, for there are undoubtedly times when a gracious host of-

61. *ST* II-II, q. 45, a. 2 [St. Paul 1285].

62. *Super Epistolam ad VIII Romanos lectura* 1 [Marietti 112]: "Et horum ratio est, quia, sicut philosophus dicit in III *Ethic.*, qualis est unusquisque, talis finis videtur ei. Unde ille cuius est animus informatus per habitum bonum vel malum, existimat de fine secundum exigentiam illius habitus."

63. *QDV*, q. 24, a. 10 [Leonine 22.3:706.246–58]: "Secundum est inclinatio habitus, qui quidem cum sit quasi quaedam natura habentis, sicut Philosophus dici in libro De memoria et reminiscentia (De mem. 6 452a 27) quod consuetudo est altera natura, et Tullius in Rhetoricis (De inventione II, C. 53) quod virtus consentit rationi in modum naturae, pari ratione vitii habitus quasi natura quaedam inclinat in id quod est sibi conveniens, unde fit ut habenti habitum luxuriae bonum videatur illud quod luxuriae convenit, quasi sibi connaturale, et hoc est quod Philosophus dicit in III Ethicorum, quod 'qualis unusquisque est talis et finis videtur ei.'"

64. Notice that one of the ways that Aquinas thinks we know that we have a habit is because we can perceive that we have this inclination: *In III Sent.*, d. 23, q. 1, a. 2 [Moos 702]: "sed ille qui habet habitum, … cognoscit se habere habitum, inquantum percipit inclinationem sui ad actum, secundum quam se habet aliqualiter ad actum illum. Et hoc quidem cognoscit homo per modum reflexionis, inquantum scilicet cognoscit se operari quae operatur."

65. Note the continuation of the passage cited two notes above (*QDV*, q. 24, a. 10): "Tertium vero est falsa aestimatio rationis in particulari eligibili: quae quidem provenit vel ex altero praedictorum, scilicet impetu passionis, aut inclinatione habitus." See also the next few lines; *QDC*, q. 12, cited above, where he is quite clear that these are two different seemings; *QDM*, q. 6 [Leonine 23:150.461–81], and cf. q. 7, a. 5 ad 7 [Leonine 23:173.242–45]; *SCG* IV.95 [Leonine manualis 565]: "Et hoc quidem sequitur in universali naturam rationalem, ut beatitudinem appetat: sed quod hoc vel illud sub ratione beatitudinis et ultimi finis desideret, ex aliqua speciali dispositione naturae contingit; unde Philosophus dicit quod qualis unusquisque est talis et finis videtur ei…. Quod enim aliquid appetatur a nobis ut ultimus finis, contingit quandoque ex eo quod sic disponimur aliqua passione, quae cito transit: unde et desiderium finis de facili removetur, ut in continentibus apparet. Quandoque autem disponimur ad desiderium alicuius finis boni vel mali per aliquem habitum: et ista dispositio non de facili tollitur, unde et tale desiderium finis fortius manet, ut in temperatis apparet; et tamen dispositio habitus in hac vita auferri potest"; and *In III Ethic.* c. 13 [Leonine 47.1:156–57.54–78].

fers something unhealthy, and surely the temperate person would not have to violate his temperance to be polite. In fact, it is precisely because he is temperate that he can be flexible in such contexts. The only possible constant variable to which the sense appetites can be reliably inclined through the messy contingents of human actions is the command of prudence.

Let me unpack this a little further. Moral virtues can only be used for the good. This means that a moral virtue cannot be actualized or used by a bad command or an imprudent reason. If someone virtuous made an imprudent choice, that is, did not use his prudence in deliberation, he could not use his virtue of temperance to carry out his imprudent command. Virtue in the sense appetite "distinguishes" between prudent and imprudent choices. But such language makes the virtuous sense appetites seem essentially rational, as if they had a little homunculus distinguishing between reason's good and bad choices. Rather, moral virtue is precisely the kind of potency that is only actualized by prudential commands. Potencies just are potencies for particular actualizations or ranges of actualizations, and this particular kind of potency is caused by and ordered to a particular kind of actualization, namely, one that is always good. It has only been caused by prudence and it can only be actualized by prudence, and as potency ordered to actualization it "seeks" or "inclines toward" the command of prudence, which is the actualization of prudence.

The inclination of the virtuous sense appetites is not outwards toward this or that particular good, as the passions are, as only the prudential judgment of reason determines the mean concerning those things. It is rather upward and inward toward the prudential command of reason. As an impression (*impressio* or *conformitas*) caused by reason's command, which inclines back toward its like, moral virtue can discriminate (in an appetitive way) between the motions of the sense appetites that are caused by reason and those that are not—the one actualizes it and the other does not.[66]

It is worth pointing out here that temperance and courage, unlike justice, are first and foremost concerned with perfecting the agent; they

---

66. In fact, an imprudent choice pains the virtuous sense appetites, as it is contrary to the habit. Cf. *In II Sent.*, d. 25, q. 1, a. 4 [Mand 655].

order the agent to himself, as he ought to be ordered.[67] Their role is to tighten the ship, so to speak. They help the parts of the potential whole to operate in a more seamless harmony, drawing them a little nearer to their original prelapsarian state, as the parts are drawn together in a more unified operation.

I could also put it this way. The natural postlapsarian function of the sense appetites is to be moved by external bodily sensible goods or evils via the internal and external sense powers. This is the normal, default, causal route; this is what they are inclined toward. However, when these same sense appetites receive the moral virtues they are also now further inclined to the goods of the soul, and this further inclination can only be received from prudence and its commands. The habit of moral virtue forms a kind of pathway by which reason's command, whatever it may be, might easily travel without interference from strong passion. It is as if the habit rewires the sense appetites so that the causal circuitry is different. They are still moved by external sensible goods, of course, but they await further intelligence and information before they are fully unleashed. We might say that the sense appetites are no longer quite so hasty for sensible material goods, and they now await whatever travels down the path from reason.

Let me offer a concrete example. Imagine a temperate man who has just walked into a room with a freshly baked plate of cookies and a vegetable platter set before him. He would undoubtedly delight in the smell of the cookies, but not in such a way as to blind him to the benefits of the vegetables. His sense appetites would be attracted to the cookies, and probably neutral with respect to the vegetables. The virtue in his sense appetites lowers the vehemence of his passion, enabling him to deliberate about whether to eat a cookie or a carrot. The intemperate man, however, who habitually thinks that sweet things ought to be pursued, does not flinch—he follows his passion and goes straight for the cookies. Those who act continently and incontinently are experiencing strong passions for the cookies and thus are having a difficult time thinking clearly about the benefits of eating vegetables, but they are trying. The habit of temperance in the temperate man is *not* inclining toward either

---

67. The virtues of the sense appetite order a person toward himself; *ST* I-II, q. 72, a. 4 [St. Paul 857].

of these two alternatives, but it is seeking or inclining toward the mean prudentially commanded.[68] It is waiting for the person to make up his mind (this would not take long, of course), and wants and seeks (*appetit*) the virtuous act, which must be commanded. It takes some delight in receiving this prudential command whenever it is given, whether the agent choses to eat a cookie or a carrot. Although the example is morally trivial, the point I wish to make is that the virtuous person is simply inclined to doing whatever he thinks is good. The habit of temperance inclines toward a temperate act, which is precisely a prudentially commanded act. The intemperate person is simply inclined to choose what is most pleasant. Those acting continently and incontinently are not so inclined in either way, but because they have vehement passions they are being drawn toward the cookies and thus are having a difficult time thinking clearly about what they should do.

But it is perhaps not quite right to say that the sense appetites of the virtuous incline to the prudential command of reason, although Aquinas does put it that way.[69] What he says is that they incline to the virtuous act. Virtuous acts, however, must always be freely chosen, and if reason is to move the lower powers, this only happens by way of command—so it is the same. If one breaks down the parts of the soul into their various roles, as Aquinas does, then the inclination of moral virtue is toward command. Fortitude, for example, is precisely concerned with finding the mean in fear and daring. When Aquinas says that the habit of courage inclines to the courageous act itself, this must refer to an act in which the mean has been found in fear and daring, and that can only be an act commanded by prudence. It certainly helps to be inclined toward this and not pulled away from it by fear.

Aquinas speaks of this technically as "that the proximate and proper end is that the likeness of the habit exists in act."[70] Thus one can say

---

68. Cf. *In III Sent.*, d. 23, q. 1, a. 4, sol. 2, ad 4 [Moos 714]: "prudentia determinat medium per modum dirigentis et ostendentis; sed virtus moralis per modum exequentis et inclinantis in medium."

69. Ibid.

70. *In Ethic.* III.15 [Leonine 47.1:165.95–118]: "Et dicit quod finis cuiuslibet operationis virtuosae est secundum convenientiam proprii habitus; movet enim habitus ex consuetudine causatus per modum naturae eo quod consuetudo est sicut quaedam natura, sicut dicitur in libro De memoria [452a27–28]. Finis autem ultimus agentis naturalis operantis est bonum universi, quod est bonum perfectum, sed finis proximus est ut similitudinem suam in aliud

that the courageous person *intends* the very courageous act itself.[71] One can also say that a habit seeks to do something like itself.[72] Of course, the cause (courageous act) is like its effect (the virtue of courage), which seeks to cause similar courageous acts. Or we can say that to the courageous man, courage seems good[73] as he is so disposed according to his habit.[74] Or we can say that he seeks to act in a manner that is connatural to his habit,[75] that is, courageously, etc. Or that he "judges" courage to be good according to his habit.[76] It is all the same.

This means that the virtues do incline to the virtuous act prior to the judgment of reason. As I mentioned before, wherever there is form, there is an inclination following that form, and in this case we are speaking of the inclination that necessarily follows upon the virtue itself, it follows the "exigency of the form" of virtue.[77] This is a kind of antecedent affective help or support. It is a habitual inclination of the sense appetites toward participating in reason. However, this antecedent help is not the help of an antecedent passion. For it is not inclined toward sensible things as passions are, but toward the command of prudence. Thus I affirm the existence of a kind of "virtuous antecedent" affectivity as an essential feature of moral virtue, as this affectivity simply follows upon the existence of the virtue, but I avoid the particular set of problems rightly associated with virtuous antecedent passions. It seems to me that many Aquinas scholars have confused these two inclinations, as if the inclination of the habit of moral virtue is identical to the inclination of pas-

---

imprimat, sicut finis calidi est ut per suam actionem calidum faciat. Similiter autem et finis virtutis operantis ultimus quidem est felicitas, quae est bonum perfectum, ut in I habitum est [1107b2], sed finis proximus et proprius est ut similitudo habitus existat in actu. Et hoc est quod dicit quod bonum quod intendit fortis est fortitudo, non quidem habitus fortitudinis qui iam praeexistit, sed similitudo ipsius in actu, et hoc etiam est finis, quia unumquodque quod est propter finem determinatur in propria ratione secundum proprium finem quia ex fine sumitur ratio eorum quae sunt ad finem; et ideo finis fortitudinis est aliquid ad rationem fortitudinis pertinens. Sic igitur fortis sustinet et operatur gratia boni et hoc est inquantum intendit operari ea quae sunt secundum fortitudinem." That this is indeed Aquinas's thought and not simply an exposition of Aristotle, see *ST* II-II, q. 123, a. 7 [St. Paul 1584].

71. See both texts in the previous note.

72. Ibid.

73. Ibid.

74. See 260n57 and 259n56.

75. See text, 261n63.

76. *QDM*, q. 7, a. 5, ad 7 [Leonine 23:173.235–45].

77. See 261n62.

sions, and because Aquinas does affirm that the habits of moral virtue incline toward virtuous acts prior to our prudent choices, he must also mean that that the passions do so as well.[78] But that is a mistake. Be that as it may, Aquinas does indeed think that the virtues provide a kind of antecedent affective support prior to our choices, but it is quite different than scholars have thought.

Summary

This chapter began with the common view that the moral virtues enable us to spontaneously feel like doing the right thing. If feeling here means passion or emotion, Aquinas denies that moral virtues can do this. They can make sudden or spontaneous passions milder, but they cannot possibly order them to the right things or actions without reason. If by "feeling" we signify any kind of sensitive affective support, then Aquinas will grant this in a limited sense. Moral virtue does offer a kind of antecedent affective support. We are somehow inclined to virtue before we have decided what to do; we might say, loosely speaking, that we feel like acting virtuously or that we are so inclined. These two facets of moral virtue, namely, the inclination toward the virtuous act and the milder antecedent passions, obviously work in tandem and reinforce one another. In any case, moral virtue does offer some antecedent sensitive support. I have no doubt, however, that some readers will not be convinced that Aquinas has gone far enough. In other words, I may be right about Aquinas, but Schiller's beautiful soul is, at the end of the day, the better and more compelling alternative. In the next chapter I will try to convince these readers that Aquinas is right for not going farther than he did.

78. See, e.g., Terence Irwin, *The Development of Ethics, vol. 1: From Socrates to the Reformation* (Oxford: Oxford University Press, 2007), 1:522–26.

13

———————

KANT, ARISTOTLE,

AND SOCIAL PSYCHOLOGY

The main goal of this book has been to discover and synthesize Aquinas's genuine position on the relation of passion and emotion in moral virtue. In the last chapter, I contrasted those findings with existing interpretations of contemporary Thomists, arguing that in their zeal to distinguish the Thomist position from other modern moral theories, they have unintentionally provided a rosier picture of the role of the passions in moral virtue than Aquinas himself offers. The reader will thus naturally be wondering where this corrected Thomist position stands in relationship to contemporary virtue theory more generally. In fact, I want to do more in this chapter than simply compare and contrast Aquinas with other theorists—I mean to offer a preliminary argument in favor of a Thomist account of the problem of the passions. A comprehensive argument for Thomist virtue theory would of course require its own book. What I can do with this chapter is offer a basic comparison with Kant and Aristotle, followed by suggestive evidence for the Thomistic position from studies in social psychology.

Although I admit that to some extent this plays into the "great men" narrative of Western thought, neglecting many other good philosophers, I believe it is worth considering the classical way this comparison has been made, in part to criticize it. Kant and Aristotle have traditionally been thought to represent two ends of a spectrum of possible philosophical positions, with Aristotle holding that the emotions can partic-

267

ipate in reason and Kant that they cannot, and here Aquinas is viewed as firmly Aristotelian. This perspective can perhaps be explained by the fact that many professors pair Kant's *Groundwork* (which does not offer his thinking on virtue) with Aristotle's *Nicomachean Ethics* in their ethics courses and simply argue that Kant's virtue is nothing but Aristotelian continence; this is how I was taught. However, the narrative also has deep historical roots, as we saw in Schiller's criticism of Kant—indeed, this way of thinking has perdured from Kant until now. It is only in the last twenty years or so that Kantians have rescued Kant from this mischaracterization, and in light of this revision, Aquinas no longer looks like Kant's opposite. But it is also worth comparing Aristotle and Kant because the three main strands of thought in contemporary ethics are Aristotelian, deontological, and utilitarian, and of these three, the Aristotelian and deontological positions have the most to say about how reason and emotion are and ought to be related, so discussing them should enable us to bring Aquinas into the contemporary discussions, at least to some extent, although my remarks will be far more suggestive than systematic. I will argue that Aquinas has a plausible position that is different enough from the classical ones to be interesting and compelling, and that it can be cast in familiar enough historical and philosophical terms to be readily intelligible to most.

I will not enter into Aristotle's or Kant's work in great detail, for that would require a book in its own right. However, because our understanding of Kant's virtue has recently been revised, I will offer a brief summary of it, but not of Aristotle's virtue, as most of this book's readers will be familiar enough with the latter. However, some readers may be less familiar with the criticisms leveled against Aristotelian virtue ethics during the last twenty years or so by philosophers with an eye on social psychology. These objections raise serious questions about the plausibility of Aristotle's account of moral virtue, and if Aquinas is basically Aristotelian, then these objections should be aimed at Aquinas as well. I will discuss these objections in some detail and argue that Aquinas is in certain important respects quite different from Aristotle and that, for this reason, he can offer better and more plausible responses to these criticisms. Moreover, drawing out this difference between the two thinkers will enable me to revisit and criticize the classical understanding of Aquinas's placement *vis-à-vis* Kant and Aristotle and also to argue that it may not be that bad if Aquinas is a bit closer to Kant and a bit less like Aristotle than previously thought.

Kant and Aquinas

Before directly engaging Kant, perhaps the paradigmatic modern moral philosopher, I will very briefly address a broader and vaguer objection from many who consider the "modern turn" in the broad sweep of the history of philosophy. The objection, which I formulated more fully in the second section of the previous chapter, goes something like this: granting reason control over passion is tantamount to denying the hylomorphic relation between soul and body, for such a dualistic view implies that the soul belongs to something like Descartes's *res cogitans* or Kant's noumenal a priori realm and is thus radically sundered from the passions' sphere of phenomenal *res extensa*.

Simply put, I fail to see any real connection between the two issues. The soul qua form is, as I discussed in the first two chapters of this book, united to the body, while qua mover or potential whole it is united as an ordered series of powers. Strictly speaking, hylomorphism is the former, but on some accounts it is the latter.[1] In either case, the details of how exactly these powers work together makes no difference to hylomorphism. In particular, the issue of whether reason should have despotic or democratic control of the passions does not call into question Aristotle's or Aquinas's metaphysics of hylomorphism. How the sense appetites and passions might participate in reason is simply a question regarding the details of how the potential whole works. In fact, I think Aquinas's views are compatible with non-Thomistic views of hylomorphism and even with the denial of hylomorphism altogether. Aquinas himself would have metaphysical problems with such a picture, of course, but he certainly could not argue from his ethical views on the relation between reason and emotion to hylomorphism or vice versa.

On the ethical front, the criticism is often made that granting reason too much control over sensibility involves descending a slippery slope

---

1. For examples of the latter position, see Marmodoro, "Aristotle's Hylomorphism"; Jaworski, "Hylomorphism" and *Structure and the Metaphysics of Mind: How Hylomorphism Solves the Mind-Body Problem* (Oxford: Oxford University Press, 2016), 53–81.

toward Kant—that is, if we emphasize choice and command in Aquinas, he looks too much like Kant—but it is taken to be obvious that Aquinas is the polar opposite of Kant, whose best was not virtue but merely continence.[2] Or so the story goes. However, given the recent groundbreaking work in Kantian ethics,[3] this story must be discarded as far too simplistic.

Here I offer a very brief sketch of Kant's position as recently understood. For Kant, cognition of the moral law causes desire, which in turn causes a feeling of pleasure that includes a feeling of respect, moral feeling, conscience, and love of human beings.[4] These are all good feelings/emotions that the virtuous person will experience. However, they are what Aquinas calls the affects of the will (as they are caused by intellectual cognition), analogous to how he is willing to call the will's movements passions. What Aquinas refers to as passions, namely, real

2. This view, as I have mentioned, stems partly from the fact that it is all too easy to read Kant's *Groundwork* and Aristotle's *Nicomachean Ethics* side by side in philosophy courses. The obvious conclusion to be drawn from this juxtaposition is that Kant offers nothing more than Aristotelian continence. But Kant is quite explicit that the *Groundwork* is only meant to establish the supreme principle of morality (4:392 [7]); it is not meant to offer his full view of what moral virtue is, which includes *both* the a priori and the empirical/subjective/a posteriori anthropology that he develops in other texts; see Baxley, *Kant's Theory*, 45–49. Philosophers who appear to hold the view that Kant's virtue is something like Aristotelian continence (which is inferior to virtue) include Rosalind Hursthouse, *On Virtue Ethics* (Oxford: Oxford University Press, 1999), 104; Julia Annas, "Virtue Ethics," in *The Oxford Handbook of Ethical Theory*, ed. David Copp (Oxford: Oxford University Press, 2006), 517, and *The Morality of Happiness* (New York: Oxford University Press, 1993), 53; Martha C. Nussbaum, *Upheavals of Thought: The Intelligence of Emotions* (Cambridge: Cambridge University Press, 2001), 172.

3. See, e.g., Baxley, *Kant's Theory*; Sherwin, *Making a Necessity of Virtue*; Randy Cagle, "Becoming a Virtuous Agent: Kant and the Cultivation of Feelings and Emotions," *Kant-Studien* 96 (2005): 452–67; Rohlf, "Emotion and Evil in Kant"; James Reid, "Morality and Sensibility in Kant: Toward a Theory of Virtue," *Kantian Review* 8 (2004): 89–114; G. Felicitas Munzel, *Kant's Conception of Character: The Critical Link of Morality, Anthropology, and Reflective Judgment* (Chicago: University of Chicago Press, 1999).

4. See Kant, *Metaphysics of Morals*, 6:211–14 (11–14). For a very helpful discussion of these terms with more textual references, see Kelly Sorensen, "Kant's Taxonomy of the Emotions," *Kantian Review* 6 (2002): 109–28, and Baxley, *Kant's Theory*, 137–43. See also Mark Packer, "Kant on Desire and Moral Pleasure," *Journal of the History of Ideas* 50, no. 3 (1989): 429–42. Although I am attempting to compare Aquinas and Kant here, I must point out that English has many different philosophical candidates for what would count as an emotion in Kant, which makes the comparison between Kant and Aquinas tricky. Sorenson's *Taxonomy* is the best guide to Kant's terms. In order to be brief, I cannot enter into the discussion about these important distinctions, but I do believe that my general comparison remains accurate even when one takes Kant's detailed distinctions into consideration.

sensible passions—as they arise from a posteriori reality for Kant—are simply disconnected from morality, which must be grounded in a priori practical reason.[5] Moreover, given that Kant thinks we have an ineradicable propensity to let such inclinations serve as sufficient motives for our acts (which he calls radical evil), they must be controlled.[6] When such passions are effectively controlled, the virtuous agent will feel great peace, cheerfulness, and joy.[7] In sum, Kant's virtuous person will take great pleasure in his or her feelings of respect, moral feeling, conscience, and love of human beings and will also feel at peace and be cheerful and joyful. Thus, although Kant does think we need to control our sensible passions (as does Aquinas), he hardly lives up to his famous robotic caricature.

Kant outlines three ways to attain such self-mastery or control over the passions: by *extirpation*, by *suppression*, and by *silencing*.[8] According to Kant, there are times when we ought just to extirpate or cut out our emotions altogether—but perhaps we cannot, and then we ought to suppress them and restrict their deliberative weight—while at other times we ought to silence our emotions so that they are not so loud in our deliberations, thus enabling us to hear the other alternatives proposed by reason. Although the difference between these three ways of controlling emotions seems obscure to me, the general point worth highlighting is simply that these emotions are obstacles that a virtuous agent needs to control, for without that control the virtuous agent cannot deliberate clearly and is not fully autocratic but rather a "plaything" at the mercy of forces beyond his or her control.[9] Choices that follow upon such feelings are animal choices, according to Kant; they are not strictly human.[10]

Aquinas, of course, makes the similar point that such passions are

5. Kant, *Metaphysics of Morals*, 6:375–78 (141–43). For an interesting discussion of the disconnect between cognition and passion in Kant, see Sherwin, *Making a Necessity of Virtue*, 176–80.

6. For Kant's views on radical evil, see his *Religion within the Boundaries of Mere Reason*, ed. and trans. Allen Wood and George DiGiovanni (Cambridge: Cambridge University Press, 1998), 6:32 (55–56). For further discussion, see Rohlf, *Emotion and Evil*, 749–73; Baxley, *Kant's Theory*, 68–69; Allison, *Kant's Theory of Freedom*, 146–61; Munzel, *Kant's Conception*, chap. 3.

7. Kant, *Religion*, 6:25n49; *Metaphysics of Morals*, 6:485 (227) and 6:409 (167).

8. For a discussion of these three ways, see Baxley, *Kant's Theory*, 64–67.

9. Kant, *Metaphysics of Morals*, 6:420 (175).

10. Ibid., 6:213 (13).

really ways that we suffer the world around us, and as such they are morally problematic. Furthermore, both agree that if such a passion should happen upon the right action, this would be by accident and thus would not be a fully human action.[11] Neither Kant nor Aquinas thinks the passions are bad *per se*, but only that they are morally unreliable and often troublesome.[12] Both agree that if someone should unthinkingly act on the passion of doing good to another (Kant's infamous beneficent man), this action would be imprudent, and perhaps even detrimental to the recipient, as the actor had not properly thought through the act.[13]

Kant, however, is much more pessimistic than Aquinas is about habits.[14] For Kant, somewhat similar to Scotus, virtue is a strength of the will to do one's duty.[15] He thinks that habits, qua second natures, operate in the realm of the sensible a posteriori and as such could never be virtuous. Virtue, in contrast, is full autocracy, that is, freedom in the most robust sense, where we make not only free choices, but good choices, and this is simply not something that sensible habits can help us do. The problem with passions for Kant, in Baxley's words, is the "deliberative weight" that we tend to give them,[16] and from what we have seen, we have good reason to think that Aquinas would agree on this point.

Additionally, for both Kant and Aquinas, it is unrealistic to say that

11. Kant, *Groundwork*, 4:390 (5–6) and 4:411 (25); see Baxley, *Kant's Theory*, 34–39. Aquinas, *QDV*, q. 26, a. 7 [Leonine 22.3:773.112–24].

12. Kant, *Metaphysics of Morals*, 6:394 (156). For discussion of this point, see Baxley, *Kant's Theory*, 70–71. Kant goes even further in *Religion* and says that "considered in themselves natural inclinations are good, i.e., not reprehensible, and to want to extirpate them would not only be futile but harmful and blameworthy as well" (6:58 and 78). Aquinas would agree that considered in themselves, the passions are good, but that trouble enters when we consider their relation to reason from a moral perspective. For Kant, like Aquinas, the problem is the "deliberative weight" we tend to grant them—this is part of Kant's radical evil, and Kant is adamant that it is we ourselves who grant them such weight; see *Metaphysics of Morals*, 6:394 (156).

13. Kant, *Groundwork*, 4:398–99 (13–15); Aquinas, *QDV*, q. 26, a. 7 [Leonine 22.3:773.112–24]. For more texts and a discussion of Kant on this point, see Baxley, *Kant's Theory*, 34–39.

14. Kant, *Anthropology from a Pragmatic Point of View*, ed. and trans. Robert Louden (Cambridge: Cambridge University Press, 2006), 149 (40). Kant saw the problem between the deterministic nature of habits and the free nature of morality—as I discussed in chapter 12—quite well. See Kant, *Metaphysics of Morals*, 6:407 (165) and 6:409 (167), as well as *Anthropology*, 199–200 (93–94).

15. Kant, *Anthropology*, 147 (38), and *Metaphysics of Morals*, 6:405 (164). "Maintenance program" is Baxley's apt phrase. See Baxley, *Kant's Theory*, 52, 114, 118–19, 131, 134, 177.

16. Baxley, *Kant's Theory*, 71 and 118.

a virtuous person would always have the right passions. For Kant, Aristotle's optimism about habituating sensibility is hopelessly unrealistic, for virtue cannot go on autopilot but is "always in progress."[17] Moreover, for Kant, as for Aquinas, having the wrong passion is compatible with being virtuous.[18]

Both Kant and Aquinas are much more interested than Aristotle in the problem of freedom, and both emphasize the role of the will as the first principle of morality. Indeed, long before Kant's famous lines in the *Groundwork*, the late Aquinas wrote that only the good will makes us unqualifiedly good.[19] Both set up the problem of reason's relation to the passions with the same classical political analogy, and both argue that what is required is the effective control of sensibility by reason, that is, despotism rather than democracy or anarchy is the solution.[20] For Kant, it is only when reason controls sensibility that a person is fully autocratic. As with Aquinas, either external factors via sensibility control our choices, in which case we are not fully free, or we have control over them.

Although Kant and Aquinas share these basic concerns, Kant, like Scotus, makes the will do all of the heavy lifting. And Kant's hatred of habits, as necessarily compelling freedom, makes it impossible for him to grant some positive role for them in the realm of the emotional life.[21] Aquinas grants the problem, but not the solution. For him the habits of moral virtue are determinate, but they are determined to prudential choices, which are themselves free. Lowering the vehemence of antecedent passions and having an inclination to prudential choice do not require any special rational power, nor can these be conceived of as impinging on autocracy.

A great part of the reason why morality must be cast in the language of duties and imperatives for Kant is the fact that we have contrary incli-

---

17. Kant, *Metaphysics of Morals*, 6:409 (167).

18. See, for instance, Kant's discussion of courage in *Anthropology*, 256–57 (154–55). Given Kant's views on radical evil and his view that habits cannot make our sensible natures go on autopilot, it follows that habitually right emotions are impossible. See *Metaphysics of Morals*, 6:408–9 (166–67).

19. It is Aquinas's mature belief that only the good will makes us unqualifiedly good; *In Ethic.* 3.6 [Leonine 47.1:136.40–59], and *QDM*, q. 1, a. 5 [Leonine 23:24.191–211].

20. See 6n16;77n41; Kant, *Metaphysics of Morals*, 6:408 (166).

21. See 272n14.

nations. Put simply, it is because we do not want to do what is right that morality has to take the form of duties. As Julia Annas notes, a "common modern view, deriving from Kant, is that the virtues are *correctives* to our feelings, and consist essentially in the strength of will to overcome feelings. For feelings might lead us in the wrong direction as well as the right one; they cannot be guaranteed to lead dependably to the right result. None of the ancient ethical schools share this view."[22] Although Aquinas would reject the claim that virtues consist essentially in the strength of the will, he would accept the rest. All of this is to say that if this is what counts as ancient, then Aquinas hardly fits the bill as the paradigmatic medieval moral philosopher faithfully carrying Aristotle's torch. If what makes morality quintessentially Kantian and deontological is the stubborn fact of contrary inclinations, then there is a strong whiff of deontology in Aquinas.

Aristotelian Virtue and Some Recent Criticisms

Let us now turn to Aristotle and consider how Aristotelian Aquinas's moral virtue is when it comes to the relation between emotion and reason. Aristotelian virtue ethics has certainly had a meteoric rise in academia during the last fifty years or so. But philosophers John Doris and Gilbert Harman have recently argued against Aristotelian virtue ethics along the following lines.[23] Empirical studies in social psychology show that most humans do not fare well when measured against the traditional virtues and vices. As a standard, we can use the following basic and relatively noncontroversial premise: virtuous people will act virtuously in various relevant situations over time. For instance, someone who is courageous will act courageously in different situations, such as helping

22. Julia Annas, *The Morality of Happiness* (Oxford: Oxford University Press, 1993), 53.

23. Gilbert Harman, "Moral Philosophy Meets Social Psychology: Virtue Ethics and the Fundamental Attribution Error," *Proceedings of the Aristotelian Society* 99 (1999): 315–31, "The Nonexistence of Character Traits," *Proceedings of the Aristotelian Society* 100 (2000): 223–26, "Skepticism about Character Traits," *Journal of Ethics* 13 (2009): 235–42; John Doris, "Persons, Situations, and Virtue Ethics," *Nous* 32 (1998): 504–30, *Lack of Character: Personality and Moral Behavior* (Cambridge: Cambridge University Press, 2002), "Heated Agreement: Lack of Character as Being for the Good," *Philosophical Studies* 148 (2010): 135–46. See also Maria Merritt, "Virtue Ethics and Situationist Personal Psychology," in *The Moral Psychology Handbook*, ed. J. Doris and the Moral Psychology Research Group (Oxford: Oxford University Press, 2000), 355–401.

someone with a contagious disease or addressing a case of sexual harassment, and this person will also act courageously over a long duration of time. Doris and Harman argue that the empirical evidence from social psychology shows a glaring lack of evidence for such behavior, and even worse, the evidence shows that it is situations rather than virtues that are primarily responsible for moral behaviors.

Consider one of Doris's and Harman's favorite empirical studies, a particularly famous and influential one. In 1972, Alice Isen and Paula Levin hired an actress to drop her papers (a thesis, or something like it) as shoppers in a mall left a phone booth.[24] Some shoppers had found a (planted) dime in the phone booth, while others had not. The undercover psychologists, Isen and Levin, blended in and watched what happened. The results were striking. Out of the twenty-five people who did not find a dime, only one person bent down to help the woman pick up her papers, but fourteen of the sixteen people who did find a dime in the booth helped her. In sum, those who found a dime helped the woman, but those who did not find a dime did not help her. Finding a dime apparently made all the difference to their moral behavior, and most people, I believe, whether they are proponents of virtue or not, will agree that virtuous people will not act morally simply depending on whether they have just found a dime in a payphone! Based on many studies like this one, Harman and Doris conclude that moral behavior is not typically ordered by the virtues, for if they were so ordered, a slight alteration of the situation (dime or no dime) would not cause such a drastic change in their moral behavior. The overwhelming evidence seems to point to the fact that it is situations, not character traits, that somehow produce moral behavior. Hence the titles of Doris's very influential book, *Lack of Character*, and one of Harman's papers, "The Nonexistence of Character Traits."[25]

The Aristotelian response to Doris and Harman has primarily been that virtue is, and has always been understood to be, rare.[26] Virtue is hu-

---

24. Alice Isen and Paula Levin, "Effect and Feeling Good on Helping: Cookies and Kindness," *Journal of Personality and Social Psychology* 21 (1972): 384–88.

25. See 274n23.

26. See, e.g., Diana Fleming, "The Character of Virtue: Answering the Situationist Challenge to Virtue Ethics," *Ratio* 19 (2006): 38; N. Athanassoulis, "A Response to Harman: Virtue Ethics and Character Traits," *Proceedings of the Aristotelian Society* 100 (2000): 217–20;

man excellence, and excellence is rare. Therefore, we should never have expected to find widespread evidence of virtue in such studies. Doris admits that there may be monsters and saints at the "tails of the bell curve,"[27] but if they exist they are so rare that we can safely ignore them. In other words, if we are thinking of virtue descriptively rather than normatively, then virtue ethics basically has nothing to offer; it simply cannot help us describe the way people actually are.[28]

Doris seems to move from the descriptive to the normative as follows: yes, he says, virtue ethics' central premise of cross-situationally consistent character traits is perhaps possible, but given the evidence, it is extremely unlikely, in fact, perhaps only slightly more likely than finding a unicorn. And if there are no virtuous people out there, why bother, from a normative perspective, trying to become one?[29] The problem with these "rarity arguments," which give virtue ethicists some breathing room from the experimental data, is that they simultaneously make virtue so rare as to seem to be ephemeral. The more perfect virtue is, the rarer it is, the more impossible it will be to empirically find, and the less believable it becomes.

This last point raises the question of how damning the data actually are, or how rare virtue in fact is. In the classic phone booth experiment, one of Doris's favorites, only one person out of twenty-five who did not find a dime helped. While the degree of spinelessness is striking, it is equally striking that a study two years later completely failed to replicate the experiment, which nevertheless—bafflingly—has become a classic.[30]

Michael DePaul, "Character Traits, Virtues and Vices: Are There None?," *Proceedings of the Twentieth World Congress of Philosophy* 9 (2000): 141–57; G. Sreenivasan, "Errors about Errors: Virtue Theory and Trait Attribution," *Mind* III (2002): 57.

27. Doris, *Lack of Character*, 60.

28. "Descriptive" here simply means describing the way people actually are, while "normative" means describing the way people ought to be.

29. Doris, *Lack of Character*, 110 and 122. See also Harman, "Nonexistence of Character Traits," 224: "If we know that there is no such thing as a character trait and we know that virtue would require having character traits, how can we aim at becoming a virtuous agent? If there are no character traits, there is nothing one can do to acquire character traits that are more like those possessed by a virtuous agent."

30. Doris buries this in a footnote; *Lack of Character*, 30n4. For the failed replication, see Gregory A. Blevins and Terrance Murphy, "Feeling Good and Helping: Further Phone Booth Finding," *Psychological Reports* 34 (1974): 326. For discussion, see Christian Miller, *Moral Character* (Oxford: Oxford University Press, 2013), 63–66. It is also worth pointing out that social psychology as a whole is currently going through a replication crisis; see Open

Despite the experiment's inadequacies, Doris seems to think that it is roughly indicative of other better and similar studies. Here, however, I think Doris is wrong. A forthcoming meta-analysis by Blaine Fowers et al. has examined 286 independent studies on helping, with a total of 46,705 participants, and found that on average roughly 40 percent of the participants helped.[31] The virtue-as-unicorn analogy would be far more compelling if the average were closer to 4 percent than to 40 percent. Nevertheless, if virtue is as rare as it is extraordinary, some Aristotelians might even think that 4 percent is a bit too high. Be that as it may, given the empirical evidence, there is plenty of breathing room for both Aristotle's and Aquinas's moral virtue.

Aristotle's Realism Problem

Even granting this breathing room, Christian Miller nevertheless thinks there is a good objection to Aristotle's account of virtue that is "lurking in the same neighborhood"[32] as Doris's objection. While Miller agrees that the rarity response is a valid argument,[33] he seriously doubts that we can become what Aristotle thinks we can. He goes after Aristotle's well-established position that the virtuous person will always have the right desires[34]—or, as Aristotle often says, the virtuous person will

---

Science Collaboration, "Estimating the Reproducibility of Psychological Science," *Science* 349 (2015): 18. For the failed replications of Roy Baumeister's ego-depletion effect see also Martin S. Hagger and Nikos L. D. Chatzisarantis, "A Multilab Preregistered Replication of the Ego-Depletion Effect," *Perspectives on Psychological Science* 11 (2016): 546–73. For a more philosophical discussion of the problem, see Brian D. Earp and David Trafimow, "Replication, Falsification, and the Crisis of Confidence in Social Psychology," *Frontiers in Psychology* 19 (2015): 621. Time will tell how bad the replication crisis is and what reseach will remain standing.

31. G. Tyler Lefevor et al., "To What Degree Do Situational Influences Explain Spontaneous Helping Behaviour? A Meta-Analysis," *European Review of Social Psychology* 28, no. 1 (2017): 1–30.

32. Miller, *Character and Moral Psychology*, 207.

33. Ibid., 202–13.

34. For discussions of this, see Amélie Rorty, "Akrasia and Pleasure: Nicomachean Ethics Book 7," in *Essays on Aristotle's Ethics*, ed. A. Rorty (Berkeley: University of California Press, 1980), 274; Jonathan Lear, *Aristotle: The Desire to Understand* (Cambridge: Cambridge University Press, 1998), 167–68; Annas, *Morality of Happiness*, 56–57; Jan Edward Garrett, "The Moral Status of 'the Many' in Aristotle," *Journal of the History of Philosophy* 31 (1993): 189; Howard Curzer, *Aristotle and the Virtues* (Oxford: Oxford University Press, 2012), 343 and 386; Sarah Broadie, *Ethics with Aristotle* (New York: Oxford University Press, 1991), 267 and 270–71. Broadie puts this quite strongly when she notes Aristotle's "stringent condition for temperance, for it is possible to be aware that something would be pleasant, and also to

desire the right thing at the right time and in the right way.[35] Aristotle is quite explicit in the crucial passage on participation that when the sense appetite participates in reason, "it speaks, on *all* matters, with the same voice as reason."[36] Miller argues that

on empirical grounds, it is reasonable to worry that this standard is psychologically unattainable for beings like us. Note that the requirement is *not* that in one particular instance of action there be no opposing desires. That would be unremarkable. It is that consistently and reliably across *all* situations relevant to virtue, there be no opposing occurrent desires. So even in cases where highly rewarding cheating could go undetected, or powerful sexual experiences be felt, or terrible carnage on the battlefield avoided, the expectation is that there be no inclinations whatsoever in those directions. That puts virtue out of our reach. And note that this is a requirement, not for maximal or full virtue, but just for *weak* virtue. It is one thing to say that full virtue is out of the reach of human beings. Few would disagree with that. But it is a much different claim to say that even minimal virtue is out of our reach.[37]

I think Miller is absolutely right—it seems absurd and highly unrealistic to suppose that anyone could always have the right desires across all situations.[38] If the point of virtue ethics is to help us become virtuous, it would be foolish to ask us to become something impossible; rather, what is realistic or possible should limit our understanding of the normative goal.[39]

---

mind foregoing it, without for a moment being actually tempted to prefer it. A person in this state with regard to some physical pleasure would not be responding temperately by Aristotle's standard. He might for instance be sorry that the rational course entails foregoing the pleasure, even though he unswervingly sets the pleasure to one side. He might even for the moment regret his general commitment to rational decency without being inclined to break out of it. For Aristotle, these conditions count as 'continence,' every bit as much as the condition of the agent who experiences and resists actual temptation" (270).

35. For example, *Nic.* 1106b16–23, 1115b11–20, 1119a11–18, 1119b15–16, 1125b32–36, 1146a10–12, 1151b34–1152a4.

36. *Nic.* 1102b28.

37. Christian Miller, "Categorizing Character: Moving Beyond the Aristotelian Framework," in *Varieties of Virtue Ethics*, ed. D. Carr, J. Arthur, and K. Kristjánsson (London: Palgrave Macmillan, 2017), 143–62.

38. Miller confirmed (personal communication) that in this quotation, "empirical grounds" does not refer to the data from empirical social psychology experiments (although his thoughts are deeply informed by them); his argument is simply an appeal to straightforward common sense.

39. One might try to argue that Aristotle wants us to strive toward something higher than is possible so that we make more progress than we would have otherwise, overshooting the mean, in a way, toward a kind of theoretical ideal. I find this highly unconvincing, for

Bonnie Kent takes this one step further, although her arguments do not stem from these contemporary debates. Besides having infallible emotions, she points out that Aristotle's virtuous man is himself morally infallible.[40] For instance, Aristotle says: "For no function of the man has so much permanence as virtuous activities.... he will be happy throughout his life; for always, or by preference to everything else, he will do and contemplate what is excellent, and he will bear the chances of life most nobly and altogether decorously."[41] Likewise, Aristotle repeatedly says that virtue is "unchangeable" and that vice is "incurable."[42] Thus, not only does Aristotle's virtuous person always have the right desires or emotions; he or she also always does the right thing. Likewise, the vicious person will always consistently act viciously. Aristotle's virtuous or vicious person is completely cross-situationally consistent, that is, the virtuous person will always act virtuously in each appropriate situation while the vicious person will always act viciously. And having the right (or wrong) desires is no doubt a great part of what enables Aristotle's virtuous and vicious agents to act with such infallible consistency.

In other words, while I believe that Doris overstated the strength of his case, I do nonetheless think there is something to be said for his argument when we consider Aristotle's virtue together with Miller's and Kent's criticisms of it. We might combine these and reformulate the argument against Aristotle's virtue as follows: There is no empirical evidence that virtuous people exist and strong empirical evidence that

---

then we do not know what Aristotle thinks actual virtue looks like, even though Aristotle devotes much time and effort to describing exactly what virtuous people are like. When Aristotle says that "the purpose of our examination is not to know what virtue is, but to become good, since otherwise the inquiry would be of no benefit to us" (*Nic.* 1103b29–30), I take him to mean that through reading the *Nicomachean Ethics*, it is possible (for some) to become virtuous in the way he describes.

40. Bonnie Kent, *Virtues of the Will* (Washington, D.C.: The Catholic University of America Press, 1995), 225, and "Losable Virtue: Aquinas on Character and Will," in *Aquinas and the Nicomachean Ethics* (ed. Hoffmann et al.), 109. Kent does somewhat qualify her claim: "Of course, the virtuous person might make a mistake and so might appear to have acted badly, just as the vicious person might be pressured or bribed into appropriate behavior and so might appear to have acted well. But at a deeper level these characters are quite consistent. The virtuous person never chooses badly; the vicious person never chooses well" (225). I gather that Kent is referring to cases in which the virtuous person acts on ignorance of some particular (*Nic.* III.1), but such cases would not be morally problematic because the person could not have known otherwise.

41. *Nic.* 1100b13–21; see also 1100b34–35 and 1128b28–31.

42. For example, *Nic.* 1105b1, 1114a10–22, 1137a29, 1150a20–23, 1150b32–35, 1165b18c.

most people are not virtuous; therefore, as it seems unrealistic and even impossible to become virtuous, there seems to be no point in trying to become virtuous or in promoting doing so.[43]

Granting Miller's and Kent's complaints, I think that we should seek a different account of moral virtue than Aristotle's, namely, one that will provide some cross-situational consistency and stability, but without going so far as claiming that the virtuous person will have perfect desires and act with perfect consistency. Indeed, some psychologists have practically begged philosophers working in normative virtue ethics to take up the interdisciplinary question of the virtues and their sensitivity to various situations (cross-situationality) and stability over time.[44] On this question, I believe that Aquinas has a worthwhile contribution to make that is more realistic and plausible than Aristotle's.[45]

Aquinas on Traits and Situations

Part of the difficulty in explaining the sense in which Aquinas thinks that virtues are responsive to situations is that there is no consensus in the field of psychology on what a situation is.[46] Be that as it may, I think our general intuitions suffice in most cases. We can at least say

43. Someone might challenge the claim that there is no evidence that virtue exists, as one might think that the 40 percent in Fower's meta-analysis suggest that there are virtuous people. But each of these studies is a one-time snapshot of human behavior. The fact that someone helps in one situation does not mean that they will help in another. They might, but they might not. To date, there is no evidence one way or the other, simply because no one has run the same people through multiple different experiments.

44. Eranda Jayawickreme et al., "Virtuous States and Virtuous Traits: How the Empirical Evidence Regarding the Existence of Broad Traits Saves Virtue Ethics from the Situationist Critique," *Theory and Research Education* 12 (2014): 289.

45. Many Aristotelians have argued that the recent objections to Aristotle attack an uncharitable or oversimplified version of Aristotle; see, e.g., Rachana Kamtekar, "Situationism and Virtue Ethics on the Content of Our Character," *Ethics* 114 (2004): 460; Julia Annas, "Virtue Ethics and Social Psychology," *A Priori* 2 (2003): 28–30; Kristján Kristjánsson, "An Aristotelian Critique of Situationism," *Philosophy* 83 (2008): 67–71; Diana Fleming, "The Character of Virtue: Answering the Situationist Challenge to Virtue Ethics," *Ratio* 19 (2006): 38. I agree with Christian Miller that even if situationists have an uncharitable or simply incorrect account of Aristotelian virtue, Aristotelians still face the same problem, namely, that most people do not come close to living up to these scholars' interpretations of Aristotle, and thus they are forced back to the rarity argument; see Miller, *Moral Character*, 214–16. However, I do not believe that I have offered an oversimplified account of Aristotle; I have referred to the relevant texts as well as the scholarship that supports my interpretation.

46. For a discussion of this see Miller, *Character and Moral Psychology*, 85–90. Here Miller also points out that there is hardly any consensus on what character traits are, but I will only be dealing with what Aquinas and Aristotle believe they are.

that situations have to do with particulars. A few examples of situations that have changed the moral behaviors of people include smelling cookies, holding a warm drink or an icy-hot therapeutic pad, or being surrounded by others.[47] These are all particulars, and for Aquinas, one way that we respond to such particulars is through emotions, as we perceive the particulars through the external and internal senses. In some of the relevant experiments, however, the situation also seems to include emotion—for instance, psychologists have changed moral behavior by making participants feel hurried or guilty.[48] In any case, for the most part these situations track particulars or our emotional response to these particulars.[49] We can say, in general, that the passions in these experiments are largely caused by the situations. For Aquinas, as I have discussed, the stronger the passion, the more it hinders reason from making a virtuous choice. Thus, the more vehement a passion is, the more likely we are to be moved by the situation rather than by ourselves through our virtue.

Thus, we should ask: how vehement do passions need to be to hinder reason? Or conversely, we might wonder: how mild do they need to be to count as virtuous propassions? If we could answer this question, we could presumably distinguish virtuous from nonvirtuous persons. Those with virtuous propassions should resist the situational manipulations of social psychologists, whereas those with vehement passions should not. Aquinas presents this in either/or terms: either such a passion is a mild propassion or it is a perfect/antecedent passion. It seems clear as day. In general, when making a distinction, one usually points to the extremes to sharpen the contrast and illuminate the distinction, as Aquinas does

47. R. Baron, "The Sweet Smell of … Helping: Effects of Pleasant Ambient Fragrance on Prosocial Behavior in Shopping Malls," *Personality and Social Psychology Bulletin* 23 (1997): 498–503; Lawrence Williams and John Bargh, "Experiencing Physical Warmth Promotes Interpersonal Warmth," *Science* 322 (2008): 606–7; and Chen-Bo Zhong and Katie Liljenquist, "Washing Away Your Sins: Threatened Morality and Physical Cleansing," *Science* 313 (2006): 1451–52.

48. Dennis Regan, Margo Williams, and Sondra Sparling, "Voluntary Expiation of Guilt: A Field Experiment," *Journal of Personality and Social Psychology* 24 (1972): 42–45; John M. Darley and Daniel C. Batson, "'From Jerusalem to Jericho': A Study of Situational and Dispositional Variables in Helping Behavior," *Journal of Personality and Social Psychology* 27 (1973): 100–108.

49. Some of them also focus on our beliefs and thoughts, e.g., Lisa L. Shu, Francesca Gino, and Max H. Bazerman, "Dishonest Deed, Clear Conscience: When Cheating Leads to Moral Disengagement and Motivated Forgetting," *Personality and Social Psychology Bulletin* 37 (2011): 330–49.

here. This does not mean, however, that in every given case it will be easy to discern whether the passion is one or the other.

Here the metaphysics of passions is crucial. Passions are real extramental accidents (in the category passion) that will have varying degrees of intensity depending on the strength of their causes. Their causes are often complex, traveling down many different kinds of pathways in causing the motion or passion in the sense appetites, as I discussed in chapter 10. As is the case with any motion, the stronger the cause(s) of the motion, whatever it (they) may be, the stronger or more vehement the motion or passion will be. My point is that these passions will fall along a scale and it will be very hard to pin down any particular one as either a propassion or a perfect passion.

For instance, let us say that Bob is justifiably angry because someone has said something incredibly offensive to his daughter, and let us also imagine the vehemence of his anger on a 10 point scale, all else being equal, where 1 is the mildest propassion and 10 is the most vehement perfect passion. When the vehemence of Bob's anger is ranked as 1, he can think clearly and prudently about the situation and respond appropriately, but when it is ranked as 10, he becomes irrationally violent. But what about when it is ranked as 3, 5, or 7? Does 3 indicate a propassion? What does 5 indicate? Clearly there is a scale here such that at one end, Bob is affected by his righteous anger while still being able to think clearly about what he should say or do, while at the other end, he is made completely irrational by the anger, and there is a possible range that falls in between these extremes.

The metaphysics of habits is also crucial here. As metaphysical accidents in the first species of quality, habits can inhere in their subjects to greater or lesser degrees. In the case of the moral virtues, which lower or dampen the motion or actualization of the sense appetite *vis-à-vis* antecedent passions, as I have discussed, the more the habit inheres in the sense appetites the more it will lower the vehemence of antecedent passions.[50] In other words, there is an inverse relation between how strongly the habit inheres in the sense appetite and how strong the antecedent passions will be, all else being equal.[51]

50. See chapter 4, 111n103, for the degrees of inherence, and chapters 8, 10, and 11 for the lowering of vehemence.

51. For a helpful discussion of how virtues come in degrees that is cast in the language of

For instance, the stronger the habit of temperance, the less powerful the temptation. This is entirely a question of degrees on a scale, both for the habit and for the passion. Let us say that Bob's virtue reduces his passion by 40 percent from what it would have been otherwise. In a normal situation, he would have experienced an anger ranked with a vehemence of 5, but his virtue inheres strongly enough to lower the vehemence to 3, so we might label this a propassion. Of course, it would be better if he could strengthen his habit and lower the vehemence to 2, but 3 is certainly better than 4. We could, very roughly speaking, say that he is virtuous if the vehemence of his passion falls somewhere between 1 and 3. But there is no clear-cut fixed line for distinguishing mild antecedent propassions from vehement antecedent perfect passions in any given situation.

The line between virtue and nonvirtue, at least concerning the passions, is quite clear for Aristotle, namely, it is determined by whether someone has such disordered passions at all. And because Aristotle's virtuous man has no disordered passions, it makes sense that such a person would never be tempted and would act with perfect cross-situational consistency. This is not the case for Aquinas, however, for whom virtuous people will have disordered passions, but these will not be very vehement. And while it is impossible to pinpoint the exact degree of vehemence that distinguishes virtue from nonvirtue in Aquinas's theory, we can say that the more vehement the passion, the more moved by the situation a person will be, and thus less cross-situational consistency can be expected.

For Aquinas, the stronger the virtue, the better. But it is important to note that the upper limit of this virtue does not involve perfect cross-situational consistency. There are a few important reasons for this. One is that Aquinas thinks that someone with moral virtue can sin out of weakness from passion.[52] In other words, for Aquinas, unlike Aristotle, it is possible for someone to be virtuous and incontinent at the same

---

the contemporary analytic discussions of categorical and dispositional properties, see Justin Matchulat, "Defending Virtue against the Situationist Challenge: Aristotle, Aquinas, and Contemporary Metaphysicians on Degree Traits," *Proceedings of the American Catholic Philosophical Association* 88 (2015): 245–58. I draw a sharper line between Aristotle and Aquinas than Matchulat does and lean towards William Jaworski's identity theory (see chapter 4 for a discussion and 116n118 for the literature) on the more metaphysical questions.

52. See, e.g., *ST* II-II, q. 47, a. 16 [St. Paul 1300–1301], and q. 53, a. 6 [St. Paul 1319]. See also Kent, *Losable Virtue*, 91–109.

time. This may seem impossible, for granting that a prudent person must have the moral virtues (because they are connected) and granting that moral virtue lowers the vehemence of the passions, it seems impossible for such a person to sin from vehement passion.

So let us revisit Bob, whose virtue dampens the vehemence of his antecedent anger by 40 percent, all else being equal, which will undoubtedly help him in most situations. As I discussed, passions are caused by all kinds of factors, and it is obvious that the intensity of Bob's anger will depend on the power of its causes. Let us say that Bob's daughter was not simply insulted, but violently accosted. In such a case, Bob's baseline anger will be much higher, perhaps with a vehemence of 10, and given the 40 percent virtue reduction, he will wind up with an antecedent passion with a vehemence of 6. Now, Bob may very well choose prudently in this situation, but he also may not; in either case, he struggles with his anger and so would count as continent or incontinent. Aquinas's point, I believe, is that no matter how virtuous we are, there will almost invariably be moments in our lives when we are under intense pressure and will have to wrestle with our passions.[53] I chalk this up as a plus for the plausibility of Aquinas's position. Virtues are helpful *vis-à-vis* passion, but they are by no means foolproof.

For Aristotle, continence and incontinence are dispositions.[54] For Aquinas, however, they seem rather to describe occurrent moments when the will wrestles with passion.[55] When we say that someone is temperate, for instance, we usually mean to signify that the person actually possesses that habit. However, because continence and incontinence are not habits, Aquinas does not think one can label people as continent or incontinent in the strong sense that the grounding truthmakers for such claims are metaphysical dispositions. Thus, we may say that Bob, in the previous case, was both virtuous and incontinent (if he chose wrongly),

---

53. Aquinas also thinks that if a passion is vehement enough, it can destroy our free choice altogether; see *QDM*, q. 3, a. 9 [Leonine 23:87.193–207], and *ST* I-II, q. 33, a. 3 [St. Paul 699].

54. E.g., *Nic.* 1150a15–16, 1151a27–30. See Curzer, *Aristotle and the Virtues*, 344; Bonnie Kent and Ashley Dressel, "Weakness and Willful Wrongdoing in Aquinas's *De malo*," in *Aquinas's Disputed Questions on Evil: A Critical Guide*, ed. M. V. Dougherty (Cambridge: Cambridge University Press, 2016), 38.

55. *ST* I-II, q. 58, a. 3, ad 2 [St. Paul 791]; II-II, q. 155, a. 3 [St. Paul 1692]. See Kent, *Losable Virtue*, 91–109.

thereby signifying both that he actually possessed the habit, which was of some help to him, but also that he was incontinent, as his will was wrestling with passion at that moment and he failed to choose rightly. Aquinas thus very much softens Aristotle's hard line between continence and virtue.

Here it is also worth briefly revisiting Aquinas's point that we only use our habits when we will to do so. For Aquinas one can have a virtue and will not to use it. A virtuous person might simply act from malice.[56] That is, a virtuous person might just choose to cheat, steal, harm someone, and so forth. Likewise, a vicious person might simply choose to act against his or her vice and do the right thing on some occasion. As Aquinas sees things, if the virtues were infallible and vices were incurable, they would rob us of the ability to do otherwise—that is, they would rob us of free choice.

From a theological perspective, of course, Aquinas has a much stronger sense of sin. He certainty holds that anyone at any time is capable of sinning. The postlapsarian state is simply one in which humans will morally fail now and again, despite their best efforts. This way of thinking is completely foreign to Aristotle: imagine trying to persuade Aristotle's great-souled man to go to confession! Kant's theory of radical evil, however, is much closer to Aquinas's way of thinking. Moral infallibility is simply off the table for Aquinas, given the heightened role he gives to the will, his view that virtue is compatible with incontinent and malicious acts, his belief that the virtuous person will have mild disordered passions, and his belief in original sin. Thus, it stands to reason that we should expect less cross-situational consistency from the virtuous person on Aquinas's model than on Aristotle's.

In any particular situation, we cannot know whether the virtuous person will act rightly. We can say, however, that the more virtuous or vicious people are, the less, on average, their acts will be caused by the situation and the more they will be caused by the people themselves through their character traits. For the virtuous person has certain tailwinds that help that person to act rightly in different situations: mild propassions, a habitual inclination toward acting virtuously and taking

---

56. This would not be malice qua habitual vice, but a malicious choice; see *ST* I-II, q. 78, a. 3 [St. Paul 893].

pleasure in doing so, as well as prudence, the habit of practical reasoning and choosing well, which enables the person to see and choose the right act in any given situation. Nevertheless, virtuous people must still make a choice and may very well choose wrongly, whether incontinently or maliciously. Such deviations from their character must be infrequent, for otherwise the acts would alter their character and we could not call them virtuous. But we can say with certainty that the more virtuous a person is, the more likely he or she will be to act with cross-situational consistency. The nice feature here is that this way of thinking aligns perfectly well with how a relatively large group of psychologists already think about character traits, namely, the stronger the character trait, the greater the cross-situational consistency we should expect to find,[57] even if Aquinas would disagree with some of them here or there. There is no need to invent a new theory of traits and their sensitivity to situations: we can simply place Aquinas in one prevalent camp.

There is one last point concerning social psychology that I wish to address, which further distinguishes Aquinas from Aristotle. Perhaps the most striking facet of the social psychology experiments is the strong evidence that situations play such a large role in the moral behavior of most people. For those who believe that most people are basically virtuous, the evidence suggests otherwise: Most people will act immorally because of some irrelevant situation. Following Aristotle, Aquinas does say that most people are followers of their passions, so the fact that the presence of guilt or even the touching of something hot or cold would make an emotional difference and thus affect moral actions is unsurprising.[58]

But Aristotle is much more pessimistic in his description of the way most people are. While Aquinas agrees with Aristotle's descriptive claim

---

57. See, e.g., Walter Mischel, "Toward an Integrative Science of the Person," *Annual Review of Psychology* 55 (2004): 2; David Magnusson and N. Endler, "Interational Psychology: Present Status and Future Prospects," in *Personality at the Crossroads: Current Issues in Interactional Psychology*, ed. D. Magnusson and N. Endler (Hillsdale, Mich.: Lawrence Erlbaum Associates, 1977), 14 and 17; David Zuroff, "Was Gordon Allport a Trait Theorist?," *Journal of Personality and Social Psychology* 51 (1986): 993; Yuichi Shoda, "A Unified Framework for the Study of Behavioral Consistency: Bridging Person x Situation Interaction and the Consistency Paradox," *European Journal of Personality* 13 (1999): 379.

58. Some of the experiments do not deal directly with passions. For instance, one study showed that reciting an honor code prior to taking an exam significantly decreased the probability of cheating; Shu, "Dishonest Deed," 330–49. But the fact that making moral principles salient lowers cheating should not be surprising, at least on Aquinas's theory. For Aquinas, of

that the many (*hoi polloi*) are followers of passion, he rejects Aristotle's further claim that the many have no knowledge of what is good and bad and that they simply obey their fear of punishment.[59] Miller plausibly argues that, contra Aristotle, the social psychology experiments show that most people do have some moral beliefs and desires.[60] Regarding, for instance, the Milgram shock experiment, it is well documented that participants were deeply uncomfortable electrocuting their fellow humans.[61] Their deep discomfort shows that they knew it was wrong—that is, most people do have moral knowledge even if they fail to act on it. Aquinas indeed believes that most people have some moral knowledge, for synderesis, the habitual first principles of moral reasoning, can never be fully effaced.[62] Thus, while both Aristotle and Aquinas agree that most people follow their passions[63] and thus should be very susceptible to situational manipulations, as the experiments strongly confirm, Aquinas would additionally predict that they would feel guilty when they fail to live up to their moral knowledge, which the experiments also confirm. Aristotle would make no such prediction, as the many apparently have no moral knowledge at all.[64] Aquinas's account of the many, considered descriptively in light of these experiments, is thus clearly preferable to Aristotle's.

Moreover, for Aquinas but not for Aristotle, being virtuous is compatible with having bad emotions now and again, and it is even com-

---

course what one thinks about as one deliberates makes a difference. As he sees things, paying or not paying attention to moral principles is a large factor when we make good or bad choices; see Hoffmann, *Angelic Sin*, 122–56.

59. *Nic.* 1179b11–16. For a discussion of Aristotle's "the many," see Garrett, *The Many*, 171–89, and Curzer, *Aristotle and the Virtues*, 369–70. Curzer argues that the many is its own separate moral category, whereas Garrett argues that it may include vice. The difference, as Curzer points out, is that the many are not incurable as the vicious are; see 369n5.

60. Miller, *Character and Moral Psychology*, 37–46.

61. Miller, *Moral Character*, 42, and *Character and Moral Psychology*, 282–85.

62. *In II Sent.*, d. 39, q. 3, a. 1.

63. *Nic.* 1179b11–16; *ST* II-II, q. 95, a. 5, ad 2.

64. Here I cannot possibly address the leading contemporary theories of the way most people are, for example, Christian Miller's Mixed Trait Theory or John Doris's Local Virtue Theory. See my review of Miller's *Character and Moral Psychology* in *The Thomist* 79 (2015): 663–68. For an insightful criticism of Doris, see Miller, *Character and Moral Psychology*, 198–202; for an insightful criticism of Miller, see Doris's review of *Character and Moral Psychology* in *Notre Dame Philosophical Reviews* (February 11, 2015), available at ndpr.nd .edu/news/55693-character-and-moral-psychology. To properly address such views from a Thomistic perspective, I believe that more work needs to be done on Aquinas's descriptive views of the way most people are.

patible with a real stumble from virtue. For this reason, it will be very difficult to say something conclusive based on any particular study. If one dips into a study of a hundred participants and finds that thirty acted morally, this gives us no basis for concluding that any one of those thirty participants was actually virtuous. Because one can act against one's virtue or vice, some of those who are virtuous may be hidden in the group of seventy, and some of those without virtue may be hidden among the thirty. Be that as it may, an aggregation of studies could give us a rough indication of the possible percentage of people who are virtuous. It would be much better to have the same hundred people participate in multiple different moral experiments and see which participants act morally across different situations and times. Moreover, if this could be done multiple times across diverse swaths of the population, then we would have even better data on how rare virtue may be. But nothing like this has been done because such experiments would be very difficult and expensive to run.

Be that as it may, in the big picture, Aristotle's account of the vicious and the many depicts them as being worse than they seem to be, while his account of virtue seems to make the virtuous seem better than they are. Aquinas moderates Aristotle's extremes and offers, in their place, a much more realistic and plausible account. Aquinas's account of virtue does not require that the virtuous always feel like doing the right thing, nor does it require that they are morally infallible, nor does he think that the vicious are utterly incurable, nor, for that matter, does he think that most people have no moral knowledge at all—he thinks they have quite a bit, even if they fail to act on it. Furthermore, as Aquinas's virtuous and vicious people are not Aristotelian fairy-tale heroes and villains who are infallibly good or bad, Aquinas's virtue, considered normatively, seems like a far more plausible and realistic goal that we can strive to reach.

Summary

In sum, for Aquinas but not for Aristotle, virtue is compatible with having bad emotions now and again, and it is even compatible with a real stumble from virtue. If Aquinas is right, there have been (and still are) virtuous people who thought Aristotle was right about virtue and were thus mistaken about their own virtue as well as that of others. No one can be perfectly virtuous, and most virtuous people (like everyone else) will have plenty of room for improvement. Some may object that the bar has been set too low here, but setting the bar unrealistically high is also undoubtedly demoralizing. From a theological perspective, as I have noted, to claim that humans are naturally capable of becoming such that they never have a contrary emotion or a stumble is tantamount to saying that they can overcome original sin by their own efforts; from a philosophical perspective, it should be clear by now that Aquinas also holds that this is impossible. If we grant his arguments, then surely our practical efforts to strive for virtue should strive for what is possible.

While it would be nice to draw a clear line between virtue and non-virtue by nailing down the exact level of vehemence at which the trouble starts *vis-à-vis* antecedent passion, this is of course impossible. It depends on the person in question, their natural dispositions, the particular context, and all kinds of other causes of any given passion. Aquinas is right to leave this vague. There are simply too many variables or different principles that are causally at play in any particular passion, and in any particular instance some of these may be more powerful than others.

Furthermore, on Aquinas's view, because the antecedent passions and propassions of the virtuous person cannot be ordered, the virtuous person will not always want to do the right thing. Indeed, at times virtuous persons will want to eat and drink more than they should, will be sexually attracted to those whom they should not pursue, will become angry about what they should not be angry about, and so forth. Because passions often stem from the external world and are our sensible natural reactions to the world around us, the virtuous person does not have blind faith in them. The virtuous person is always prudently a little distrustful of them, as he or she should be. The passions may be right, but they may very well not be, and that is simply the way life is. Because antecedent passions are normally mild, they are not threatening and here there is no real power struggle between the virtuous person's emotions and reason. But there will most likely be more difficult moments in life when the virtuous person will struggle.

Granting that the virtuous person will have some bad emotions and will occasionally have to do what is right despite them, the virtuous person does seem a bit Kantian/deontological. Aquinas leans toward Kant in his emphasis on the will and free choice, his skepticism about the passions, his views on the need to control them, his belief that being virtuous is compatible with having the wrong passions, and his views that are similar to Kant's view of radical evil. However, Aquinas agrees with Aristotle that our sensitive natures can and ought to be habituated and that we can have virtuous sensible passions (albeit consequent ones); he simply thinks that Aristotle went too far, and I suspect he would think that Kant did not go far enough.

We can safely say that Aquinas is hardly the polar opposite of Kant and a faithful follower of Aristotle on the emotions' participation in reason, so we may abandon that classical narrative. It is also worth mentioning that this classical story has often been used as a way to understand the debates between the intellectualists and the voluntarists of the thirteenth and fourteenth centuries. Some hold that Aquinas was the last great bastion of Aristotelianism and that after his death the voluntarists put philosophy on an express train headed for Kant. But as I have argued, although Aquinas is no voluntarist, he is hardly an intellectualist. Furthermore, if there really was such a train, then Aquinas himself was on it, given his later more muscular account of will and his views that the sense appetites only participate in reason insofar as they are commanded, that we only use our habits when we will to do so, and so forth. I am, quite frankly, unable to offer some kind of compelling counternarrative about the history of philosophy, and I am also uninterested in doing so. I simply want to point out that the classical way in which this story has been told cannot be right.

Moreover, why should anyone accept, as Schiller does, that the only viable alternatives are that *either* we have a beautiful soul with perfect emotions *or* we are all will and reason, quashing passion? I think Aquinas is right to argue that perfect emotions are not possible, but that does not mean that the sense appetites cannot be habituated in other helpful and virtuous ways, as I have argued. For there is a huge space between no habituation of the emotions at all (which was never really Kant's view) and perfect habituation of the emotions (which does seem to be Aristotle's view) for various possible philosophical and psychological accounts of how the virtues might habituate our emotions. I think Aquinas's position is a very good one, but there are of course many others that are worth considering.

On the other hand, there is something right about Schiller's complaint regarding Kant. Schiller's account of the beautiful and harmonious soul is undeniably attractive and moving. In chapter 12, I responded to the Thomists who argue for some form of Schiller's/Aristotle's position. But the general worry held by those who are attracted to variations of Schiller's views, regardless of the textual niceties and evidence in Aquinas, is that Aquinas's mild virtuous passions seem to make our lives less full and worthwhile. Even if we have been wrong about Kant's views of virtue until recently, some, perhaps, will nevertheless complain that Kant's real views are still too close to the caricature of Kant and that Aquinas is also too close to this. There simply seems to be too much controlling and commanding of emotion. A good life is a passionate life, and when lowering the intensity of emotion is coupled with the choosing and commanding, it seems that we are moving too far in the wrong direction, with too much despotism. Perhaps it seems like plain suppression of emotion and feeling at the end of the day. Perhaps those who object nevertheless think that the main goal of moral virtue is precisely emotional spontaneity, that is, simply loving the good and having the right emotions without so much thought and command. While I will not rehash the arguments about why I think such a position is unrealistic, I want to conclude this chapter—and the third part of this book— by offering a sketch (and partial summary) of Aquinas's virtuous person in the hope of mollifying these worries.

First, I would like to point out that for Aquinas, deliberation—that is, thinking through what particular thing we should do—must simply be full of passion. These passions need not be vehement, but deliberation is hardly dry. The thinking through various possible things that we might do in deliberation looks, roughly, like this: if I do this, that will happen, but if I do that, this will happen, and so forth. And in thinking through all of these different particular scenarios, we imagine ourselves doing them, which will inevitably cause a number of passions. For instance, when we consider ourselves doing something good, we imagine ourselves doing it, and this causes pleasure, or if we think of ourselves doing something bad, this will cause pleasure regarding whatever advantage we expect to get but also pain at the thought of, perhaps, having to harm someone. In any case, for Aquinas, all deliberation, whether virtuous or nonvirtuous, will have its concomitant emotions, as the internal senses are used in thinking through various possible scenarios. Aquinas's account of deliberation can hardly be construed as dry.

Furthermore, at least in English, we can call the movements of the will feelings or emotions. The will, after all, moves toward whatever seems good to it in an affective way, and it feels pleasure regarding the good and pain regarding what is understood as bad. This is as true for virtuous people as it is for nonvirtuous ones. The wills of virtuous people, however, will be more moved toward (or affected by) the good things, that is, they will take more pleasure in the good things and be more pained by the bad ones, simply because they more clearly understand them to be respectively good and bad. This is much like Kant's way of thinking.

Concerning the sensible emotions that are not caused by deliberation, such as those that follow seeing an old woman falling on the sidewalk, Aquinas's position is hardly unfeeling. Aquinas does not believe that virtuous people first deliberate about whether or not to feel pity, then decide that they should feel it, and then command themselves to feel it. That would be absurd. For the most part, passion and deliberation happen almost simultaneously. It is immediately obvious what one should do in such a case, and as quickly as one knows this, one also feels compassion. Sometimes one may happen before the other, but there is no reason to assume that deliberation is a slow process. Deliberation is only slow in complicated cases in which one should slow down and think through the various scenarios. I think most people would agree that we should slow down in such cases and think though the various possible consequences of our actions, and that here the emotions are not always our best guides. Nevertheless, these kinds of sensible emotions are often caused by external events, and there is no reason to assume that the virtuous person will have any fewer of these than anyone else.

Furthermore, as deliberation is for the most part quite fast, most of our passions will be consequent passions, and there is no reason to think that virtuous consequent passions are any less vehement than others.[65]

65. Command, through choice, adds the crucial cause to the already present causal

In other words, most passions will be consequent passions, these will be right and may be vehement, and thus the virtuous life will be as passionate as any other, nonvirtuous life. In the big picture, the virtuous person will by and large have good and right emotions, even if the antecedent passions are not always right.

But virtuous people have another affective advantage that others lack. The virtue itself, as I have discussed, inclines them to acts of virtue, that is, virtuous people simply feel like doing the right thing. They are more inclined to act virtuously than those who do not have virtue. It may be bit of a stretch to call this an emotion or feeling, as it is more permanent and less occurrent than what we usually mean by a feeling or emotion, but these English words are loose and ill-defined enough to allow us to say this. Be that as it may, this is an affective facet of life that the virtuous person has that the nonvirtuous lacks.

The antecedent emotions of the virtuous, however, will be less intense than those of persons without virtue. Here there is a real sense in which the virtuous life will be less emotional or feeling than the lives of the nonvirtuous. But in the big picture, this seems to me to be a good thing, for I think it is obvious that our emotions are not always right. There are times when we fear things that we should not fear and we want things that we should not want—there is no way around this. And I think Aquinas is correct that antecedent emotions that are too strong will obscure our deliberations and hence negatively impact our choices. Besides, it seems to me (and I think most would agree) that always following emotion, or assuming that our emotions will always lead to good outcomes, will frequently lead us astray. It is often good to think through what is the best thing to do and then to do it, even if our emotions may be pulling us in other directions. If this makes Aquinas rationalistic or quasi-Kantian, then so be it.

I also do not think it is quite right to call virtuous deliberation "dry" or unemotional simply because vehement antecedent passions are absent.

mixture of an antecedent passion, morphing it into a consequent passion, and one could just as well argue that choice would have a vehemence-increasing role here. In fact, in *QDM*, q. 3, a. 13, ad 5 [Leonine 23:95.158–59], Aquinas claims that habits make the motion of the will more vehement. Here he is talking about vice, but I see no reason why the same would not apply to virtue. If this is correct, then the increased vehemence of the good will would causally increase the vehemence of consequent passions.

Of course, as most of us are not virtuous, our own deliberations (mine included) are rather "wet" and often a bit too passionate. It seems to me that virtuous deliberations should rather be considered to be, for the most part, peaceful, serene, and in a certain sense passionate, referring both to the analogous way that one may call the will's motions passions and to the experience of real but mild passions. I doubt that virtuous people would consider their deliberations to be dry and sterile. Whenever I have moments of calm deliberation, I am always grateful for them; they seem more lucid and are even at times pleasant in a way that "wetter" deliberations cannot be.

Such deliberation enables the higher powers of the soul to rule the lower. In virtuous humans, this happens rather peacefully and despotically; many of us, however, are more like democracies, where all sorts of differing constituents with relatively equal power are loudly arguing with one another and claiming their right to decide the course of events. The political analogy, which goes back to the *Republic*, is repugnant to our modern sensibilities, of course, but we should lay our correct political sensibilities aside to grasp the point. Either the higher rules the lower with pleasure and ease or it often painfully struggles with it.[66] For my part, I long for peace and quiet.

Even more broadly, the point of virtue is increased happiness, not increased passion. Aquinas is adamant that it is better to be moved to the good by both reason and passion than simply by reason alone,[67] and that the more vehement an antecedent passion is, the harder it will be to order that passion to a human good that is conducive to happiness. If we want to be happy, which means being moved to the good both by reason and by the emotions, Aquinas thinks milder antecedent passions are crucial.

In sum, the virtuous person's deliberations will be full of sensitive

---

66. Part of the analogy is also that the sense appetites have a motion and causality of their own that is not diminished or taken away when the higher powers become more despotic as the lower powers participate in or obey them. What happens in the despotic case is that the sense appetites act according to their own causal efficacy at the command of reason, rather than more simply responding to external sensibles and/or vice versa. As Aquinas sees it, in either case, the sense appetites act according to their full integrity. But the latter, more despotic alternative is even better, as then it acts according to its natural capacity to participate in reason, as the prelapsarian powers were intended to act.

67. *ST* I-II, q. 24, a. 3 [St. Paul 664].

passions, and we may call the movements of that person's will emotions as well, which will be frequent and better than those of the person who is not virtuous. Most of the virtuous person's passions will be consequent passions and will be just as frequent and vehement as anyone else's, but they will be ordered to the right things. Although virtuous people lose some vehemence in their antecedent passions, they gain some affectivity from their virtue, which makes them feel like acting virtuously and gives them pleasure when doing so. All in all, their virtue enables them to have better feelings and emotions than other people. Whatever else one might want to say, Aquinas's virtuous life is hardly a dry and unfeeling life.

Schiller's and Aristotle's harmonious soul would be wonderful, if it were possible. As I discussed in the first part of this book, virtue does make the soul's parts more harmonious (the parts of the potential whole); it makes them work together better and more seamlessly with less internal struggle. But in our messy and complicated lives, this harmony can only reach a certain point, and going further is simply unrealistic. As Aquinas sees things, the desire for perfect harmony is really a natural desire for paradise, which is possible, just not in this life.

Ackrill, John L. *Aristotle: Categories and De Interpretatione*. Oxford: Clarendon Press, 1963.

———. "Aristotle's Definitions of psuchê." *Proceedings of the Aristotelian Society* 73 (1972–73): 119–33.

Adams, Marilyn McCord. *William Ockham*. 2 vols. Notre Dame, Ind.: University of Notre Dame Press, 1987.

Adams, Robert. *A Theory of Virtue: Excellence in Being for the Good*. Oxford: Oxford University Press, 2006.

Aertsen, Jan A. *Medieval Philosophy and the Transcendentals*. Leiden: Brill, 1996.

Albert the Great. *Alberti Magni Opera omnia*. Edited by Bernhard Geyer et al. Münster: Aschendorff, 1951.

———. *Alberti Magni Ratisbonensis episcopi, Ordinis Praedicatorum, Opera omnia*. Edited by Auguste Borgnet. 38 vols. Paris: Vivès, 1890–99.

Allison, Henry E. *Kant's Theory of Freedom*. Cambridge: Cambridge University Press, 1990.

Annas, Julia. *The Morality of Happiness*. New York: Oxford University Press, 1993.

———. "Virtue Ethics." In *The Oxford Handbook of Ethical Theory*. Edited by David Copp. Oxford: Oxford University Press, 2006.

Aristotle. *The Complete Works of Aristotle*. Edited by Jonathan Barnes. Princeton, N.J.: Princeton University Press, 1984.

Arlig, Andrew. "Medieval Mereology." *The Stanford Encyclopedia of Philosophy*, Fall 2015 Edition. Edited by Edward N. Zalta. Available at plato.stanford.edu/entries/mereology-medieval/.

Aquinas, Thomas. *Opera omnia*. Rome: Marietti, 1926–65.

———. *Opera omnia, iussu impensaque Leonis XIII P.M. edita*. Rome: S. C. de Propaganda Fide, 1882–.

———. *Scriptum super libros sententiarum magistri Petri Lombardi*. 4 vols. Edited by R. P. Mandonnet and R. P. Maria Fabianus Moos. Paris: Lethielleux, 1929–47.

———. *Summa theologiae*. Rome: Editiones Paulinae, 1955.

Athanassoulis, Nafsika. "A Response to Harman: Virtue Ethics and Character Traits." *Proceedings of the Aristotelian Society* 100 (2000): 217–20.

Baker, Richard R. "The Thomistic Theory of the Passions and Their Influence upon the Will." PhD diss., University of Notre Dame, 1941.

Baldner, Steven. "Is St. Albert the Great a Dualist on Human Nature?" *Proceedings of the American Catholic Philosophical Association* 67 (1993): 219–29.

———. "St. Albert the Great on the Union of the Human Soul and Body." *American Catholic Philosophical Quarterly* 70 (1996): 103–20.

Barad, Judith. "Aquinas's Assent/Consent Distinction and the Problem of Akrasia." *The New Scholasticism* 62 (1988): 98–111.

———. *Consent: The Means to an Active Faith According to St. Thomas Aquinas*. New York: Peter Lang, 1992.

Barnes, Corey L. *Christ's Two Wills in Scholastic Thought: The Christology of Aquinas and Its Historical Context*. Toronto: Pontifical Institute of Mediaeval Studies, 2012.

Baron, Robert. "The Sweet Smell of … Helping: Effects of Pleasant Ambient Fragrance on Prosocial Behavior in Shopping Malls." *Personality and Social Psychology Bulletin* 23 (1997): 498–503.

Baxley, Anne Margaret. *Kant's Theory of Virtue: The Value of Autocracy*. Cambridge: Cambridge University Press, 2010.

Bazán, B. Carlos. "Le dialogue philosophique entre Siger de Brabant et Thomas d'Aquin: à propos d'un ouvrage récent de E. H. Wéber." *Revue philosophique de Louvain* 72 (1974): 55–155.

———. "The Human Soul: Form *and* Substance? Thomas Aquinas' Critique of Eclectic Aristotelianism." *Archives d'histoire doctrinale et littéraire du Moyen-âge* 64 (1997): 95–126.

Blevins, Gregory A., and Terrance Murphy. "Feeling Good and Helping: Further Phone Booth Finding." *Psychological Reports* 34 (1974): 326.

Bonaventure. *S. Bonaventurae Opera Omnia*. Edited by PP. Collegii a S. Bonaventura. 10 vols. Quaracchi: Collegium S. Bonaventurae, 1882–1902.

Bos, E. P., and A. C. van der Helm. "The Division of Being over the Categories According to Albert the Great, Thomas Aquinas and John Duns Scotus." In *John Duns Scotus: Renewal of Philosophy*, edited by E. P. Bos, 187–89. Amsterdam: Rodopi, 1998.

Bourke, Vernon. "Habitus as a Perfectant of Potency in the Philosophy of St. Thomas Aquinas." PhD diss., University of Toronto, 1938.

———. "The Role of Habitus in the Thomistic Metaphysics of Potency and Act." In *Essays in Thomism*, edited by Robert E. Brennan, 103–9. New York: Sheed and Ward, 1942.

———. "Human Tendencies, Will and Freedom." In *L'homme et son destin, d'après les penseurs du Moyen Age*, 76–79. Louvain: Nauwelaerts, 1960.

Boyd, Craig. "Participation Metaphysics in Aquinas's Theory of Natural Law." *American Catholic Philosophical Quarterly* 79 (2005): 431–45.

———. "Participation Metaphysics, The Imago Dei, and the Natural Law in Aquinas' Ethics." *New Blackfriars* 88 (2007): 274–87.

Brams, Jozef. "The Revised Version of Grosseteste's Translation of the Nicomachean Ethics." *Bulletin de philosophie médiévale* 36 (1994): 45–55.

Broadie, Sarah. *Ethics with Aristotle*. New York: Oxford University Press, 1991.

Brock, Steven. "Natural Inclination and The Intelligibility of the Good in Thomistic Natural Law." *Vera Lex* 6, nos. 1–2 (2005): 57–78.

Brower, Jeffrey E. *Aquinas's Ontology of the Material Word: Change, Hylomorphism and Material Objects*. Oxford: Oxford University Press, 2014.

Brown, Barry F. *Accidental Being: A Study in the Metaphysics of St. Thomas Aquinas*. Lanham, Md.: University Press of America, 1985.

Brungs, Alexander. *Metaphysik der Sinnlichkeit: Das System der Passiones Animae bei Thomas von Aquin*. Halle: Hallescher Verlag, 2002.

Butera, Giuseppe. "Thomas Aquinas on Reason's Control of the Passions in the Virtue of Temperance." PhD diss., The Catholic University of America, 2001.

———. "On Reason's Control of the Passions in Aquinas's Theort of Temperance." *Mediaeval Studies* 68 (2006): 133–60.

Butler, Joseph. *The Analogy of Religion, Natural and Revealed, to the Constitution and Course of Nature*. Oxford: Oxford University Press, 1907.

Cagle, Randy. "Becoming a Virtuous Agent: Kant and the Cultivation of Feelings and Emotions." *Kant-Studien* 96 (2005): 452–67.

Campbell, Keith. *Abstract Particulars*. London: Blackwell, 1990.

Carlisle, Clare. *On Habit*. New York: Routledge, 2014.

Cates, Diana Fritz. "The Virtue of Temperance (IIa–Iae, qq. 141–170)." In *The Ethics of Aquinas*, edited by Stephen J. Pope, 321–40. Washington, D.C.: Georgetown University Press, 2002.

———. *Aquinas on the Emotions*. Washington, D.C.: Georgetown University Press, 2009.

Cessario, Romanus. *The Moral Virtues and Theological Ethics*. Notre Dame, Ind.: University of Notre Dame Press, 1991.

Charlton, William. "Aristotle's Definition of Soul." *Phronesis* 25 (1980): 170–86.

Clagett, Marshall. "Richard Swineshead and Late Medieval Physics: I. The Intension and Remission of Qualities." *Osiris* 9 (1950): 131–61.

Clark, Patrick. *Courage, Death and Virtue in Aquinas and His Philosophical Inheritance*. PhD diss., University of Notre Dame, 2009.

———. "Is Martyrdom Virtuous?: An Occasion for Rethinking the Relation of Christ and Virtue in Aquinas." *Journal of the Society of Christian Ethics* 30 (2010): 141–59.

Clark, Russell, and Larry Word. "Why Don't Bystanders Help? Because of Ambiguity?" *Journal of Personality and Social Psychology* 24 (1972): 392–400.

———. "Where is the Apathetic Bystander? Situational Characteristics of the Emergency." *Journal of Personality and Social Psychology* 29 (1974): 281–82.

Clarke, W. Norris. "The Meaning of Participation in St. Thomas." *Proceedings of The American Catholic Philosophical Association* 26 (1952): 147–57.

Cohoe, Caleb. "There Must be a First: Why Thomas Aquinas Rejects Infinite, Essentially Ordered, Causal Series." *British Journal for the History of Philosophy* 21, no. 5 (2013): 838–56.

Corcilius, K., and P. Gregoric. "Separability vs. Difference: Parts and Capacities of the Soul in Aristotle." *Oxford Studies in Ancient Philosophy* 39 (2010): 81–120.

Cory, Therese. *Aquinas on Human Self-Knowledge.* Cambridge: Cambridge University Press, 2013.

Craemer-Ruegenberg, Ingrid. "The Priority of Soul as Form and Its Proximity to the First Mover: Some Aspects of Albert's Psychology in the First Two Books of His Commentary on Aristotle's De Anima." In *Albert The Great: Commemorative Essays*, edited by Francis J. Kovach and Robert W. Shahan, 49–65. Norman: University of Oklahoma Press, 1980.

Cunningham, Stanley B. *Reclaiming Moral Agency: The Moral Philosophy of Albert the Great.* Washington, D.C.: The Catholic University of America Press, 2008.

Curzer, Howard. *Aristotle and the Virtues.* Oxford: Oxford University Press, 2012.

Dales, Richard. *The Problem of the Rational Soul in the Thirteenth Century.* Leiden: E. J. Brill, 1995.

Damasio, Antonio R. *Descartes' Error: Emotion, Reason, and the Human Brain.* New York: Putnam, 1994.

Darley, John, Lawrence Lewis, and Allan Teger. "Do Groups always Inhibit Individuals' Responses to Potential Emergencies?" *Journal of Personality and Social Psychology* 26 (1973): 395–99.

Darley, John M., and Daniel C. Batson. "'From Jerusalem to Jericho': A Study of Situational and Dispositional Variables in Helping Behavior." *Journal of Personality and Social Psychology* 27 (1973): 100–108.

Davenport, Anne Ashley. *Measure of a Different Greatness: The Intensive Infinite 1250–1650.* New York: Brill, 1999.

Decosimo, David. *Ethics as a Work of Charity.* Stanford, Calif.: Stanford University Press, 2014.

De Haan, Daniel D. "Moral Perception and the Function of the Vis Cogitativa in Thomas Aquinas's Doctrine of Antecedent and Consequent Passions." *Documenti e studi sulla tradizione filosofica medievale* 25 (2014): 289–330.

———. "Perception and the *Vis Cogitativa*: A Thomistic Analysis of Aspectual, Actional, and Affectional Percepts." *American Catholic Philosophical Quarterly* 88 (2014): 397–437.

DePaul, Michael. "Character Traits, Virtues and Vices: Are There None?" *Proceedings of the Twentieth World Congress of Philosophy* 9 (2000): 141–57.

De Young, Rebecca Konyncyk. "Power Made Perfect in Weakness: Aquinas's Transformation of the Virtue of Courage." *Medieval Philosophy and Theology* 11 (2003): 147–80.

Doig, J. C. "Aquinas on Metaphysical Method." *Philosophical Studies* 13 (1964): 20–36.

———. "Aquinas and Jaffa on Courage as the Ultimate of Potency." In *Tradition and Renewal: Philosophical Essays Commemorating the Centennial of Louvain's Institute of Philosophy: Lectures Delivered at Leuven and Louvain-la-Neuve, 21–24 May 1991*, edited by D. A. Boileau and J. A. Dick, 13–21. Leuven: Leuven University Press, 1993.

———. *Aquinas's Philosophical Commentary on the Ethics: A Historical Perspective.* Dordrecht: Kluwer, 2001.

Doolan, Gregory T. *Aquinas on the Divine Ideas as Exemplar Causes.* Washington, D.C.: The Catholic University of America Press, 2008.

———. "Aquinas on the Metaphysician's vs. the Logician's Categories." *Quaestiones Disputatae* 4, no. 2 (2014): 133–55.

———. "Aquinas and the Categories as Parts of Being." In *The Discovery of Being: Philosophical and Theological Perspectives on Thomas Aquinas*, edited by Doolan. Washington, D.C.: The Catholic University of America Press, forthcoming.

Doris, John. "Persons, Situations, and Virtue Ethics." *Noûs* 32 (1998): 504–30.

———. *Lack of Character: Personality and Moral Behavior.* Cambridge: Cambridge University Press, 2002.

———. "Heated Agreement: *Lack of Character as Being for the Good.*" *Philosophical Studies* 148 (2010): 135–46.

Drost, Mark. "Intentionality in Aquinas's Theory of Emotions." *International Philosophical Quarterly* 31 (1991): 449–60.

Duham, Pierre. *Etudes sur Leonard de Vinci.* Ser. 3. Paris: A. Hermann, 1955.

Dumont, Stephen. "The Necessary Connection of Moral Virtue to Prudence according to John Duns Scotus—Revisited." *Recherches de théologie et philosophie médiévales* 55 (1988): 184–206.

———. "John Duns Scotus." In *A Companion to Philosophy in the Middle Ages*, edited by Jorge J. Gracia and Timothy B. Noone, 353–69. Oxford: Blackwell, 2005.

Durling, R. "The Anonymous Translation of Aristotle's *De generatione et corruptione (Translatio Vetus).*" *Traditio* 49 (1994): 320–30.

Earp, Brian D., and David Trafimow. "Replication, Falsification, and the Crisis of Confidence in Social Psychology." *Frontiers in Psychology* 19 (2015): 621.

Eberl, Jason T. "Aquinas on the Nature of Human Beings." *Review of Metaphysics* 58 (2004): 333–65.

d'Eysden, Fidèle. "La distinction de la substance et de ses puissances d'opération d'après saint Bonaventure." *Etudes Franciscaines* 2 (1951): 5–23 and 147–71.

Fabro, Cornelio. *Participation et causalité selon s. Thomas d'Aquin.* Louvain: Publications Universitaires de Louvain, 1961.

———. "Elementi per una dottrina tomistica della partecipazione." In his *Esegesi tomistica,* 421–48. Rome: Libreria editrice della Pontificia Universita Lateranense, 1969.

———. "The Intensive Hermeneutics of Thomistic Philosophy." *Review of Metaphysics* 27 (1974): 449–91.

———. "Le *'Liber de bona fortuna'* de l' *'Ethique à Eudème'* d'Aristote et la dialectique de la divine Providence chez Saint Thomas." *Revue Thomiste* 88 (1988): 556–72.

———. *La nozione metafisica di partecipazione secondo san Tommaso d'Aquino.* Opere Complete 3. Segni: Editrice del Verbo Incarnato, 2005.

Feingold, Lawrence. *The Natural Desire to See God According to St. Thomas and His Interpreters.* Ave Maria, Fla.: Ave Maria Press, 2010.

Ferry, Leonard. "Sorting our Reason's Relation to the Passions in the Moral Theory of Aquinas." *Proceedings of the American Catholic Philosophical Association* 88 (2016): 227–44.

Feser, Edward. *Scholastic Metaphysics: A Contemporary Introduction.* Heusenstamm: Editiones Scholasticae, 2014.

Field, Richard W. "St. Thomas on Properties and the Powers of the Soul." *Laval théologique et philosophique* 40 (1984): 203–15.

Flanagan, Owen. *Varieties of Moral Personality.* Cambridge, Mass.: Harvard University Press, 1991.

Fleming, Diana. "The Character of Virtue: Answering the Situationist Challenge to Virtue Ethics." *Ratio* 19 (2006): 24–42.

Furth, Montgomery. *Substance, Form and Psyche: an Aristotelian Metaphysics.* Cambridge: Cambridge University Press, 1988.

Gallagher, David M. "Thomas Aquinas on the Causes of Human Choice." PhD diss., The Catholic University of America, 1989.

———. *"Aquinas on Moral Action: Interior and Exterior Acts."* *Proceedings of the American Catholic Philosophical Association* 64 (1990): 118–29.

———. "Thomas Aquinas on the Will as a Rational Appetite." *Journal of the History of Philosophy* 29 (1991): 559–84.

———. "Aquinas on Goodness and Moral Goodness." In *Thomas Aquinas and His Legacy,* edited by David M. Gallagher, 37–60. Washington, D.C.: The Catholic University of America Press, 1994.

———. "Free Choice and Free Judgement in Thomas Aquinas." *Archiv für Geschichte der Philosophie* 76 (1994): 247–77.

Garrett, Jan Edward. "The Moral Status of 'the Many' in Aristotle." *Journal of the History of Philosophy* 31 (1993): 171–89.

Garrigou-Lagrange, R. *God: His Existence and his Nature*, vol. 1. Translated by Dom Bede Rose. St. Louis, Mo.: Herder, 1934.

Gauthier, R. A. *Ethica Nicomachea*. Leiden: E. J. Brill, 1972–74.

Geiger, Louis B. *La participation dans la philosophie de s. Thomas d'Aquin*. Paris: Librairie Philosophique J. Vrin, 1953.

Gondreau, Paul. "The Passions and the Moral Life: Appreciating the Originality of Aquinas." *The Thomist* 71 (2007): 419–50.

———. *The Passions of Christ's Soul in the Theology of St. Thomas Aquinas*. Scranton, Penn.: University of Scranton Press, 2008.

Gorevan, Patrick. "Aquinas and Emotional Theory Today: Mind-Body, Cognitivism, and Connaturality." *Acta Philosophica* 9 (2000): 141–51.

Grant, Edward. *The Foundations of Modern Science in the Middle Ages*. Cambridge: Cambridge University Press, 1996.

Grant, Matthews S. "God, The Sinner, and The Act of Sin." *The Thomist* 73 (2009): 455–96.

Hagger, Martin S., and Nikos L. D. Chatzisarantis. "A Multilab Preregistered Replication of the Ego-Depletion Effect." *Perspectives on Psychological Science* 11 (2016): 546–73.

Harak, G. Simon. *Virtuous Passions: The Formation of Christian Character*. New York: Wipf and Stock, 1993.

Harman, Gilbert. "Moral Philosophy Meets Social Psychology: Virtue Ethics and the Fundamental Attribution Error." *Proceedings of the Aristotelian Society* 99 (1999): 315–31.

———. "The Nonexistence of Character Traits." *Proceedings of the Aristotelian Society* 100 (2000): 223–26.

———. "Skepticism about Character Traits." *Journal of Ethics* 13 (2009): 235–42.

Hasse, Dag. "The Early Albertus Magnus and his Arabic Sources on the Theory of the Soul." *Vivarium* 46 (2008): 232–52.

Hause, Jeffrey. "Aquinas on the Function of Moral Virtue." *American Catholic Philosophical Quarterly* 81 (2007): 1–20.

Hause, Jeffrey, and Claudia Murphy. *Aquinas: Disputed Questions on Virtue*. Indianapolis, Ind.: Hackett, 2010.

Heil, John. *From an Ontological Point of View*. Oxford: Clarendon Press, 2003.

———. *The Universe as We Find It*. Oxford: Oxford University Press, 2012.

Henle, Robert J. *Thomas and Platonism*. The Hague: Martinus Nijhoff, 1956.

Henninger, Mark G. "Aquinas on the Ontological Status of Relations." *Journal of the History of Philosophy* 24 (1987): 491–515.

Hoffmann, Tobias. "Aquinas on the Moral Progress of the Weak Willed." In *Das*

Problem der Willensschwäche im mittelalterlichen Denken / The Problem of Weakness of Will in Medieval Thought, edited by Tobias Hofmann, Jörn Müller, and Matthias Perkams, 221–47. Recherches de Théologie et Philosophie médiévales Bibliotheca 8. Leuven: Peeters, 2006.

———. "Aquinas and Intellectual Determinism: The Test Case of Angelic Sin." *Archiv für Geschichte der Philosophie* 89 (2007): 122–56.

———. "Intellectualism and Voluntarism." In *The Cambridge History of Medieval Philosophy*, edited by Robert Pasnau, 414–27. Cambridge: Cambridge University Press, 2010.

———. "Conscience and Synderesis." In *The Oxford Handbook of Aquinas*, edited by Brian Davies and Eleonore Stump, 255–64. Oxford and New York: Oxford University Press, 2012.

———. "Prudence and Practical Principles." In *Aquinas and the Nicomachean Ethics*, edited by Tobias Hoffmann, Jörn Müller, and Matthias Perkams. Cambridge: Cambridge University Press, forthcoming.

Hursthouse, Rosalind. *On Virtue Ethics*. Oxford: Oxford University Press, 1999.

Inagake, Bernard Ryosuke. "*Habitus* and *Natura* in Aquinas." In *Studies in Medieval Philosophy*, edited by John F. Wippel, 159–75. Washington, D.C.: The Catholic University of America Press, 1987.

Inglis, John. "Aquinas's Replication of the Acquired Moral Virtues." *Journal of Religious Ethics* 27 (1999): 3–27.

Irwin, Terence. *The Development of Ethics, vol. 1: From Socrates to the Reformation*. Oxford: Oxford University Press, 2007.

Isen, Alice, and Paula Levin. "Effect and Feeling Good on Helping: Cookies and Kindness." *Journal of Personality and Social Psychology* 21 (1972): 384–88.

Jaeger, Andrew J. "Back to the Primitive: From Substantial Capacities to Prime Matter." *American Catholic Philosophical Quarterly* 88 (2014): 381–95.

Jakob, Josef. *Passiones: Ihr Wesen und ihre Anteilnahme an der Vernunft nach dem Hl. Thomas von Aquin*. Vienna: Pontificiae Universitatis Gregorianae, 1958.

James, Helen John. *The Thomist Spectrum*. New York: Fordham University Press, 1966.

Jaworski, William. "Hylomorphism and the Metaphysics of Structure." *Res Philosophica* 91 (2014): 179–201.

———. *Structure and The Metaphysics of Mind: How Hylomorphism Solves the Mind-Body Problem*. Oxford: Oxford University Press, 2016.

Jayawickreme, Eranda, Peter Meindle, Erick Helzer, Michael Furr, and William Fleeson. "Virtuous States and Virtuous Traits: How the Empirical Evidence Regarding the Existence of Broad Traits Saves Virtue Ethics from the Situationist Critique." *Theory and Research Education* 12 (2014): 283–308.

Jensen, Steven. "Virtuous Deliberation and The Passions." Forthcoming in *The Thomist*.

Johansen, Thomas. *The Powers of Aristotle's Soul.* Oxford: Oxford University Press, 2012.

Johnston, Rebekah. "Aristotle's *De Anima*: On Why the Soul is Not a Set of Capacities." *British Journal for the History of Philosophy* 19 (2011): 185–200.

Kahm, Nicholas. "Aquinas on Quality." *British Journal for the History of Philosophy* 24, no. 1 (2016): 23–44.

———. "Aquinas and Aristotelians on Whether the Soul Is a Group of Powers." *History of Philosophy Quarterly* 34 (2017): 115–32.

Kainz, Howard P. *Active and Passive Potency in Thomistic Angelology.* The Hague: Nijhoff, 1972.

Kamtekar, Rachana. "Situationism and Virtue Ethics on the Content of Our Character." *Ethics* (2004): 458–91.

Kant, Immanuel. *The Metaphysics of Morals.* Translated and edited by Mary Gregor. Cambridge: Cambridge University Press, 1996.

———. *Critique of Practical Reason.* Translated by Mary Gregor. Cambridge: Cambridge University Press, 1997.

———. *Religion within the Boundaries of Mere Reason.* Translated and edited by Allen Wood and George DiGiovanni. Cambridge: Cambridge University Press, 1998.

———. *Anthropology from a Pragmatic Point of View.* Translated and edited by Robert Louden. Cambridge: Cambridge University Press, 2006.

———. *Groundwork of the Metaphysics of Morals.* Translated and edited by Mary Gregor and Jens Timmermann. Revised by Jens Timmermann. Cambridge: Cambridge University Press, 2012.

Kent, Bonnie. *Virtues of the Will.* Washington, D.C.: The Catholic University of America Press, 1995.

———. "Habits and Virtues." In *The Ethics of Aquinas*, edited by Stephen J. Pope, 116–29. Washington, D.C.: Georgetown University Press, 2002.

———. "The Moral Life." In *The Cambridge Companion to Medieval Philosophy*, edited by A. S. McGrade, 231–53. Cambridge: Cambridge University Press, 2003.

———. "Virtue Theory." In *The Cambridge History of Medieval Philosophy*, edited by R. Pasnau, 2:493–505. Cambridge: Cambridge University Press, 2010.

———. "Losable Virtue: Aquinas on Character and Will." In *Aquinas and the Nicomachean Ethics*, edited by Tobias Hoffmann, Jörn Müller, and Matthias Perkams, 108–9. Cambridge: Cambridge University Press, 2013.

Kent, Bonnie, and Ashley Dressel. "Weakness and Willful Wrongdoing in Aquinas's *De malo.*" In *Aquinas's Disputed Questions on Evil: A Critical Guide*, edited by M. V. Dougherty, 34–55. Cambridge: Cambridge University Press, 2016.

Kim, Yul. "A Change in Thomas Aquinas's Theory of the Will." *American Catholic Philosophical Quarterly* 82 (2008): 221–36.

King, Peter. "The Inner Cathedral: Mental Architecture in High Scholasticism." *Vivarium* 46 (2008): 253–74.

Klubertanz, George P. *The Discursive Power: Sources and Doctrine of the Vis Cogitativa According to St. Thomas Aquinas*. St. Louis, Mo.: Messenger Press, 1952.

———. "St. Thomas' Treatment of the Axiom *omne agens agit propter finem*." In *An Etienne Gilson Tribute*, edited by C. J. O'Neill, 101–17. Milwaukee, Wis.: Marquette University Press, 1959.

Knasas, John F. X. "Aquinas on the Cognitive Soul: Metaphysics, Physics, or Both?" *American Catholic Philosophical Quarterly* 77 (1998): 501–27.

Kristjánsson, Kristján. "An Aristotelian Critique of Situationsim," *Philosophy* 83 (2008): 55–76.

Künzle, Pius. *Das Verhältnis der Seele zu ihren Potenzen*. Freiburg: Universitätsverlag, 1956.

Laporta, Jorge. *La Destinée de la nature humaine selon Thomas d'Aquin*. Paris: J. Vrin, 1965.

———. "Pour Trouver le Sens Exact des Terms Appetitus Naturalis, Desiderium Naturale, Amor Naturalis, etc. chez Thomas D'Aquin." *Archives d'histoire doctrinale et littéraire du Moyen-âge* 48 (1973): 66–71.

Lear, Jonathan. *Aristotle: The Desire to Understand*. Cambridge: Cambridge University Press, 1988.

Lee, Jaekying. "The Intellect-Body Problem in Aquinas." *Archiv für Geschichte der Philosophie* 88 (2006): 239–60.

Little, Arthur. *Platonic Heritage*. Dublin: Golden Eagle Books, 1949.

Lofy, Carl A. "The Meaning of 'Potential Whole' in St. Thomas Aquinas." *The Modern Schoolman* 37 (1959): 39–47.

Lombard, Peter. *Magistri Petri Lombardi Parisiensis Episcopi Sententiae In IV Libris Distinctae*. 2 vols. Grottaferrata: Collegii S. Bonaventurae, 1971.

———. *The Sentences: Book 1, The Mystery of the Trinity*. Translated by Giulio Silano. Toronto: Pontifical Institute of Mediaeval Studies, 2007.

Lombardo, Nicholas E. *The Logic of Desire: Aquinas on Emotion*. Washington, D.C.: The Catholic University of America Press, 2011.

Long, Steven. *Analogia Entis*. Notre Dame, Ind.: University of Notre Dame Press, 2012.

Lottin, Odon. *Psychologie et morale aux XIIe et XIIIe siècles*. 6 vols. Leuven / Gembloux: Abbaye du Mont César / J. Duculot, 1942–60.

MacIntyre, Alasdair. *After Virtue*. Notre Dame, Ind.: University of Notre Dame Press, 1981.

Magnusson, David, and N. Endler. "Interactional Psychology: Present Status and Future Prospects." In *Personality at the Crossroads: Current Issues in Interactional Psychology*, ed. Magnusson and Endler. Hillsdale, Mich.: Lawrence Erlbaum Associates, 1977.

Maier, Annelise. *Zwei Grundprobleme der scholastischen Naturphilosophie. Das Prob-*

lem der intensiven Grösse. Die Impetustheorie. Rome: Edizioni di storia e letteratura, 1951.

Mansfield, Richard K. "Antecedent Passion and the Moral Quality of Human Acts According to St. Thomas." *Proceedings of the American Catholic Philosophical Association* 71 (1997): 221–31.

Maritain, Jacques. *St. Thomas and the Problem of Evil.* Milwaukee, Wis.: Marquette University Press, 1942.

———. *The Ranger of Reason.* New York: Charles Scribner's Sons, 1952.

Martin, Charles Burton. "On the Need for Properties: The Road to Pythagoreanism and Back." *Synthese* 112 (1997): 193–231.

Martin, Charles Burton, and John Heil. "The Ontological Turn." *Midwest Studies in Philosophy* 23 (1999): 34–60.

Marmodoro, Anna. "Aristotle's Hylomorphism without Reconditioning." *Philosophical Inquiry* 36 (2013): 5–22.

———. *Aristotle on Perceiving Objects.* Cambridge: Cambridge University Press, forthcoming.

Martino, Carla Di. *Ratio Particularis Doctrines Des Sens Internes D'Avicenne à Thomas D'Aquin.* Paris: Vrin, 2008.

Matchulat, Justin. "Defending Virtue against the Situationist Challenge: Aristotle, Aquinas, and Contemporary Metaphysicians on Degree Traits." *Proceedings of the American Catholic Philosophical Association* 88 (2015): 245–58.

Mattison, William C. "Thomas's Categorizations of Virtue: Historical Background and Contemporary Significance." *The Thomist* 74 (2010): 189–235.

McCluskey, Colleen. "Happiness and Freedom in Aquinas's Theory of Action." *Medieval Philosophy and Theology* 9 (2000): 69–90.

McKay Knobel, Angela. "The Infused and Acquired Virtues in Aquinas' Moral Philosophy." PhD diss., University of Notre Dame, 2004.

———. "Prudence and Acquired Moral Virtue." *The Thomist* 69 (2005): 535–55.

———. "Can the Infused and Acquired Virtues Coexist in the Christian Life?" *Studies in Christian Ethics* 23, no. 4 (2010): 381–96.

———. "Two Theories of Christian Virtue." *American Catholic Philosophical Quarterly* 84, no. 3 (2010): 599–618.

———. "Aquinas and the Pagan Virtues." *International Philosophical Quarterly* 51 (2011): 339–54.

———. "Relating Aquinas's Infused and Acquired Virtues: Some Problematic Texts for a Common Interpretation." *Nova et Vetera* 9, no. 2 (2011): 411–31.

McLaughlin, Thomas. "Act, Potency, and Energy." *The Thomist* 75 (2011): 207–43.

Merritt, Maria. "Virtue Ethics and Situationist Personality Psychology." *Ethical Theory and Moral Practice* 3 (2000): 365–83.

Miller, Christian. *Moral Character.* Oxford: Oxford University Press, 2013.

———. *Character and Moral Psychology*. Oxford: Oxford University Press, 2014.

———. "Categorizing Character: Moving beyond the Aristotelian Framework." In *Varieties of Virtue Ethics*, edited by David Carr. London: Palgrave Macmillan, 2017.

Miner, Robert. *Thomas Aquinas on the Passions. A Study of Summa Theologiae, 1a2ae 22–48*. Cambridge: Cambridge University Press, 2009.

Mischel, Walter. "Toward an Integrative Science of the Person." *Annual Review of Psychology* 55 (2004): 1–22.

Mitchell, Jason A. "Being and Participation: The Method and Structure of Metaphysical Reflection according to Cornelio Fabro." PhD diss., Pontifical Athenaeum Regina Apostolorum, 2013.

Montagnes, Bernard. *The Doctrine of the Analogy of Being according to Thomas Aquinas*. Translated by E. M. Macierowski. Translation reviewed and corrected by Pol Vandevelde. Edited with revisions by Andrew Tallon. Milwaukee, Wis.: Marquette University Press, 2008.

Munzel, G. Felicitas. *Kant's Conception of Character: The Critical Link of Morality, Anthropology, and Reflective Judgement*. Chicago: University of Chicago Press, 1999.

Murphy, Claudia Eisen. "Aquinas on Our Responsibility for Our Emotions." *Medieval Philosophy and Theology* 8 (1999): 163–205.

Nemesius. *De Natura Hominis: Traduction de Burgundio de Pise*. Edited by G. Verbeke and J. R. Moncho. Leiden: Brill, 1975.

Nussbaum, Martha C. *Upheavals of Thought: The Intelligence of Emotions*. Cambridge: Cambridge University Press, 2001.

O'Meara, Thomas F. "Virtues in the Theology of Thomas Aquinas." *Theological Studies* 58 (1997): 254–85.

Open Science Collaboration. "Estimating the Reproducibility of Psychological Science." *Science* 349 (2015): 1–8.

Osbourne, Thomas M. "The Augustinianism of Thomas Aquinas's Moral Theory." *The Thomist* 67 (2003): 279–305.

———. "Perfect and Imperfect Virtues in Aquinas." *The Thomist* 71 (2007): 39–64.

Owens, Joseph. *An Elementary Christian Metaphysics*. Houston: Center for Thomistic Studies, 1983.

Packer, Mark. "Kant on Desire and Moral Pleasure." *Journal of the History of Ideas* 50 (1989): 429–42.

Pasnau, Robert. *Thomas Aquinas on Human Nature*. Cambridge: Cambridge University Press, 2002.

Pegis, Anton Charles. *St. Thomas and the Problem of the Soul in the Thirteenth Century*. Totonto: Pontifical Institute of Mediaeval Studies, 1934.

Perler, Dominik. "Faculties in Medieval Philosophy." In *The Faculties*, edited by Dominik Perler, 97–139. Oxford: Oxford University Press, 2015.

Pierson, Daniel J. "Thomas Aquinas on the Principle *Omne Agens Agit Aibi Simile*." PhD diss., The Catholic University of America, 2015.

Piliavin, Irving, Judith Rodin, and Jane Piliavin. "Good Samaritanism: An Underground Phenomenon." *Journal of Personality and Social Psychology* 13 (1969): 289–99.

Pilsner, Joseph. *The Specification of Human Acts in St. Thomas Aquinas*. Oxford: Oxford University Press, 2006.

Pini, Giorgio. *Categories and Logic in Duns Scotus: An Interpretation of Aristotle's Categories in the Late Thirteenth Century*. Leiden: Brill, 2002.

———. "Scotus on Deducing Aristotle's Categories." In *La tradition médiévale des Catégories (XIIe–XIVe siécles). XIIIe Symposium européen de logique et de sémantique médiévales. Avignon 6–10 juin 2000*, edited by J. Biard and I. Rosier-Catach, 23–35. Philosophes médiévaux 45. Louvain-la-Neuve / Leuven: Éditions de l'Institut supérieur de Philosophie / Éditions Peeters, 2003.

Pinkaers, Servais. "Virtue Is Not a Habit." *Cross Currents* 12 (1961): 65–81.

———. *The Sources of Christian Ethics*. Translated by Sr. Mary Thomas Noble. Washington, D.C.: The Catholic University of America Press, 1995.

———. *The Pinkaers Reader: Renewing Thomistic Moral Theology*. Edited by John Berkman and Craig Steven Titus. Washington, D.C.: The Catholic University of America Press, 2005.

Porter, Jean. *The Recovery of Virtue: The Relevance of Aquinas for Christian Ethics*. Louisville, Ky.: Westminster John Knox Press, 1990.

Regan, Dennis, Margo Williams, and Sondra Sparling. "Voluntary Expiation of Guilt: A Field Experiment." *Journal of Personality and Social Psychology* 24 (1972): 42–45.

Reid, James. "Morality and Sensibility in Kant: Toward a Theory of Virtue." *Kantian Review* 8 (2004): 89–114.

Renard, Henri. "The Habits in the System of St. Thomas." *Gregorianum* 29 (1948): 88–117.

Rhonheimer, Martin. *Natural Law and Practical Reason: A Thomistic View of Moral Autonomy*. Translated by Gerald Malsbary. New York: Fordham University Press, 2000.

Roberts, Robert C. "Temperance." In *Virtues and Their Vices*, edited by Kevin Timpe and Craig A. Boyd, 93–115. Oxford: Oxford University Press, 2014.

Rohlf, Michael. "Emotion and Evil in Kant." *Review of Metaphysics* 66 (2013): 749–73.

Romano, Joseph J. "Between Being and Nothingness: The Relevancy of Thomistic Habit." *The Thomist* 44 (1980): 427–40.

Rorty, Amélie Oksenberg. "Akrasia and Pleasure: Nicomachean Ethics Book 7." In *Es-*

says on Aristotle's Ethics, edited by Amélie Oksenberg Rorty. Berkeley: University of California Press, 1980.

Royce, James E. "St. Thomas and the Definition of Active Potency." *The New Scholasticism* 34 (1960): 431–37.

Ryan, Thomas. "Aquinas' Integrated View of Emotions, Morality and the Person." *Pacifica* 14 (2001): 55–70.

———. "Revisiting Affective Knowledge and Connaturality in Aquinas." *Theological Studies* 66 (2005): 52–53.

Rziha, John. *Perfecting Human Actions: St. Thomas on Human Participation in Eternal Law*. Washington, D.C.: The Catholic University of America Press, 2009.

Scaltsas, Theodore. "Is a Whole Identical to Its Parts?" *Mind* 99 (1990): 583–98.

Schiller, Friedrich. "On Grace and Dignity." *The Complete Works of Friedrich Schiller, vol. III: Aesthetical and Philosophical Essays*. New York: P. F. Collier and Sons, 1902.

———. *Xenien*, "The Philosophers." In Johann Wolfgang von Goethe, *Werke*, vol. 1. Edited by Erich Trunz. Munich: Beck, 1982.

Shanley, Brian J. "Divine Causation and Human Freedom in Aquinas." *American Catholic Philosophical Quarterly* 72 (1998): 99–122.

———. "Aquinas on Pagan Virtue." *The Thomist* 63 (1999): 553–77.

———. "Beyond Libertarianism and Compatibilism: Thomas Aquinas on Created Freedom." In *Freedom and the Human Person*, edited by Richard Velkley, 70–89. Washington, D.C.: The Catholic University of America Press, 2007.

Sherwin, Michael S. *By Knowledge and by Love: Charity and Knowledge in the Moral Theology of St. Thomas Aquinas*. Washington, D.C.: The Catholic University of America Press, 2005.

———. "Infused Virtue and the Effects of Acquired Vice: A Test Case for the Thomistic Theory of Infused Cardinal Virtues." *The Thomist* 73 (2009): 29–52.

Sherwin, Nancy. *Making a Necessity of Virtue: Aristotle and Kant on Virtue*. Cambridge: Cambridge University Press, 1997.

Shoda, Yuichi. "A Unified Framework for the Study of Behavioral Consistency: Bridging Person x Situation Interaction and the Consistency Paradox." *European Journal of Personality* 13 (1999): 361–87.

Shu, Lisa, Francesca Gino, and Max Bazerman. "Dishonest Deed, Clear Conscience: When Cheating Leads to Moral Disengagement and Motivating Forgetting." *Personality and Social Psychology Bulletin* 37 (2011): 330–49.

Simplicius. *Commentaire sur les Catégories d'Aristotele: Traductione de Guillaume de Moerbeke*, vol. 2. Edited by A. Pattin. Leiden: Brill, 1975.

Sorabji, R. "Body and Soul in Aristotle." In *Aristotle's De Anima in Focus*, edited by Michael Durrant, 162–69. London: Routledge, 1993.

Sorensen, Kelly. "Kant's Taxonomy of the Emotions." *Kantian Review* 6 (2002): 109–28.

Sreenivasan, Gopal. "Errors about Errors: Virtue Theory and Trait Attribution." *Mind* 111 (2002): 47–68.

Studtmann, Paul. *The Foundations of Aristotle's Categorical Scheme*. Milwaukee, Wis.: Marquette University Press, 2008.

Stump, Eleonore. "Aquinas's Account of Freedom: Intellect and Will." *The Monist* 80 (1997): 576–97.

———. "Substances and Artifacts in Aquinas's Metaphysics." In *Knowledge and Reality: Essays in Honor of Alvin Plantinga*, edited by Tom Crisp, Matthew Davidson, and David Vander Laan, 63–80. Dordrecht: Springer, 2006.

———. "Emergence, Causal Powers, and Aristotelianism in Metaphysics." In *Powers and Capacities in Philosophy: The New Aristotelianism*. Edited by Ruth Groff and John Greco. London: Routledge, 2013.

Suto, Taki. "Virtue and Knowledge: Connatural Knowledge According to Thomas Aquinas." *Review of Metaphysics* 58 (2004): 61–79.

Svoboda, David. "Thomas Aquinas on Whole and Part." *The Thomist* 76 (2012): 273–304.

Symington, Paul. "Thomas Aquinas on Establishing the Identity of Aristotle's Categories." In *Medieval Commentaries on Aristotle's Categories*, edited by Lloyd Newton, 119–44. Leiden: Brill, 2008.

———. *On Determining What There Is: The Identity of Ontological Categories in Aquinas, Scotus and Lowe*. New Brunswick, N.J.: Ontos, 2010.

te Velde, Rudi A. *Participation and Substantiality in Thomas Aquinas*. New York: E. J. Brill, 1989.

———. "Metaphysics, Dialectics and the *Modus Logicus* According to Thomas Aquinas." *Recherches de Theologie Et Philosophie Medievales* 63 (1996): 15–35.

———. "Evil, Sin, and Death." In *The Theology of Thomas Aquinas*, edited by Rik Van Nieuwenhove and Joseph Wawrykow, 143–66. Notre Dame, Ind.: University of Notre Dame, 2005.

Titus, Craig Steven. "Passions in Christ: Spontaneity, Development, and Virtue." *The Thomist* 73 (2009): 53–87.

Tomarchio, John. "Aquinas's Division of Being according to Modes of Existing." *Review of Metaphysics* 54 (2001): 585–613.

———. "Aquinas's Concept of Infinity." *Journal of the History of Philosophy* 40 (2002): 163–87.

Toner, Chris. "Angelic Sin in Aquinas and Scotus and the Genesis of Some Central Objections to Contemporary Virtue Ethics." *The Thomist* 69 (2005): 79–125.

Torrell, Jean-Pierre. *Saint Thomas Aquinas, vol. 1: Person and Work*. Revised edition. Translated by Robert Royal. Washington, D.C.: The Catholic University of America Press, 2005.

———. "Nature and Grace in Thomas Aquinas." In *Surnaturel: A Controversy at the Heart of Twentieth-Century Thomistic Thought*, edited by Serge-Thomas Bonino, OP, translated by Robert Williams, and revised by Matthew Levering, 155–90. Naples, Fla.: Sapientia Press, 2009.

Uffenheimer-Lippens, Elisabeth. "Rationalized Passion and Passionate Rationality: Thomas Aquinas on the Relation between Reason and the Passions." *Review of Metaphysics* 56 (2003): 525–58.

Vuillemin-Diem, Gudrun, and Marwan Rashed. "Burgundio de Pise et ses manuscrits grecs d'Aristote: Laur. 87.7 et Laur. 81.18." *Recherches de Théologie et Philosophie médiévales* 64 (1997): 136–98.

Wawrykow, Joseph P. *God's Grace and Human Action: 'Merit' in the Theology of Thomas Aquinas*. Notre Dame, Ind.: University of Notre Dame Press, 1995.

———. "Grace." In *The Theology of Thomas Aquinas*, edited by Rik Van Nieuwenhove and Joseph Wawrykow, 192–221. Notre Dame, Ind.: University of Notre Dame Press, 2005.

Wéber, E.-H. *La controverse de 1270 à l'Université de Paris et son retentissement sur la pensée de S. Thomas d'Aquin*. Paris: Vrin, 1970.

Westberg, Daniel. "Did Aquinas Change His Mind about Will?" *The Thomist* 58 (1994): 41–61.

———. *Right Practical Reason: Action, Aristotle and Prudence in Aquinas*. Oxford: Oxford University Press, 1994.

White, Kevin. "Aquinas on the Immediacy of the Union of Soul and Body." In *Studies in Thomistic Theology*, edited by Paul Lockey, 209–80. Houston: Center for Thomistic Studies, 1996.

———. "The Passions of the Soul (IaIIae, qq.22–48)." In *Essays in the Ethics of St. Thomas Aquinas*, edited by Stephen Pope, 103–15. Washington, D.C.: Georgetown University Press, 2002.

Williams, Donald C. "The Elements of Being." *Review of Metaphysics* 7 (1953): 3–18.

Williams, Lawrence, and John Bargh. "Experiencing Physical Warmth Promotes Interpersonal Warmth." *Science* 322 (2008): 606–7.

Williams, Thomas. "The Libertarian Foundations of Scotus's Moral Philosophy." *The Thomist* 62 (1998): 193–215.

Wippel, John F. "Godfrey of Fontaines on Intension and Remission of Accidental Forms." *Franciscan Studies* 39 (1979): 316–55.

———. *Thomas Aquinas on the Divine Ideas*. Etienne Gilson Series 16. Toronto: Pontifical Institute of Mediaeval Studies, 1993.

———. "Thomas Aquinas and the Condemnation of 1277." *The Modern Schoolman* 72 (1995): 233–75.

———. *The Metaphysical Thought of Thomas Aquinas: From Finite Being to Uncreated Being*. Washington, D.C.: The Catholic University of America Press, 2000.

———. "Thomas Aquinas on the Separated Soul's Natural Knowledge." In *Thomas Aquinas: Approaches to Truth*, edited by J. McEvoy and M. Dunne, 114–40. Dublin: Four Courts Press, 2002.

———. "Metaphysical Foundations for Christian Humanism in Thomas Aquinas." *Doctor Communis* fasc. 1–2 (2004): 124–42.

———. *Metaphysical Themes in Thomas Aquinas II*. Washington, D.C.: The Catholic University of America Press, 2007.

———. "Thomas Aquinas on the Divine Ideas." In his *The Gilson Lectures on Thomas Aquinas*, 233–72. Toronto: Pontifical Institute of Mediaeval Studies, 2008.

———. "Essence and Existence." In *The Cambridge History of Medieval Philosophy*, edited by Robert Pasnau, 2:622–34. Cambridge: Cambridge University Press, 2010.

———. "Thomas Aquinas and the Unity of Substantial Form." In *Philosophy and Theology in the Long Middle Ages: A Tribute to Stephen F. Brown*, edited by Kent Emery, Jr., Russell L. Friedman, and Andreas Speer, 117–54. Leiden: Brill, 2011.

Wolter, Allan. "Duns Scotus on the Natural Desire for the Supernatural." *New Scholasticism* 23 (1949): 281–317.

Wood, Adam. "The Faculties of the Soul and Some Medieval Mind-Body Problems." *The Thomist* 75 (2011): 585–636.

Wood, Allen. *Kant's Ethical Thought*. Cambridge: Cambridge University Press, 1999.

Wright, John H. "Human Freedom and Divine Action: Libertarianism in St. Thomas Aquinas." In *Human and Divine Agency: Anglican, Catholic, and Lutheran Perspectives*, edited by F. M. McLain and W. M. Richardsom, 41–47. Lanham, Md.: University Press of America, 1999.

Zavalloni, R. *Richard de Mediavilla et la controverse sur la pluralite des formes*. Louvain: Éd. de l'Institut Supérieur de Philosophie, 1951.

Zhong, Chen-Bo, and Katie Liljenquist. "Washing away Your Sins: Threatened Morality and Physical Cleansing." *Science* 313 (2006): 1451–52.

Zuroff, David. "Was Gordon Allport a Trait Theorist?" *Journal of Personality and Social Psychology* 51 (1986): 993–1000.

Aquinas on Emotion's Participation in Reason was designed in Garamond with Meta display type and composed by Kachergis Book Design of Pittsboro, North Carolina. It was printed on 60-pound Maple Eggshell Cream and bound by Maple Press of York, Pennsylvania.